Praise for *Terrorists or Freedom Fighters?*

Finally, a serious look at the latest liberation movement from both a historical, philosophical and activist perspective. Regardless of what one thinks about the tactics of the Animal Liberation Front, this long overdue book is a must-read for anyone concerned about the future of the movement for animal liberation.

—**Michael Greger, MD**, Chief BSE Investigator for Farm Sanctuary, Mad Cow Coordinator for the Organic Consumers Association

In a world driven by profit margins, utilitarianism, speciesism, and in this generalized climate of political swindle, *Terrorists or Freedom Fighters?* speaks truth to power. It is a work destined to shape the politics of a new generation of militant activists.

—**Peter McLaren**, Professor, Graduate School of Education and Information Studies, University of California, Los Angeles, and author of *Che Guevara, Paulo Freire, and the Pedagogy of Revolution*

In a century, will people look back on the era of routine human exploitation of non-human animals as we now look at slavery? Moral progress on this front likely will come because of efforts like *Terrorists or Freedom Fighters?*. This timely collection will help anyone interested in challenging the conventional approach to animals and thinking more generally about the state of our society.

—**Robert Jensen**, Associate Professor, School of Journalism, University of Texas at Austin

Too often, scholarly works about social movements seem to have little to do with the movement, while activist works often have little substance. Not this book, which combines both viewpoints. Here, readers have access to the logic and philosophy of animal liberation as well as its practice and reflections on our current social era. Best and Nocella have filled a huge void. Bravo!

—**Rik Scarce**, author of *Eco-Warriors: Understanding the Radical Environmental Movement*

Terrorists or Freedom Fighters? exposes readers to compelling ideas that will undoubtedly make them think, and make them question. It is a valuable contribution to the most critical of public discourse.

—**Bob Linden**, GoVeganRadio.com

An outstanding collection of writings and an excellent antidote for the corporate welfare state's corruptness and propaganda.

—**Chris Hannah**, Propagandhi, co-founder of G7 Records

A serious and essential book on animal liberation theory and practice, a revolutionary bellwether for the Patriot Act political climate of our times and a multiperspectival social critique and defense of animal lives, this book should find a place in university classrooms, activist bookshelves, and Homeland Security offices everywhere. The greatest aspect of this great collection may be its success in generating a foundation for greater understanding and dialogue between those in higher education, in policy organizations and government, and in grassroots groups like the ALF.

—**Richard Kahn**, Ecopedagogy Chair of the UCLA Paulo Freire Institute, and founder of GetVegan.com

This groundbreaking collection of essays addresses one of the most important issues of our times: the role of the ALF in the animal liberation movement. By examining the philosophical and ethical underpinnings of the ALF, and by demonstrating that a strong defense can be mounted on behalf of ALF actions and principles, Best and Nocella's volume promises to breathe new life into the debates concerning militant animal activism. This book will be an invaluable resource for teachers, students, and activists interested in animal liberation.

—**Matthew Calarco,** Sweet Briar College

One of the most powerful and thought-provoking books I have ever read. Please read it and ACT NOW!!!

—**John Feldmann,** Goldfinger

2004
Lantern Books
One Union Square West, Suite 201
New York, NY 10003

Printed in Canada

Library of Congress Cataloging-in-Publication Data

Terrorists or freedom fighters? : reflections on the liberation of animals / edited by Steven Best, Ph.D. and Anthony J. Nocella.
p. cm.
Includes bibliographical references.
ISBN 1-59056-054-X (alk. paper)
1. Animal experimentation—United States. 2. Animal Liberation Front. 3. Animal rights movement—United States. 4. Terrorism. I. Best, Steven. II. Nocella, Anthony J.
HV4930.T47 2003
179'.3—dc22
2003016251

cover illustration by Sue Coe © 2004

printed on 100% post-consumer waste paper, chlorine-free

TERRORISTS
OR FREEDOM
FIGHTERS?

Reflections on the Liberation of Animals

Edited by Steven Best, PhD and Anthony J. Nocella II

NEW YORK • LANTERN BOOKS
A DIVISION OF BOOKLIGHT INC.

Acknowledgments

We wish to thank all the authors for their thoughtful contributions to this groundbreaking book. We are indebted to various people from Lantern Books: Anne Sullivan for encouraging us to put this project together, and Martin Rowe and Sarah Gallogly for their assistance and faith in this work. Dilip Barman, Rick Bogle, Rod Coronado, Karen Davis, Josh Harper, Ali Hossaini, Craig Marshall, pattrice jones, Richard Kahn, and Jim Mason provided valuable critical remarks on the Introduction of the book. We are immensely grateful to Sue Coe for her stunning cover image that beautifully captures the pathos of liberation; the eyes of the dog held by the liberator (mirroring the look of so many animals freed in real life) perhaps provides the best answer to the question we pose in the title of the book. We warmly thank Ward Churchill for his powerful words in the Foreword of this volume. Thanks to *No Compromise* and *Animal's Agenda* for permission to use essays originally published in their pages. Finally, we wish to thank various friends and supporters: David Barbarash, Gail Eisnitz, Sunshine Swallers, Joe and Lauren, Patrick and Natalie, Megan Lewis, Jay, Brian, Becca, Jeremy, Tim, Zack, Sarah, Ozzy, Ben, Cameron Naficy with Live Oak Alliance, Toshi, Mario, Peter McLaren, Mike Lee, Leslie James Pickering, Craig Rosebraugh, Robin Webb, Kevin Jonas, Michael Greger, Yvone Pollock, Paul Shapiro, Mike Becker, Mark Somma, Robert Jensen, Bob Linden, Rik Scarce, Derrick Jensen, Matthew Calarco, Elliot Katz, Erica and Nick, Rock Star Productions, Miyun Park, Sean with UARC, Pierre with The Fund for Animals, Ramsey Kanaan with AK Press, Kate Timko, John Sorenson, Anna and Megan from PETA, John Feldmann with Goldfinger, Chris with G7 and Propagandhi, Alma Williams, Jerry Vlasak, Tom Regan, Joe Miele, DeLora Frederickson, Felix Valenzuela, Sangeeta, Jay and Jason from PeTA2.com, Will to Live, Eye Against, the Basement, the Center on

Animal Liberation Affairs, *Arkangel* magazine, *Bite Back* magazine and, most importantly, the late Shadow, Sy, Sparkle, Scooter, and Dos, and our families.

This book is dedicated to all those who have the courage to speak and act the truth no matter what the consequences, to the late animal rights activist Barry Horne, who died in prison from a hunger strike, to a future where our species fulfills its potential for compassion and reverence for life, and especially to all the animals (human and non-human) who have suffered because of human ignorance, greed, alienation, and violence.

Contents

Foreword
Illuminating the Philosophy and Methods of Animal Liberation
Ward Churchill 1

Introducing the Animal Liberation Front 7

Animal Liberation Front Guidelines 8

Introduction
Behind the Mask: Uncovering the Animal Liberation Front
Steven Best, PhD, and Anthony J. Nocella II 9

History 65
Thirty Years of Direct Action
Noel Molland 67
Animal Liberation—By "Whatever Means Necessary"
Robin Webb 75
A Personal Overview of Direct Action in the United Kingdom
and the United States
Kim Stallwood 81

Liberation 91
Legitimizing Liberation
Mark Bernstein, PhD 93
At the Gates of Hell: The ALF and the Legacy
of Holocaust Resistance
Maxwell Schnurer, PhD 106
Abolition, Liberation, Freedom: Coming to a Fur Farm
Near You
Gary Yourofsky 128

Mothers with Monkeywrenches: Feminist Imperatives
and the ALF
  pattrice jones 137

Motivation 157
Aquinas's Account of Anger Applied to the ALF
  Judith Barad, PhD 159
Direct Actions Speak Louder than Words
  Rod Coronado 178
Touch the Earth
  Lawrence Sampson 185
Take No Prisoners
  Western Wildlife Unit 189

Perception 193
Understanding the ALF: From Critical Analysis
to Critical Pedagogy
  Anthony J. Nocella II 195
Open Rescues: Putting a Face on the Rescuers
and on the Rescued
  Karen Davis, PhD 202
From the Front Line to the Front Page — An Analysis
of ALF Media Coverage
  Karen Dawn 213

Tactics 229
How to Justify Violence
  Tom Regan, PhD 231
Direct Action: Progress, Peril, or Both?
  Freeman Wicklund 237
Defending Agitation and the ALF
  Bruce G. Friedrich 252
Bricks and Bullhorns
  Kevin Jonas 263
Revolutionary Process and the ALF
  Nicolas Atwood 272

Terror 277
ALF and ELF — Terrorism Is as Terrorism Does
  Paul Watson 279

The Rhetorical "Terrorist": Implications of the USA
Patriot Act for Animal Liberation
  Jason Black and Jennifer Black 288
It's War! The Escalating Battle Between Activists
and the Corporate-State Complex
  Steven Best, PhD 300

Afterword: The ALF: Who, Why, and What?
  Ingrid Newkirk 341

Appendices 345
1: My Experience with Government Harassment
  Rod Coronado 345
2: Letters From the Underground: Parts I and II
  Anonymous 354
3: Defining Terrorism
  Steven Best, PhD, and Anthony J. Nocella II 361

Contact Resources 379

About the Authors 383

Index 393

FOREWORD

Illuminating the Philosophy and Methods
of Animal Liberation

WARD CHURCHILL

The fire *this* time.—Eldridge Cleaver, 1969

For the past four decades, an entity loosely referred to as the "animal rights movement" has conducted an increasingly concerted series of direct actions against industries, "sports," and scientific enterprises guilty of the confinement, abuse, torture and mass death of nonhuman beings. From physical disruptions of English fox hunts during the early 1960s to a raid upon Oxford Laboratory animal colonies in 1974, from infiltration/disruption of New York University Medical Center's experimental facility in 1977 to the torching of an animal diagnostics lab at the University of California-Davis a decade later, from the 1997 rescue of over 10,000 mink from the Arritola Mink Farm in Oregon to the still more recent arson of a partly complete ski resort near Vail, Colorado, that was eradicating the habitat of the local lynx population, animal rights activists have engaged in several thousand noteworthy actions in two dozen countries for forty years. Along the way, they have extracted penalties from their opponents running into the hundreds of millions of dollars.

Often stunning in their sheer audacity—and in the dexterity with which they've been carried out—these assaults upon the sites of carnage have commanded considerable public attention. They've also been systematically decontextualized, sensationalized, and otherwise distorted by the minions of the establishment media with the result that, although every action has been crafted in such a way that not a single fatality has resulted from the movement's lengthy campaign of sabotage, the activists responsible are commonly viewed as "terrorists." Hence, the methods, if not the objectives, of groups like the Animal Liberation Front, the Earth Liberation Front, the Sea Shepherd Conservation Society, and Earth First! have been as readily condemned by all too many self-styled progressives as they have by the governmental and corporate officials most directly under attack.

To be valid, however, denunciation requires an accurate understanding of that which is denounced. And, unquestionably, those committed to the struggle for animal liberation are among the least understood of all contemporary oppositionists, not only in tactical terms, but philosophically. It is therefore fortunate that Steven Best and Anthony Nocella have teamed up to provide the present volume, providing as it does what is undeniably the most detailed and comprehensive overview of the thinking that has underpinned the sustained and to all accounts growing activism on behalf, not only of nonhuman animals, but the natural order in its entirety. One will finish reading this book agreeing or disagreeing with what is said herein, or more likely some combination of the two, but one cannot read it and at the same time remain functionally ignorant of what the animal liberationists are doing and why they are doing it. *Terrorists or Freedom Fighters?* is thus a perfect antidote to the falsehoods spewed on a regular basis by the likes of CNN and Fox News; it provides the basis, that is, for constructing genuinely informed opinions on its subject matter. Suffice it to say that no more can be asked of any book.

The probability is that those who avail themselves of the essays that follow, regardless of their preexisting political perspectives, will find themselves holding far more in common with the most militant animal rights advocates than they'd previously imagined. The logic employed by the movement is, in a word, compelling. It cannot be evaded even by those, such as myself, who explicitly privilege humans over other species by taking as the centerpiece of our posture an active resistance to genocide and such corollaries as racism, colonialism and aggressive war. Given that the key to the "genocidal mentality" resides, as virtually all commentators agree, in the perpetrators' conscious "dehumanization of the Other" they have set themselves to exterminating, it follows that removal of the self-assigned license enjoyed by humans to do as they will to/with nonhumans can only serve to better the lot of humans targeted for dehumanization/subjugation/eradication.[1]

In sum, it is more than superficially arguable that to attack the grotesqueries of scientific/medical experimentation using live simians is to seriously undermine the psychointellectual foundation upon which the nazi doctors stood when using dehumanized humans to the same purpose at Dachau and elsewhere (and upon which the nazis' American counterparts stand when undertaking projects like the Tuskegee Experiment, MK-ULTRA, and so on).[2] By the same token, to assault the meatpacking industry is to mount a challenge to the mentality that allowed well over a million dehumanized humans to be systematically slaughtered by the SS einsatzgruppen in eastern Europe during the early 1940s, and the nazis' simultaneous development of truly industrial killing techniques in places like Auschwitz, Sobibor and Treblinka[3] (one might look to the penal labor camps of America's Deep South and American Indian residential schools in both the US and Canada during a slightly earlier period to find counterpart examples[4]). The implications embodied in such connections are, of course, theoretically profound.

Among other issues raised is the manner in which those purporting to oppose a genocidal—or, in the terms posed by animal liberationists, *omnicidal*—reality are obliged to confront it. Can the constraints of dialogue or debate concerning the ethics and morality of genocide/omnicide *really* be appropriate to a context in which one side of the debate entitles itself to perpetrate such crimes even while the supposed "dialogue" is being conducted? The answer, to be sure, is—*must* be—an unequivocal "no." The niceties attending this sort of civic discourse pertain *only* to situations in which commission of the offending course of action has yet to be undertaken or in which the perpetrators are willing to suspend their activities pending resolution of the debate. Neither of these circumstances prevailing, direct action of the sort designed to disrupt—and at an optimum halt—the process of commission is absolutely essential. In the alternative, the "opposition" is an utter farce.

That said, the question becomes which varieties of direct action may be warranted. The answer is to a significant extent situational; that is, determined by the nature of the offense confronted. Abridgements of civil rights—those evident under a regime of Jim Crow racial segregation (apartheid), for example—can perhaps be addressed more or less exclusively by reliance upon such methods as mass demonstrations, strikes, boycotts, sit-ins, and the like. So, too,

problems like wage inequity and occupational safety. But is there anyone deluded enough to believe that such tactics might in themselves
have been effective—and thus appropriate as a set of methodological
constraints—as a means of confronting/stopping the Hitlerian genocide?[5] That making condemnatory statements, sending petitions, refusing to buy German products, staging rallies/marches in protest, and/or
conducting prayer vigils and other such bearings of witness to the nazi
slaughter constituted *all* that "moral" or "responsible" persons
could/should have done in response?

Animal liberationists, unlike the great majority of oppositionists in
other vectors, appear, at least in principle, to have drawn the correct
conclusions from these and comparable queries. To this extent, if none
other, there is much to be learned from their praxis. At the same time,
however, it seems to be a consensus position within groups like the
ALF and the ELF that infliction of property damage upon entities
engaged in the willful perpetration of omnicide constitutes the limit of
legitimate response to the crimes at hand. Plainly, if there is the least
merit to the above-discussed nazi analogy—which is advanced with
regularity by proponents of animal rights—then the drawing of such a
figurative line in the tactical sand is as arbitrary as that drawn by those
who would restrict the range of responses to symbolic gestures.

The crux of the issue is revealed by the positing of another hypo-
thetical: Given the opportunity to do either in, say, 1942, would it have
been more effective/appropriate to have torched the office of Adolf
Eichmann, the nazi bureaucrat whose peculiar expertise made an
orderly implementation of the Final Solution possible, or to have eliminated Eichmann himself?[6] The answer need not be rendered as an
abstraction. Instead, it is bound up in the esteem in which the Czech
partisans who assassinated Eichmann's boss, SS Obergruppenführer
Reinhard Heydrich, continue to be held even by those inclined most
vociferously to revile the ALF/ELF brand of "ecoterrorism."[7] Similarly,
the degree of valorization now all but universally accorded the so-
called June Plotters—i.e., the group of German military officers and
diplomats who attempted to assassinate Adolf Hitler himself in 1944—
speaks eloquently to the conclusion which must be drawn.[8] Neither a
principle or an analysis, after all, is more valuable than the consistency with which they are applied.

Whether and how such unification of principle, analysis and action
should—or can—be actualized in the present setting are matters that
Terrorists or Freedom Fighters? only begins to address. Nonetheless,
and to their everlasting credit, the authors whose work is assembled

herein lay much of the informational/conceptual groundwork necessary for such questions to be interrogated on a rational rather than
merely visceral basis. Best and Nocella are to be commended for having brought this collection of voices together. As well, Lantern Books
for having displayed the courage to make the result available to a general readership.

Notes

1. For explication of the quoted phrases, see Robert Jay Lifton and Eric Markusen, *The Genocidal Mentality: Nazi Holocaust and Nuclear Threat* (New York: Basic Books, 1988), and Tzvetan Todorov, *The Conquest of America: The Question of the Other* (New York: Harper & Row, 1984). Also see the section title "Yea Rats and Mice or Swarms of Lice," in my *Little Matter of Genocide: Holocaust and Denial in the Americas, 1492 to the Present* (San Francisco: City Lights Books, 1997), 169–78.

2. Robert Jay Lifton, *The Nazi Doctors: Medical Killing and the Psychology of Genocide* (New York: Basic Books, 1986); James H. Jones, *Bad Blood: The Tuskegee Syphilis Experiment* (New York: Free Press, 1981); John Marks, *The Search for the "Manchurian Candidate"* (New York: W.W. Norton, [2ⁿᵈ ed.] 1991); Martin A. Lee and Bruce Shlain, *Acid Dreams: The Complete Social History of LSD: The CIA, the Sixties, and Beyond* (New York: Grove Press [2ⁿᵈ ed.] 1992).

3. See Richard Rhodes, *Masters of Death: The SS Einsatzgruppen and the Invention of the Holocaust* (New York: Alfred A. Knopf, 2002); the section titled "Killing Center Operations" in Raul Hilberg's *The Destruction of the European Jews* (Chicago: Quadrangle Books, 1961), 555–638.

4. The death rate in the nazis' notorious Dachau concentration camp was 36 percent. At Buchenwald, it was 19 percent. At Mauthausen, generally considered to be the harshest of all nazi facilities other than outright extermination centers like Auschwitz, it was 58 percent; Michael Burleigh, *Ethics and Extermination: Reflections on the Nazi Genocide* (Cambridge, UK: Cambridge University Press, 1997), 211. By comparison, *no* prisoner is known to have survived a 10-year sentence under the conditions prevailing in Mississippi's convict leasing system from its 1866 inception to formal abolition in 1890; David M. Oshinsky, *"Worse Than Slavery": Parchman Farm and the Ordeal of Jim Crow Justice* (New York: Free Press, 1996), 46. On the residential schools, the conditions in which were so abysmal that a 50 percent mortality rate prevailed among the American Indian children incarcerated therein from roughly 1880 to 1930, see David Wallace Adams, *Education for Extinction: American Indians and the Boarding School Experience, 1875–1928* (Lawrence: University Press of Kansas, 1995); John S. Milloy, *"A National Crime": The Canadian Government and the Residential School System, 1879 to 1986* (Winnipeg: University of Manitoba Press, 1999).

5. Gandhi apparently filled the bill in this regard. As has been noted elsewhere, "Civil disobedience as a strategy of political opposition can succeed only with a govern-
ment ruled by conscience. In 1938, after Kristallnacht, when Gandhi advised the Jews in Germany to employ *Satyagraha*, the Indian version of passive resistance, he disclosed his inability to distinguish between English and German political morality"; Lucy S. Dawidowicz, *The War Against the Jews* (New York: Free Press, [2ⁿᵈ ed.] 1985), 274.

6. Hannah Arendt, *Eichmann in Jerusalem: A Report on the Banality of Evil* (New York: Penguin, 1964); Jochen von Lang and Claus Sibyll, eds., *Eichmann Interrogated: Transcripts from the Archive of the Israeli Police* (New York: De Capo Press, 1999).
7. Callum MacDonald, *The SS Obergruppenführer Reinhard Heydrich* (New York: Free Press, 1989).
8. Peter Hoffmann, *The History of the German Resistance, 1933–1945* (Montréal/Kingston: McGill-Queens University Press, [3ʳᵈ ed.] 1996), 263–534.

Introducing the
Animal Liberation Front

Reprinted from the ALF Primer

The Animal Liberation Front consists of small autonomous groups of people all over the world who carry out direct action according to the ALF guidelines.

These groups, called cells, range from one individual to many individuals working closely together. Activists in one cell do not know ALF activists in another cell because they remain anonymous. This is what helps to keep activists out of jail, and free to be active another day.

Since there is not a central organization or membership guide to the ALF, people are driven only by their own personal conscience or cell decisions to carry out actions. The ALF is non-hierarchical in its structure, which allows for only those people involved directly in the action to control their own destiny.

Anyone in your community could be part of the ALF without you knowing. This includes PTA parents, church volunteers, your spouse, your neighbor, or your mayor. No one is immune to the suffering of animals, which includes even the workers themselves in any animal abuse industry who cannot bear to watch animals withering in pain any longer.

Any action that adheres to the strict nonviolence guidelines, which follow, can be considered an ALF action. Economic sabotage and property destruction are considered ALF actions, as well as live liberations. Volunteers carry out actions across the world to bring animal liberation a little closer to the victims of untold agony.

Since there isn't a way to contact the ALF in your area, it is up to each of us to take the responsibility ourselves to stop the exploitation of fellow animals. In the words of a convicted ALF activist, "when you see the pictures of a masked liberator, stop asking who's behind the mask and look in the mirror!"

ANIMAL LIBERATION FRONT GUIDELINES

Reprinted from the ALF Primer

To liberate animals from places of abuse, i.e., laboratories, factory farms, fur farms, etc., and place them in good homes where they may live out their natural lives, free from suffering.

To inflict economic damage to those who profit from the misery and exploitation of animals.

To reveal the horror and atrocities committed against animals behind locked doors, by performing nonviolent direct actions and liberations.

To take all necessary precautions against harming any animal, human and nonhuman.

Any group of people who are vegetarians or vegans and who carry out actions according to ALF guidelines have the right to regard themselves as part of the ALF.

INTRODUCTION

Behind the Mask: Uncovering the Animal Liberation Front

STEVEN BEST, PhD, AND ANTHONY J. NOCELLA II

The world only goes forward because of those who oppose it.—Goethe

But if you have no relationship with the living things on this earth, you may lose whatever relationship you have with humanity.—Krishnamurti

On September 11, 2001, the political landscape changed dramatically. Instantaneously, it became unpatriotic to criticize President Bush, the government, or US policy on any front. Activist groups like the Sierra Club announced that they were indefinitely suspending all criticism against Bush's pro-corporate agenda as the nation tried to pull together. Without question, there were real enemies outside our continent to be wary of, but the government exaggerated the threat as it began to identify imaginary enemies within. The "war on terrorism" quickly became an attack on civil liberties, free speech, and domestic dissent. While flags waved everywhere, the Bush administration was gutting freedoms and shredding the Constitution, moving America ever closer to tyranny.

Nowhere was this dynamic more obvious than with the October 26, 2001 passage of the USA Patriot Act, which endowed the government with unprecedented powers of surveillance, search and seizure, and suppression of dissent (see Best and Black and Black in this volume).[1] As liberty was being attacked in the name of "security," activists in the post-9/11 world confronted a threatening new terrain where political action against the state and corporations decimating animals and despoiling the earth was suppressed and conflated with "terrorism" in order to legitimate severe political repression.

During this turbulent time when the nation and its patriots called for unity—a "unity" that masks deep divisions, injustices, and conflicts inherent in the US—the war between animal rights and environmental activists on one side, and corporate exploiters and the state on the other, began to heat up as never before (see Best in this volume).[2] Animal rights and environmental activists refuse to ignore the plight of the natural world as the country focuses on the human costs of global conflicts; rather, they emphasize the bloody war the human species has perennially waged on nonhuman species and the violence and terrorism of the human pogrom against the earth. Far from backing down in the face of government repression, the militant wings of the animal rights and environmental movements have escalated their struggles and thereby provoked an intense confrontation with their enemies in the state and corporate worlds.

We have entered a neo-McCarthyite period rooted in witch-hunts against activists and critics of the ruling elites. The terms and players have changed, but the situation is much the same as in the 1950s: the terrorist threat usurps the communist threat, Attorney General John Ashcroft dons the garb of Senator Joseph McCarthy, and the Congressional Meetings on Eco-Terrorism stand in for the House Un-American Activities Committee. Now as then, the government informs the public that the nation is in a permanent state of danger, such that security, not freedom, must become our overriding concern. As before, the state conjures up dangerous enemies everywhere, not only outside our country but, more menacingly, ensconced within our borders, lurking in radical cells. The alleged dangers posed by foreign terrorists are used to justify the attack on "domestic terrorists" within, and in a hysterical climate the domestic terrorist is any and every citizen expressing dissent.

But the state's tactic can only backfire, for if every dissenting group is branded as "terrorist," none are terrorist, and the true enemies become harder to identify. As US policy fails miserably in Afghanistan and Iraq, with chaos, anti-American hostilities, soldier casualties, public opposition, and terrorist threats growing, the government nonetheless squanders significant resources to persecute animal rights and environmental activists whom the state, corporations, and mass media smear as "violent" and demonize as "terrorists." The new ecowarriors, however, insist that their only crime is a principled defense of the earth and the billions of animals massacred in an ongoing global holocaust. As ecowarriors see it, the human individuals, corporations, and state entities that promote or defend the exploitation of the natural world are the true violent forces and the real terrorists.

Thus, in the post-9/11 climate, intense controversy brews around the discourse of violence and terrorism. And so the questions arise: Who and what are "terrorists"? And, conversely, who and what are "freedom fighters"? What is "violence," and who are the main perpetuators of it? It is imperative that we resist corporate, state, and mass media definitions, propaganda, and conceptual conflations in order to distinguish between freedom fighters and terrorists, between nonviolent civil disobedience and "domestic terrorism," and between ethically justified destruction of property and wanton violence toward life.

I. The ALF: The Newest Liberation Movement

Where there is disharmony in the world, death follows.
—Ancient Navajo saying

Animal liberation is the ultimate freedom movement, the "final frontier."—Robin Webb, British ALF Press Officer

This is a book about a new breed of freedom fighters—human activists who risk their own liberty to rescue and aid animals imprisoned in hellish conditions. Loosely bonded in a decentralized, anonymous, underground, global network, these activists are members of the Animal Liberation Front (ALF). Their daring deeds have earned them a top spot on the FBI "domestic terrorist" list as they redefine political struggle for the current era. An intense sense of urgency informs their actions. They recognize a profound crisis in the human relation with the natural world, such that the time has long passed for moderation, delay, and compromise. They can no longer fiddle while the earth burns and animal bodies pile up by the billions; they are compelled to take immediate and decisive action.

ALF activists operate under cover, at night, wearing balaclavas and ski masks, and in small cells of a few people. After careful reconnaissance, skilled liberation teams break into buildings housing animal prisoners in order to release them (e.g., mink and coyotes) or rescue them (e.g., cats, dogs, mice, and guinea pigs). They seize and/or destroy equipment, property, and materials used to exploit animals, and they use arson to raze buildings and laboratories. They have cost the animal exploitation industries hundreds of millions of dollars.[3] They willfully break the law because the law wrongly consigns animals to cages and confinement, to loneliness and pain, to torture and death. They target a wide range of animal exploiters, from vivisectors and the fur industry to factory farmers, foie gras producers, and fast food restaurants.

Resolved not to harm living beings, motivated by love, empathy, compassion, and justice, animal liberationists are the antithesis of the "terrorists" that government, industries, and mass media ideologues impugn them to be. They are not violent aggressors against life; they are defenders of freedom and justice for any enslaved species. They uphold rights not covered by law, knowing that the legal structure is defined by and for human supremacists. The goal of the ALF is not simply to liberate individual animals here and there; it is to free all animals from every form of slavery that binds them to human oppressors. The ALF, like the animal rights movement as a whole, is attacking the entire institutional framework of animal exploitation along with the domineering values, mindset, identities, and worldviews of the human species.

Although human slavery has been outlawed in "liberal democracies" where many dispossessed and disenfranchised groups gain more rights and respect (while industries still command slave trades in domestic and foreign sweatshops), animal slavery in many ways has become worse than ever. This is the case in the sheer number of animals killed, the degree of violation of their natural lives (culminating in the technological manipulations of genetic engineering and cloning), and often in the intensity and prolonged nature of their suffering (as evident in the horrors of vivisection, fur farming, factory farming, mechanized slaughter, puppy mills, and so on).[4] Animal "welfare" laws do little but regulate the details of exploitation.[5]

Just as nineteenth-century white abolitionists in the US worked across racial lines to create new forms of solidarity, so the new freedom fighters reach across *species* lines to help our fellow beings in the animal world. In this endeavor, they unleash a frontal assault on the prevalent mentality that says animals are objects, resources, or property, and they advance the universalization of rights that is the key marker of moral progress.[6]

By expanding the definition of the moral community, animal liberationists challenge long-entrenched prejudices. These relate not only to class, gender, race, sexual orientation, or specific interest groups, but also to the human species itself—to the arrogant conception of its place in the web of life and its ugly, condescending, vicious, and violent attitudes toward other species. *Speciesism* is the belief that nonhuman species exist to serve the needs of the human species, that animals are in various senses inferior to human beings, and therefore that one can favor human over nonhuman interests according to species status alone.[7] Like racism or sexism, speciesism creates a false dualistic division between one group and another in order to arrange the differences hierarchically and justify the domination of the "superior" over the "inferior." Just as society has discerned that it is prejudiced, illogical, and unacceptable for whites to devalue people of color and for men to diminish women, so it is beginning to learn how utterly arbitrary and irrational it is for human animals to position themselves over nonhuman animals because of species differences. Among animals who are all sentient subjects of a life, these differences—humanity's claim to be the sole bearer of reason and language—are no more ethically relevant than differences of gender or skin color, yet in the unevolved psychology of the human primate they have decisive bearing. The theory—speciesism—informs the practice—unspeakably cruel forms of domination, violence, and killing.

The animal liberation struggle is the most difficult battle human beings have ever fought, because it requires widespread agreement to abandon what most perceive as their absolute privileges and God-given rights to exploit animals by sole virtue of their human status. Moreover, where the stakes of human liberation struggles were largely confined to particular interests, the failure of human beings to drastically reframe their attitudes and relations to animals—such as inform trophy hunting of endangered species and factory farming on a worldwide scale—will have catastrophic and global consequences for all humanity, if for no other reason than systemic environmental collapse resulting from ecological disruption, pollution, rainforest destruction, desertification, and global warming.

In a capitalist society, human struggles for freedom—especially those of gender, race, or sexual "identity politics"—can easily be co-opted and absorbed into the channels of affirmative action, "representative democracy," "liberal pluralism," and multicultural consumerism, where their critical edge is blunted.[8] Similarly, animal welfare advocacy is easily absorbed by current systems of domination. But the fight for animal liberation demands radical transformations in the habits, practices, values, and mindset of all human beings as it also entails a fundamental restructuring of social institutions and economic systems predicated on exploitative practices. The philosophy of animal liberation assaults the identities and worldviews that portray humans as conquering lords and masters of nature, and it requires entirely new ways of relating to animals and the earth. Animal liberation is a direct attack on the power human beings—whether in premodern or modern, non-Western or Western societies—have claimed over animals since Homo sapiens began systematically hunting them over two million years ago. The new struggle seeking freedom for other species has the potential to advance rights, democratic consciousness, psychological growth, and awareness of biological interconnectedness to higher levels than previously achieved in history.

Animal liberation is the next logical development in moral evolution. Animal liberation builds on the most progressive ethical and political advances human beings have made in the last 200 years and carries them to their logical conclusions. Animal liberation demands that human beings give up their sense of superiority over other animals and tear down the Berlin Wall between species. It challenges people to realize that power demands responsibility, that might is not right, and that an enlarged neocortex is no excuse to rape and plunder the natural world. Animal liberation requires that people transcend the comfortable boundaries of humanism in order to make a qualitative leap in ethical consideration, thereby moving the moral bar from reason and language to sentience and subjectivity. Distorted conceptions of human beings as demigods who command the planet must be replaced with the far more humble and holistic notion that they belong to and are dependent upon vast networks of living relationships. Unless human beings radically alter their relations toward animals and the earth by creating new worldviews, identities, sensibilities, and an ethic of reverence for life, animals will continue to die by the billions and one third to one half of the earth's life forms may go extinct in the next few decades.

Since the fates of all species on this planet are intricately interrelated, the exploitation of animals cannot but have a major impact on the human world itself. When human beings exterminate animals, they devastate habitats and ecosystems necessary for their own lives. When they butcher farmed animals by the billions, they ravage rainforests, exacerbate global warming, and spew toxic wastes into the environment. When they construct a global system of factory farming that squanders vital resources such as land, water, and crops, they aggravate the problems of desertification and world hunger. When humans are violent toward animals, they often are violent toward one another. The connections may go far deeper. Some theorists argue that the cruel forms of domesticating animals at the dawn of agricultural society created the technologies and conceptual model for hierarchy, state power, and the exploitative treatment of other human beings, as many feminists argue speciesism and patriarchy emerged together with the rise of male power (see jones in this volume).[9]

In countless ways, the exploitation of animals rebounds to create crises within the human world itself. The vicious circle of violence and destruction can end only if and when the human species learns to form harmonious relations with other species and the natural world. Thus, animal liberation and human liberation are interrelated projects.

II. Direct Action and Democracy

Power concedes nothing without a demand. It never did and it never will.—Frederick Douglass

Even voting for the right thing is doing nothing for it. It is only expressing to men feebly your desire that it should prevail. A wise man will not leave the right to the mercy of chance, nor wish it to prevail through the power of the majority.—Henry David Thoreau

Direct action is always the clamorer, the initiator, through which the great sum of indifferentists become aware that oppression is getting intolerable.—Voltairine de Cleyre (1866–1912), American anarchist and feminist writer

We always obeyed the law. Even if you don't agree with a law personally, you still obey it. Otherwise life would be chaos. —Gertrude Scholtz-Klink, chief of the Women's Bureau under Adolf Hitler

Anyone quick to condemn the tactics of the ALF needs a history lesson and logical consistency check. Especially amid the current hysteria over war and terrorism, it is easy to forget that the United States won its independence not only by war with England, but also through acts of nonviolent civil disobedience, including property destruction. As dramatically evident in the Boston Tea Party, when in 1773 fifty members of the underground Sons of Liberty group dumped 342 chests of

British tea into the Boston harbor to protest the high tax on tea and British tyranny in general, the colonies employed sabotage tactics to undermine the power of the British and to galvanize the will of the newly emerging nation. Of this form of "terrorism," John Adams said, "There is a dignity, a majesty, a sublimity, in this . . . effort of the patriots that I greatly admire."[10]

Not merely an act of senseless demolition, property destruction was and still is a legitimate cry for justice and a powerful means of achieving it. Civil disobedience and sabotage have been key catalysts for many modern liberation struggles. As James Goodman succinctly puts it,

> The entire edifice of western liberal democracy—from democratic rights, to representative parliament, to freedom of speech—rests on previous acts of civil disobedience. The American anti-colonialists in the 1770s asserting "no taxation without representation"; the French revolutionaries in the 1780s demanding "liberty, equality, fraternity"; the English Chartists in the 1830s demanding a "People's Charter"; the Suffragettes of the 1900s demanding "votes for women"; the Gandhian disobedience movement from the 1920s calling for "Swaraj"/self-government; all of these were movements of civil disobedience, and have shaped the political traditions that we live with today.[11]

Few things are more American and patriotic than dissent, protest, civil disobedience, and property destruction in the name of freedom and liberation. From the Boston Tea Party to the Underground Railroad, from the Suffragettes to the Civil Rights Movement; from Vietnam War resistance to the Battle of Seattle, key struggles in US history employed illegal direct action tactics—and sometimes violence—to advance the historical movement toward human rights and freedoms. Rather than being a rupture in some bucolic tradition of Natural Law guiding the Reason of modern citizens to the Good and bringing Justice down to earth in a peaceful and gradual drizzle, the movements for animal and earth liberation are a continuation of the American culture of rights, democracy, civil disobedience, and direct action, as they expand the struggle to a far broader constituency.

American history has two main political traditions. First, there is the "indirect" system of "representative democracy" whereby citizens express their needs and wants to elected local and state officials whose sole function is to "represent" them in the political and legal system.

The system's "output"—laws—reflects the "input"—the people's will and interests. This cartoon image of liberal democracy, faithfully reproduced in generation after generation of textbooks and in the discourse of state apologists and the media, is falsified by the fact that powerful economic and political forces co-opt elected officials, who represent the interests of the elite instead of the majority.[12] From the realization that the state is hardly a neutral arbiter of competing interests but rather exists to advance the interests of economic and political elites, a second political tradition of direct action has emerged.

Direct action advocates argue that the indirect system of representative democracy is irredeemably corrupted by money, power, cronyism, and privilege. Appealing to the lessons of history, direct activists insist that one cannot win liberation struggles solely through education, moral persuasion, political campaigns, demonstrations, or any form of aboveground, mainstream, or legal action. Direct action movements therefore bypass pre-approved efforts to influence the state in order to immediately confront the figures of social power they challenge. Whereas indirect action can promote passivity and dependence on others for change, direct action tends to be more involving and empowering. In the words of Voltairine de Cleyre, "the evil of pinning faith to indirect action is far greater than any . . . minor results. The main evil is that it destroys initiative, quenches the individual rebellious spirit, [and] teaches people to rely on someone else to do for them what they should do for themselves. . . . [People] must learn that their power does not lie in their voting strength, that their power lies in their ability to stop production."[13]

Direct action tactics can vary widely, ranging from sit-ins, strikes, boycotts, and tree sits to hacking Websites, email and phone harassment, home demonstrations, and arson, as well as bombings and murder. Direct action can be legal, as with home demonstrations against a vivisector, or illegal, as in the case of the civil disobedience tactics of Mohandas Gandhi and Martin Luther King Jr. Illegal direct action, moreover, can be nonviolent or violent, and can respect private property or destroy it.

Opponents of direct action often argue that illegal actions undermine the rule of law, and they view civil disobedience as a threat to political order. Among other things, this perspective presupposes that the system in question is legitimate or cannot be improved. It misrepresents direct activists as people who lack respect for the principles of law, when arguably they have a higher regard for the spirit of law and its relation to ethics and justice than those who fetishize political order for its own sake.[14] Moreover, this argument fails to grasp that many direct action advocates (such as in the ALF and ELF) are anarchists who seek to replace the states and legal systems they hold in contempt with the ethical substance of self-regulating decentralized communities. Whatever their approach, champions of direct action renounce uncritical allegiance to a legal system. To paraphrase Karl Marx, *the law is the opiate of the people*, and blind obedience to laws and social decorum led German Jews to their death with little resistance. All too often, the legal system is simply a Byzantine structure designed to absorb opposition and induce paralysis by deferral, delay, and dilution.

III. Origins of the ALF

We are a nonviolent guerrilla organization, dedicated to the liberation of animals from all forms of cruelty and persecution at the hands of mankind.—Ronnie Lee, ALF founder

Not to hurt our humble brethren is our first duty to them, but to stop there is not enough. We have a higher mission—to be of service to them whenever they require it.—St. Francis of Assisi

During the 1970s, environmental and (to a lesser extent) animal welfare and rights organizations became important forces in the US political landscape, taking their place alongside various social movements that emerged in the 1960s. While environmental and animal advocacy groups were increasingly influential and passed a number of laws protecting the environment and animals, they were compromise- and reform-oriented movements that became institutionalized, co-opted, and limited in the change they could effect. Their main tactics were letter writing, lobbying, boycotts, and sometimes protests and demonstrations. By the late 1970s and early 1980s, it became increasingly apparent that mainstream approaches had failed to bring about the substantive changes necessary to protect animals and the natural world, and that animal advocacy and environmental protection groups often had become part of the status quo they set out to change. Despite huge amounts of time, money, and energy invested in various strategies, the situation for animals and the earth was steadily worsening.[15]

Animal and environmental activists began looking for more radical and effective tactics of struggle. In 1977, for example, Paul Watson was voted out of Greenpeace for increasingly confrontational tactics with the butchers of newborn harp seals.[16] Rejecting Greenpeace's timid condemnation of sabotage tactics against animal exploiters, Watson formed a new organization that became the Sea Shepherd Conservation Society. With a 206-foot ship purchased with the help of Cleveland Amory and the Fund for Animals, Captain Watson and crew set sail on the high seas in defense of marine mammals everywhere. Watson rammed pirate whaling ships, impeded dolphin massacres, destroyed driftnets, and did whatever it took to defend his constituency, all without ever injuring human life (although his own life was often threatened, jeopardized, and nearly ended by sundry sealing thugs). Similarly, in 1981, Dave Foreman abandoned mainstream environmental politics in order to join with friends to create Earth First! and conduct campaigns of sabotage and monkeywrenching against loggers and other plunderers of nature.[17] Through tactics such as tree spiking, tree sitting, road blockades, chaining bodies to fences, pulling up survey stakes, and destroying equipment used to clear forests and build roads, Earth First! reinvented environmental politics for the new era of ecotage. As Watson, by his own count, has saved millions of animals, Earth First! successfully delayed, weakened, or stopped numerous development and logging projects.[18]

While direct action movements for radical ecology and animal rights were dawning in the US, a powerful new group known as the Animal Liberation Front was gaining strength in England and would forever change the struggle to protect animals and the earth. The roots of the ALF in England can be traced to the Bands of Mercy, a nineteenth-century Royal Society for the Prevention of Cruelty to Animals youth organization (see Molland and Webb in this volume). Originating in 1824, the Bands of Mercy focused their efforts on thwarting hunting. A similar English group, the Hunt Saboteurs Association (HSA), was established in 1963 to contest hunting and continues today.[19] HSA members disrupt hunting activities by blowing horns, blockading roads, setting off smoke bombs, distracting dogs with meat and false scents, and setting themselves in the path between the hunters and the hunted.

Women often played an important role in the HSA and were singled out by pro-hunt thugs as easy targets for violent physical attacks.[20] These courageous women challenged both the speciesism of the hunt and the patriarchal identities and authority of the hunters. The empowering ability of direct action is particularly important for women because it provides a potent vehicle to subvert traditional gender roles. As one author points out, "Women are gendered emotional and empathetic, but also passive and weak. Direct action on behalf of animals takes the desirable aspects of that gendered analysis (compassion, empathy) and destroys the oppressive aspects (passive, weak). In this way, women in the animal liberation movement who use direct action can be seen as creating new conceptions of gender."[21]

By 1965 HSA members grew tired of being assaulted by hunters and the courts, and sought more effective means to stop hunting. They decided to work underground and shift to property destruction tactics. In 1972 some HSA members formed a new organization in Luton, reviving the name of the Band of Mercy. Led by Ronnie Lee and Cliff Goodman, the group had a more militant philosophy and tactical approach. To stop hunting on land and at sea, they destroyed vans, boats, and equipment, and often succeeded in halting the slaughter. When Lee learned more about the horrors of animal testing, the group targeted vivisectors. On November 10, 1973, Lee's group set fire to a half-completed building at Milton Keynes—their first attack on the vivisection industry and their first use of arson.[22] Through such actions, the Band of Mercy sought to wreak enough property destruction that insurance companies would end coverage to exploitation industries, and in many cases they succeeded.

The Band of Mercy grew increasingly strong and bold, expanding their activities to include animal rescues. Through arson, destruction, and liberation, the group halted many hunts, saved many lives, undermined or shut down animal exploitation businesses, and helped to stop some possible ventures from even starting. The successes continued until Lee and Goodman were arrested in August 1974 for the raid on Oxford Laboratory Animal Colonies in Bicester. The two soon achieved national political fame as the "Bicester Two." Both were given three years in prison but served only a third of the time and received parole. Once released, the two took completely different paths. While Goodman became the first-ever police informer on the animal liberation movement, Lee evolved into an even stronger warrior for the animals. Lee organized more than 30 people to begin a potent new liberation campaign, choosing a name that would intimidate exploiters yet demonstrate the ethic of compassion. In 1976 Lee christened his group the Animal Liberation Front. The ALF soon became an international force, and currently has active cells in over 20 countries. The US in particular has become a hotbed of action.

Migration to the US

> We ask nicely for years and get nothing. Someone makes a threat, and it works.—Ingrid Newkirk

> We should never feel like we're going too far in breaking the law, because whatever laws you break to liberate animals or to protect the environment are very insignificant compared to the laws that are broken by that parliament of whores in Washington. They are the biggest lawbreakers, the biggest destroyers, the biggest mass-murderers on this planet right now.—Paul Watson

The facts of how the ALF started in the US are somewhat sketchy. According to Freeman Wicklund and Kim Stallwood (see this volume), the first ALF action in the US happened in 1977, when activists released two dolphins from a research facility in Hawaii.[23] Others identify the origin of the ALF in the raids that took place on March 14, 1979, at the New York University Medical Center, where activists disguised as lab workers liberated one cat, two dogs, and two guinea pigs.[24] The most complete account of the ALF in the US is chronicled in Ingrid Newkirk's book, *Free the Animals: The Amazing True Story of the Animal Liberation Front.*[25] Newkirk gives yet another genealogy, arguing that the ALF first emerged in the US in late 1982, with a Christmas Eve raid on a Howard University laboratory in order to rescue 24 cats whose rear legs were being crippled in a cruel experiment.

Newkirk's book eloquently captures the pathos of compassion, the drama of liberation, the courage of ALF activists, and their dedication to finding emergency and long-term medical care for the animals they liberate. To read Newkirk's book is to understand what the ALF does and why. Where references to the ALF might conjure up images of male warriors, it is significant that in this account the founder and key organizer of the ALF in America was a woman. Newkirk writes that witnessing the horrors of monkey experiments at the Institute for Behavioral Research in Silver Spring, Maryland, inspired "Valerie" to launch a US branch of the ALF. "Valerie" led numerous break-ins and liberations; funded vehicles, supplies, and transportation costs; served as transporter and facilitator; and overall was the principle force for establishing ALF cells throughout the country.

The first wave of ALF actions included the liberation of cats, dogs, rabbits, guinea pigs, pigs, and primates from experimental laboratories at Howard University, Bethesda Naval Research Institute, various branches of the University of California, the University of Oregon, the University of Pennsylvania, Texas Tech University, the City of Hope, SEMA lab, the Beltsville Agricultural Research Center, and elsewhere. One of the most important raids took place in May 1984, when the ALF broke into the University of Pennsylvania's head injury laboratory, where primates' heads were strapped in metal helmets and forcefully struck by a pneumatic device in order to research human head injuries. The ALF unleashed $60,000 in property damage and, more importantly, stole 60 hours of researchers' tapes that documented sadistic acts of cruelty and callous indifference to the suffering of the monkeys. The rescue led to the shocking movie *Unnecessary Fuss*, which helped to shut down the lab and, with public relations assistance from PETA, spread awareness of animal confinement and torture to the public.[26]

Similarly, liberations in January 1985 at the City of Hope National Medical Center, Los Angeles, exposed an appalling hellhole behind a façade of progressive science and "humane research." ALF rescues and follow-up media work via PETA news conferences brought national attention to deplorable conditions where dogs and other animals endured sloppy surgeries and inadequate or no post-operative care, and frequently bled to death in their cages or suffocated in their own fecal matter. Newspapers were inundated with letters from an outraged public, government investigations found serious violations of the federal Animal Welfare Act, the National Institutes of Health suspended over $1 million in federal research grant funds, and the experiments were stopped. Three months later, the ALF raided the University of California-Riverside laboratory to rescue Britches, a three-week-old macaque monkey separated from his mother, isolated in a wire cage with his eyes sewn shut. PETA filed formal complaints about this extreme abuse to government agencies, urged its members to write their representatives in Congress, and made a moving video of Britches. The "before" and "after" liberation pictures were stirring, and the justice of the action was obvious. Once again, the public learned about the kind of horrors that truly transpire behind the closed doors of "science," and Riverside received a well-deserved black eye. Eight of the 17 research projects interrupted by the ALF the night of Britches' liberation were closed forever.

The ALF was able not only to free innocent animals, but also to expose the sadism that masquerades as science, to educate the public about institutionalized animal abuse, to spark public debate about rarely discussed issues such as vivisection, and, in many cases, to bring about welfare reforms or to shut down some operations altogether. After numerous well-publicized raids and rescues, Newkirk writes, "Society's comfortable belief that all animal research was conducted humanely began to collapse."[27]

Whereas the early raids involving "Valerie" concentrated on rescues, the emphasis gradually shifted to property destruction and arson. One of the most devastating blows was dealt in 1987, with the torching of the animal diagnostics lab and 20 vehicles at the University of California at Davis, causing $5.1 million in damage. In February 1992 Rod Coronado and other ALF members set fire to a Michigan State University mink research facility, causing $100,000 in estimated damage and wiping out 32 years of research data accumulated to breed mink in fur farms. In an April 1989 raid on the University of Arizona at Tucson, activists liberated over 1,200 animals, costing the university an estimated $700,000. In May 1997 10,000 mink were released from Arritola Mink Farm in Oregon, the largest liberation in the US to date. In economic terms, the most costly act of arson destruction was inflicted on the Alaskan Fur Company in Minnesota in November 1996, creating over $2 million in damage to fur coats and other merchandise and over $250,000 to the building. While perhaps not as pleasing to the public as pictures of rescued animals, these actions had powerful economic effects on industry targets.

IV. Philosophy and Structure of the ALF

> We're very dangerous philosophically. Part of the danger is that we don't buy into the illusion that property is worth more than life . . . we bring that insane priority into the light, which is something the system cannot survive.—David Barbarash, former spokesman for the ALF

If one is looking for groups with which to compare the ALF, the proper choice is not Al Qaeda or Saddam Hussein's Republican Guard, but rather the Jewish anti-Nazi resistance movement and the Underground Railroad. The men and women of the ALF pattern themselves after the freedom fighters in Nazi Germany who liberated war prisoners and Holocaust victims and destroyed equipment—such as weapons, railways, and gas ovens—that the Nazis used to torture and kill their victims. Similarly, by providing veterinary care and homes for many of the animals they liberate, the ALF models itself after the US

Underground Railroad movement, which helped fugitive slaves reach free states and Canada. Whereas corporate society, the state, and mass media brand the ALF as terrorists, the ALF has important similarities with some of the great freedom fighters of the past two centuries, and is akin to contemporary peace and justice movements in its quest to end bloodshed and violence toward life and to win justice for other species.

On the grounds that animals have basic rights, animal liberationists repudiate the argument that scientists or industries can own any animal as their property.[28] Simply stated, animals have the right to life, liberty, and the pursuit of happiness, all of which contradict the property status that is often literally burnt into their flesh. Even if animal "research" assists human beings in some way, that is no more guarantee of legitimacy than if the data came from experimenting on non-consenting human beings, for the rights of an animal trump utilitarian appeals to human benefit. The blanket privileging of human over animal interests is simply speciesism, a prejudicial and discriminatory belief system as ethically flawed and philosophically unfounded as sexism or racism, but far more murderous and consequential in its implications. Thus, the ALF hold that animals are freed, not stolen, from fur farms or laboratories—and that when one destroys the inanimate property of animal exploiters, one is merely leveling what was wrongfully used to violate the rights of living beings.

The ALF is any individual or group in any area of the world who at any time decide to strike against animal exploitation in the name of animal rights while following ALF guidelines (see this volume). To join the ALF, one does not consult the local *Yellow Pages*; rather, one goes into stealth action. There is no national leader to capture in order to decapitate the movement, only a host of individuals and affinity groups that spread rhizomatically and clandestinely. A given ALF cell is probably unaware of the identities and activities of other cells. This decentered structure defies government infiltration and capture, and thereby thwarts the kind of success the FBI had in its illegal surveillance, penetration, and disruption of the Students for a Democratic Society, the Black Panthers, the American Indian Movement, the Committee in Solidarity with the People of El Salvador, and numerous other groups.[29] Given the decentralized and anonymous nature of ALF actions, the ALF in principle is not about authority, ego, heroism, machismo, or martyrdom; rather, it is about overcoming hierarchy, patriarchy, passivity, and politics as usual so that creative individuals can dedicate themselves unselfishly to the cause of animal liberation. The structure and philosophy of the ALF thereby has some key affinities with anarchism and radical feminism (see Jones in this volume).

Crucially, the ALF follows a strict code of nonviolence whereby they carefully avoid causing physical injury to animal oppressors when they attack their property. The ALF claims that in thousands of actions and over three decades of operation, they have never harmed a single human being: "The ALF does not, in any way, condone violence against any animal, human or nonhuman. Any action involving violence is by definition not an ALF action, any person involved is not an ALF member."[30] Some critics, however, allege that on at least one occasion someone inadvertently was hurt (see Stallwood in this volume), while others question the validity of the claim to nonviolence by a philosophy that accepts that small animals may be injured or killed in arson attacks (see below). Still other detractors argue that the decentralized and anonymous nature of the ALF allows it to engage in physical violence and deny that the act was authentically ALF. The same structure, however, permits any rogue individual to wreak havoc in the name of the ALF in violation of its nonviolent principles.

In an "organization" where anyone can claim membership, there may be individuals who join the ALF for the wrong reasons—less because they believe in justice for other species than because they have destructive and violent temperaments or enjoy media attention from their actions. Such individuals clearly are ill-suited to the cause they betray, but do not discredit it. When position papers and manifestos signed by ALF members proliferate, and when there is no significant opposition to violence by other ALF members, then one can say that the ALF is a violent organization. For now, the ALF holds to a nonviolent stance that its opposition cannot claim, since police and thugs such as sealers and hunters often have violently assailed and killed animal activists.[31] But this point is never made by the apologists of animal exploitation, who arbitrarily define violence and terrorism as attacks on the property of industries and exploiters but not as assaults on animals, the earth, or defenders of the natural world.

While the ALF renounces physical violence against human beings, it also rejects the claim that destroying property is violence. The ALF is grounded in the principle that laws protecting animal exploitation industries are unjust, and they break them in deference to the higher moral principle of animal rights. As former ALF spokesperson David Barbarash sums up the ethical foundations of the ALF, "The basic premise is that if someone's property is used to inflict pain, suffering, and death on innocent animals' lives, then the destruction of that property is morally justified. It is not unlike freedom fighters in Nazi Germany destroying the gas chambers. The ALF believe that life is more important than things."[32]

Following a basic tenet of civil disobedience philosophy, the ALF believes that there is a higher law than that created by and for the corporate-state complex, a moral law that transcends the corrupt and biased statutes of the US political system. When the law is wrong, the right thing to do is to break it. This is often how moral progress is made in history, from defiance of American slavery and Hitler's anti-Semitism to sit-ins at "whites only" lunch counters in Alabama. Thoreau's maxim that one ought to obey one's own conscience rather than an unjust law is a good start toward critical thinking, autonomy, and political responsibility, but it can also provide a formula for violence.[33] To be consistent with its principles, the ALF must abide by the belief that however righteous their anger, no one must ever be harmed in the struggle for liberation of others; only property is to be damaged as a necessary means to the end of animal liberation. Despite their zeal, ALF members are unlike some radical anti-abortionists who kill their opponents, and the vast differences should never be conflated.

The ALF can be likened to peace and justice movements with the pronounced differences that it militates for other species and challenges the arbitrary boundaries of the community of rights-bearers as set by "progressive" humanist philosophies and struggles. The ALF demands justice for animals so that they may not be discriminated against, exploited, injured, and murdered solely because of their species. The ALF struggles for peace in the animal world so that nonhuman species may live among their families, fellow beings, and natural habitats unimpeded by the pain and violence human beings gratuitously inflict on them. The ALF is not a "hate group" motivated by appetites for destruction, wrath, and revenge; rather it is comprised of people who love animals and the earth, and who are guided by a positive vision of a world where human and nonhuman animals co-exist more harmoniously.

The activist thrust of the ALF shows that there is a clear distinction between animal welfare and animal rights, as well as between animal rights and animal liberation.[34] While those who adopt the animal welfare position seek merely to reduce animal suffering, supporters of animal rights aim to abolish it, demanding not bigger cages and "humane treatment," but rather empty cages and total liberation. Animal welfare philosophy accepts the property status of animals, but animal rights philosophy insists that animals are subjects of their own life and no one's to own. Whereas animal welfare philosophy reinforces the moral gulf between human and nonhuman animals and allows any use of animals so long as it furthers some alleged human interest, animal rights theory puts human and nonhuman animals on an equal moral plane and rejects all exploitative uses of animals, whether human beings benefit or not.[35]

Clearly, animal rights is the guiding moral philosophy of the ALF, but whereas animal rights often is a legal fight without direct action, animal liberation is an immediate confrontation with exploiters. ALF tactics move beyond protests and demonstrations outside animal prisons in order to illegally break into these compounds, to free their tormented captives, and to destroy the instruments of pain. While appreciating the value of education and philosophizing, working in aboveground and legal channels, and striving for long-term changes for the animals, ALF activists feel compelled to take immediate action, to directly free as many prisoners as possible, and to break any security system or law that stands between them and a suffering animal they can help. For the ALF, animals have fundamental rights to freedom, and these rights entail human duties to secure them.

V. The "Principled" Critique of the ALF

The question is not whether we will be extremists, but what kinds of extremists we will be. The nation and the world are in dire need of creative extremists.—Martin Luther King, Jr.

If the ALF uses "extreme" tactics, it is only because the evil done to animals is extreme and emergency measures are required in conditions where laws rigorously protect the holocaust unleashed by animal abusers. Despite ever-escalating government repression and penalties for animal and earth liberation actions, today's guerrilla warriors are not deterred or intimidated. "The only way to stop the ALF and ELF," asserts the North American Animal Liberation Front Press Office, "is for our society at large to seriously deal with the issues which have brought these people to take such dramatic actions, and that does not seem to be happening very quickly."[36]

Whether voiced by advocates within the movement or opponents outside of it, there are two common criticisms of ALF tactics, which we will call the "principled" or "intrinsic" and the "pragmatic" or "extrinsic" objections. The principled critique examines the intrinsic ethical nature of property destruction (is the action right or wrong?), while the pragmatic critique considers the extrinsic consequences of sabotage tactics (do sabotage actions help or hinder the movement?). The distinction between principled and pragmatic objections is an analytic one drawn for clarity's sake, and it should be clear that detractors can and often do conflate both critiques into one.

Proponents of the principled objection tend to uncritically define property destruction as violence and reject it as inherently wrong on this ground. Their argument assumes the form of a classic syllogism: (i) property destruction is violence, (ii) violence is always wrong, (iii) therefore, property destruction is wrong. These critics rarely define what they mean by "violence," they dogmatically cling to the pacifist positions of Gandhi and King, and they make unqualified universal judgments that violence is always wrong and never works politically to achieve liberation.

ALF opponents assert that the animal rights movement is grounded in the values of nonviolence and that "violent tactics" contradict these values. Consequently, they argue that groups like the ALF and Stop Huntingdon Animal Cruelty (SHAC) disarm the movement's moral advantage, which is best exerted in ethical persuasion and education efforts intended to create legislative changes. Some may criticize any effort at illegal direct action, while others may only object to property destruction and allow other means of illegal direct action such as open rescues. Those who use violence in the fight for animal rights, ALF opponents say, degenerate into the same mindset they are challenging and reproduce destructive social dynamics. The end does not justify the means; rather, the end must be reflected in the means. The argument here could be summarized in Gandhi's phrase, "Be the change you seek."

Advocates of the principled critique believe that illegal actions and "violence" are unnecessary for a cause strong enough to prevail on the logical arguments supporting it. Peter Singer, for example, affirms "animal liberation" as a just cause, so long as it remains "nonviolent."[37] Violence can only beget more violence, he argues, recommending that animal liberationists emulate Gandhi and King in their goal to divest themselves of hatred, anger, and the will to revenge. Singer thinks that direct action is most effective when it brings results other tactics cannot, and uncovers evidence of extreme animal abuse that awakens public understanding about the plight of animals. As an example of a just and effective raid, he points to the ALF break-in at the University of Pennsylvania head injury research laboratory, which exposed a truth never meant to be seen by the public. Singer argues that to stop or reduce animal suffering "we must change the minds of reasonable people in our society. . . . The strength of the case for Animal Liberation is its ethical commitment; we occupy the high moral ground and to abandon it is to play into the hands of those who oppose us. . . . The wrongs we inflict on other species are . . . [undeniable] once they are seen plainly; and it is in the rightness of our cause, and not the fear of our bombs, that our prospects of victory lie."[38] The motto here is not Burn Baby Burn, but Learn Baby Learn.

Education and ethical argumentation are indeed potent forces of change. In many cases, argumentation—especially if reinforced by powerful images of animal suffering—can sway reasonable, open-minded, and decent people whose problem is that they do not know, not that they do not care. Passionate and eloquent animal rights educators like Gary Yourofsky have changed many minds and lives across the country. Indeed, many of the leading figures in the animal advocacy movement such as Don Barnes, Steve Hindi, and Howard Lyman are, respectively, former vivisectors, hunters, and cattlemen who had a profound awakening and were transformed through education. Moreover, the movement continues to innovate powerful new means of education, communication, and legislation because more can be done within the mainstream paradigm, and advocates proclaim that one must not prematurely close any doors to respectful dialogue with the public and animal oppressors.[39]

While Singer and many others appeal to the "minds of reasonable people," the ALF believes that far too many are unreasonable and closed-minded, rendering the force of reason and persuasion insufficient. Industries and the state have strong institutional and monetary biases against justice for animals that no amount of persuasion or education is likely to change. Those who champion education and legislation as the sole tools of struggle project a rationalist belief that discounts the irrational forces often ruling the human psyche, the sadistic pleasure all too many derive from torture and killing, the deep psychological mechanisms human beings use to resist change and unpleasant realities, the mechanisms of detachment and compartmentalization that allow them to ignore the enormity of animal suffering, the vested interests they have in exploiting animals, and their identities as members of a species they believe is the preordained master of the earth.

Semantic Quagmires: Defining "Violence" and "Terrorism"

It's a strange kind of terrorist organization that hasn't killed anyone.—*The Observer*

A man that should call everything by its right name would hardly pass the streets without being knocked down as a common enemy.—George Savile, first Marquess of Halifax

A key controversy surrounding the ALF concerns whether or not their actions are "violent" and whether they are "terrorists." Before one can productively address these questions, it is important to provisionally define the terms; yet rarely do critics undertake this task, and when they do their definitions typically are flawed, biased, inconsistent, and politically motivated.[40] Because their definitions are vague and circular, dictionaries are a problematic place to start. But if we consult them we find that they define violence in broad terms, such that a "violent" act involves "exertion of physical force to injure or abuse" (Merriam Webster Collegiate Dictionary, Tenth Edition) or the "purpose of violating, damaging, or abusing" (American Heritage Dictionary). Terms such as "injure" or "abuse" themselves need precise definitions, and dictionaries tend not to specify whether violence applies only to living beings or also to physical objects—obviously a key question in discussions of animal liberation through illegal direct action.

Some key questions immediately arise: Is property destruction violence, or is this an unwarranted extension of the term that distorts its meaning? If property destruction can legitimately be called violence, and the ALF might therefore be labeled a violent organization, is violence always wrong? Or are there times when violent actions in defense of human and nonhuman animals are legitimate and necessary?

A reasonable definition of "violence" would seem to be an intentional act of one individual or group against another individual or group that inflicts physical damage or harm upon their bodies, possibly resulting in death. The word "intentional" is important. If one willfully and purposively intends to physically harm another person, that is violence, but it is not violence if one does it unwittingly or by mistake. If an enraged person intentionally shoots another person with a gun or runs over him or her with a car, that person has committed a violent act, but if the gun fires by mistake or the driver falls asleep at the wheel, that is sheer accident or possibly neglect (even though there may be "violent" consequences involving bloodshed, injury, and death).

But there are many ways to harm, injure, or abuse another person without causing physical damage, and so violence might require a broader definition. Violence could involve the intentional infliction of psychological as well as physical injury, such as in a situation of domestic verbal abuse. Verbal battering can cause far more harm to a person than a physical attack and might legitimately be construed as a form of violence. One can also intentionally injure a person by maliciously damaging his or her name, reputation, or career, although it is questionable whether "violence" is the best term for this kind of harm (whereas "slander" fits the bill).

If violence entails the intentional causing of physical or psychological harm to a sentient human subject, then this applies equally as well to sentient nonhuman subjects. "In suffering," Peter Singer notes, "animal are our equals." Without question, human beings can and do act violently toward animals in a sickening litany of practices, including branding, tail docking, teeth cutting, debeaking, castration, confinement, beating, clubbing, trapping, shooting, shocking, scalding, burning, blinding, mutilating, chemical poisoning, anal electrocution, and boiling, skinning, or dismembering animals who are still alive and conscious. Once society drops its speciesist blinders to define nonhuman animals as sentient beings and complex subjects of a life who can be maliciously victimized, traumatized, and hurt just like human animals, and who can experience not only physical but also psychological pain, then it is quite logical to conclude that those who intentionally harm animals for whatever dubious purposes are violent malefactors.

Since violence is related to terrorism—easily the most abused term of the present era—we must also ask: What is terrorism? (see below, "Defining Terrorism," and Watson in this volume). Can a movement be violent but not terrorist? Is the ALF a "terrorist" organization—or a counter-terrorist resistance force? Are animal exploitation industries and the state that defends them the true terrorists in this conflict?

Any valid definitions of violence and terrorism must include the obscene suffering humans inflict on animals, yet common usage conveniently ignores this barbarity toward animals while targeting activists who protest the enormity of such evil. If society used non-speciesist definitions of violence and terrorism, ones that acknowledge and respect both human and nonhuman beings as subjects of a life, then the outcry against terrorism would shift from the activists trying to prevent injury, loss of life, and environmental degradation to the industries and individuals profiting from bloodshed, torture, and destruction.[41] Those who cry "eco-terrorist" the loudest are typically those who profit the most from violence and killing, and those who seek to disguise their own crimes against life by vilifying others.

But what if we follow Gandhi, King, and ALF critics both inside and outside the animal advocacy movement and expand the concept of violence to include property destruction (see Regan in this volume)? Is the concept still logically coherent, or have we exceeded its definitional boundaries? How can one "hurt," "abuse," or "injure" a nonsentient thing that does not feel pain or have awareness of any sort—e.g., a van, a laboratory, or a fur farm? One simply cannot—unless a human being or another animal is involved indirectly in the attack.

Proponents of the "sabotage is violence" argument seem to assert that there is violence (1) in the action itself and (2) in its effect on human targets. First, in the act of property destruction, objects are defaced, smashed, burned, and demolished. Anger, aggression, hatred, and hostility are exerted rather than calmness, peace, love, and compassion. If this is violence, then one certainly ought to open up the definition of violence and terrorism to include corporate destruction of oceans, rivers, marshes, mountains, forests, and ecosystems of all kinds, for certainly their peace and integrity are disturbed and it is doubtful love informs such pillage and annihilation.

Second, by destroying property, activists do cause some kind of harm or injury to those who own the property or have a stake in it. People whose homes, cars, or offices are damaged suffer fear, anxiety, and trauma. Their business, livelihood, research, or careers may be ruined, and they may be harmed psychologically, emotionally, economically, professionally, and in other ways. From this line of reasoning, one could conclude that property destruction is violence. If sabotage is violence, it pales in comparison to what industries inflict on animals in the speciesist Gulags, factories, and killing fields/seas of industrial capitalism. Animal liberationists rightly underscore the ironic disparity between the outcry over home demonstrations, liberations, and property damage and the silence over the obscene violence inherent in the torture and killing of billions of animals every year for food, fashion, sport, entertainment, and science. Let moral outrage be put in proper perspective.

Depending on the motivation and act, one might call intentional damage done to property vandalism, defacement, or theft, but not necessarily violence. In the context of animal liberation, however, property destruction is not vandalism, which entails sheer hooliganism and lack of a noble ethical purpose; rather, it is destruction for a just cause—a principled act of sabotage. The ALF believes that the ends justify the means, and that if property destruction is an evil, then certainly it is the lesser of two evils when compared to the suffering it is designed to mitigate or to end. Strict pacifism is a self-defeating position. As Paul Watson (who accepts the argument that property destruction is violence) puts it,

> To remain nonviolent totally is to allow the perpetuation of violence against people, animals, and the environment. The Catch-22 of it—the damned-if-you-do, damned-if-you-don't dilemma—is that, if we eschew violence for ourselves, we often thereby tacitly allow violence for others, who are then free to settle issues violently until they are resisted, necessarily with violence. . . . Sometimes, to dramatize a point so that effective steps may follow, it is necessary to perform a violent act. But such violence must never be directed against a living thing. Against property, yes. But never against a life.[42]

Typically, those who vilify saboteurs as "violent" leap to the conclusion that they are "terrorists," failing to realize the differences between the two terms insofar as one can use violence in morally legitimate ways in conditions ranging from self-defense to a "just war" (see Bernstein in this volume).[43] A viable definition of "terrorism" contains at least three specific conditions, namely that there is: (1) an intentional use of physical violence (2) directed against innocent persons ("noncombatants") (3) for the ideological, political, or economic purposes of an individual, corporation, or state government. The intent to create fear (terror) in the mind of the victim might be viewed as a necessary condition of terrorism, but it is not a sufficient condition to be privileged apart from or over the use of physical harm in identifying a wrong. Besides ignoring state terrorism, a key omission from prevailing definitions is *species terrorism*, whose innocent victims are the billions of animals tortured and slaughtered by human beings and animal exploitation industries any given year (see "Defining Terrorism" in this volume). Just like human animals, nonhuman animals experience the trauma, pain, torment, and injury of terrorism; they are not (human) people, but they are *persons*. If property destruction is violence, it is not necessarily terrorism, for in a just war to save animals it avoids "-non-combatants" (ordinary citizens), targets only "combatants" (executives and managers of industries exploiting animals and the earth), and does not even physically harm its opponents.

The distinction between physical and psychological violence provides a key to understanding the indiscriminate deployment of the word "terrorism," whose root is "terror." Using another broad definition, a "terrorist" is someone who causes the feeling of panic or fear in another's mind. SHAC is a vivid example of liberation soldiers using psychological warfare or "psychological terrorism." To accomplish its goal of bringing down Huntingdon Life Sciences, SHAC deploys tactics of harassment and persecution—ranging from a hailstorm of faxes, emails, and phone calls to home demonstrations—to harass executives who work for HLS or their supporting companies (accounting firms, janitorial services, food providers, and so on). If one's definition of "terrorism" involves only a conscious effort to instill fear and anxiety in the mind of others (as a sufficient condition of terrorism), then SHAC is a kind of "terrorist" organization—and so too is the Internal Revenue Service. In fact, since society is inherently conflict-ridden and fraught with tension among actors with competing goals and antagonistic viewpoints, political struggle often involves giving and receiving injury, harm, and fear in some sense.

Dilemmas and the Politics of Language

> In our time, political speech and writing are largely the defense of the indefensible.—George Orwell

The act of destroying objects can be construed as violence if the premises of the argument are clear enough from the start, but these premises are shaky and this definition takes one into some very gray semantic territory that has potentially problematic consequences.

First, broadening the term "violence" to include store windows, buildings, laboratory equipment, and assorted physical objects can easily trivialize the violence done to human and nonhuman animals and may blur the critical distinction between living beings and nonliving things. There is a huge difference between breaking the neck of a mink and smashing a fur store window, but the values of society are revealed all too clearly when only the latter action is condemned as a crime worthy of intense opprobrium and legal action.

Second, animal advocates who accept the state's argument that property destruction is "violent" may unwittingly contribute to the demonization of saboteurs and freedom fighters as "terrorists," and thereby help legitimate FBI suppression of the animal rights movement and activists alleged to be involved with or supportive of the ALF. Suppose the ALF agreed that property destruction is violence and publicly announced that indeed they are a pro-violence group. This would solidify the prejudice in the public mind that they are terrorists—a mistaken impression, for, as noted, a political group can be violent yet not fit the definition of terrorists who aim to traumatize, injure, or kill innocent people to bring about their political goals. The ALF might be counter-terrorists, but not terrorists. We suspect, however, that such subtleties would escape the propaganda machines of the state, animal exploitation industries, the mass media, and much of the public. Consequently, the ALF's status would be sealed as a "terrorist" organization, bringing disastrous political results for anyone suspected or convicted of ALF activity or "support" of it.

Just as, in the 1980s, Latin American peasants asking for land and fair wages were denounced as communists, so today's activists defending the natural world against corporate attacks are called terrorists. Just as the US corporate-state complex used the term "communism" to export violence under a morally acceptable cover (fighting the "communist threat") through brutal dictatorships, juntas, and death squads, it now deploys the discourse of "terrorism" to discredit activists and promote the terrorist agendas of the ruling powers. Past Red Scares effectively weakened social justice movements by casting suspicion on the patriotic integrity of labor and reform movements; similarly, the corporate-state complex and mass media now manufacture "green scares" to legitimate a war against the movements defined as dangers to the fabled American way of life.

Detractors insist that it is only a matter of time before the ALF inadvertently kills someone or pursues a course of violence. Some critics argue that the ALF has already injured or killed people, but they confuse the ALF with ultra-radical English groups such as the Animal Rights Militia and the Justice Department. While in solidarity with the ALF on many points, the Animal Rights Militia, the Justice Department, and the Revolutionary Cells feel the ALF is too *conservative* in its policy of nonviolence. In contrast, they openly espouse physical violence against animal oppressors, unable to fathom why some believe that a human life has absolute value, especially if it involves a person inflicting violence upon animals. Consequently, these pro-violence groups employ fake poisoning scares to force companies to pull their products from the shelves. They target exploiters with booby-trapped letters fitted with poisoned razor blades. They set off bombs and they issue death threats.[44] The Animal Rights Militia, the Justice Department, and the Revolutionary Cells graduated from the "all is justified" school, and they aim to ratchet up the conflict between activists and industry to new levels (see Best in this volume).[45] Razor blade letters, bomb threats or bomb attacks, arson, harassment, death threats, and physical assaults have proven to be effective means of preventing and ending animal exploitation, and therefore will continue to be used by the most militant elements of the struggle.

But it is important to clearly distinguish between such groups and the ALF, and to keep in mind that when a "radical" animal rights group threatens or commits violence, it is not acting in conformity with the ALF philosophy.[46] Indeed, it could easily be a framing action by the state or an animal exploitation industry, intended to discredit the cause of animal liberation. True, ALF spokespersons and supporters have sometimes expressed violent sentiments against animal abusers, and phrases such as "do whatever it takes" and "animal liberation by any means necessary" can give credence to charges that the ALF has a violent edge. But given the enormity and magnitude of animal suffering, and the righteous anger that animal liberationists feel, one should notice that the ALF has demonstrated remarkable *restraint* in their war of liberation. When it comes to violence against living beings, even animal abusers, the ALF believes that the means do *not* justify the end, and therefore they renounce physical violence against their human adversaries.

Death threats and bomb scares, while effective tools of intimidation, may inflict considerable psychological harm, and on this ground one might argue that such tactics are inconsistent with ALF nonviolent principles—while recognizing the absurdity tainting those critics who exonerate animal abusers from moral wrong in causing intense physical and psychological pain to animals. Booby-trapped letters sent by the Justice Department and baseball bat attacks against HLS executives are clear-cut cases of violent actions intended to cause a person physical harm; while fine for those who endorse violence, they contradict ALF principles. In April 2002, however, an avowed ALF cell placed 38 unidentified bottles of Pantene Pro V shampoo contaminated with a diluted solution of ammonia and hydrogen peroxide in 13 supermarkets throughout New Zealand to coincide with World Week for Laboratory Animals. Although their communiqué stated that the dilution was harmless, it mimicked a bona fide terrorist action by targeting innocent people for a political cause.

Arson is a valuable weapon for destroying laboratories and research facilities, but it also is a problematic tool for nonviolent direct action because fire is so destructive and unpredictable. More than anything, acts of arson conjure up images of violence and terrorism in the public mind and pose credibility problems for the ALF.[47] For many animal advocates, the question is not whether illegal direct action is defensible, but rather where to draw the line with such tactics, and some in this camp draw it at the use of arson.[48] If the arsonist does not accidentally injure or kill a human being who was not known to be in the target building after careful reconnaissance, small animals in the vicinity might be injured or killed, as could any firefighter called to put out the flames.

It is not unreasonable to conclude that small animals have been injured or killed in arson strikes, thereby calling into question the nonviolent character of the ALF in an absolute sense. Robin Webb poses the problem thus: "In my opinion, arson does not fall under the classification of 'damage to property' but rather, actions that endanger life. The ALF is proud of its claim never to have harmed human life but arson has, almost undisputedly, taken life, whether it be a mouse, rat or spider. One cannot check every nook and cranny of a department store or broiler shed; the presence of a small creature is not so obvious as that of a human and they do not understand fire alarms and emergency exits. If one does not or cannot take at least as great a care to ensure that spiders are not present as one does to ensure the absence of humans then that is not only endangering life but also practical speciesism."[49]

Seemingly, if the ALF wishes both to be nonviolent and to continue using arson, the only philosophical resort it has in the face of this dilemma is (1) to claim it never intentionally causes violence to any form of life, or (2) to shift from deontological (absolute) defenses of the rights of all beings to a utilitarian justification of possibly harming animals or firefighters in order to save the maximum of animal life through sabotage. The ALF seeks to do no harm to any living being, but no action carries any guarantees and, like all human beings, ALF activists unavoidably injure life (the ant beneath one's footstep) simply by existing, raising the question of what "nonviolence" means and to what extent it is possible.

VI. The "Pragmatic" Critique of the ALF

Until the last fur farm burns to the ground, expect to hear from us.—ALF press release

We played the game, we played the rules. We were moderate, reasonable, and professional. We had data, statistics, and maps. And we got fucked. That's when I started thinking, "Something's missing here. Something isn't working."—Earth First! activist Howie Wolkie on attempts to protect wilderness through compromise with the US Forest Service

The pragmatic argument brackets the ethical status of sabotage tactics in order to scrutinize their possible or actual consequences for the animal advocacy movement. Like the principled critique, the pragmatic critique advocates legislation and education as the proper tools of progressive change, arguing that sabotage is premature and counterproductive. Following Tom Regan's line of argument (in this volume), if significant options for nonviolent change have not been fully explored, then "violence" (which for Regan includes property destruction) is not a legitimate option. Hence, many animal advocate critics argue that sabotage tactics seek a perilous shortcut to the hard work to be done through education and legislation.

As we have seen, however, the ALF believes that there is no virtue in following the legal path if it is a road to futility, and legalistic dogmas ought to be overturned in favor of a more realistic appraisal of effective tactics. If the legal system were open to justice for animals, the ALF would not have to exist. Animals are slaves. Society views them as property and resources for human use. As such, animals have no legal standing, whereas their exploiters have constitutional rights of property ownership. When laws protecting animals are passed, they typically are rewritten and watered down over time, rendering them toothless. Frequently, they are not even enforced.[50] The vast majority of animals used in research—95 percent—are rats, mice, and birds who have no legal protection whatsoever in the Animal Welfare Act, and so any form of abuse is permitted.[51] Furthermore, in the age of global capitalism dominated by treaties and institutions such as the General Agreement of Trades and Tariff, the North American Free Trade Agreement, the World Trade Organization, and the International Monetary Fund, legislative changes for the animals are especially precarious. The WTO has overridden numerous progressive laws such as those protecting sea turtles or banning steel-jawed leghold traps as "barriers to free trade."[52]

The inadequacies of adopting a strictly legal approach are obvious if one studies the history of Paul Watson's efforts to protect whales and baby harp seals. Despite the laws of the International Whaling

Commission that prohibit whaling, Russia, Japan, Iceland, and other nations kill thousands of whales every year with impunity while governments such as the United States turn their backs. If not for the interventions, documentation, and publicity efforts of Watson and members of the Sea Shepherd Conservation Society, many more whales would be dead and the carnage would have gone uncontested and unnoticed. When Watson innovated new tactics to protect harp seals, such as spraying them with a harmless dye to render their beautiful white coats valueless to their killers, the Canadian government immediately created new laws to proscribe his actions. The Orwellian "Seal Protection Act"—which guards only the sealers and bans others from even witnessing seal slaughters—was made and modified with seal defenders like Watson in mind. The beauty of the Sea Shepherd example is that Watson is not even breaking the law; instead, after exhausting all conventional means of saving whales, he is upholding the law against pirate whalers who otherwise kill with impunity in the waters of international indifference

That said, critics counter with the argument that sabotage is counterproductive insofar as it (1) alienates the public and (2) invites state repression. Short of rigorous sociological polling, it seems true that animal liberationists increasingly are coded by the mass media as "terrorists," and that their message and the context for their actions frequently do not reach the public. But the argument that sabotage always precludes discussion and has no educational value has been disproved, for it is often the case that a provocative hit—such as the August 2003 attacks on Bay Area foie gras chefs and restaurants—brings publicity to the conditions of animal exploitation being challenged and creates debate and change on issues that otherwise would not have been exposed or discussed (see Dawn in this volume). Watson brought unprecedented international attention to the bloodbaths on the high seas only through provocative direct action and sabotage strategies.

More often, of course, the ALF and ELF are negatively coded in mainstream media as "eco-terrorists," and liberation groups seem to lack a coherent strategy for jamming the corporate airways, getting out their perspective, educating the public about the plight of animals and their choice of tactics, and exposing the real terrorists. The first waves of ALF liberations were often accompanied by press conferences with the assistance of PETA, and successfully exposed cruelties of animal research while portraying the ALF in a positive light. "Before" and "after" pictures of animals such as Britches, liberated from the University of California-Riverside, were particularly powerful means of delegitimating vivisectors while portraying the ALF as genuine free-dom fighters whose actions, though illegal, were just.

At a certain point, however, perhaps with the change in focus from liberation to sabotage, strategic ALF media work in the US became increasingly rare. Some critics observe a parallel shift in media cover-age of the ALF, from a positive "Robin Hood" coding of bandits breaking the law to realize a higher good, to extremists and terrorists enamored with violence and destruction (see Stallwood in this volume). Consequently, one can ask: Does the ALF appear just and heroic in media representations, or ludicrous and violent? Are the animal exploitation industries condemned, or is the ALF? Are people encour-aged to feel sympathetic to the ALF and the animals they are trying to save, or to "owners" of the animals and the animal exploitation indus-tries? Are the exploiters, rather than the animals themselves, portrayed as victims?

This media framing problem explains why many activists embrace "open rescues" without property damage, and go so far as to replace broken locks or damaged property (see Davis in this volume). As Paul Shapiro of Compassion Over Killing explains, "We found that these rescues generate extremely positive media coverage because we're not painted as so-called terrorists with ski masks or somebody who's ashamed to admit what they've done. . . . And because we're openly admitting that we did this, the public reaction is much more sympa-thetic. Another advantage of open rescues is that because there is no property destruction, the issue isn't muddled by the press. The issue stays on the fact that there is animal cruelty going on and that the ani-mals are suffering. The issue isn't, 'Should they have broken property? Are they terrorists? Can we condone these types of tactics?' "[53]

Clearly, animal liberation and illegal direct action are not depend-ent on property destruction or "violence," and are fully compatible with Gandhian principles that a public unsympathetic to animal rights might find more palatable than arson and bombing attacks. Yet amidst the current insanity open rescues too are increasingly stigmatized as acts of terrorism. Open rescues work well when activists penetrate hell-holes like factory farms that are not popular with the public and whose owners will not prosecute for fear of negative publicity, but in some more sensitive areas such as laboratories or military bases, the risk of a long jail term makes them a less plausible approach. Legally, the dis-tinction between open and closed rescues is beginning to blur, as for instance on January 1, 2004 a new California law went into effect making trespassing on animal farms a misdemeanor punishable by six months in jail and/or a $1,000 fine. Soon enough, open rescuers may get more jail time than they bargained for.

Unavoidably, animal liberationists are caught in a war of publicity and propaganda, and they must defeat the mendacity of the state and animal exploitation industries to fight for the hearts and minds of the people. While public opinion may indeed be secondary to the impact direct action can have on an industry, and potential negative media coverage should not deter activists from sabotage operations, it is a tactical mistake to act as if public thinking were irrelevant.[54] If negative images of ALF actions prevail, industries will win support, liberationists will lose sympathy, and few will protest when the state pounces on the ALF with fierce repression. One might argue that the mass media is incorrigibly corrupt and cannot positively represent ALF viewpoints or actions, but media representations are more ambiguous and complex than this. Sometimes the media does fairly balanced or even positive stories that represent the ALF point of view and discuss the conditions of exploitation they challenge in an educational manner. Activists do not necessarily face a choice between illegal direct action and good press. Liberation activists can apply direct pressure to exploiters as they work media relations after the action—much as the ALF did with great success after the raids on the University of Pennsylvania, the University of California-Riverside, and the so-called City of Hope.[55]

Opponents of sabotage also have good reason to fear that property destruction and arson will invite a severe counterattack by the government. Clearly, state repression of the movement as a whole has increased sharply since the early 1990s, when the ALF was very active in the mink releases and arson attacks of the Operation Bite Back campaign. Repression by a state that supposedly protects democracy and free speech is unavoidable whenever a political movement becomes effective and seriously threatens "the rule of law" and corporate hegemony. The blowback mainstream organizations might receive is not necessarily the result of ALF actions alone, but also stems from the effectiveness of the animal advocacy movement in general and the will of the corporate-state complex to crush all dissent. The fallacy in this argument against the ALF is the assumption that the state will repress the entire movement only if and when an underground element consistently breaks the law. In fact, from the 1960s onward, FBI COINTELPRO surveilled, invaded, and attacked nonviolent social justice movements working within the constraints of the legal system, and the situation is no different in animal rights or environmental movements. One way or the other, the insidious and entrenched interests of the state must be taken on squarely and the naiveté of substantive change through the legal system must be abandoned.

Exploiters on the Run

The pump don't work 'cause the vandals took the handles.
—Bob Dylan, "Subterranean Homesick Blues"

In response to the pragmatic argument that ALF tactics are counterproductive, set the animal rights movement back, and weaken its credibility in the public eye, it is instructive to underscore the fact that illegal direct action tactics have succeeded in ways no other tactics could (see Webb and Coronado in this volume). The ALF has rescued thousands of animals that other groups had ignored, were unaware of, or were unable to assist through legal means. Moreover, the ALF has slowed down or shut down many brutal operations other groups were powerless to stop, and prevented other ventures from even starting. Where legal tactics often stall interminably within bureaucratic channels, the ALF has eliminated threats to animals in one night's work. In November 1986 Rod Coronado and David Howitt demolished a whale "processing" plant in Reykjavik and then sank two Icelandic whaling ships, half of their fleet. They caused $1.8 million in damage to the processing plant and $2.8 million to the ships.

In the early 1990s, Coronado and others from the Western Wildlife Unit of the ALF attacked fur farms and universities doing research on behalf of the fur industries. Dubbed "Operation Bite Back," the raids devastated the fur industry. Six months after a June 1991 ALF break-in, Oregon State University's Experimental Fur Farm shut down: head researcher Ron Scott admitted to the media that the closure was a direct result of the raid. In December 1991 Malecky Mink Ranch in Yamhill, Oregon was permanently retired after multiple incendiary attacks. In February 1992 the ALF broke into Michigan State University's Experimental Fur Farm. They liberated two minks and set fire to mink researcher Richard Aulerich's office, destroying 32 years of data invaluable to the mink farm industry. In 1993 an arson attack on the USDA's Predator Research Facility ended its bloodletting. Along with dozens of devastating assaults on the fur farming industry, Operation Bite Back also liberated thousands of mink, including a record release of 10,000 mink in 1997 at the Arritola Mink Farm in Mount Angel, Oregon.[56]

To gauge the effectiveness of ALF actions, one need only ask: What tactics do industries such as fur farms and vivisection laboratories fear the most—education and lobbying, protests and demonstrations, or sabotage? Even industry opponents of the ALF admit that it is a potent foe blocking "progress" in their fields. Susan Paris, president of the pro-vivisection group Americans for Medical Progress, wrote: "Because of terrorist acts by animal activists, crucial research projects have been delayed or scrapped. More and more of the scarce dollars available to research are spent on heightened security and higher insurance rates. Promising young scientists are rejecting careers in research. Top-notch researchers are getting out of the field." Similarly, a report to Congress on Animal Enterprise Terrorism states that "Where the direct, collateral, and indirect effects of incidents [of sabotage] are factored together, the ALF's professed tactic of 'economic sabotage' can be considered successful, and its objectives, at least toward the victimized facility, fulfilled."[57]

Critics argue that industries can recover from ecotage in order to build bigger and better facilities, to use more animals, or to cut down more trees. But it is also true that ecotage tactics have eliminated or economically weakened corporations, forcing them to bear increased insurance and security costs. Even when acknowledging the efficacy of ALF actions, opponents insist that they are of short-term, not long-term, significance. Property destruction, arson attacks, and illegal actions can win some dramatic battles, they say, but contribute little toward winning the war, a process they argue demands patience, public support, moral integrity, and planting more deeply rooted seeds of change. To this objection, the ALF insists that animals and the earth are in crisis and resistance can no longer afford to be moderate, compromising, or complacent about time.

Then again, perhaps victory in war requires a multi-faceted attack of numerous tactics and strategies working as one.

VII. Rifts in the Movement

"Politics is the art of the possible."—Otto von Bismarck

Many in the mainstream are choosing to distance animal advocacy from association with the "extreme fringe" of the ALF, employing such criticisms as are discussed above. Wayne Pacelle, senior Vice President of the Humane Society of the United States, says, "There's sympathy for the motive but increasing antipathy for the means. It's clearly counterproductive. We believe you lose your moral authority when you resort to vandalism, threats of violence and other means of illegal conduct."[58] Reverend Professor Andrew Linzey frames the point in even stronger terms:

> I believe that our movement is facing a Rubicon. If animal rights is not to become synonymous with terror tactics, individuals and organizations must move, and move fast, to dissociate themselves completely from violent militancy. . . . I understand something of the despair that leads to violence. None of us are immune from hateful thoughts or coercive desires. But to indulge such pathology, even as a psychological release, invites counterviolence and rightful social derision. Most importantly of all, it constitutes living proof that we really don't believe in our own vision of a peaceful world. I beg my fellow peaceable animal advocates to take their stand now, as a matter of urgency, before others take their stand against us. . . . It has been said that ours is not a cause to win, ours is a cause to lose. I believe it. But we shall not only lose, we shall also deserve to lose, if we fail to break free of the taint of terror tactics. It is nothing less than tragic that a movement that contains so many honorable and conscientious people should be publicly held to ransom by a small group of violent zealots.[59]

As dialogue about animal liberation begins within the animal advocacy movement, we hope for pluralism and tolerance for different approaches. There will never be a homogenous unity or consensus over complex philosophical and tactical issues within the animal advocacy movement, nor will people intent on pursuing one strategy yield to the arguments of others. And so the best one can expect is mutual respect and recognition that a tactical tool kit contains many useful devices, ranging from letter writing, legislative measures, and vegan outreach to home demonstrations, open rescues, and smashing vivisection labs. In the words of David Barbarash,

> We need to be smart about how we move forward, and not discard any tactics. We shouldn't overlook the legal avenues to change, nor should we dismiss illegal means just because our society, at this moment in its history, has deemed these actions illegal (while sanctioning the horrendous pain and suffering inflicted on animals). I believe the most successful way for-

ward to animal liberation is a multi-pronged attack on all fronts by different people: while one group is lobbying government representatives for changes to legislation, another group is protesting and blockading the labs, and at another time the ALF will enter those labs to rescue the animals and destroy the implements of torture. If we all work together in solidarity and respect each other's paths we will move forward much quicker.[60]

In recognizing the respective strengths and contributions of different approaches, we help to bridge the gap between the animal welfare and animal rights camps as well as the underground and aboveground communities. Like an ecosystem, the strength of the movement lies in its diversity, so long as there is mutual respect, understanding, and solidarity. Not everyone, however, wants to live under one happy roof. Pacelle, Linzey, and others decry illegal direct action tactics as an invasive species that weakens the ecosystem, while Gary Francione brashly insists that welfarism handicaps the goal of abolition and does more harm than good.[61] Although direct action advocates often charitably acknowledge the great value of aboveground or welfarist approaches, mainstream organizations such as the Humane Society of the United States and Friends of Animals denigrate direct action, animal liberation, and property destruction. Philosophical and tactical disagreements aside, mainstream organizations are pressured, in today's climate of assigning guilt by association, to criticize the ALF, to distance themselves from it, and even to boycott conferences that include direct activists so that they do not have to fight the kind of rearguard battles against "terrorist" accusations that pester PETA.

In response to mainstream criticism of the ALF, a Western Wildlife Unit document states,

The ALF leaves the path of moderation to those who sincerely believe that that is the road to victory. But we must also ask that those who approach the legal means of reform with the same conviction in which the ALF approaches its own, not be so quick to condemn avenues of illegal direct action. Without illegal direct action on the path of liberty and justice, many of this century's greatest social changes never would have been achieved . . . all avenues of action must be utilized and recognized because without them our battle appears to be that of a splintered faction unable to share basic common goals. . . .

Not only do we rescue individuals and utilize guerrilla warfare to sabotage industries destroying earth and animals, but whether others recognize it or not, the ALF also brings issues to light and creates the catalyst for others in the movement to continue pressuring for change.[62]

A respectful pluralism would benefit this movement considerably, but the ideal to attain beyond that is synthesis and mediation of the two faces of struggle. The work the ALF did with PETA in earlier actions such as the raids on the University of Pennsylvania, the University of California-Riverside, the City of Hope, or, more recently, with SHAC, shows how underground and aboveground facets of the movement can cooperate with great success, throwing bricks while raising bullhorns (see Jonas in this volume). In today's ultra-repressive social environment, however, cooperation between overt and covert groups is difficult to achieve. Targeted with a RICO lawsuit, In Defense of Animals was forced to promise not to work with or support "violent" organizations such as SHAC, as PETA was compelled to disavow connections with SHAC and the ALF. Both organizations had to pay lawyers and court costs to settle cases and were able to absorb legal fees that might devastate a smaller outfit.

But mainstream organizations don't have to openly cooperate with or support the ALF to benefit from their actions. The ALF enhances their credibility and effectiveness by providing a militant alternative that makes them seem reasonable and temperate in comparison. The "moderate" and acceptable path of change is defined only in relation to a more controversial and "extreme" road. Mainstream wilderness organizations often got additional land designated as wilderness areas only because Earth First! was demanding far more.[63] Similarly, Dr. Martin Luther King, Jr.'s tactics of nonviolent civil disobedience were more easily embraced by the state because they were less threatening than the fiery radicalism of Malcolm X and the Black Panthers. Unlike the aboveground animal rights movement, King was well aware that the "extremists" were in fact his allies, for, as he said, "I am only effective as long as there is a shadow on white America of the black man standing behind me with a Molotov cocktail."[64]

VIII. Against Hypocrisy

Do you think then that revolutions are made with rose water?—Alain Chamfort

There are two faces of the ALF—the "benign" one that breaks into prisons to release and rescue animals, and the "malign" one that smashes windows, wrecks equipment, and torches buildings. The public seems sympathetic only to the benign side because it believes that property destruction is violence. Many animal rights advocates embrace both sides of the ALF, while others feel that its emphasis has changed from liberation to sabotage, leading it to take a more "violent" turn. In fact, the ALF has always pursued both pathways and views them as inseparably related to the project of animal liberation.[65] As the ALF sees it, animals must be released and rescued whenever possible to bring about good in the short run, but sabotage must also inflict maximal damage to undermine exploitation industries in the long run and to mitigate or prevent the need for future liberations. Yet the argument that the more the ALF destroys property, the more the public will view them as terrorists and not freedom fighters, may warrant paying more attention to rescue, releases, education, and media relations. It must be acknowledged, however, that rescue operations are likely more difficult to conduct than sabotage, so a preponderance of ALF strikes may continue to be sabotage.

Animal rights or welfare advocates who condemn the liberation and property destruction tactics of the ALF succumb to hypocrisy. We imagine that few people who care passionately about animals would not clandestinely "steal" a dog from a neighbor who neglects and abuses the animal, understanding that calls to the local animal pound or police could take time the dog cannot afford and ultimately may be futile. Similarly, we suspect that few people would not seize or destroy traps set by a sadist in their community who captures and tortures cats. Who would not break down the door of a killer and use violence if necessary to rescue a human or nonhuman family member? How many people truly disagree with Paul Watson's actions when he pulls up miles of driftnets from the ocean used to destroy thousands of marine animals such as turtles and dolphins? Who, like Watson, would not take away a sealer's spiked club if that act could prevent the sealer from smashing the skulls of baby seals? Who (besides Greenpeace) wishes to uphold the monstrous sealer's "right to property" over the innocent seal's right to life?

And who wants to find fault with the Jewish resistance fighters who killed every Nazi and destroyed every gas oven they could? If one supports that kind of struggle and property destruction, why not support the ALF? Is it because that was the 1940s and this is now? Is it because that was Germany and this is the US? Or is it because those acts defended human beings while the ALF defends animals? Is it because those who criticize the ALF are speciesists who condone sabotage on behalf of humans but not animals? Is it the tactics people disagree with—or the cause and constituency?

One of the central ironies of our time is that within the exploitative and materialist ethos of capitalism, property and inanimate objects are more sacred than life, such that to destroy living beings and the natural world is a legal and (to all too many) ethically acceptable occupation, while to smash the things used to kill animals and to plunder the earth is illegal, immoral, and even an act of "terrorism." Mink farmers are good citizens, but those who release their captives before their necks are snapped are ecoterrorists. Individual or corporate property rights over animals and the earth are protected and privileged over our common inheritance of the planet and the well-being of all future generations. The state unleashes draconian rule with legislation such as the Patriot Act, but champions of animal rights and radical ecology are smeared for using intimidation tactics. In the mass media, the courts, the legislature, and corporate discourse, the ALF is denounced as a criminal force that operates illegally, while society largely ignores the illegalities of corporations (as evident in recent cases such as the Enron and WorldCom scandals) and the state (ranging from the routine violations of politicians and the murderous acts of the CIA and FBI to the subversion of the Constitution by Ashcroft and Bush).

Torching a research or vivisection laboratory is considered more heinous than anally electrocuting foxes or conducting LD50 tests, which pour industrial chemicals into the bodies of animals until half of them die. The loss of one building is deemed more noteworthy than the devastation of rainforests or the eradication of species. Critics whine about the *possibility* of physical violence by the ALF but fall silent before the *actuality* of state terrorism, animal massacres, and environmental destruction on a global scale. They decry death threats, but never death. They condemn activist pressure against animal exploiters but condone the violence thugs direct against activists. The US is rife with volatile anti-government and hate groups—ranging from neo-Nazis militiamen to right-wing Christian zealots—that have a long record of violence, including killing hundreds of people in the Oklahoma City bombing, yet the state positions the ALF above all of them as the more dangerous "domestic terrorist" threat. While Al Qaeda and sundry terrorist cells openly threaten more attacks on the nation, the FBI deploys hundreds of agents and squanders millions of dollars to harass activists who rescue cats and dogs. Those who exploit human beings, animals, and the earth are dignified with labels such as "scientist," "developer," or "businessman" as those who dare attack the property of the powerful are branded as "terrorists." It's a game of corrupt semantics where those who monopolize power monopolize meaning.

The staggering hypocrisies, inanities, ironies, distortions, lies, and contradictions that pervade a barbaric society posing as civilized are numbing to contemplate. In this Orwellian world—where slavery is freedom and war is peace, where timber companies raze forests under the "Healthy Forest Restoration Act" and governments guard seal massacres under the "Seal Protection Act"—it is difficult to find truth and logic. It is not the ALF's tactics that deserve vehement condemnation, but rather the industries that exploit animals so viciously, the legal systems that institutionalize their interests, the media moguls that denigrate animal rights, and the states that run the whole insane asylum.

IX. About This Volume

Sentiment without action is the ruin of the soul.—Edward Abbey

As we let our own light shine, we unconsciously give other people permission to do the same. As we are liberated from our own fear, our presence automatically liberates others. —Nelson Mandela

This book is unique in many ways. To begin, it is the first volume ever written on the ALF, and as such is long overdue. *Terrorists or Freedom Fighters?* is an anthology of essays by leading supporters and critics of the ALF from *within* the animal rights movement (with the exception of Lawrence Sampson). While unanimous about the goal of total animal liberation, the animal rights community differs considerably over the proper means to achieve this end, and so this book presents both defenses and critiques of the ALF. In addition, this anthology brings together the thoughts of prominent activists and academics, thereby creating a rare encounter of perspectives, although many figures in the book combine both roles and approaches.

The tactics of illegal direct action and property destruction are complex and controversial. Rather than seek any definitive, absolute, or final answers to the multitude of important questions that emerge, this anthology wishes to begin serious discussion and debate about a host of crucial issues surrounding the history, philosophy, ethics, politics, and strategies of the ALF; its relation to other resistance movements; and the role it plays in the overall animal advocacy community. The book is subtitled "Reflections on the Liberation of Animals," rather than "Reflections on the ALF," because the ALF represents only one tactic of direct action animal liberation, with pro-violence groups like the Justice Department on one side, and aboveground open rescue groups like Mercy For Animals and Compassion Over Killing on the other side.

Since nothing can be understood without history and context, we begin with three valuable essays on the history of the ALF. Noel Molland and Robin Webb each trace the beginnings of the ALF in England during the 1970s, and Kim Stallwood describes this history from his personal relationships with Ronnie Lee and other members of the ALF. Stallwood narrates what he found to be a disturbing shift in the ALF toward embracing "violent methods." Against Lee's and Webb's philosophy of animal liberation "by any means necessary," Stallwood suggests four core values that animal liberation actions should meet, including nonviolence to human beings and to property.

Just what type of liberation movement is the ALF, and what connections does it have with human liberation movements? In "Legitimating Liberation," Mark Bernstein nicely dissects the arguments for and against animal liberation. Bernstein grounds the intelligibility and legitimacy of animal liberation in the undeniable fact of animal sentience and subjectivity, well established in the vast literature of cognitive ethology.[66] He underscores the analogies between human and animal liberation movements and concludes that animal liberationists are soldiers in a "just war." In his essay, "At the Gates of Hell: The ALF and the Legacy of Holocaust Resistance," Maxwell Schnurer finds that the key to understanding the ALF lies less in comparing it to human liberation movements in the US than to the German Holocaust resistance movement. Schnurer explores a number of significant analogies between the two struggles and argues from the validity of human opposition to genocide to the justness of animal liberation. For Schnurer, the boldness of direct action has the unique power to challenge human "mindlessness" in the face of systemic violence, and is therefore a critical tool for restoring the lost ethical relationships between humans and animals. Gary Yourofsky addresses the hot topic of mink liberation in his essay, "Abolition, Liberation, Freedom: Coming to a Fur Farm Near You." Noting that the US tragically failed to make the right connections and choices in the aftermath of 9/11, Yourofsky defends the rationale for animal liberation and debunks the standard lies the mink industry and press spew after an ALF release. Convicted for the crime of "random acts of kindness and compassion," Yourofsky concludes with a stirring statement of resistance to his court of accusers. pattrice jones' "Mothers with Monkeywrenches: Feminist Imperatives and the ALF" draws the organic connections between "eco-feminism" or "anarcha~feminism" and animal liberation, arguing that "animal liberation is a feminist project." If power over women and domination over animals emerged hand in hand in history, it follows that an important part of the feminist project is animal liberation and a vital component of animal liberation is overturning patriarchy

One cannot evaluate the ALF unless one properly understands its motivations and why activists like Coronado, Yourofsky, and Watson have risked their freedom and lives in the service of animals. Judith Barad believes that love is central to ALF philosophy and motivation, but in "Aquinas's Account of Anger as Applied to the ALF" she also finds an important place for anger. Developing the insights of medieval philosopher Thomas Aquinas, Barad argues that anger can be a galvanizing, cathartic, and productive force, but only if coupled with reason, understanding, and love; otherwise it becomes destructive to the activist, the cause, and possibly to other human beings. In "Direct Actions Speak Louder than Words." Rod Coronado eloquently manifests the spiritual ecowarrior ethos motivating many ALF activists. Coronado defends the ALF from the pragmatic critique, ticking off an impressive list of ALF victories and challenging pacifist interpretations of modern freedom struggles such as led by Gandhi and King, while maintaining that no one tactic alone is adequate to win. Lawrence Sampson, a member of the American Indian Movement, is not an animal rights activist or a vegetarian. Unlike fellow American Indian Rod Coronado, Sampson defends the Makah nation's tradition of killing whales and is critical of what he feels is an ethnocentric bias in the animal rights community. Yet he supports the ALF because he admires their courage to challenge the "legal criminals" who comprise America's corporate elite. Sampson believes that the ALF and Native Americans are fighting the same foes, and his essay demonstrates the kind of solidarity warriors for human and animal nations must forge before either can mount a credible challenge to the killing machines of modernity. The Western Wildlife Unit sends a stirring call to action in "Take No Prisoners." This essay beautifully captures the biocentric, spiritual ethic and worldview that animates Sampson and Coronado, and infuses the souls of many who take direct action to protect Mother Earth. The Indian peoples' resistance was not in vain; their courage lives on through the new warriors who slip into the night and live proudly with the belief that each blow they inflict on oppressors is a healing touch.

For a variety of reasons, the ALF are poorly understood, perceived, and represented within the movement and society as a whole. In "Understanding Animal Liberation: From Critical Analysis to Critical Pedagogy," Anthony Nocella asks critics to steer past the stereotypes of the ALF as "extremist" and "terrorist" in order to grasp its true nature and reasons for being. Nocella suggests a method for such rethinking, with the goal of understanding the ALF from within, through empathy and lived experience, rather than from without, through detachment and "objective" distance. If they truly tried to understand the ALF, critics might have a different perception of its struggle. Karen Davis's essay "Open Rescues: Putting a Face on the Rescuers and the Rescued" shifts the debate from the "closed" (underground) rescues of the ALF to the relatively new "open" (aboveground) rescues tactics pioneered by Australian activist Patty Mark. Both types of rescue methods break the law to liberate animals, but open rescue tactics resonate more with the Gandhian approach than the confrontational style of Coronado and others. Davis emphasizes the importance of narrative and drama for effective video documentation of animal cruelty and rescue and calls for a more sophisticated *cinema verité*. In "From the Front Line to the Front Page: An Analysis of ALF Media Coverage," Karen Dawn offers a much-needed study, perhaps the first, of the relationship between the ALF and the mass media that underground activists so often disdain. Dawn skewers a few trusty dogmas of some in the ALF and movement critics in the nonviolence camp. She convincingly argues that the ALF ought to take media coverage more seriously and use the media to its advantage—as it did in its earlier history. Against ALF critics, Dawn uses recent case studies to show that sabotage tactics are not necessarily alienating and counterproductive, as they often generate positive press and social debate.

The controversy surrounding the ALF stems principally from their chosen methods and tactics of struggle and the question of whether or sabotage is violent and effective. Tom Regan brings a provocative argument to the table with his essay "How to Justify Violence." Though influenced by Gandhi, Regan nonetheless rejects the Gandhian dogma that violence is always wrong. Against many figures in the book, Regan insists that property destruction should be considered violence, and believes activists should shift their strategy from *denying* that it is violence to *defending* it as violence. Regan specifies three conditions that must hold for such a defense. Freeman Wicklund writes as a former ALF advocate who adopted a more critical tone the more deeply he probed the nonviolent philosophies of Gandhi and King. As Wicklund sees it in "Direct Action: Progress, Peril, or Both?", there are two roads to animal liberation, the "road of coercion" and the "road of persuasion."[67] Although social movements follow both paths, Wicklund believes that the latter is the best avenue of change, and he argues that the ALF skips important stages of struggle before using direct action. Writing a direct rebuttal to Wicklund in "Defending Agitation and the ALF," Bruce Friedrich rejects the arguments that clandestine, illegal direct action alienates the public, always gets bad press, reduces activists to the same ethical level of animal oppressors, and impedes the cause. Friedrich analyzes the discontinuities between the struggles of Gandhi and King and animal liberation, and shows why "strategic nonviolence" tactics are inadequate in the struggle against human supremacy. Kevin Jonas' piece, "Bricks and Bullhorns," describes SHAC's legal and aboveground methods of liberation through intimidation. Jonas provides an important history of the SHAC movement and offers an instructive comparison of its highly focused approach to the scattershot strikes of the ALF. Through the oblique relation between the ALF and SHAC, Jonas also explains how the underground can and must work with the aboveground movement to deliver a powerful "one-two punch" to animal oppressors. Akin to Sampson, Nicolas Atwood's essay "Revolutionary Process and the ALF" commends the ALF for being a "dynamic and inspirational" movement and a catalyst of social change. But she also insists that "the ALF is not revolutionary. . . . ALF actions can only be part of a revolutionary process" to liberate animals and transform society as a whole. This opens the door to alliances with other social movements of the kind envisioned by Best, Sampson, and jones, but, akin to Jonas, Atwood argues that the ALF must move from striking random targets to developing a coherent strategy of attack.

The ALF increasingly is excoriated as a "terrorist" organization (a sign of its increasing effectiveness), but terrorism is a highly relative and problematic term. In "ALF and ELF: Terrorism is as Terrorism Does," Captain Paul Watson brilliantly punctures the fallacies that plague hypocrites who abuse the T-word. Whereas most deployments of the term "terrorism" are subjective, arbitrary, and politically motivated, Watson clarifies what the concept means "objectively defined" and shows why it does not apply to the actions of the ALF and ELF. Like Friedrich, Watson takes on pacifist interpretations of history and debunks standard readings of social movements led by Gandhi and King. The earth is in serious crisis, Watson argues, and the only escape is through militant resistance of the kind represented by the ALF and ELF, along with widespread adoption of a new ecocentric ethic that overcomes human arrogance and alienation from nature. Jennifer and Jason Black's essay, "The Rhetorical 'Terrorist': Implications of the USA Patriot Act on Animal Liberation," provides an excellent historical and political contextualization of animal liberation struggles in the era of Bush and Ashcroft. The authors describe the nature of the Patriot Act, how it wrongly frames liberation activities as "terrorism" under its sweeping purview, and its implications for animal rights activism. Steven Best continues the sharp political analysis of the Patriot Act and extends it to some of the Act's repressive offspring in his timely essay, "It's War! The Escalating Battle Between Activists and the Corporate-State Complex." Best argues that tensions have been steadily mounting between animal and earth liberationists on one side and various exploitation industries and the state on the other, such that we are approaching a new type of civil war. Warning of the danger of impending fascism, Best shows how human and animal rights are interconnected projects.

Finally, in "The ALF: Who, Why, and What?", Ingrid Newkirk beautifully summarizes the arguments in favor of an underground presence within the animal rights struggle. If every human liberation movement had a militant and "violent" component, she asks, why should it be any different for the animal liberation movement? Moral progress does not work through gentle nudges or ethical persuasion alone, rather, "Society has to be pushed into the future." Newkirk cuts through the hypocrisy of ALF detractors to show that opposition to sabotage supports the greater over the lesser "violence," as she illuminates the empathy and urgency that motivates ALF actions for animals trapped in the torture chambers of a violent speciesist world. The book concludes with appendices and resources for further study. "My Experience with Government Harassment" is Rod Coronado's chilling testimony about government repression and its impact on the unity of the animal rights movement.[68] "Letters from the Underground (Parts I and II)" comes from an anonymous female ALF member. Part I describes how she joined the underground and gravitated toward her first ALF action—a brave and empowering solo foray. Part II discusses how to find the right people with which to form a cell or affinity group. These letters provide some insight into how ALF actions are conducted and how an ALF activist thinks. In "Defining Terrorism," Best and Nocella probe the complexities of the term "terrorism." Citing numerous definitions of the term, they underscore the momentous consequences of politically motivated definitions and call for a more adequate definition that includes both state-sponsored and species terrorism. Finally, the Resource list provides the most current information on the various media and organizations that address animal and earth liberation issues, including prisoner support.

Difference in Unity, Unity in Difference

While certainly there is room for disagreement among the contributors, they all defend the liberation of animals; they believe in the legitimacy of nonviolent civil disobedience as a political tactic to drive progressive political change; and they renounce, repudiate, and revile animal exploitation industries and the bloody stain speciesists leave on this planet and the human soul. The authors concur on the goal of animal liberation, while sometimes disagreeing about the best means to achieve that goal. Many, like Bernstein, Schnurer, Watson, Coronado, Jonas, Friedrich, Newkirk, and Yourofsky support sabotage or direct pressure tactics and reject the argument that property destruction is "domestic terrorism." Others, like Stallwood, Wicklund, and Regan, link property destruction to violence and advocate more Gandhian tactics of liberation. Hence, Coronado and Friedrich embrace the closed rescues of the ALF, while Davis and Stallwood prefer the open rescues of Compassion Over Killing. Coronado, Yourofsky, and Jonas question the value of media coverage, while Dawn upholds its importance. Some, like Watson, focus exclusively on animal rights and environmental protection in their activism, as others, like Best, jones, Nocella, and Atwood seek to build bridges among radical movements.

At a time when the animal advocacy movement is divided over the nature and effects of the ALF, contributors such as Coronado, Friedrich, jones, and Jonas call for a rapprochement, advocating more solidarity between the underground and aboveground elements of the movement. They reject the debilitating logic of either/or—either closed or open rescue, either legislation or agitation, either covert or overt operations—as both strategies clearly are useful and necessary. Arguably, activists like Coronado and Yourofsky are even more subversive and dangerous in their current aboveground roles as educators than in their former underground incarnations as ALF liberators, but to a significant degree this effectiveness stems from their experience underground.

Like the ALF Press Office and the Center on Animal Liberation Affairs, an academic forum tank for animal liberation issues, the writers in this volume provide an open network of support for the liberation of animals and they reclaim the rights to free thought and speech that as we write are being dismantled by the US government under the rubric of Homeland Security and defense against "terrorism."[69] The point of this volume is not to advocate property destruction, break-ins, arson, or physical violence against animal abusers. Rather, the book aims to begin a dialogue about what people can and should do in a world where animals are so severely oppressed and tortured, where the law serves to protect the profits of a few abusers rather than to prevent the exploitation and massacre of billions of animals, and where animals need immediate and not just long-range help. The book, moreover, seeks to dispel a number of misconceptions about the motivations and philosophy of the ALF. It should be clear that the ALF is supported not only by what society views to be "naïve" young people or "confused" spiky-haired anarchists, but rather by a diverse array of thinking people that includes seasoned activists, serious academics, and the above-mentioned youth and anarchists. Indeed, the ALF can be your respectable neighbor or fellow Parent Teacher Association member who destroys traps set by those who intend to harm animals or steals and trashes free circus passes left on store counters.

Additionally, we emphasize that members of the ALF are not hateful and violent people; they are concerned and compassionate citizens who cannot tolerate violence toward animals, and who will go to extraordinary lengths to stop extraordinary wrongs. Ultimately, we would like to see more informed public debate and dialogue about the ALF, as well as rigorous academic writing on the history, ethics, tactics, and politics of animal liberation. We also hope there can be more understanding and harmonious relations between the aboveground and underground components of the animal rights struggle. May this volume be a modest beginning toward these ends.

X. Into the Future

This is no time to engage in the luxury of cooling off or to take the tranquilizing drug of gradualism.—Dr. Martin Luther King, Jr.

Boldness has genius, power and magic in it. Begin it now.
—Goethe

The Nuremberg Trials accused those aware of Nazi atrocities
with gross apathy and inaction. Will our generation one day
be questioned as to why we did not take greater action to stop
violence that engulfs the world of animals on earth?—Rod
Coronado

The time will come when men such as I will look upon the
murder of animals as they now look upon the murder of
men.—Leonardo Da Vinci

The way forward to total animal liberation is as difficult as it is
unclear. No one can predict the future course of struggles, but it is safe
to say that different visions, philosophies, and tactics of animal advocacy and liberation will continue to compete. There is strength in diversity, so the best one can hope for is that multiple approaches can coex-
ist, positively reinforce one another, and learn to repel the state repression that unavoidably will grow. Every aspect of the animal advocacy
movement should learn to appreciate or at least tolerate different
approaches. If they support the ALF, activists should not hesitate to say
so, and defend free speech and constitutional rights in the process; if
they disagree with the ALF, let them state their criticisms in constructive ways that advance the movement and not flee from debate.

The challenge for the ALF is to be as militant and effective as possible without losing the moral high ground, without alienating public
support, and without diluting the values of freedom and compassion.
Animal exploiters have no such burden; they seek only to oppress and
to profit from their violence and terrorism. The state has no such burden; it is an apparatus that monopolizes power and violence and exists
primarily to crush dissent and promote corporate agendas. The task of
the ALF, clearly, is fraught with great tension and difficulty. The ALF
cannot achieve the goal of animal liberation alone or only through sabotage and occasional rescues and releases. By themselves and with their
chosen methods, they are not and cannot be a revolutionary force,
which by definition requires systemic social change. They can slow the
machines of death and destruction but alone cannot destroy them in
their entirety. To achieve its abolitionist goals and win freedom for animals, the ALF—as only part of a process of total social transformation—requires a huge army of warriors to join its ranks, an exponen-

tial increase in liberation and sabotage actions around the globe, and mass support by a diversity of people working in consort against the prevailing systems of hierarchy and domination.

The ALF will win popular support only when enough people understand the motivation and legitimacy of its actions, and begin to view its members as freedom fighters, not terrorists. This in turn demands widespread education about the ALF and the unspeakable horrors that billions of animals suffer in the entertainment industries, rodeos, circuses, zoos, fur farms, factory farms, slaughterhouses, and other extensions of the global Gulag for the animal slaves of the human species.

During the nineteenth century, abolitionists in the US broke every law protecting the ownership of slaves and were condemned by the press as violent criminals. Now, we uphold these abolitionists to schoolchildren as heroes far ahead of their time. We hope history will someday view the ALF in the same light, and that the ALF proves worthy of the honor.

Notes

1. For additional analyses of the impact of the Patriot Act on civil liberties, see Cynthia Brown, ed., *Lost Liberties: Ashcroft and the Assault on Personal Freedom* (New York: The New Press, 2003); David Cole and James X. Dempsey, *Terrorism and the Constitution: Sacrificing Civil Liberties in the Name of National Security* (New York: The New Press, 2002); David Cole, *Enemy Aliens: Double Standards and Constitutional Freedoms in the War on Terrorism* (New York: The New Press, 2003); Nancy Chang, *Silencing Political Dissent: How September 11 Anti-Terrorism Measures Threaten Our Civil Liberties* (New York: Seven Stories Press, 2002); and Nat Hentoff, *The War on the Bill of Rights and the Gathering Resistance* (New York: Seven Stories Press, 2003).

2. Throughout this essay, we use the phrase "exploitation of animals" to refer to the cultural, institutional, and technological structures whereby human beings expropriate animals from their natural habitats, behaviors, and social relations, disrupt their existence, confine them, cause them pain and suffering, force them to labor in some way, and/or kill them in order to serve human purposes. We therefore call fur, hunting, meat and dairy, vivisection, and other industries that profit from animal suffering and death "animal exploitation industries."

3. See www.animalliberation.net.

4. "Forty-eight billion farm animals are killed each year around the world—nearly eight times the human population, more than 130 million a day, more than five million every hour, almost 100,000 a minute. These numbers do not include the billions of other animals whose lives are taken, bodies injured, and freedom stolen in the name of entertainment, sport, or fashion." Tom Regan and Martin Rowe, "What the Nobel Committee Also Failed to Note," *International Herald Tribune*, December 19, 2003.

5. See Gary Francione, *Animals, Property, and the Law* (Philadelphia: Temple University Press, 1995).

6. For the argument that moral progress can measured by the degree of the universal-ization of rights, see Roderick Nash, *The Rights of Nature: A History of Environmental Ethics* (Madison: University of Wisconsin Press, 1989). Also see Steven Best (forthcoming), *Animal Rights and Moral Progress: The Struggle for Human Evolution* (Lanham, MD: Rowman & Littlefield).

7. For the classic critique of speciesism, see Peter Singer, *Animal Liberation*, second edi-tion (New York: Random House, 1990). Richard Ryder first coined the term "speciesism"; see his *Animal Revolution: Changing Attitudes Toward Speciesism* (Oxford: Berg, 2000).

8. On the problems with "identity politics," see Steven Best and Douglas Kellner, *Postmodern Theory: Critical Interrogations* (New York: Guilford Press, 1991).

9. See Jim Mason, *An Unnatural Order: Uncovering the Roots of Our Domination of Nature and Each Other* (New York: Simon and Schuster, 1993), and Marjorie Spiegel, *The Dreaded Comparison: Human and Animal Slavery* (New York: Mirror Books, 1996).

10. Cited in James Tracy, ed., *The Civil Disobedience Handbook: A Brief History and Practical Advice for the Politically Disenchanted* (San Francisco: Manic D. Press, 2002).

11. James Goodman, "Why do we need a Forum on Civil Disobedience?" www.interna-tional.activism.uts.edu.au/civildis/goodman.html.

12. On the corporate domination of the American political system, see William Grieder, *Who Will Tell the People? The Betrayal of American Democracy* (New York: Touchstone Books, 1993), and Michael Parenti, *Democracy for the Few* (Belmont, CA: Wadsworth, 2001).

13. See www.spunk.org/library/writers/decleyre/sp001334.html.

14. On communitarian anarchist ethics, see Murray Bookchin, *Remaking Society: Pathways to a Green Future* (Boston: South End Press, 1990) and Janet Biehl, *The Politics of Social Ecology: Libertarian Municipalism* (Montréal: Black Rose Books, 1998).

15. On this theme, see Mark Dowie, *Losing Ground: American Environmentalism at the Close of the Twentieth Century* (Cambridge, MA: MIT Press, 1995).

16. Although Greenpeace had developed a militant and media-savvy form of direct action that included actions such as sailing ships into nuclear test areas, they had a strict Gandhian code against "violence toward property." For an excellent account of Greenpeace and Watson's departure from the group, see Rik Scarce, *Eco-Warriors: Understanding the Radical Environmental Movement* (Chicago: The Noble Press, 1990). Also see Watson's own account in *Sea Shepherd: My Fight for Whales and Seals* (New York: Norton, 1982), *Ocean Warriors: My Battle to End the Illegal Slaughter on the High Seas* (Toronto: Key Porter Books Limited, 1994), and *Seal Wars: Twenty-five Years on the Front Lines with the Harp Seals* (Toronto: Key Porter Books Limited, 2002).

17. Applied to the contemporary context of ecology and animal rights, industrial sabo-tage becomes ecotage and monkeywrenching involves attacks on the machines and property of industries slaughtering animals and raping the natural world for profit. A seminal influence on the direct action environmental movement was Edward Abbey, a radical environmental writer outraged by the devastating impact of indus-try on the American Southwest. Best known among Abbey's works is *The Monkey Wrench Gang* (New York: Perennial, 2000), a 1975 novel about a ragtag band of characters united in their will to break the law and to destroy the property of indus-tries harming the environment. Abbey's fictional vision inspired non-fictional action.

For more on the origins of Earth First! and their militant ecotage tactics, see Foreman's books, *Ecodefense: A Field Guide to Monkeywrenching* (Chico, CA: Abbzug Press, 1993), which gives expert advice about how to employ ecotage tactics to dismantle the industrial machine, and, *Confessions of an Eco-Warrior* (New York: Crown Trade Paperbacks, 1991).

18. After intense FBI harassment, surveillance, and a setup with an agent provocateur leading to the 1989 arrest of Foreman and other Earth First! members for allegedly plotting to sabotage nuclear power plants in three states, the organization ceased doing ecotage, although today a more socio-political incarnation of the group continues to support direct action and radical resistance movements of all kinds. As Scarce describes, another factor leading to the abandonment of ecotage by Earth First! was the effort by Judi Barr, Darryl Cherney, Mike Roselle, and others to forge alliances with loggers against the timber corporations that exploited workers and forests alike. Since the first use of ecotage in Earth First!, however, there were sharp disagreements within the group about whether or not property destruction is violence and a sound tactic, just as there are in the animal advocacy movement today. As more social and anarchist ideas influenced Earth First!, Dave Foreman left and started *Wild Earth* magazine in order to maintain his focus on wilderness issues.

19. See the Hunt Saboteurs Association Website at hsa.enviroweb.org/hsa.shtml.

20. On the risks that hunt sabs, particularly female activists, face, see www.geocities.com/CapitolHill/Lobby/5342/hsa5.html.

21. "Gender and the Animal Rights Movement," www.utanimalrights.com/gender.htm.

22. See Noel Molland, "Thirty Years of Direct Action," in this volume.

23. Seven years earlier, however, in 1970, former Flipper trainer Ric O'Barry, while obviously not an ALF member, liberated a dolphin from the Lerner Marine Laboratory on Bimini, one of the Bahama islands. O'Barry describes the break-in and jail time and notoriety he received in his book, *Behind the Dolphin Smile* (Los Angeles: Renaissance Books, 1999).

24. "Monumental Animal Liberation Front Actions—United States," www.animalliberationfront.com/ALFront/alfusa.htm.

25. Ingrid Newkirk, *Free the Animals: The Amazing True Story of the Animal Liberation Front* (New York: Lantern Books, 2000).

26. On the documentary *Unnecessary Fuss*, see "The ALF and the 'Unnecessary Fuss' Video," Lawrence Finsen and Susan Finsen in Kelly Wand, ed., *The Animal Rights Movement* (Farmington Hills, MI: Greenhaven Press, 2003), pp. 203–209. For a recent list of ALF actions, see "North American Animal Liberation Front Press Office 2001 Year-End Direct Action Report," www.tao.ca/~naalfpo/2001_Direct_Action_Report.pdf.

27. Newkirk, *Free the Animals*, 267.

28. See the In Defense of Animals campaign, "They are not our property, we are not their owners," www.idausa.org/index.shtml.

29. On the FBI counterintelligence program (COINTELPRO) and its infiltration of political groups during the 1960s and onwards, see Ward Churchill and Jim Vander Wall, *Agents of Repression: The FBI's Secret Wars Against the Black Panther and the American Indian Movement* (Boston: South End Press, 1990). As the authors make clear, the FBI and allied police forces did not hesitate to kill, let alone frame, opponents such as Fred Hampton and members of the American Indian movement. For collected COINTELPRO documents, see Ward Churchill and Jim Vander Wall, *The COINTELPRO Papers: Documents From the FBI's Secret Wars Against Dissent in the United States*, updated edition (Boston: South End Press, 2002).

30. "The ALF Primer," www.animalliberationfront.com/ALFront/ALFPrime.htm.

31 On the brutal repression faced by the hunt saboteurs in England, see www.geocities.com/CapitolHill/Lobby/5342/hsa5.html. Many animal and earth warriors and other victims have been killed. Dian Fossey was murdered in 1985 by the gorilla hunters she fought against. Cattle ranchers and perhaps other interests assassinated Chico Mendes in 1988. In 1985 agents of the French government sank the Greenpeace ship, Rainbow Warrior, in New Zealand, and killed a photographer who was aboard. Loggers have purposely cut down trees occupied by tree sitters, injuring them, and purposely felled a tree on David Gypsy Chain, killing him. Thugs have injured Dave Foreman and attempted to kill Paul Watson numerous times. There is much evidence that the timber industry and possibly the FBI tried to kill Judi Bari and Darryl Cherney in the 1990 bombing of their car. Not so curiously, no one cries "violence" or "terrorist" when activists are hurt and killed, rather they save their moral outrage for activist attacks on property.

32. "The ALF Unmasked—Interview with David Barbarash," www.animal-lib.org.au/more_interviews/barbarash.

33. Henry David Thoreau, *Civil Disobedience and Other Essays* (Mineola, NY: Dover Publications, 1993).

34. The ALF meaning of "animal liberation" is not the same as Peter Singer's usage, which is concerned with animal welfare, not animal rights—with utilitarianism, not deontology (the philosophical basis for rights theory).

35. For helpful discussions of the philosophy of animal rights that distinguishes it from animal welfare, see Tom Regan, *The Case For Animal Rights* (Berkeley: University of California Press, 1983), Gary Francione, *Introduction to Animal Rights: Your Child or the Dog?* (Philadelphia: Temple University Press, 2000), and Steven Best, "Chewing on the Rights Vs. Welfare Debate: Do Corporate Reforms Delay Animal Liberation?" in *The Animals' Agenda*, March/April 2002, pp. 14–16. Of course, many effective animal rights activists employ welfare measures to help animals, and we in no way seek to denigrate their efforts. Our differences are not so much with those who use welfare tactics within a larger framework of rights and abolition but rather those who embrace the welfarist philosophy or worldview and its sundry speciesist implications and practices.

36. "North American Animal Liberation Front Press Office 2001 Year-End Direct Action Report."

37. See Peter Singer, *Animal Liberation*.

38. *Animal Liberation*, pp. xii–xiii. Singer, of course, is a utilitarian, and so his main line of reasoning against ALF tactics logically would be that they could have negative consequences for the movement; thus he might push the pragmatic objection.

39. Steve Hindi, for example, is one who has led the way in using mobile education squads similar to his Tiger Truck—a huge van fitted with digital video screens on all sides, electronic message boards, and amplified sound, showing graphic images of animal abuse. Hindi skillfully uses undercover video footage to expose the lies of animal exploitation industries and educate the public about animal cruelty. Humane education programs and powerful films like *The Witness* and *Peaceable Kingdom* (created by Jenny Stein and James LaVeck) are changing minds throughout the country. Wayne Pacelle and the Humane Society of the United States have pioneered important new legal tactics that bypass corrupt national and state legislatures and bring votes concerning animal welfare to the people through the open referendum ballot.

40. For a definition of violence by an ALF supporter and an argument in support of

property destruction as a justifiable nonviolent action, see Ronnie Webb, "Is Violence in the Pursuit of Animal Rights Morally Justifiable?" *Arkangel* #4, archived at www.arkangelweb.org/index.php.

41. On the concept of persons, see Peter Singer, *Rethinking Life and Death: The Collapse of Our Traditional Ethics* (New York: St. Martin's Griffin, 1994), pp. 180–183. If certain minimal psychological criteria are required for a being to count as a "person," Singer points out an interesting irony that some humans are not persons, while some animals are. The morally relevant distinction then is not between human and nonhuman, but between person and non-person.

42. Paul Watson, *Sea Shepherd: My Fight for Whales and Seals*.

43. For the classic statement of just war theory, see Thomas Aquinas, *Summa Theologiae*. For a useful online resource, see "Just War Theory" in the Internet Encyclopedia of Philosophy, www.utm.edu/research/iep/j/justwar.htm.

44. See "Animal Rights Militia Fact Sheet" and "Justice Department Fact Sheet," at www.animalliberation.net.

45. In August and September 2003 a new group called the Revolutionary Cells bombed Chiron and Shaklee corporations because of their ties to Huntingdon Life Sciences. Although the group only caused minor damage, this was the first time in recent history that an animal rights group used a bomb. They also sent out a communiqué threatening "the endgame for animal killers" and signed off with "for animal liberation through armed struggle." See www.directaction.info/news_aug29_03.htm.

46. In two infamous cases, however, three people attacked HLS British managing director Brian Cass with baseball bats outside his home (he was not seriously injured), and Cass's marketing director was accosted on his doorstep and temporarily blinded with a searing spray. SHAC disavowed any connection to these actions and criticized them as them as violent tactics incompatible with their legal and nonviolent orientation. No evidence ever surfaced linking the assault to SHAC.

47. In a 2003 interview, Rod Coronado described the importance of arson to the ALF: "When we address buildings and institutions that have no other purpose but to destroy life, fire is the only way to stop them." *LA Weekly*, August 29–September 4, 2003.

48. See for instance an "ALF response" to a letter challenging the rationale of using arson, in which the pro-ALF author concludes that "arson is NOT recommended" for numerous reasons relating to possible injury to life and negative media coverage (www.animalliberationfront.com/_disc2a/0000006c.htm).

49. "Is Violence in the Pursuit of Animal Rights Morally Justifiable?" *Arkangel* #4.

50. On the gross inadequacy of animal welfare laws, see Gary Francione, *Animals, Property, and the Law*. For a specific example of how wildlife smuggling laws are routinely flouted, see Charles Seabrook, "Wildlife smuggling refuses to be caged," *Atlanta Journal-Constitution*, December 21, 2003.

51. See the American Anti-Vivisection Society bulletin at www.aavs.org/welfare01.html.

52. See Steven Best, "WTO and Animal Rights," in Andrew Linzey, ed., *The Animal World Encyclopedia* (forthcoming).

53. See "Taking Compassion to New Levels," by Paul Shapiro, *Satya* magazine, September 2001.

54. "Our aim is to destroy property and force laboratories to close—publicity is neither here nor there." Interview with a former ALF activist in "Terrorists or Altruists?" *New Internationalist*, Issue 215, January 1991.

55. This type of work, presumably, is the function of an ALF press office and spokesperson, but since David Barbarash stepped down in January 2003 no one has officially

assumed the role of ALF spokesperson, and there are debates as to whether or not there should be a single spokesperson instead of a network of activists, philosophers, scientists, and doctors on hand to discuss ALF actions with the media. Official spokesperson(s) or not, media relations is one area where underground and above-ground aspects of the movement can work in unison and harmony, although in the age of the Patriot Act it is becoming increasingly dangerous for the aboveground to be associated with or to defend the underground.

56. For an account of Operation Bite Back, see www.animalliberation.net.
57. Both quotes cited at www.angelfire.com/pa/veganresist/alfhistory.html.
58. "2 Strategies, same goal in activism for animals," *The Chicago Tribune*, February 16, 2003.
59. "Putting Our House in Order," *The Animals' Agenda*, September–October 2001.
60. "The ALF Unmasked—Interview with David Barbarash."
61. See Gary Francione, *Rain Without Thunder: The Ideology of the Animal Rights Movement* (Philadelphia: Temple University Press, 1996).
62. "Memories of Freedom," www.djurratt.org/bocker_tidningar/memoriesoffreedom.pdf.
63. In an interview with *E Magazine*, David Brower said: "The Sierra Club made the Nature Conservancy look reasonable. I founded Friends of the Earth to make the Sierra Club look reasonable. Then I founded Earth Island Institute to make Friends of the Earth look reasonable. Earth First! now makes us look reasonable. We're still waiting for someone else to come along and make Earth First! look reasonable" (cited in "The Wildlands Project: The Nature Conservancy," by Judy Keeler, on OutdoorWire.com). That group would be the Earth Liberation Front.
64. Cited in Christopher Manes, *Green Rage: Radical Environmentalism and the Unmaking of Civilization* (Boston: Little, Brown and Company, 1990).
65. A glance at the 2001–2003 ALF reports shows that the preponderance of their actions involved sabotage.
66. Donald Griffin was the pioneer of cognitive ethology, rocking the prejudices of his peers and blazing new trails with works such as *The Question of Animal Awareness* (1974), *Animal Thinking* (1984), and *Animal Minds: Beyond Cognition to Consciousness* (2001). His legacy is being carried forth innovatively in studies on chimpanzees, birds, whales, dolphins, and other animals, and in the work of writers such as Marc Bekoff. The human understanding of animals clearly is undergoing a major revolution.
67. See also Wicklund's defense of nonviolent direct action, "Strategic Nonviolence For Animal Liberation," at articles.animalconcerns.org/snv/snv1.html.
68. For a detailed and compelling account of his own experiences of FBI persecution, see Craig Rosebraugh, *Burning Rage of a Dying Planet: Speaking For the Earth Liberation Front* (New York: Lantern Books, 2004).
69. For information on CALA, see www.cala-online.org.

History

Our ignorance of history causes us to slander our own times.—Gustave Flaubert

The past is never dead; it's not even past.—Gwen Stevens (William Faulkner)

History teaches everything, even the future.—Alphonse de Lamartine

Thirty Years of Direct Action

NOEL MOLLAND

It is hard, if not impossible, to say when the animal/earth liberation movement first started. A study of the subject literally takes you back thousands of years to 200 BCE, when people like Pythagoras advocated vegetarianism and animal compassion on spiritual grounds, and to the first century CE, when Plutarch wrote what is widely regarded as the first animal rights literature.

However, you will be delighted to know that I am not going to bore you to death with 2,000 years of waffle. Instead, I merely intend to look at what occurred 30 years ago this year [2002]. But first, to fully understand the events of 30 years ago, we must look slightly further back than that, to the events of 1964.

During the nineteenth and twentieth centuries Britain saw a wealth of animal welfare and rights groups established. However, these groups by and large relied upon the parliamentary system of legal reform to achieve their aims. This process was incredibly slow and achievements were minor. Even the 1911 Animal Protection Act treated animals as property and offered no protection to wild-born creatures. By the mid-1960s people were looking around for other ways of campaigning, and in 1964 John Prestige found that new style.

In 1964 in Brixham, Devon, England, Prestige founded the Hunt Saboteurs Association (HSA), a group that would actively oppose blood sports. Rather than campaigning for parliamentary reforms, the members of John's new group were prepared to directly go out into the fields of Britain and do everything they could, within the law, to prevent the killing of British wildlife.

The popularity of this new form of campaigning was instant. Just a year after the HSA was founded, hunt saboteur groups were active across the English West Country in Devon, Somerset and Avon. Groups also started to emerge outside of the West Country in places like Birmingham, Hampshire and Surrey. Originally a single, Devon-based group, the HSA soon became a national network of dedicated activists using lawful methods to disrupt hunts and to prevent the "green and pleasant land" from literally becoming a killing field.

And so it was that, in 1971, as part of the ever-expanding HSA network, a new hunt sab group was formed in Luton, founded by a law student named Ronnie Lee. The Luton hunt sabs, like a lot of other hunt sab groups, soon became very successful in saving the lives of animals. Many a hunt soon found its sadistic day's entertainment ruined by the Luton Gang.

However, despite the success of the Luton hunt sabs in the field, it soon became apparent to some people within the groups that the strictly legal actions of the HSA could only ever go so far toward preventing animal suffering. The problem was that if a hunt is allowed to be active, no matter how good a hunt sab group may be, there is a chance that an animal may be harmed or killed.

Even if the sabs do manage to prevent an animal from being killed, the fear the hunted animal goes through is tremendous. Contemporary vet reports, gathered at the end of the twentieth century, corroborate this fact. Recognizing that strictly legal hunt sabotage couldn't totally prevent the hunted animals' suffering, Ronnie Lee and a few close friends came to the conclusion that the only real way to do so was to ensure that the hunt was never allowed to become active in the first place. With this aim in mind, Ronnie Lee and Cliff Goodman, and possibly two or three other people, decided to form the Band of Mercy in 1972.

The group's name was chosen because it had been the name of an earlier animal liberation direct action group. During the nineteenth century, an anti-slavery activist named Catherine Smithies had set up a youth wing of the RSPCA called the Bands of Mercy. By and large these youth groups were just normal young supporters of the RSPCA who told stories of heroic animal deeds and took oaths of compassion to the animals. However, some of these young Victorian animal rights activists were a little more zealous than others and went around sabotaging hunting rifles. The activities of the Victorian Bands of Mercy became so well known that there was even a theatrical play written in which a group of children sabotages a hunting rifle.

For Ronnie Lee and his companions, the Victorian Bands of Mercy were a fine example of direct action, so they decided to adopt their not-strictly-legal approach to saving lives. At first, the Band of Mercy concentrated on small actions directed against the hunt during the cub-hunting season. (Cub hunting is when young hounds are taught to tear young fox cubs apart in order for the hound to get the taste for killing.) The initial actions of the Band of Mercy were very simple and were basically designed around the idea of disabling the hunt vehicles in order to slow down or even stop the hunt from carrying out its murderous activities.

However, the Band of Mercy was very clear from the beginning that it was not merely carrying out acts of wanton vandalism against those whom they opposed; rather, their actions were designed around the idea of "active compassion." Accordingly, the Band always left a message to the hunters explaining the reasons behind their actions and the logic of animal liberation. They also wished to show that the attacks were not motivated by personal animosity against any one individual.

The success of the Band of Mercy soon became apparent. By carrying out illegal direct action, the Band was able to prevent the hunts from starting, thus not only saving the lives of innocent animals, but also preventing the psychological suffering of "the chase." Inspired by their early successes, the Band soon became much more daring. Toward the end of 1973 the Band learned about the construction of a new vivisection laboratory. The research laboratory was being built near Milton Keynes for a company called Hoechst Pharmaceuticals. As they visited the building site, two of the Band's activists realized that if they prevented the building from ever being completed, they could also prevent the suffering of the animals destined to be tortured within its four walls. The Band eventually decided that the best way to destroy the construction was through the use of arson. Even if the damage caused by the fire could be repaired, the restoration work would have to be paid for by Hoechst Pharmaceuticals (thus leaving the company with less money to spend on torturing animals).

On November 10th, 1973, the Band of Mercy conducted its first-ever action against the vivisection industry. Two activists gained entry into the half-completed building at Milton Keynes. Once inside, the activists set fire to the building. This action was a double watershed for the movement, as it was not only the Band's first action against the vivisection industry; it was also the Band's first use of arson. In that first fire an amazing £26,000 worth of damage was caused. Six days later, the Band of Mercy returned and started another fire in the same building, causing a further £20,000 worth of damage.

To make sure everyone knew why the building had been set alight, the Band of Mercy sent a message to the press. The statement read:

The building was set fire to in an effort to prevent the torture and murder of our animal brothers and sisters by evil experiments. We are a nonviolent guerrilla organization dedicated to the liberation of animals from all forms of cruelty and persecution at the hands of mankind. Our actions will continue until our aims are achieved.

After the Milton Keynes arson, the next major action occurred in June 1974, when the Band turned its attention to the bloody seal cull of the Wash along the Norfolk coast. The seal cull was an annual event and involved hunters going out in two Home Office–licensed boats and butchering seals. Seal culling is a bloody attack and the seal has no hope of escape. With the goal of preventing the cull from ever starting, and regarding the successful use of arson in the November 1973 action, the Band once again decided to use arson as a campaign tool to destroy the tools of animal murder.

In June 1974 the Band of Mercy set out on their second major action. Under the cover of darkness, two activists sought out the Home Office–licensed boats and set them alight. One of the boats was only slightly damaged by the fire; the other, however, was totally destroyed. This time, the Band of Mercy decided they wouldn't leave a message claiming responsibility. Instead, they wanted to leave the sealers wondering what on earth had happened, whether those responsible would return and whether, if new boats were provided, those vessels would meet with the same fiery fate.

That year there was no seal cull at all due to the actions of the Band of Mercy. Not only that, but because of the fire the owner of the two Home Office–licensed boats went out of business. Having seen one person's business totally destroyed by the actions of these anonymous arsonists, no one was keen to invest in a new business that might very well go the same way. Because of this fear, no one has ever attempted to re-start a seal culling business, and there has never been a seal cull at the Wash since. Because of the actions of two activists, countless numbers of seals have been saved from the bloody annual seal cull.

Looking back on the June 1974 action, it is clear that the attack on the boats was an amazing success. Not only de facto seals, but generations of seals to come, were saved from the seal cullers. Despite this success, however, not everyone in the animal liberation movement approved of the Band's tactics. In July 1974 a member of the Hunt Saboteurs Association offered a reward of £250 for information that would inform upon the Band of Mercy. Speaking on behalf of a local sab group, the spokesperson told the press, "We approve of their ideals, but are opposed to their methods."

Fortunately, despite this act of treachery, the Band of Mercy had by now realized its power. By performing illegal actions the Band was able to directly save the lives of animals through destroying the tools of torture and death. Even if the weaker members of the movement rejected the Band's ideas, the Band realized its work had to continue. To stop would be to let the animals down.

Following the anti–seal cull action, the Band of Mercy launched its first intensive wave of campaigning against the vivisection industry. In the months leading up to the action at the Wash, the Band of Mercy had been able to gather some inside information about vivisection laboratory animal suppliers. All of this information was gathered and stored, waiting for the day it could be used to its fullest effect. And so it was that, following the action at the Wash, the Band was able to launch straight into a wave of actions against the vivisection industry. Between June and August 1974 the Band of Mercy launched eight raids against vivisection lab animal suppliers. The main emphasis of the actions was to cause economic sabotage by either damaging buildings or vehicles. But the Band also reached another landmark in their history by carrying out their first-ever animal rescue during this period.

The first Band of Mercy animal rescue happened in Wiltshire in the English West Country. A guinea pig farm was targeted and the activists managed to rescue half a dozen of the inmates. Besides being a landmark action for being the first Band of Mercy animal rescue, the action also produced an unexpected but very welcome outcome. The guinea pig farm owner was so shaken by the raid that she began to fear that more activists would turn up during the night. Fearing that masked strangers might break into her home, this woman who profited from animal torture took the only sensible course of action: she closed her business.

Besides targeting the vivisection industry, the Band of Mercy continued to take actions against the hunt. But, not wanting to limit their actions to just two forms of animal abuse, the Band also targeted chicken breeders and the firearm lobby. In July 1974 a gun shop in Marlborough was attacked and damaged. The original Victorian Bands of Mercy could surely be proud that their great deeds were being continued in a twentieth-century form.

For a small group of friends, consisting of less than half a dozen activists, the Band of Mercy was able to make a tremendous impact against the animal abusers. In August 1974, however, the Band's luck ran out. After a successful action against Oxford Laboratory Animal Colonies in Bicester, the Band of Mercy made the mistake of returning to OLAC two days later. (I should point out that it's very easy with hindsight to say that it was a mistake to return, but back then it was a perfectly logical action.) On this second raid, a security guard spotted the activists, Ronnie Lee and Cliff Goodman, and called the police. Ronnie and Cliff were promptly arrested.

If the police had hoped that the arrests would bring an end to the Band of Mercy, they were mistaken. The arrest of Ronnie Lee and Cliff Goodman brought the group a fresh wave of publicity. Many people viewed the Band not as terrorists but as heroes, latter-day Robin Hoods for the animals. Ronnie and Cliff were soon lionized as the Bicester Two. Throughout the hearing, daily demonstrations took place outside the court. Support for the Bicester Two was very strong and came from the most unlikely of quarters. Even Ronnie Lee's local Member of Parliament, the Free Church Minister Ivor Clemitson, joined in the campaign for their release.

Despite the strong public support for the Bicester Two, both Ronnie Lee and Cliff Goodman were given three years' imprisonment. A letter published in the *Daily Telegraph* shows the anger felt at the outcome of the first animal liberation trial.

> Many would sympathize with their action against the utterly diabolical and largely unnecessary form of cruelty involved in animal experimentation. These young men, while defying the law, showed great courage, and the sentences of three years' imprisonment seems unrealistic and harsh.

Now, it is said you can't keep a good animal/earth liberation activist down. This is certainly true in the case of Ronnie Lee. After the sentencing, Ronnie and Cliff split up. Cliff went back to Oxford prison, where he and Ronnie had both been inmates while on remand, and Ronnie was moved to Winchester prison.

At Winchester prison Ronnie discovered that provisions for vegans in prison were less than desirable. So, in order to get a decent meal and vegan clothing, Ronnie went on a hunger strike. This hunger strike gained a great deal of media attention, bringing animal liberation again into public discussion. Ronnie soon expanded his hunger strike demands to include issues revolving around Porton Down, the Government's chemical and biological warfare research station, a site of horrific animal experimentation.

Faced with a rush of unwanted attention, Winchester prison soon had to back down and supply Ronnie with his vegan provisions. Sadly, the success of the strike did not extend to Porton Down. In order to keep the Ministry of Defense out of the media spotlight, all of the attention was focused on Ronnie himself, against his wishes. Recognizing that the media was moving the focus from animal abuse to the hunger strike, Ronnie decided to end his protest.

Despite Ronnie's good example, the other activists in the Band of Mercy brought the Band almost to a grinding halt while the Bicester Two were jailed. The only major event to take place during the time of the Bicester Two's imprisonment was in 1975, when Mike Huskisson managed to rescue two beagles from Imperial Chemical Industries (ICI). The beagles were being used in tobacco smoking experiments and were appropriately labeled as the "smoking beagles." Mike was arrested for the action and charged with burglary. However, knowing how much public support there had been for the Bicester Two, ICI feared the adverse publicity of a trial. This meant Mike was acquitted of the charges, ICI's pointless animal testing was revealed, and the Bicester Two were given a moral boost by Mike's action.

Cliff Goodman and Ronnie Lee served only a third of their sentence and were paroled after 12 months in the spring of 1976. Being in jail had affected the two activists in totally different ways. Cliff Goodman came out of prison with just one thought: he didn't want to go back inside. He decided he wasn't a revolutionary and wanted to stick to strictly legal campaigning in the future. Sadly, Cliff decided to turn informer in prison and gave the police a great deal of information about the use of radios by the Band of Mercy. For this act of treachery, Cliff was given the title of the movement's first "grass" (police informer).

Ronnie, on the other hand, emerged with new determination. For him, prison life had called to mind the plight of imprisoned animals, inmates who, unlike human prisoners, have no "release date"—all that awaits them is suffering and death. Being a prisoner had reminded Ronnie how defenseless the animals are and how they need someone to stand up and fight on their behalf. Living in a cage gave him a new sense of solidarity and understanding and strengthened his resolve to fight for animal liberation.

Ronnie realized that there was widespread public support for animal liberation through illegal direct action. Upon his release, he gathered together the remains of the Band of Mercy along with about two dozen new recruits. This was a revolutionary group and everyone knew it. The only problem was that the name "Band of Mercy" no longer seemed appropriate. It didn't fit the new revolutionary feel. A new name was needed—a name that would haunt animal abusers, and whose very mention could symbolize the whole ideology of a revolutionary movement. With this in mind Ronnie selected the name, the Animal Liberation Front—the ALF.

This article originally appeared in No Compromise *magazine.*

Animal Liberation—By "Whatever Means Necessary"

ROBIN WEBB

This article originally appeared in a slightly different form as the sleeve notes to a benefit CD compilation album, This Is the ALF, *published by Mortarhate Records of London.*

"Animal lib loonies," "terrorists," "people haters" . . . all terms used by power-hungry, profit-motivated animal exploiters and the mass news media to describe the Animal Liberation Front (ALF) and similarly inclined groups that work outside "The Law"—whose law?—in pursuit of justice for our brothers and sisters of other species, of the other nations much older than ours upon this earth.

The truth is very different. People from all walks of life and social backgrounds, of all ages, of all beliefs and of none—these are the compassionate commandos who constitute the ALF and like-minded groups.

Driven by an abhorrence of *all* abuse and exploitation of the weak and innocent, the activists break unjust laws and risk their freedom in pursuit of a rightful cause—animal liberation—in much the same way that campaigners in past struggles fought for the abolition of slavery and the emancipation of women. It used to be a "crime" to help a slave escape from bondage. It was—indeed, still is!—a "crime" to torch empty buildings in order to commit economic sabotage. How many thinking people would now condemn the abolitionists and Suffragettes for taking such extra-parliamentary actions?

So, what *is* animal liberation? It's not difficult to understand, it doesn't need a philosopher's lifetime work to explain and it won't take years wrestling with your conscience to come to terms with its logic.

It was once argued that the black races were inferior to whites and could therefore justifiably be used as slaves. It was also once argued that women were subordinates of men and thus could also be exploited. Sensible folk now know that such reasoning is offensive nonsense. All sentient beings are individuals to whom life is of intrinsic value; it's the only life they knowingly have. Each individual of whatever species has, in his or her own way, feelings of social awareness and family ties, together with the ability to suffer. So it *must* follow that we as humans do not have the right to abuse and exploit those of other species for our own ends, merely because we have the *power* so to do, any more than we had the right to use those of other races for the same reason. As was rightly said, "Power corrupts, absolute power corrupts absolutely."

Animal liberation covers *all* abuse and exploitation. It is the *ultimate* freedom movement, the "final frontier." Once we learn to respect the right of individuals from other species to live their lives without abuse, exploitation or needless interference, we shall also have learned to respect that same right for our fellow members of the human race (after all, humans are animals, too).

That, all too briefly, is why the ALF exists. But how and when did it begin standing up to the animal-abusing Establishment and the State, asserting, "We won't *allow* it anymore—you either stop the obscenities or you pay the price!"?

Direct action against hunting with hounds began in England during 1963 when the Hunt Saboteurs Association (HSA) was formed. Going out into the fields to place themselves between the hunters and the hunted, "sabs" were brutally attacked by blood-junkies with monotonous regularity. At that time many HSA members were pacifists who rarely fought back against the hunt thugs, amongst whom "sab-bashing" became a rewarding alternative when the usual quarry wasn't around to be terrorized and tortured. This surely couldn't last, and it didn't.

By 1972 some sabs in the Home Counties of England became weary of spending their Saturdays being thrown into ditches, appreciating that if the hunt can't start, then it can't kill. Immobilizing hunt vehicles, including the hound van, super-gluing locks on gates—these and other tactics frustrated the hunters' evil exploits whilst protecting imaginative sabs from harm and giving them more free time to use fighting animal abuse.

This new radical group adopted the name "Band of Mercy" from the nineteenth-century Royal Society for the Prevention of Cruelty to Animals' youth organization. Much to the pro-hunting RSPCA's embarrassment, the original Bands of Mercy performed plays, one of which, E. S. Turner's *All Heaven in a Rage*, features a scene in which

Sarah Jane, the maid, empties a jug of water down the barrels of Mr. Quickshot the pigeon-shooter's gun and dips all his cartridges in warm water. The gun barrels subsequently burst in Mr. Quickshot's face. Was this really a course of action recommended by the RSPCA of days gone by?

Within a year the new Band of Mercy had expanded its range of targets to other areas of animal abuse, particularly the vivisection industry. Arson also began to be used as a tactic alongside liberation. Interestingly, the first Band of Mercy activist to be convicted (for torching boats owned by seal hunters) later went on to serve six years as a member of the RSPCA's national council . . . perhaps anticipating the late-1990s emergence of the Provisional RSPCA?[1]

More Band of Mercy activists were subsequently jailed for their deeds, but this in no way deterred others from taking up and continuing the fight against animal abuse with a total disregard for "The Law." In 1976 the radical activists adopted the soon-to-be-infamous title of "Animal Liberation Front." During those formative years many high-profile actions were carried out in the name of animal liberation, from the popularly acclaimed rescue of the "smoking beagles" from the hellhole laboratories of multinational Imperial Chemical Industries (ICI) to the digging up of blood-junkie folk-legend John Peel's grave. Everyone kept wondering what would happen next.

The late 1970s and early '80s saw the media treating activists, to a large extent, as well-intentioned animal-lovers who, as true British eccentrics, were just taking things a little too far; they were the Robin Hoods of the animal welfare world. "Liberation Leagues" also sprang up for a while around this time, with mass daylight raids freeing animals and obtaining valuable information that revealed the greed-driven evils practiced behind the closed doors of animal Belsens.

By the mid-1980s economic sabotage had become a common tactic, from smashing windows of butchers' shops to the sustained campaign of arson attacks against department stores that sold furs. This really began to hurt the animal abuse–based institutions and multinationals in a way that demonstrations, leafleting and marches never could: It hurt them financially. The great god Profit was under threat.

Around that time, two even more radical groups emerged. The Hunt Retribution Squad, which began in 1984, concentrated on waging war against blood sports by extending the ALF's remit, stating that it *would* be prepared to inflict physical harm on blood-junkies to prevent them murdering wild animals. The Animal Rights Militia followed quickly in 1985, soon establishing its credentials. Early actions included sending letter bombs to prominent vivisectors. The ARM would surface sporadically to ever more dramatic effect; its city center arson attacks in 1994 caused over $6 million in damages on the Isle of Wight alone. My late friend Barry Horne was subsequently convicted of the latter action, and I narrowly escaped a conspiracy charge for the same deed.

The powers behind the news media began to lean hard on editors, and almost overnight the beagle-rescuing darlings were made over into dangerous fanatics who posed a threat to the very fabric of society. In other words, the State and the Establishment were getting a metaphorical kicking for a change and didn't like it at all.

Reprisal from the State was heralded by the creation of the Animal Rights National Index (ARNI) at Metropolitan (London) Police Headquarters, which, although a police department, was intended to work closely with the security services. ARNI's first major offensive came in 1986 with the arrest of ALF Supporters Group volunteers and other activists. The Sheffield show trial that followed in 1987 imposed jail terms of up to 10 years. An immediate flood of animal liberation actions ensued, completely destroying the claim that the trial had "smashed the ALF." The oppressive sentences had proved conclusively that direct action worked and that the animal abusers were fighting a rearguard battle to protect their hellish interests. Nothing prompts a fiercer defense than the knowledge that you're losing.

With the fur trade now decimated and vivisection an established target, more attention was focused on the largest area of all animal abuse—the meat industry. Butchers' shop windows disappeared and locks were super-glued; shrink-wrapped meat on supermarket shelves was mysteriously pierced, prompting fears of contamination; and, in the major league, slaughterhouses and refrigerated meat trucks were torched. (And, of course, many individual chickens, goats, pigs, rabbits, turkeys and others of different nations found a new life free of pain and suffering.) A young vegan child observed that "If there weren't any slaughterhouses there wouldn't *be* any butchers' shops." The financial year 1991–1992 saw around 100 refrigerated meat trucks destroyed by incendiary devices at a capital cost of some $10 million. Add to that the invisible costs of increased insurance premiums and security precautions, and you begin to get the kind of losses that worry the richest of businesses.

Late 1993 saw the birth of yet another group, as radical as the ARM. The Justice Department's first wave of anti-personnel devices was intercepted, but others—booby-trapped videocassette boxes and poster tubes, metal mousetraps primed with razor blades—soon began to reach their targets. Siding firmly with the Animal Rights Militia, the JD declared "We won't be asking anyone to stop messing with animals and will make no excuses for our violent intervention—they've had it too good for too long."

Just a few months later the ARM began a series of attacks using powerful timed incendiary devices against "High Street animal abuse," including pharmaceutical giant Boots, which at that time still owned laboratories that tortured animals in useless tests, intended as nothing more than protection against possible compensation claims from human victims of drug-induced side effects. Boots soon rid itself of those concentration camps.

The ALF has always followed a triad of policies within which anyone who was a vegetarian or, preferably, a vegan, could claim responsibility as an activist under its umbrella, and enjoy the backing of the ALF Supporters Group if unlucky enough to be caught. They were, basically:

> To liberate animals from suffering or potential suffering and place them in good permanent homes or, where appropriate, release them into their natural environment.
>
> To damage or destroy property and equipment associated with animal abuse by
>> a. taking that property out of the arena of animal abuse so it could no longer cause harm, and
>> b. inflicting economic loss on the abusers with the intention of driving them out of business.
>
> To take all reasonable precautions not to endanger life of any kind.

As popular as those policies had been within the movement and despite the powerful effects wrought against animal abuse by their implementation, it became clear from the ARM, HRS and JD that anger was boiling over at the all-too-slow rate of progress towards animal liberation. The third ALF policy was becoming strained, even amongst some dedicated ALF supporters.

The arguments presented in favor of inflicting serious injury, even death, upon animal abusers were quite straightforward. Do you believe in animal liberation? Do you therefore believe that speciesism is as indefensible as racism? Did you support the African National Congress during its policy of armed struggle against apartheid? Would you therefore support an "armed struggle" by the ARM or Justice Department? Having answered each question honestly you may find some contradictions, and it's up to you to resolve them in your own mind; even Gandhi said "Where there is only a choice between cowardice and violence, I would advise violence."

That argument continues so: while politicians talked and negotiated, Nazi Germany invaded neighboring countries and began building the concentration camps. It took the overwhelming violence of World War II, including the loss of many millions of innocent lives, to rid the world of that evil. Such an example suggests that short-term violence may be justifiable in pursuit of a longer-term peace.

Whatever form it takes, direct action in pursuit of animal liberation has now spread across the whole world. From New Zealand to New York, from Sweden to South Africa, the ultimate freedom movement is growing in strength and determination.

Animal liberation is not a campaign, not just a hobby to put aside when it becomes tiresome or a new interest catches your eye. It's a war. A long, hard, bloody war in which all the countless millions of its victims have, so far, been on one side only, have been defenseless and innocent, whose tragedy was being born nonhuman. The oceans, the land and the sky should be free to all rather than be the domain of whoever is most powerful in the human world. The methods to achieve a just world are many and varied, but all tactics are important. So many are working in so many different ways, the important thing is to work for the common goal and let your heart tell you what course of action is right for you.

Notes

1. The Provisional RSPCA began as a joke on British TV, "If you don't know who the ALF are, they're like the Provisional RSPCA." This was, of course, based on the Provisional IRA in Ireland. Some people began undertaking liberations and sending out threatening letters to animal abusers using the name, thus highlighting the inadequacies of the RSPCA whilst annoying them at the same time.

A Personal Overview of Direct Action in the United Kingdom and the United States

KIM STALLWOOD

In the July–August 1998 issue of The Animals' Agenda, *I published "Direct Action: Progress, Peril, or Both?" by Freeman Wicklund. This cover feature attracted a large reader response, some samples of which were published in a special Letters to the Editor section in the November–December 1998 issue. Freeman's article also inspired Karen Davis, President of United Poultry Concerns, to organize a conference, "Direct Action for Animals," in 1999. This paper is based upon the presentation that I made at the conference.*

My presentation will consist of a history of illegal direct action as well as personal observations of its evolution in the United Kingdom, and its impact on the future of the animal rights movement in the United States. I will also summarize the rationale behind publishing Freeman's article, and discuss readers' and others' responses. My presentation is based upon my own experiences as a professional animal advocate since 1976 in the UK. I also consulted three books, which were *Animal Revolution* by Richard Ryder, *Animal Century* by Mark Gold, and *The Animal Rights Movement in America* by Lawrence Finsen and Susan Finsen. Finally, I mined my own extensive personal collection of animal rights materials for original documents and publications by and about the ALF from the 1970s and 1980s. I conclude with my personal feelings on direct action for animals.

Two things are important for me to make clear at the beginning. First, the Animal Rights Network Inc., the not-for-profit publisher of *The Animals' Agenda*, has a policy of support for nonviolence. Second, I have never been involved with ALF actions. I know myself well enough to know that I would not be very good at clandestine activities.

I would be more of a hindrance than a help. Soon after I became involved with animal rights in 1976 I was close with those who did do direct action. I may not have been a firsthand participant but I did carefully watch what happened and was indirectly involved.

The first direct action for animals in the present era of animal advocacy, which I date as being post–Second World War, began in England in the early 1960s with the Hunt Saboteurs Association (HSA). In 1963 journalist John Prestige was assigned to report on the Devon and Somerset Staghounds. When he witnessed the hunters drive a pregnant deer into a village and kill her, he vowed to act. The first hunt he and his friends sabotaged was the South Devon Foxhounds on the day after Christmas Day, which is traditionally an important date in the fox hunting calendar. They fed meat to the hounds to satisfy any appetite that the dogs may have had for chasing and killing a fox.

"Sabbing" really came into its own in the mid-1970s after enjoying some favorable publicity in the British media. "Sabs" (now using vegan tactics!) disrupted the hunt by laying false scents, wiring up gates to slow down the hunt's progress, and setting off fireworks in woods to scare the foxes away. Some sabs developed an amazing expertise with a hunting horn and even succeeded in gaining control of the pack from the hunt master.

Hunters, of course, retaliated by attacking sabs. In 1976 the Joint Master of the Essex Union Foxhunt was widely quoted as saying, "Horsewhipping a hunt saboteur is rather like beating a wife—they're both private matters." In 1991 Mike Hill became the first sab to die while sabotaging a hunt in Cheshire. In 1993 15-year-old Thomas Worby died when a vehicle from the Cambridgeshire Hunt struck him during a sab.

In 1972 some sabs thought that more militant action for animals was required and consequently formed the Band of Mercy. The original Bands of Mercy were formed in the 1870s as children's clubs that were dedicated to fostering kindness to animals. Those Bands of Mercy modeled themselves on Bands of Hope, which were clubs for children who pledged themselves never to drink alcohol. I often read that the Victorian Bands of Mercy sabotaged fox hunts, but I have never been able to find evidence to substantiate this claim.

In 1975 the first animal activist to be convicted was Robin Howard, who had damaged two Lincolnshire sealing boats. Later that year Ronnie Lee and Cliff Goodman were sentenced to three years in prison for causing damage to equipment at various animal research laboratories in England and Wales during the two preceding years.

Released after one year, Goodman established an animal rescue group and Lee, acting as spokesperson for the Band of Mercy, renamed it the Animal Liberation Front in 1976. In 1977 Lee served another prison sentence for stealing some laboratory mice.

The ALF's early actions were premised upon a philosophy of non-violence. In April 1974 Ronnie Lee wrote in *Peace News*, a biweekly nonviolent revolution newsmagazine, that militant action should be "limited only by reverence for life and hatred of violence." In a 1979 issue of the anarchist biweekly newsmagazine *Freedom*, Gary Treadwell and Ronnie Lee wrote:

> The ALF is not violent in that much care is taken to prevent injury to people and many raids have been called off because of possible confrontation. In any case our aims are for human as well as (other) animal liberation. The ALF is destructive, but only to property used to inflict, promote or transport animal exploitation.

The first illegal direct action activities elicited surprisingly sympathetic coverage in the media. For example, in 1975 Mike Huskisson rescued two beagles from tobacco research at Imperial Chemical Industries (ICI)'s laboratories. The media portrayed Huskisson as a liberator and ICI as a callous corporation. Media coverage of illegal direct action at this time tended to focus on the liberated animals and less on any damage caused. The imprisoned activists were accurately portrayed as caring people who put their own liberty at risk to save animals from cruel situations.

At first the publicity inspired others with the same altruistic motivation for animal liberation, and they organized independent cells of activists. They did not always seek publicity. They met their own costs of organizing direct action. They simply wanted to liberate animals and place them quietly into good homes. It is, of course, very difficult to succeed in breaking into research laboratories and factory farms to liberate animals. This was the late 1970s and early 1980s, however, when the animal exploitation facilities had yet to become as security-conscious as they are today. What's more, the police were not particularly interested in the ALF actions.

The media coverage tended to glamorize the people and the actions and, as it continued, a new wave of activists became interested in direct action. This new group tended to be younger, unemployed, and anarchist. They placed animal liberation within a larger context of opposi-

tion to the state, the military-industrial complex, capitalism and social-
ism. They did not embrace nonviolence. They saw illegal direct action
for animals as opportunities to violently confront the society they
rejected. Consequently, their motivation for helping animals was not
exclusively focused on liberating animals from exploitation, as it was
for the ALF founders and originators. At the same time, it became
increasingly more difficult to successfully liberate animals because
security and police activity increased. This caused a shift primarily
toward acts of "economic sabotage," which included "bricking"
butcher's shop windows, arson, food poisoning threats, letter bombs,
incendiary devices, and so on. What's more, Ronnie Lee began speaking out in favor of violence toward people as an acceptable direct
action tactic. For example, in an article signed "R.L." in the October
1984 ALF newsletter he proposed that activists should set up "fresh
groups . . . under new names whose policies do not preclude the use of
violence towards animals abusers."

From 1981 to 1986 I was the national organizer for the British
Union for the Abolition of Vivisection (BUAV) in London. From 1981
to 1984 the BUAV donated part of its offices rent-free to the ALF
Supporters Group (ALF SG), which included Ronnie Lee and Vivien
Smith. BUAV's board of directors and staff, including myself, were pro-
ALF. We routinely reported on ALF actions in BUAV's bimonthly newspaper, *The Liberator*, which I edited. The BUAV was the only established organization in the early to mid-1980s that was willing to stand
alongside the ALF and its supporters' group. The BUAV probably
extended more support to the Animal Liberation Front in the form of
free office space, resources, and uncritical publicity than any other animal rights group ever has.

This was also the same period that the ALF moved from a position
of nonviolence to support violence toward people. It also became
apparent that despite BUAV's support and generosity, the ALF SG was
attempting to seize control of BUAV through the latter's democratic
membership structure. There was also a disagreement over strategy.
BUAV's leadership believed in a dual strategy of political action and
direct action; the ALF leadership, who were anarchists, believed all
political action was a waste of time and money. The ALF wanted
BUAV and its considerable resources so that they could redirect all of
it toward direct action. BUAV's board could not accept that the ALF
SG was moving to a position of no longer supporting nonviolence.
They also could not accept that the ALF SG was attempting to challenge BUAV's leadership when it had provided so much support to

them. Finally, the BUAV board, although a supporter of illegal direct action, reluctantly expelled the ALF SG from its offices in 1984.

It is important to note that ALF SG/BUAV disagreement over political action coincided with the unsympathetic Conservative government's passage of legislation that regulated the use of animals in scientific research. The coalition of four national anti-vivisection organizations that I helped lead at that time laid the foundation for the progress that the present Labor government is now making. This includes the abolition of animal research for cosmetic testing, including ingredients, alcohol and tobacco research, and all experiments with great apes. This movement-wide political campaign would have stopped if the ALF SG had seized control of the BUAV.

The change in philosophy, from a nonviolent strategy of illegal direct action to a violent one, cost the ALF its sympathetic media coverage and growing public support. It also forced other animal advocacy organizations to defensive positions, thereby making their already difficult work that much harder. The ALF SG became isolated and received little or no support from the animal rights movement once it had lost BUAV's assistance. Further alienation occurred in 1984 when *Peace News*, which since the early 1980s had provided the ALF with a mailing address, withdrew its support because ALF actions were increasingly about causing economic sabotage and threatening human life, not freeing animals.

The Animal Liberation Front was not the only organization that organized illegal direct action in the 1980s. The Northern Animal Liberation League (NALL) was the first of a series of regional liberation leagues whose strategy was to organize the largest number of people to illegally enter a research laboratory or a factory farm in broad daylight on a Sunday when the institution had little or no staff on duty. The minimum amount of damage was caused to gain entry. The raid's objective was to rescue animals, take photographs, and steal information, to enable the greatest number of people to witness animal exploitation hidden from public view. These raids, which were well planned and disciplined in their execution, usually lasted about 30 minutes. This ensured that the activists had dispersed by the time the police arrived. The information taken from the raids was then distributed in towns near the action so that local residents could learn what was happening on their doorstep. A 1981 NALL raid on Sheffield University's laboratories resulted in returning a stolen dog to his human companions.

The liberation league raids became a regular feature on the animal rights calendar. Some of the raids involved two groups of activists. One group demonstrated outside the gates to a laboratory while a second group was inside. The second "inside" group quickly joined the first "outside" group who were legally demonstrating; thus by the time the police arrived they could not prove who had been inside and who had not.

In 1977 the first US animal liberation action was conducted by the Undersea Railroad, who released two porpoises from a Hawaii research lab. The first US ALF raid was in 1979, when five animals were rescued from the New York University Medical Center. Slowly, ALF actions began occurring throughout the US. Perhaps one of the most notable was the 1984 raid on the University of Pennsylvania's Head Injury Lab, operated by Thomas Gennarelli. More than 60 hours of videotape taken by the researchers themselves was stolen by ALF and given anonymously to People for the Ethical Treatment of Animals (PETA). PETA produced a videotape summary, called *Unnecessary Fuss*, which was widely distributed. After a year-plus campaign, which included demonstrations, civil disobedience, and political and media lobbying, the laboratory's funding from the National Institutes for Health was canceled.

The trend in illegal action for animals in the UK and US over the last two decades has not been as sophisticated in its ability to combine it with other forms of action. Instead, it has tended toward the use of violent methods that place humans and animals at a perceived and/or real risk. For example, an explosion at a research laboratory at Bristol University in England used high-powered explosives that placed people at risk. A pipe bomb underneath a car owned by a researcher in England exploded and harmed a nearby baby in a stroller. In the US several pipe bombs were placed at the Utah Fur Breeders Agriculture Cooperative near buildings that housed mink. Telephoned bomb threats have also been made to hotels hosting fur sales. Allegations of poison-laced turkeys have coincided with recent Thanksgiving holidays.

Clearly, much more can be said about the evolution of illegal direct action for animals, the organizations, and the players. I have chosen to focus on this early history because it is important to know that direct action began as nonviolent direct action and later became violent direct action. It was initially carried out by people whose paramount interests were to rescue animals and cause damage only to property that directly harmed animals while taking extraordinary measures to not place anyone—human or animal—at risk.

It was in this context that I wanted to publish a cover article on this subject in *The Animals' Agenda*. I was seriously concerned that illegal direct action had lost its ethical foundation; that it had become an opportunity for misfits and misanthropes to infiltrate the ALF and perhaps seek personal revenge for some perceived social injustice. Where was the intelligent debate about tactics and strategies that went beyond the mindless rhetoric and emotional elitism pervading much of the self-produced direct action literature? In short, what had happened to the animals' interests?

When *Agenda*'s managing editor, Kirsten Rosenberg, brought to my attention the strategy guide called *Strategic Nonviolence for Animal Liberation*, I at last thought I had found some serious writing on illegal direct action. Although I had only met the author, Freeman Wicklund, once, and was not familiar with the activities of the Animal Liberation League, which published the guide, I was impressed with its contents. Kirsten and I proceeded to work with Freeman on the writing of the cover feature, which was published in 1998.

Readers' response to the article was polarized; some liked it, some hated it. *The Animals' Agenda* was subjected to a letter-writing and e-mail campaign, including a petition, that demanded we publish a cover feature on the ALF in the next issue. I remember reading a number of letters and e-mails that were remarkably alike and were clearly written by people who hadn't read the article. The cover feature preceding Freeman's was about animal rights and abortion. I had deliberately structured that article so that there were two viewpoints equally alongside each other. Some readers felt that this was how the article on direct action should have been structured, but to do so would have missed the point of Freeman's article. His article discussed the history of illegal direct action and critiqued its overall effectiveness. It was not—nor was it intended to be—an anti-ALF article, which is how some readers saw it.

I carefully considered all of the comments received, especially the critical ones. Our response was to: (1) publish two pages of readers' letters in the second issue after the one that included Freeman's article; (2) start publishing in every issue a new department, "ALF Action Digest," reporting recent ALF activities; and (3) publish a cover feature interview with Rod Coronado, who had completed a five-year prison sentence for ALF actions.

I am very proud to have published Freeman's outstanding article. It has significantly contributed to the debate about illegal direct action for animals. I applaud Karen Davis and United Poultry Concerns

(UPC) for organizing a forum on direct action, and hope that one result of forums such as theirs is that illegal direct action for animals will return to its original and ethical foundation of nonviolence to all beings.

Finally, my personal feelings on direct action for animals have considerably evolved over the last 30 years. I supported the ALF in its formative period in the 1970s and the emergence of the Animal Liberation Leagues (the precursor to open rescues) in the 1980s.

Currently, I view animal advocacy within the framework of four core values: compassion, truth, nonviolence or *ahimsa*, and "interbeing" (the understanding that everything, including thoughts and actions, is interrelated). I evaluate all actions for animals, including direct action, by these four core values. Consequently, I believe in direct action that

- is motivated by a sense of compassion for all beings (human and nonhuman alike);
- tells the truth about animal cruelty and all resulting harms it causes to people and the environment;
- is accomplished with adherence to nonviolent principles to all beings (human and nonhuman alike) and property; and
- is undertaken only after all consequences of the direct action and its impact on all people and animals are carefully considered by the protagonists, who are willing to honestly and openly accept the consequences.

I therefore conclude that much of what is done in the name of illegal direct action for animals is harmful to animals, humans, and the environment because it conflicts with the four core values.

Conversely, the actions of the Animal Liberation Leagues in Britain in the 1980s, and the more recent development of the open rescue strategy started in Australia and adopted by groups in the United States, are to be encouraged because I believe they sufficiently meet the standards of the four core values. I like open rescues because

- they tell the truth about cruel practices toward animals by documenting them with videotape footage, photographs, and reports, which are used to educate the public, secure media coverage, and challenge appropriate authorities;
- they clearly demonstrate a compassionate attitude among the advocates toward the cruelly exploited animals by, for example,

providing bottled water to dehydrated chickens in battery cages, which inspires others to think positively about animal advocates and the animal advocacy movement;

- they respect the property of others, causing the minimum amount of damage to gain entry, including leaving replacement locks if any have been destroyed; and

- the truth telling, compassionate action, and demonstrated respect reveal the animal advocates' larger understanding ("interbeing") of their actions.

With respect to violence against humans, animals, and inanimate property as a strategy and tactic in the animal rights movement, I conclude that all acts of violence toward humans and animals as well as the vast majority of acts of violence toward property are incompatible with the four core values in animal advocacy of truth, *ahimsa*/nonviolence, compassion, and interbeing.

I believe that the only compatible acts of violence against property are those that meet the four core values. For example, as in acts of open rescue, prying open and permanently damaging a lock or padlock is acceptable when the intent is to gain access to documents and evidence of animal cruelty and suffering. As in the practice with open rescues, a replacement lock is left at the site of the damaged lock. Also, in certain circumstances, carefully selected property damage that renders inoperable equipment that is directly used to cause suffering and pain to animals is compatible with the four core values. This also includes similar minimal property damage to free animals from oppression. As with leaving a replacement lock, some form of compensation to the minimal damage caused should be made, which serves as a symbolic and actual reparation.

Clearly, what is incompatible with the four core values of animal advocacy is gratuitous violence, including graffiti, wanton property destruction or vandalism, and home demonstrations.

Compatible with the four core values of animal advocacy is a statement explaining why such action was taken and urging the owners, management, and workers of the business or institution to end their practices of animal exploitation and explaining why such action will benefit humans and animals.

Finally, the application of the four core values of animal advocacy to direct action also helps to prevent the media from framing the action as a "caring scientific researcher dedicated to saving humanity versus a misanthropic animal activist who cares more about a rat than a baby."

Instead, as in the case of Mike Huskisson, the media is more likely to accurately portray animal advocates as caring passionately about animals and acting compassionately and nonviolently to protect them.

LIBERATION

Take sides. Neutrality helps the oppressor, never the victim. Silence encourages the tormentor, never the tormented.—Elie Wiesel

If we are trespassing, so were the soldiers who broke down the gates of Hitler's death camps; if we are thieves, so were the members of the Underground Railroad who freed the slaves of the South; and if we are vandals, so were those who destroyed forever the gas chambers of Buchenwald and Auschwitz. —anonymous ALF activist

The fight is not for us, not for our personal wants or needs. It is for every animal that has ever suffered and died in the vivisection labs, and for every animal that will suffer and die in those same labs unless we end this evil business now. The souls of the tortured dead cry out for justice, the cry of the living is for freedom. We can create that justice and we can deliver that freedom. The animals have no one but us, we will not fail them.—Barry Horne

Legitimizing Liberation

MARK BERNSTEIN, PhD

It is for good reason that a positive connotation is universally asso-ciated with the notion of liberation. To liberate is to free, and to make free—or, at least to make more free—is largely a measure of allowing a group of individuals to behave in conformity with their natural instincts and act in accordance with their desires and preferences. Prior to being liberated, individuals are oppressed, subjugated, and unduly restricted. Blacks were liberated in this country in 1863 with the enact-ment of the Emancipation Proclamation, Indians were liberated from British colonial rule in 1947, and Afghans were liberated from the Taliban regime in 2001. Undoubtedly, liberation is a matter of degree. No reflective person believes that Blacks or Afghans are fully free at this time. Moreover, despite the dating of seminal events, liberation is a process and is rarely accomplished by a particular edict on a partic-ular date. The Emancipation Proclamation, important as it was, was just one step toward the end of slavery and racial discrimination.

The logic of liberation mandates that candidates for liberation have the possibility of living more fulfilling and happier lives. They must, in other words, have welfares. This is why it is senseless to query the mer-its of liberating chairs or vegetables. Although one can paint and rein-force a chair to make it both more aesthetically pleasing and more functional, the chair, in and of itself, is not made better off by such modifications. Similar considerations apply to vegetables. Adding fer-tilizer may help them grow more quickly and salting them may enhance their taste, but vegetables cannot be made better (or worse) off, any more than chairs can. One does not know where to begin to liberate chairs and vegetables, not from ignorance, but in virtue of the fact that there is no point of departure.

Nonhuman animals are prime subjects of liberation. To be sure, there are still some rather perverse neo-Cartesians who cling to the idea that animals are devoid of consciousness and are nothing more than relatively complex automatons.[1] For these philosophers, there is no issue of animal liberation. Without any awareness, animals cannot feel pain, frustration, discouragement, and depression. Nor, of course, can they experience pleasure, satisfaction, hope, or joy. Lacking any consciousness, they are absent any well-being. The only criterion of an animal being better or worse than it was at an earlier time resides in its serviceability to us. Just as the function of a clock is to tell time—and so a better clock is one that more accurately tells time—the function of a burro, say, is to carry loads. The heavier loads the pack beast can bear, the better and more valuable he is.

There are those who would deny the intelligibility of liberating animals by arguing that they unfailingly lack the capacity to form desires and preferences.[2] These theorists are not quite as radical as the neo-Cartesians; they allow that animals have consciousness and feelings but deny that, for example, they can prefer that they not be in a state of intense pain. The avenue to this conclusion inevitably turns on the idea that only language users have the capability to create preferences. Since nonhuman animals are considered linguistically deprived, desires can never form part of their mental lives. The reasoning fails for a host of reasons. Conditioning the possibility of desires upon actual language use would entail that we are mistaken in believing that *human* infants desire their mother's milk, let alone their mother's attention and comfort. Secondly, at least some animals seem to have language ability; witness the sign language capacity of some primates. Perhaps most importantly, were such an unlikely hypothesis true, it would still carry little weight in denying the coherence of animal liberation. After all, these theorists still accept the commonsense idea that animals can feel pain and suffer, and so have a welfare. Even if they are incapable of forming desires to rid themselves of pain, their welfare would still be compromised by it; a dog relieved of his pain is surely made better off even if he could not—by virtue of limited language skills—form a preference to be rid of his suffering.

Although strictly unnecessary to the argument for a meaningful liberation, recent studies in cognitive ethology have supported the intuitive belief that the difference between animal and human minds is, at most, one of degree rather than kind. Darwin, himself, insisted upon a continuity between animal and human experience, a point forcefully advanced by zoologists, physiologists, and primatologists, as well as ethologists. Discarding *a priori* prejudices that impose an unbridgeable chasm between animals and humans allows us to appreciate the unsurprising results of scientific research. Most will not find it revelatory to read that many animals communicate, play, deceive, make tools, and have intimate social relationships.[3] In the ways that matter most, they are like us.

So much for the intelligibility of liberating animals. Outside the offices of a few philosophers, the urgent question is not whether the notion of liberation can be meaningfully applied to animals, but is rather whether the liberation of animals is justified. We want to know whether the liberation of animals is a morally right (or at least morally permissible) course of action to pursue or whether it is morally wrong or impermissible. Not surprisingly, the simplicity of the question is deceptive.

Liberation is, as are all intentional processes, a means toward an end. One therefore might object to the propriety of animal liberation on either of two grounds. First, the argument may be aimed at the end of liberation, accusing this goal of being immoral in its own right. Here, the means that liberationists employ are simply irrelevant to the moral issue; if the aim is unworthy, it is superfluous to discuss the validity of the means of reaching it. A second argument may concede that the goal of animal liberation is a just one, but insist that the usual means that liberationists use to try to attain their goals are morally repellent. In this case, there is more hope of agreement; it may be possible to find a mutually acceptable instrument to efficaciously carry out the purposes that both parties deem worthy of completion.

Those who believe that the purposes of animal liberationists are unjust would appear to inherit the burden of proof. After all, there is little dissension concerning the liberation of slaves, Indians, and Afghans. The objective of freeing a group of individuals from a repressive regime so that they can live autonomous lives hardly seems in need of vindication. Thus, the anti-liberationist bears the onus of showing why the animal liberation movement is relevantly different from these other lauded campaigns. Effectively, he or she needs to demonstrate why, although improving the plight of oppressed human animals is a good, taking measures to try to enhance the lot of nonhuman animals is not.

Once we adopt the commonsense, anti-Cartesian position that animals have consciousness and can feel pain and suffer, it becomes extremely difficult to see how any sort of compelling argument can be mounted. What reasons can be forwarded suggesting that the pursuit of bettering nonhuman lives is either wrong or unworthy?

Perhaps one can argue that nonhuman animals, by their very nature, have no value. In this case, one would deny the radical Cartesian portrayal of animals as deprived of consciousness (let alone sentience) but insist the pain and suffering that animals endure are of no moral significance whatsoever. Animals hurt, of course, when they experience unpleasant feelings, but since their lives are of no inherent importance, there is no intrinsic reason why their pains should concern us. From this point of view, it is at best a waste of time and energy to care for the plight of animals, and more likely is an indulgence of a superstitious attitude that unfortunately pervades much of contemporary society.

When alleging that animals "by their very nature" lack value or that animal lives are of no "inherent importance," apologists are tacitly relying on a time-honored distinction between two sorts of values. An individual has *instrumental* value insofar as it contributes to the performance of some goal. Money is paradigmatic of an object with instrumental value. Few of us care about the green rectangular pieces of paper in and of themselves; their worth is purely a function of how well they serve as a means toward an end. Money serves as a means to own the food, shelter, and clothing that we desire. If the pieces of paper lost their commercial function, money would lose its value. On the other hand, an item has *intrinsic* value insofar as it has value in and of itself. The value of an object is intrinsic if it has worth independently of any use that we may make of it. Pleasure is frequently cited as something with intrinsic value. We value pleasant sensations for their own sake and not for their serviceability.

The objection, then, can be reconfigured: Animal lives are merely instrumentally valuable. The worth of animals reduces to the benefits that they can provide us. So, for example, burros are valuable for their ability as pack animals, butterflies have value in virtue of giving us visual pleasure, and dogs and cats are valuable because they provide us with companionship. Subtract the services that animals supply and their value is eliminated; therefore, to concern ourselves with the feelings of animals *per se*, i.e., independent of how their interior lives may affect our own lives, is just plain silly.

But why should we accept the notion that animals possess only instrumental value? Pain and suffering are bad states to endure for the creature who experiences them regardless of color, race, ethnicity, national origin, sexual orientation, intelligence or species. Making the world a better place is a venerable aim, and relieving individuals of pain and suffering, especially intense pain and suffering of innocent creatures, is one way of improving it. Conceiving of animals as nothing more than conscious commodities, as the objection does, is an unwarranted reduction. The argument against liberation on the grounds that its goal is unworthy therefore fails. It rests upon a counterintuitive, provincial assumption that has nothing to recommend it.

A second anti-liberationist argument concedes that, in a perfect world, animals should be liberated, but reminds us that, *pace* Leibniz, we do not inhabit the best of all possible worlds. The charge is that liberationists are starry-eyed idealists who are oblivious to the real-life contingencies that pervade our everyday lives. Millions of people are employed in industries that consume animals. It is rhetorically asked whether the liberationists would have us dismiss the workforce of those who work in the agricultural, hunting, and pharmaceutical industries, thereby escalating unemployment to unknown heights and effectively ruining our entire economy. Perhaps there is a historical scenario in which our nation might have developed in ways to be far less dependent upon our use of animals, but, for better or worse, this is not the world in which we currently live. This objection may allow that certain segments of particular industries are so cruel and so peripheral to their maintenance that relatively minor modifications are justified. Perhaps we should make the cages somewhat larger for battery hens who now live most of their lives in ultra-confinement; perhaps more care should be exercised in the slaughterhouses of cows and pigs so that they do not, respectively, get skinned or scalded alive; perhaps minks should not have to suffer anal electrocution on their route to becoming fur coats. Still, goes the objection, we should not be so ingenuous to believe that major institutional changes can be instituted without enormous negative implications for our society.

We should take note that, at bottom, this is a utilitarian argument. It suggests that, given the situation in which we currently find ourselves, the consequences of animal liberation would be dire; we are incalculably better off if, at most, we tinker with the present system, making just minor concessions to the demands of pro-animal forces. Of course, the "we" here conveniently refers to our human community. If we were to consider the interests of all the nonhuman animals that lie at the lifeblood of our institutions, the calculus would undoubtedly be quite different.

Consider a similar argument purveyed by a slaveowner in early nineteenth-century Virginia. He rails against the abolitionists, reminding them that the agricultural industry would suffer untold economic setbacks were the practice of slavery abandoned. He reminds his idealistic, tender-hearted opponents that cheap labor is what makes the cotton industry, among so many others, profitable. Being a kind and decent fellow, he is willing to make some minor modifications. He will provide his slaves with slightly larger living quarters and not beat them quite as severely if they fail to give him an honest day's work.

We need not belabor the analogy. If we want to employ a utilitarian or consequentialist criterion to determine the right course of action, we cannot, without being arbitrary and self-serving, limit the interests to be calculated to a group of persons of which we, *mirabile dictu*, happen to be members. The welfare of *all* must be considered, be it that of black slaves on colonial plantations or animals in contemporary institutions.

Animal liberationists may, as have many others, question the utilitarian presumption. There seems to be more to determining right and wrong behavior than merely subtracting bad from good. Suppose that an unsuspecting innocent walks into a hospital to visit a sick friend. Several very ill patients are waiting for life-saving organ transplants. If our visitor donated his kidneys and heart, he would save the lives of three deserving human beings. Understandably, our visitor, although feeling sympathy for the dying patients, does not want his organs extracted. Surely, we believe that by refusing donation he acts permissibly, and we just as certainly believe that if the doctors compelled him to involuntarily undergo the fatal operation to get his organs, they would be doing something horribly wrong. Yet, on utilitarian grounds, our innocent visitor ought to give up his organs and the doctors, if need be, ought to force him to yield his life. After all, although we are killing one, we are saving three.

There are limits on what others can do to us without our voluntary consent. Although the general good may be served by our discomfort and death, our lives have a certain value that allows us not to sacrifice ourselves to this end. Cases vary, of course, but to deny animal liberationists the use, in general, of non-utilitarian considerations will also impoverish our moral interactions among humans.

Far and away, the most frequent complaint hurled against animal liberationists vilifies the means they use to try to reach their ends. At least for the sake of argument, the goal of liberation—to free animals to allow them, as far as possible, to lead autonomous lives without artificial restrictions—is conceded as good. What cannot be accepted, goes the objection, are the instruments that the liberationists employ to reach their justifiable aim. In short, anti-liberationists remind us of the longstanding moral adage that the end does not justify the means, especially when the means employed often result in great property damage, societal disruption, and personal harm.

The openly conservative are not the only ones who decry liberationist methods. Some anti-liberationists who pride themselves on being progressive believe that activists ought to proceed with their campaigns "within the system." They encourage liberationists to forswear their illegal ways and write letters to their local newspapers and congressional representatives. Instead of breaking into laboratories and animal farms, they claim, activists should hold peaceful demonstrations and protests. Progressives find these lawful and peaceful actions perfectly permissible—even laudable—but rescind their support once activism steps beyond the legal boundaries.

So liberationists need to vindicate their conduct not only to those who are ideologically opposed to their views, but also to those who are somewhat sympathetic to their crusade to aid animals' interests. I want to argue that liberationists have an excellent justification for their illegal activities. Let me emphasize that what I will suggest is a moral justification for past—and perhaps future—liberationist actions; the means that have been employed, and even more "radical" ones that may later be employed, are in fact morally justified by the conditions in which billions of animals find themselves. This is quite different from claiming that these behaviors would constitute the best strategy for accomplishing their worthwhile goals. This latter question is not one that is particularly situated in the province of philosophers. Although my discipline may have something useful to add to this discussion—probably in the form of game-theoretic considerations—my guess is that empirical psychologists and Madison Avenue mavens are more likely sources of wisdom on how best to effect the change of hearts and minds of the general public. In the end, a different *Weltanschauung* is probably necessary for the grand changes that the liberationists hope for.

We begin by issuing a couple of caveats to those who have this legitimate concern about liberationists' means. First, we should be careful to resist the temptation to exaggerate the harm caused by liberationists. To my knowledge, no human has ever died as a result of any liberationist activity, nor has anyone been the intentional target of physical injury. Furthermore, the extent of social disruption has been minimal. Procter and Gamble, the firm that has killed more animals than any other in cosmetic testing, scarcely skipped a beat when animal activists invaded their offices, nor did their home city of Cincinnati suffer any noticeable lasting consequences. Still, there can be no doubt that animal liberationists have caused property damage. Vivisection laboratories have been severely damaged, cages and grounds of mink farms have been destroyed, furs in "upscale" stores have been sprayed with paint, and hunting blinds have been trampled. As a result, people have lost money and families have been disrupted. Some individuals may have experienced psychic problems; having your workplace (and even recreational arena) violated, like enduring a home burglary, may be a traumatic event.

Secondly, we need to be careful not to turn this very important substantive moral issue into one of mere semantics. Much of the contemporary media is wont to label animal liberationists "terrorists," a term that carries a great deal of emotive and normative baggage; terrorists and their actions are evil just as surely as heroes and their actions are good. Given this ordinary understanding of the term, it is blatant question-begging to categorize animal liberationists in this way. More fairly, we should withhold the rubric and directly investigate whether their behavior is justifiable. The notion of terrorism, however, does prove useful as a mode of entry into our examination.

Terrorists use violence partly as a means to accomplish an immediate objective, and partly as a way of creating fear or intimidation to prevent future objectionable—by their lights—acts. Inculcating fear is not an end in itself. Terrorists view the introduction of fear as a further means to change the behaviors of others. In truth, terrorists would rather do without terrorizing; if they could bring about the societal changes that they deem legitimate, they would just as soon do without it. They believe, rightly or wrongly, that frightening people is a necessary means to bringing about a desirable end.

When "terror" is used with wide scope, I believe that animal liberationists must admit that there are times when they intentionally terrify. They want certain people who indulge in particular practices to feel uncomfortable. In the best of all worlds, this discomfort would provide an opportunity for reassessment, but, whether a considered reflection occurs or not, the liberationist ultimately hopes for a change of behavior. Obviously, the liberationist who illegally enters an animal laboratory is aiming for the experimenters to quit and the business to shut down. Liberationists, by and large, do not intend that the scientists feel concerned about their own personal safety, but they do want them to realize that their working conditions will degrade if they continue maiming and killing animals.

On the other hand, insofar as terrorist attacks are conceived as essentially indiscriminate, as tactics that do not distinguish between those who actually participate in the undesired action and those who are innocent, there is little connection with the animal liberation movement. On the contrary; liberationist actions are quite focused, meant only to interfere with the working lives of those who conduct their anti-animal behaviors.

Even with these qualifications, there is no dispute that liberationists' activities are illegal, disruptive of places of business, discomforting to those who work in the selected workplaces, and violent to property. Without a potent justification, animal liberation would be an immoral movement, no better than the practices that liberationists strive so diligently to abolish. I submit that the prime justification for animal liberation is that the activists are proxies for subjugated animals who unwillingly find themselves in a war against their oppressors. When viewed as representatives of an oppressed group who, by their very nature, are incapable of fighting their own battles, rather than being labeled as scofflaws, animal liberationists are cast in a far more flattering light. No more should they be characterized as a fringe element violently attempting to change the social structure to reflect their warped picture of how our community should be shaped. Risking humiliation and incarceration, these activists should be understood as brave, self-sacrificing, and honorable persons who should be embraced and emulated rather than marginalized and dismissed.

In this conception, animal liberationists continue a hallowed line of heroic visionaries; the Suffragettes fighting in the early twentieth century, those in the 1960s engaged in the Civil Rights Movement, and, perhaps most fittingly, the courageous men and women who harbored Jews in Nazi-occupied Europe. Although at first blush the analogy with the Holocaust may strike some as offensive,[4] it is most apt. In both cases the number of individuals tortured is enormous, the treatment of the oppressed is indescribable, and the possibility of freedom fully resides in the hands of some benefactors.

I have claimed that animal liberationists should be viewed as being at war with animal oppressors, those who most directly expose animals to great pain, suffering, and distress, e.g., factory farmers, vivisectionists, fur ranchers, and hunters. It is an unusual war in certain respects. Most significantly, the aim of the liberationists is altruistic; they fight for the improvement of the lot of nonhuman animals. Liberationists do not covet territory, riches, or glory. They seek no person's death or harm. They use no torpedoes, rockets, bombs, or guns. Still, they engage in war—a physical war—and not merely a war of words or ideas.

One advantage in characterizing animal liberation in this manner is that it suggests a means of testing its legitimacy. There is a traditional template for investigating whether a war is just or not. It would be probative to discover how good the fit is between a just animal liberation movement and a just war, keeping in mind, of course, that the rules of war were devised with states or regimes constituting the warring parties. To the extent that the animal liberation movement conforms to the criteria set forth by an orthodox rendering of a just war, the movement gains justification.

The so-called just war doctrine (*bellum justum*) contains two components. The *jus ad bellum* component concerns the grounds for entering a conflict. This part of the doctrine deals with the conditions that must be met in order to justifiably go to war. The *jus in bello* component concerns the prosecution of the war, including the moral conditions governing the actual waging of war.

Jus ad bellum informs us that engagement in war must come as a last resort. We must have the practical certainty that peaceful means of resolving the conflict are not adequate to the task. The declaration of war must derive from a legitimate authority. The initiation of combatants must be preceded by an intention to bring about a defense against aggression in an attempt to reestablish a peaceful and just society. Finally, *jus ad bellum* allows engagement in a war even if the injustice that requires redress occurs somewhere other than in the state that joins the battle.

Animal liberation, I believe, conforms quite well to these requirements. For decades, activists have implored, cajoled, debated, and sued those who oppress animals. Very little progress has been made, and in many ways the plight of the animals has worsened. Lust for money is a difficult incentive to blunt. Vivisectors are still not legally required to keep records of the number of rodents and birds that are savaged in laboratory experiments. Farm animals, thought of as "resources," objects to be exploited for their product, are now consumed in the US at the staggering annual rate of 10 billion. Technology has allowed farmers to have chickens, turkeys, and cattle grow to unnatural sizes at unnatural rates. Manipulating the natural life cycles of animals is a recipe for disaster—for the animals, that is.[5] Statutes have done little. Vague and virtually unenforceable, they carry almost no practical bite. From my own experience, reflective of many on the "pro-animal" side, reason has had little effect. I have had literally a dozen debates on my campus with vivisectionists with no noticeable effect on animal testing—this despite the fact that these experimenters are frequently "gracious" enough to concede that they cannot answer my objections to their use of animals.

Since this war is not state sponsored, there is no venue for a formal declaration. In this respect it is unlike most—but not all—wars. Korea was a "police action." Vietnam, Kosovo, and Afghanistan were campaigns of indeterminate character. Here, the requirement of *jus ad bellum* is not so much unsatisfied as inapplicable. Liberationists want—in fact, yearn—for peace; the idyllic picture painted by the prophet Isaiah (Isaiah 11:6) well captures the liberationist wish. Finally, the altruistic nature of the liberationist's battle harmonizes perfectly with the sanction to intervene on the behalf of another who suffers injustices.

Turning to the prerequisites of prosecuting a war, we find that the idea of proportional violence is key; we are not justified in creating more injustice than that produced by those who use animals as resources. In fact, it would be extremely difficult to violate this condition, in virtue of the horrendous manner in which animals on farms and in laboratories are treated. The ways in which these animals are raised, treated, and eventually slaughtered almost defies description. Liberationists' maneuvers are inordinately mild by comparison. *Jus in bello* also demands that the force be used discriminately, a requirement that calls for not harming innocents. As a practical matter, it is all but impossible not to harm innocents in war and, *a fortiori*, to know in advance that no innocents will suffer. Unless we want to abandon the possibility of a just war altogether, we must, then, concoct an escape hatch. The traditional way out is to use the church-honored "doctrine of double effect." Simplifying, this doctrine allows the killing of innocents in war as long as they are not the intended targets of the violence. Thus, although we may know with practical certainty that innocents will die in our bombing Afghanistan, for example, as long as they are not the intended targets of the bombing (as they presumably are not), this "collateral damage," unfortunate as it is, is consistent with a just war.

My purpose here is neither to defend this doctrine nor even to defend the viability of a just war. But, if there are just wars and the doctrine of double effect must be employed in order to legitimate wars, then the liberationist's war is at least as proper as any ordinary war carried out by any regime. Animal liberationists never intend to harm innocents, and the probability of any guilty party, let alone an innocent person, being physically harmed approaches zero. Since no missiles are launched, bombs dropped, or machine guns fired, the chance of innocents directly suffering is minimal. Economic losses are the worst that are likely to plague non-combatants.

In fact, animal liberationists can absorb even further limitations on the constitution of a just war. They can sincerely avow the justified belief that more violence will not follow their own intentional violence, effectively admitting that their tactics would be verboten were they to believe that their intended activities would beget a net increase in pain and suffering. One should not be deluded into believing that this addendum is vacuous. Consider a scenario in which the US is attacked by North Korea, and our destruction is assured whether or not we retaliate. If we do launch our own missiles, we will cause millions of foreign deaths. Some may urge that, despite the fact that even more suffering and death will be produced, we are justified, perhaps even morally required, to militarily respond. In meeting the burden of an additional restriction, the justification of the liberationists' case becomes further strengthened.

Moreover, liberationists can satisfy a demand that they be motivated by a strong and intuitive moral principle. The Principle of Utility in its classical form serves this purpose. Here we are told that we ought to produce the action that creates the greatest net balance of pleasure over pain. Given the enormous number of animals involved in the oppressive practices and the extent and degree of the pain and suffering they continually experience, this principle would certainly encourage liberation. The motivating moral principle need not be consequentialist. Once we realize that the capacity to experience pain and pleasure confer non-instrumental value (i.e., dignity) upon its possessor, we can understand how a principle morally sanctioning us to respect an individual's autonomy naturally elicits the adoption of a liberationist stance.

Animal liberation is an honorable cause. The enlightened have always known that improving the lot of the oppressed is just. There are none more oppressed than animals and none more innocent. We welcome you to the battle.

Notes

1. See Peter Carruthers, *The Animal Issue: Moral Theory in Practice* (Cambridge: Cambridge University Press, 1992) and Peter Harrison, "Do Animals Feel Pain?" *Philosophy*, 66, 1991.
2. See my *On Moral Considerability: An Essay On Who Morally Matters* (Oxford: Oxford University Press, 1998), esp. ch. 2.
3. See, for example, D.R. Griffin, *Animal Thinking* (Cambridge: Harvard University Press, 1984); B. Rollin, *The Unheeded Cry: Animal Consciousness, Animal Pain, and Science* (New York: Oxford University Press, 1989); and D.L. Cheney and R.M. Seyfarth, *How Monkeys See the World: Inside the Mind of Another Species* (Chicago: University of Chicago Press, 1990).

4. In a recently completed book, titled *Without a Tear* (forthcoming, University of Illinois Press), I speak to this very important psychological issue. Having lost five ancestors to the Nazi death camps, I have great empathy for those who believe that the term "holocaust" should be reserved for what occurred under Hitler's regime. I ask only that people educate themselves about the happenings in factory farms, slaughterhouses, animal laboratories, and the like. One may come to discover, as I have, that when the term is used to cover these activities as well, it denigrates none and honors all.

5. And, indeed, for humans as well. There have been very recent studies strongly suggesting that the antibiotics routinely injected into cows and chickens have made the consumers of these animals far more susceptible to various diseases. This should not strike anyone as surprising; we have known for many years that bacteria, in virtue of the replicative prowess, can become resistant to antibiotics fairly quickly.

At the Gates of Hell: The ALF and the Legacy of Holocaust Resistance

Maxwell Schnurer

The ALF (Animal Liberation Front) has been the subject of heated debate in the popular media, with intense scrutiny applied to its tactics. This concentration on tactics obscures the ALF's capacity to bring issues of animal liberation into focus in the larger public. This essay attempts to reframe the discussion of ALF tactics by placing the ALF within the historical legacy of Jewish resistance fighters who struggled against the Nazi regime. Approaching the ALF from the context of a scattered guerrilla militant movement opposing a totalitarian state, we can help to explore two aspects of ALF actions that have been hidden: the impact of direct action animal liberation on the ethical relationship of humans and animals, and the role of ALF actions in challenging the technological infrastructure vital for animal oppression.

The Animal Liberation Front represents a part of activist culture that is foreign to most people. The actions of the ALF are not part of the traditional framework of American political participation. The ALF do not lobby for legal change or elect members to Congress. The goals of their activism (animal liberation) are not a familiar topic, and their midnight-creeping, balaclava-wearing image blurs the definitions of "activist" and "terrorist." Given this popular conception of the ALF, how can we position their tactics to better understand the ramifications of their actions?[1]

This essay suggests that the ALF should be read in a particular way. Rather than engaging in a systematic analysis of their tactics in comparison to other American social movements, this essay proposes that we juxtapose the ALF and the underground partisan militants that fought against the Nazi Holocaust.[2] When we place the ALF in the historical footsteps of Holocaust resistance movements, we can explore the role of direct action animal liberation politics in exposing the ethical disjuncture between animals and humans. In addition, the ability of ALF actions to expose and disrupt networks of technological infrastructure and control becomes evident.

This analysis can help us to understand how evil can be perpetuated in our world and how direct action exposes and resists this evil. This essay argues that the ALF must be understood as a part of our culture, and that the meaning of the ALF extends far beyond the animals saved. The first section of this paper explores the mental categories that enable racism, speciesism, and sexism to continue. More importantly, it positions direct action as an important tool in helping to restore the lost ethical relationship between humans and animals. The second section discusses how the creation of bureaucratic infrastructure and networks of control are vital for the success of mass violence. This section also suggests that direct action can expose this infrastructure and create new meanings in the face of overwhelming destruction of life.[3]

Exposing the Ethical Tension

To those who believe that America could never be a totalitarian state, Stanley Milgram proposes an eloquent and terrifying rejoinder. In a series of 1962 experiments, Milgram tested Americans to explore their willingness to obey authority. Rigging a laboratory so that the subjects believed they were testing a partner (in reality a co-conspirator of Milgram's) about word pairs, Milgram asked participants to give a series of increasingly powerful electric shocks whenever the wrong answer was given. More than half of Milgram's subjects were willing to obey the researcher's orders and give 450-volt shocks to humans who were screaming in pain or whose silence presumably indicated that they had passed out from the experience.[4]

Milgram's work can be read in the context of the Nazi experience. When it was exposed that hundreds of thousands of average, everyday people had participated in the slaughter of millions of Jews, Romany, Gays, Lesbians, Anarchists, Communists, and other "undesirables," thinkers across the globe wondered what would make a person perpetuate such evil on the suffering face of another person. Milgram suggested that the human personality could not be trusted to respond to ethical situations with compassion. The Nazi experience and his own experiments led Milgram to conclude that there was widespread possibility for evil to be perpetuated even in the United States.

We can explore Milgram's experiments and the Nazi experience in terms of mindlessness, a concept that Ellen Langer introduces in her book *Mindfulness*. According to Langer, mindlessness is a mental position that creates patterns of knowledge that enable us to make quick judgments based on categories.[5] In Milgram's example, the participants were able to justify the terrible shocks they were doling out because an administrator was telling them that the experiment was of the utmost importance. For Milgram, our values associated with science and the unwillingness to disobey orders are positions of mindlessness. In the case of Nazis, the mindless categorization of Jews and other unwanted races/classes coupled with a hierarchical industrial order created a context in which concentration camps made sense. Participants in the systems of these orders were willing to engage in evil and become complicit with the evil around them because that *was simply the way the world was.*

The experience of living within these regimes of thought cannot be simply criticized or exposed. Any notion that liberation from mindlessness simply requires information suggests a shallow comprehension of a very complex problem. The nature of being within a system of meaning precludes certain approaches or resistance. Those living within a system of mindlessness (obedience to authority, the Third Reich, nationalism, etc.) have a very difficult time understanding the nature of the problem because from their perspective, the injustice is a necessary part of their existence. Oppression is not only acceptable, but often it is made to be a fundamental part of how we come to know the world.

Obedience to authority cultivates a mindset that allows one to commit violence toward another. In the case of the oppression of animals, philosopher Carol Adams has argued that acts of violence are made acceptable through cultural symbols that encourage dominance of humans. Adams parallels the oppression of animals through a comparison to the oppression of women. She argues that humans learn to ignore the lived nature of animals (and women) through a process of objectification, fragmentation, and consumption.

Objectification encourages humans to think of animals as objects (a cow has value because it can be made into a meatball). Fragmentation encourages people to break apart the bodies of animals to further distance them from their ethical subjectivity (turkeys become known as drumsticks or dark meat). Consumption is the final act of violence that solidifies the secondary ethical status of the animal (eating or abusing an animal).

Adams uses these same tools to explore how violence against women becomes normalized. She argues that objectification encourages men to think about women as two-dimensional objects, fragmentation teaches men the eroticization of body parts (fixation on specific body parts), and consumption teaches men that women's bodies are available for their pleasure through non-consensual consumption (rape). Her theory helps to explain how the human subject can commit violence against humans and animals and avoid feeling responsible. More importantly, she suggests that challenging these normative processes can help to restore the absent referent (i.e., the lived nature that is ignored) to animals and women.[6]

In the case of the Holocaust, Charles Patterson's book *Eternal Treblinka* points to the methods of distancing used by the Nazis in regard to Jews. Patterson points out that the "use of animal terms to vilify and dehumanize the victims, combined with the abominably degraded conditions in the camps, made it easier for the SS to do their job, since treating prisoners like animals made them begin to look and smell like animals."[7]

Understanding the process of obscuring the face of the other is only part of this project; the other half argues that militant direct action can help to restore that ethical relationship. This approach can help us to understand how a person participating in oppression can internally justify oppression. Realizing this process of numbing leads us to ask how a person might resist this process. Adams suggests that activists struggle to restore the absent referent by reminding people that animals and women are living, complex beings. Langer proposes that we work to become mindful by fighting the simple mental categories that can emerge. But how do we do this? How can we overcome these mental categorizations that perpetuate injustice? And if Milgram is right, that governments and leaders contain the potential to simply reframe an injustice into a new path of obedience, then can these mental gymnastics have any effect on the systems of violence?

The ALF and Holocaust resistance represent a method of bringing about new understanding that challenges these mental habits. The actions of these militants blaze new paths of meaning far beyond the direct actions that they participate in. The meaning of active militant resistance can pervade the popular consciousness of entire societies, and in the case of the ALF and of the Holocaust resistance, their actions work to make mindlessness more difficult.

The Ethical Challenge of Holocaust Resistance Fighters

The actions of militancy are done a disservice when we think of them as singular campaigns or even as terrorist actions. Militant activists operate in a cultural space, bringing new ideas and rebutting popular ideas about *what is important*. More significantly, direct-action militants open up new pathways of resistance that can become echoed (either by copying the method or by expounding/defending the method) by other activists. These actions challenge the categories of oppression by crying out "Here I am"—a living breathing being, whose very existence necessitates an ethical rejoinder.

The actions of Holocaust resistance certainly fulfill this mandate. Werner, a Jewish fighter who struggled against the Nazis in Poland, described the importance of their first attack against the Germans. "It was a tremendous uplift to our morale to be able to hit back at the Germans. It was also important to us to show the villagers that Jews, once armed, would strike back."[8]

Werner's comments are important because they suggest that direct action has communicative value. Actions of liberation communicate a message far beyond those directly involved. In the case of the Holocaust resistance fighters, their actions sent notice to potential Nazi collaborators that their actions would be noticed and could have dangerous ramifications for them. This communicative act was vital considering the difficulties resistance fighters encountered when dealing with local villagers.

A Polish Jew, Werner fled to the countryside, where a local farmer provided him shelter and food while he worked as a farmhand. At one point the Nazis passed a law that forbade farmers to employ Jews. "According to the order, the assembled Jews were to be transported by horse and buggy to the Wlodawa ghetto. Effective immediately, if a Jew was discovered in a village or on a farm, the punishment was death, both to the Jew and the farmer who sheltered him. Stephan told me that he could not risk his life and the lives of his family by keeping me any longer.[9]

Werner's band of partisan resistance fighters struck back after hiding in the winter forests. Their actions not only directly attacked the German Nazis, but also sent a message to Polish villagers that the Jews were not empty of value and passive. The message restored the absent referent and challenged the categories of meaning associated with being a fugitive Jew in Nazi-controlled Poland. For the Polish farmers, the popular idea of Jews as objects of derision came fully into clash with the reality of a living, breathing band of resistance fighters.

Simha Rotem, a leader of the Jewish resistance fighting organization ZOB, describes the beginning of the Warsaw uprising that led to the protracted battles against Nazis. The Germans had been clearing Jews out of the ghettos, dispatching them to concentration camps and exterminating them. Rotem described the outbreak of fighting in the ghetto.

> I was nailed to the spot, almost paralyzed—a tremendous explosion! I had a fervent desire to see it with my own eyes. And I did see: crushed bodies of soldiers, limbs flying, cobblestones and fences crumbling, complete chaos. I saw and I didn't believe; German soldiers screaming in panicky flight, leaving their wounded behind. I pulled out one grenade and then another and tossed them. My comrades were also shooting and firing at them. We weren't marksmen but we did hit some. The Germans took off. But they came back later, fearful, their fingers on their triggers. They didn't walk, they ran next to the walls. We let the first group of six pass—a shame to waste ammunition on a small group. Then we burst out, with two homemade grenades, 10 Molotov cocktails and pistols in our hands. "Shlomek—the gasoline!" I shouted to one of my comrades, and hurled a grenade at the Germans. We threw the Molotov cocktails at them and they burst into flames, so we shot at the fire. A waste of the only grenade we had, and we retreated up the street, taking a position with the rest of the fighters.[10]

Rotem's powerful narrative highlights two important things about Jewish resistance. First, the very action of resistance disrupts the minds of the oppressors. The Germans in Rotem's passage had only encountered peaceful Jews, Jews who went to the gas chambers with passive resistance. They had never encountered Jews *organized to fight*, and their mental categories of Jews and resistance were challenged. Second, the experience of resistance was transformative. Rotem describes "a fervent desire" to see the Germans die. All of his experience with his oppressors had come from one direction, Nazis dictating Jewish behavior. This single act of militant armed resistance fulfilled desires for vengeance and simultaneously opened up the idea of resistance.

This creation of the idea of a particular kind of resistance is one of the most powerful parts of direct action. Those in power easily dismiss traditional political protest. In the case of direct action, there is no negotiation or compromise; the action communicates the most intense distaste. Direct action is visceral empowerment. Participants immediately feel in control of a situation that was previously defined by others. This change transforms the understanding of all involved. The act of killing Germans affirms and makes concrete the very possibility of a particular kind of resistance. In this case, the direct actions of the Jewish resistance fighters reframed the identity of Jews, and of Nazis. For Polish citizens terrified of Nazi punishment, the militant actions of the Holocaust fighters placed ethical weight on the side of the Jews, making complicity all the more difficult. For Nazis, unfamiliar with Jews as anything but objects to be destroyed, the actions of resistance fighters sent a clear message that Jews were living entities who demanded ethical respect.[11]

The establishment of this possibility is of vital importance, because in the ontology of oppression the oppressed only exist as objects. The Nazis removed the lived nature that necessitated ethical relationships with Jews (e.g., farmers no longer felt the need to protect them). This establishment of a process of control can only make sense if the victims of that system are willing to participate. The very act of violent resistance sends the signal that the victims are opposed to that system, and that the oppressors' system of understanding must be revised.[12]

In this process of discovery about the lived subjectivity of Jews, the experience of resistance can expand beyond the immediate struggle. For many, the act of resistance against the Nazis was a bold move that enlarged the circle of humanity to include these Jewish humans. For many others, the experience of intense suffering during the Holocaust became the justification for widening the ethical circle of all life. Many Jews became aware of animal suffering because of their experiences of human suffering in the Holocaust. Patterson profiles several such individuals who chose to speak out for animals in his book *Eternal Treblinka*. One of these people is the famed author Isaac Bashevis Singer, who is quoted in Patterson's book as writing: "There is only one little step from killing animals to creating gas chambers à la Hitler and concentration camps à la Stalin. . . . There will be no justice as long as man will stand with a knife or with a gun and destroy those who are weaker than he is."[13] Singer's experiences as a Jew who lived through the Holocaust came to gird his vegetarianism and his lifelong commitment to alleviate the suffering of animals.

The ethical frame that develops from Singer's experience highlights the constant need to challenge and resist the reduction of living beings to objects. The Jews who became fighters against the Nazi regime were potent reminders to all who encountered them that they were not objects to be destroyed. Their call for recognition expanded the idea of liberation far beyond the precise actions that they took. The actions and experiences of suffering are not soon forgotten. Singer and many other Jews took their horrible experiences and built a system of ethics that included animals. A vital part of that ethical relationship is not simply being considerate to animals, but also acting on their behalf. Today, activists attempt to act for animals, and, like the Jews who fought against the Nazis and racism, the actions of the Animal Liberation Front represent a potent challenge to animal exploitation industries and to speciesism.

The Ethical Challenge of the Animal Liberation Front

When we consider the status of animals in our society, we are dealing with a very strict system of social meaning. Speciesism holds an extremely tight grip on this culture's consciousness. Much like the system of meaning that allows genocide to "make sense" to a community, speciesism is a system that makes sense not only to those who benefit from that system, but also those who simply live within that system.

Some may criticize the claim that ALF direct action can change people's opinions about animals. I agree with this argument. A person who owns a butcher shop will not shut down his or her business after reading an article about an ALF attack on a laboratory. At the most pragmatic level, the actions of the ALF, like the actions of Holocaust resistance fighters, can best be justified by their ability to directly slow or stop the actions of their enemies. On another level, the meaning of the ALF is in the argument presented to those who are listening: that some humans are willing to sacrifice everything for animals.[14]

Dave Foreman is one of the founders of the radical environmental organization Earth First!, a group that explicitly supported direct action destruction (or "monkeywrenching") of logging and mining equipment. Foreman's autobiography, *Confessions of an Eco-Warrior*, focuses the justifications for direct action as an effective means of stopping loggers and others from hurting the environment. While Foreman acknowledges that for those who are opposed to environmentalism "there may be no effective argument for ecodefense," he also recognizes that direct action can elicit some new meaning in an oppositional public. "Even a small-town John Bircher," he writes, "might monkeywrench to protect his backyard or his favorite fishing hole."[15]

Ron Eyerman and Andrew Jamieson argue that the very nature of social movements is to change the way people think. The arguments in their book, *Cognitive Approach to Social Movements*, suggest that social movements are effective precisely at this moment when they alter the very fabric of meaning that people cling to. Social movements create change by transforming patterns of knowledge. For example, homophobia may recede only when a person has some stake in changing his or her opinion about gay people (e.g., a family member reveals his or her homosexuality).[16] Eyerman and Jamieson argue that social movements can serve the same cognitive function and elicit new meaning from an old situation: they can help people re-interpret everyday life and make new meaning from it. Functioning like the Holocaust resistance fighters, the ALF makes a pointed rebuttal to the ideas of speciesism, and their actions represent a vigorous rejoinder to those whose system of meaning allows them to commit evil.

Three elements make the ALF's actions uniquely challenging to the system of animal oppression. First, the ALF documents a world hidden from view. Photographing and videotaping animals trapped in the most intense states of cruelty provides an immediate ethical challenge to an audience. Second, the ALF communicates a direct sense of warning to all who participate in animal oppression. The actions of the ALF resonate in the minds of those who profit from animal abuse.[17] This combined with financial cost can make industries unwilling to defend particularly high-profile animal abusers.[18] Third, the actions of the ALF send a message to all who might encounter, or consider taking part in, animal oppression, that they must be aware of the stakes of the issue. The ALF encourages reflection on the part of anyone considering animal experimentation or any other form of exploitation. These three implications elevate animal oppression from the position of "ethically contested" in our society and call upon audiences to consider their own ethical role in relationship to animals.

The ALF acts to fundamentally challenge the notion that animals are objects that humans can consume and exploit. The ALF elevates a previously non-considered group (animals) to the level of humanity. By constantly risking their freedom ALF activists may create a wedge of analysis in an audience's brain. Just as the actions of militant Jewish resistance forces disrupted the German concept that Jews were objects for destruction, ALF actions call upon us all to relocate animals to the sphere of respect. Not everyone will receive or even acknowledge such a message, but the possibility exists that some change will occur because of ALF tactics.

For those who doubt that ALF actions forward such a radical readjustment, keep in mind that ALF activists and supporters constantly highlight their actions in terms of animal suffering. Consider Gina Lynn's essay in a 1996 volume of *No Compromise* magazine:

> So what if they put us in jail for a few days or a few weeks or a few years. . . . It's an old but relevant argument: it's nothing compared to what the animals go through. There is NOTH-ING that "they" could do to us that could come close to the suffering that animals endure for hours, days, years, on end. I know I don't need to remind anyone of the pictures we've all seen of monkeys in stereotaxic devices, cows being shackled and their throats slit, foxes being anally electrocuted. . . .[19]

Lynn's argument resonates with some people—challenging assumptions and transforming static notions of being in regard to animals. Some argue, however, that the wider community misses the ALF's message, and that traditional methods of persuasion (protest, lobbying, leafleting) should be the focus of animal rights activism. The problem with this argument is that the wider community has the largest commitment to the system of meaning that holds animals under slavery. It is this very system of control that makes animal cruelty a "fact of life." Like the Polish citizens who willingly participated in the oppression of Jews, the average American has no reason to step out of his or her comfort zone to challenge speciesism; he or she has not yet encountered the strong voice that requires respect and may prompt rethinking one's relation to animals. However, even if the general public ignores the message of ALF attacks, the people who experiment and trap and kill animals feel the impact of these direct actions. In the same way that the actions of the Jewish resistance fighters sent a message for Polish farmers who might turn Jews in to the Nazis, the ALF actions communicate a message of warning for researchers, contractors, and others who might be complicit with those who harm animals. In a secret interview with an ALF activist who helped liberate animals from the University of Arizona, *No Compromise* asked about the use of fire and vandalism during the liberation. The ALF activist replied:

> . . . you make people who are considering experimenting on animals . . . think twice about going into that. I do think that,

in a way, it is much the same thing as the abolitionists who fought against slavery going in and burning down the quarters or tearing down the auction block o[r] the wiping [sic] post— whatever was being used to subjugate the slaves. It's very much the same thing. I think it sends a message to researchers about how serious this is. Sometimes when you just take animals and do nothing else, perhaps that is not as strong a message.[20]

The ALF causes significant financial and systemic cost for people who harm animals, and for these actions liberators should be commended.[21]

The legacy of the Jewish activists who fought against Nazis during the Third Reich can help us to understand how the communications of the ALF spread ideas through the communities of meaning. For the Jewish militants, the stakes were personal survival; in the case of the ALF, the stakes are the survival of animals in our world. The messages of these activists outline an ethical understanding and then punctuate those messages with action that reinscribes the lived nature of the subjects. Jews fighting back against their oppressors' forces every interaction to be rethought, as previously passive subjects become transformed into strong resisters. ALF activists engaging in direct action to free animals calls for a reevaluation of the role of animals and what the ramifications might be for those who harm them.

Exposing the Methods of Destruction

To discuss the Animal Liberation Front or the Holocaust resistance movements in terms of numbers of lives saved does not get at the vital importance of these agents of cultural transformation. Rather, we should examine these militants in terms of their strategies. These activists choose to apply pressure to particular industries and individuals, and we can get a more meaningful sense of the value of direct action by exploring how and where these activists strike.

The mental boundaries described by Adams and Langer are only part of the problem of systems of destruction. Along with these mental justifications of mindlessness comes a complicated system of industrial mechanisms designed to perpetuate oppression. These infrastructures are a fundamental support mechanism for the continued destruction of subjects whose lived nature has been obscured. Whereas the absent referent and mindlessness remove the essential nature of lived beings in order to enable violence, the bureaucratic infrastructure of an industrial society allows the remaining responsibility for violence to be spread among many people. The responsibility for suffering becomes obscured by the complex process of implementing mass slaughter.[22]

That process of obscuring is vital to the reduction of living beings to objects upon whom atrocities can be heaped. In the case of the Holocaust, it was necessary to sustain a complex infrastructure that enabled each participant to disguise his or her responsibility. Patterson describes death camp efficiency as vital in checking the compassion of the killers. He argues that the high-speed efficiency and industrial technological structure were crucial "to minimize the chance of panic or resistance that will disrupt the process."[23] In the case of animals, as Adams notes, it is essential that the acts of killing, enslaving, and torturing animals be well hidden from sight, so that the consumer only ever sees the finished "product." For both systems of oppression, it is critical that the process of destruction be as compartmentalized as possible. The reason to obscure the face of suffering is as obvious as it is hidden—the vision of terrible actions can elicit sympathy and compassion, and often call for remedy.

For both Nazis and the animal oppression industries, it was essential that the general public never comprehend the vast system used to divert responsibility away from consumers and participants in the process of destruction. It is at this point that the ALF and the Holocaust resistance movements clash with this system. Their actions expose the mechanisms of oppression and not only make public the hidden secrets, but also strike at the points of weakness. It is this exposure of the clear system of power that enables change to occur. Michel Foucault argues that through exposing lines of power and control individuals can envision new ways of thought. The Animal Liberation Front risks imprisonment to bring the horrible images of research laboratories, slaughterhouses, and fur farms to the public, exposing the cruelty inherent in these industries. In the example of the Holocaust, resistance fighters made clear the systems of oppression that allowed the Nazis to hide their actions. By bombing train tracks and destroying records, their actions opened up the Nazi machine to scrutiny.

When we analyze this process, it is important to recognize that industrial capitalism was essential for the Holocaust and the widespread oppression of animals. This is not a claim of causality; I am certainly not arguing that capitalism created either of these catastrophes. Rather I am arguing that the creation of industrial capitalism was an essential function for the networks of power that enabled mechanized animal exploitation and the networks of railways, disbursement, and control of the Nazi order. Because Jews were shipped out of the ghetto in carefully coordinated train journeys, their disappearances were hardly missed by non-Jews. Because fur farms exist far away from the luxury boutiques that sell their skins, the process of trapping, breeding, shipping, and killing is hidden from consumer sight.

In many ways, the actions of the ALF and Holocaust resistance fighters implicate not only these mechanisms of control, but the entire system of industrial capitalism. Their actions call into question the process that necessitates destruction. Especially when it comes to the ALF, we are beginning to see a larger criticism that exposes the destruction of animals as fundamental to the current order; thus the ALF calls to account the very nature of our current system.[24]

In the following section we will examine the primary texts of several ALF and Holocaust resisters who applied direct action pressure to the networks of control and surveillance that made the gates of hell obvious for all to see.

Holocaust Resistance, The ALF, and Direct Action Against a System of Destruction

Werner describes two examples of sabotage in his book *Fighting Back*. Of the first occasion, he writes: "During the late summer of 1943, we burned and destroyed dozens of large estates which supplied or served as food storage depots for the Germans."[25] Well aware of the dangerous ramifications of food supplies for Germans, these partisan armies of Polish Jews engaged in direct sabotage to slow the network of oppression. It was only the functioning of the well-oiled machine that enabled the genocide to continue, and enough pressure on the hinges of the machine could destroy its feasibility.

Later on in his book, Werner justifies their actions of sabotage. "Part of our sabotage work was aimed at wiping out all German/Polish outposts. We wanted to destroy their administrative records to diminish their ability to collect food quotas from the farmers, and in general to disrupt their control of the area."[26] This quotation is remarkable in that the enemy is described as data. Militant activists are well aware that the Nazi mechanisms only survived so long as orders and files were maintained.

Similarly, Krakowski describes Polish/Jewish resistance groups desperately attacking train tracks south of Lublin in Poland. Anxious to destroy the mechanisms that were shipping Jews to their deaths all over the continent, these militants attempted to bomb and shatter train tracks. Realizing the essential nature of these transportation routes, the German government quickly dispatched Nazi troops to protect sections of the train tracks in these partisan-heavy areas.[27]

In the case of the ALF, we see similar strategic attacks. The Western Wildlife Unit of the ALF describes a fierce action against the Oregon State University Experimental Fur Animal Research Station:

> While one warrior busied themselves [sic] with removing breeding identification cards from the mink cages (to confuse the researchers as there was no other way to identify the animals), two others slipped through the still unlocked bathroom window into the main records building. Research photos, slides and documents were loaded into backpacks along with the vivisector phone books, address books and other material that would [alert] supporters and financiers to the station's dirty work. After this, every single file, research paper and archive in the station was spilled onto the floor and every available liquid poured onto them until a water line from the bathroom was broken that would flood the entire floor.[28]

The attacks outlined seem strange without the context of an assault on the infrastructure of injustice. Why would activists destroy the files and labels on cages? Isn't the goal of the ALF to liberate animals? Of course it is, but beyond freeing individual animals the ALF activists in this action recognize that the damage they can do to the organized system of fur research is perhaps the most powerful blow they can strike in the service of animal liberation. These activists recognize that exposing the hidden structures that enable destruction to continue is the highest goal of their activism.

Consider the continued attacks not only on the farms and cages that hold animals, but also on the transportation mechanisms that bring the animals to slaughter. In an anonymous article in *No Compromise*, a member of an ALF cell describes the justification to turn toward strategic arson rather than just liberating animals, based on the notion that significant damage could slow an industry. Describing an attack on a veal processor near San Francisco, the activist wrote: "Gasoline was liberally spread throughout and a crude cigarette timer was used to ignite the building which suffered tens of thousands of dollars in damages. Before the year was out, a slaughterhouse, livestock auction yard and a fur shop all went up in flames without any injuries.[29]

When we recognize that not only individual acts of cruelty but the institutional means to harm animals is the focal point of ALF action, we can begin to reposition ALF tactics as strategic assaults on the infrastructure of oppression.[30]

The application of force to these targets is only part of the situation; sabotage also has a symbolic and communicative function. Robin D.G. Kelley describes the sabotage tactics of African-Americans in his book *Race Rebels*, arguing that attacks on employers who are unfair to working-class African-Americans is a vital part of reclaiming public space and communal self-worth. He describes a series of examples from North Carolina in which African-Americans thwart factory mechanisms in order to slow down production capability and recapture personal time from their employers.[31] Like the ALF and the Holocaust resistance fighters, these workers were well aware of the bureaucratic structures that had to be targets. Whether packing bins of tobacco more loosely to enable others to keep up, sabotaging a train that would take Jews to a death camp, or pulling the identifying labels from breeding cages, those who enact resistance are well aware of the weak points of industrial oppression.

Kelley's argument, which applies equally well to both ALF and Nazi resistance, is that sabotage has a vital and productive function in the world. It reaffirms the value of the individual participating, reframes the capitalist-oriented authority of the employer, and opens up the space for more collective affirmation.[32] Solidarity among those who are oppressed is one of the strongest elements of resistance. Sabotage unifies the oppressed and outlines the parameters of a struggle against oppressors.

For both the ALF and the Holocaust resistance fighters, the very targets chosen suggest a realization that infrastructure is an enemy. The Jews facing death in Poland were aware of the dangers of seemingly innocuous objects like train tracks, and the ALF are aware that the loss of breeding files can damage a fur farm. The importance of the ALF is at least threefold: they set individual animals free, they inflict significant damage to institutions that harm animals, and they challenge the very structures that enable oppression.

Exposing Liberation

ALF literature often uses the Holocaust as a frame of reference. Open any ALF/direct action–oriented publication and you will find a metaphorical connection to the victims of the Holocaust who "broke open the gates of Auschwitz." Consider the front page of the magazine *Resistance* by the Earth Liberation Front, where this well-known quotation appears:

> If we are trespassing, so were the soldiers who broke down the gates of Hitler's death camps; if we are thieves, so were the members of the Underground Railroad who freed the slaves of the South; and if we are vandals, so were those who destroyed forever the gas chambers of Buchenwald and Auschwitz.

This quotation is certainly not the only one of its kind that is popular within the direct action–oriented animal rights community. For years I wondered about this comparison. I felt faintly uncomfortable positioning the animal rights movement in the shadow of the Holocaust, because I view the Holocaust as the most significant evil moment in our history. Being ethnically Jewish, I felt a connection to the Holocaust as the ultimate evil, and those who sacrificed their lives to fight back against their oppressors I considered to be the bravest of heroes.

In October of 2002 I traveled to Krakow and was able see the death camps of Auschwitz. I walked through the gates labeled *Arbeit Macht Frei* and felt the palpable history of hundreds of thousands of lives that had been taken by a regime of evil. As I walked through the barracks uncovering the smallest historical data of the suffering, I was overcome by a great depression. By the time I walked into the remaining gas chamber I was simply overwhelmed—the tears flowed uncontrollably. After I saw Auschwitz, I went to see the Birkenau concentration camp that was created several miles away when Auschwitz became crowded with Jews.

Auschwitz is dedicated as a museum of the Nazi system of evil, with each barrack showcasing some horrible element of the plan of genocide. Birkenau was virtually unadorned. A few signs and a single labeled barrack were all that were available to instruct the visitor about what life was like in this death camp.

What I could see at Birkenau were the artifacts of a system of destruction that was massive in scale. I had never realized the size of the infrastructure that was needed to control, enslave, and exterminate that many people. There were hundreds of barracks covering square miles of ground fanning out from my gaze, with nothing but desolate wind between them. Long views of barracks juxtaposed against barbed wire were my only guides as I walked across the concentration camp.

At the far end of the camp were the remains of the gas chambers and incinerators. These gas chambers were far away from the public—with a wide zone of exclusion around these two death camps, citizens would never be exposed to the horrors of the camps unless they worked there or were entering to be killed. At this point I began to think about the geographical position of slaughterhouses in America. Kept far away from the public view, the institutions of slaughter in America are equally massive and hidden from sight.[33]

Unlike Auschwitz, where the gas chambers seemed terrible simply for their historical meaning, these four gas chambers were overwhelmingly large. Each gas chamber, as big as a football field, had been destroyed and lay crumbling as monuments to the evil that somehow remained possible. It was at Birkenau that the inspiration for this essay emerged.[34] In the scale of destruction lay the understanding that enables us to tie these two struggles together. Killing of this scope requires that people who kill (and who are complicit in that killing) have a moral excuse to let it continue and that the industrial bureaucracy be so expansive as to obscure the specific acts of violence.

What the Nazis needed more than anything was a system to exterminate undesirables. They required large-scale destruction and a bureaucratic system that allowed each person to wash his or her hands of ethical responsibility. What they needed most was a populace willing to set aside ethics and compassion when given orders by someone in a position of authority. The six million Jews and tens of thousands of others who were exterminated stand as testament to their intent and their success. In the United States, billions of animals die each year in structures like death camps that are hidden from public view. Like the manufacturers of the Holocaust, animal killers need a justification to abandon caring for animals, and they need an industry that efficiently kills and keeps the blood from seeping into public consciousness.

In the face of despair and overwhelming oppression, I found a moment of inspiration in an exhibit on the wall of Auschwitz that chronicled the lives of women prisoners in the camp. Out of a desperate feeling of helplessness I started to read every single caption and exhibit. Almost at the end I came across Roza Robota, who had the dubious honor of being the last woman ever killed in Auschwitz.

The exhibit explained that she and several other conspirators had helped to smuggle explosives to Jewish resistance fighters in Birkenau several miles away. They had smuggled tea packet–sized packages of gunpowder to colleagues in Birkenau, risking their lives. These hundreds of packets of gunpowder enabled Jewish resistance fighters to blow up one of the gas chambers in Auschwitz and sabotage another in the last days of the war.

At this point, the Nazis were exterminating everyone they could and destroying as much evidence as possible. The sabotaging of two of the four gigantic gas chambers represented a vital spark of light against the darkness of death. I found in Roza Robota a certain amount of hope that even in the worst of situations resistance is possible. These women had sacrificed their lives to cripple a death machine, and they had succeeded.

The ALF activists who face incarceration in order to save animals use direct action to stop oppression. Their actions not only disrupt killing, but also challenge the two most vital mechanisms of speciesism: ethical distancing and the bureaucratic mechanisms that remove responsibility. Both the ALF and the Holocaust resistance fighters expose indifference and bureaucracy to the light of public scrutiny and challenge the systems of meaning that allow evil to triumph.

The Holocaust stands as a pattern of evil. Nazis created a process that allowed ordinary people to participate in and benefit from the systematic extermination of a group of people based on their race or ethnicity. In examining the response from militant Jewish resistance fighters, we can reframe the actions of the Animal Liberation Front. The ALF, like the Holocaust resistance fighters, acts to directly stop oppression, but their actions also call upon humans to examine their own ethical relationship with animals. The direct action liberations help to bring attention to the system of thought that excludes animals from that ethical relationship, and encourages a process of self-reflection about animal cruelty. In addition, the ALF exposes the lies of industry that obscure the suffering of animals. The documentation that emerges from ALF actions is invaluable in the struggle to bring animal rights to public consciousness, and the destruction of the bureaucracy that enables violence is vitally important. Perhaps more importantly, the ALF focuses attention not only on the animals who suffer, but also on the people who benefit from that suffering.

The ALF offers us all a call to conscience about animals in our society, it exposes institutions that profit from suffering, and it pressures those who would turn their face from a world of suffering. ALF actions follow in the footsteps of Roza Robota and the women of Auschwitz whose actions saved lives in the most evil of places. The ALF's continued willingness to articulate a world free of animal cruelty and to do what is necessary for the creation of that world furthers the cause of liberation everywhere.

Notes

1. "An Animal Liberation Primer" (ALF pamphlet on file with the author) defines members of the ALF as "activists who directly intervene to stop animal suffering at the risk of losing their own freedom while following ALF guidelines" (3).

2. For a good description of one Jewish resistance organization, ZOB (Jewish Fighting Organization), see Simha Rotem, *Memoirs of a Warsaw Ghetto Fighter*, translated and edited by Barbara Harshav (New Haven: Yale University Press, 1994), p. viii: "[T]he organization consisted almost entirely of young men and women (the oldest were in their late twenties; most were between 18 and 21) who had virtually no weapons, no influence, no money, and no experience in warfare. All they had were a remarkable strength of will, tremendous reserves of intelligence and courage, and amazing talents for initiative and innovation" (viii). In this paper, I will use the examples put forward in several books of primary data by the resistance fighters themselves. Most of them are Jewish.

3. It is important to recognize that many Jews consider the Holocaust to be a unique event whose horror can never be compared to other events. There is significant debate about the danger in lessening the impact of the Holocaust by comparing it to any other suffering. This paper does not directly compare the suffering of animals to the suffering under the Holocaust. Instead, I argue that the processes that helped make the Holocaust possible continue in the continuation of speciesism and that the resistance movements to both of these horrors can benefit from a comparison. For those who are upset with the comparison of these two killing regimes, I would point you to Charles Patterson's book *Eternal Treblinka: Our Treatment of Animals and the Holocaust* (New York: Lantern Books, 2002), which carefully connects the methodology of destruction of both of these systems. It is important to point out, as Patterson does, that many Jews were made aware of animal suffering by their experience in the Holocaust. For many Jews, like Isaac Bashevis Singer, the Holocaust became the initial spark of consciousness about animal suffering.

4. Stanley Milgram, *Obedience to Authority: An Experimental View* (New York: Harper & Row Publishers, 1974).

5. Ellen Langer, *Mindfulness* (Reading, MA: Addison-Wesley Publishing Company, 1989). It is interesting that Langer is willing to engage in mindlessness in some areas, but reduce their significance in others. Consider the section of her book where she takes a niece to feed the ducks during the day and then finds the contradiction emerge when she orders duck for dinner. Langer quips that "Luckily we hadn't visited an entire farm before dinner" and then orders another animal for dinner (49). Langer seems unwilling to challenge her own mindlessness regarding her speciesism.

6. Carol J. Adams, *The Sexual Politics of Meat* (New York: Continuum Books, 1990).

7. Patterson, p. 47.

8. Harold Werner, *Fighting Back: A Memoir of Jewish Resistance in World War II*, edited by Mark Werner (New York: Columbia University Press, 1992), p. 110. It is important to remember that the active members of the Jewish resistance movement were by far in the minority. "Some of the Jews in the Ghetto, who couldn't imagine the evil intentions of the Germans, were steeped in delusions, one of which was that they had to fight the resistance movement and its allies. Other Jews said, 'This too shall pass. There have been similar things in the history of our nation.' Religious people put their faith in God. Some in the Ghetto were simple cowards, paralyzed with fear. Others were collaborators" (Rotem, p. 23).

9. Werner, p. 73.

10. Rotem, p. 34.
11. Dhoruba Bin Wahad, a former Black Panther in New York City, described the danger of the Panthers as the danger of ideas. He argues that the Black Panthers were relatively few, but the idea of armed resistance of African-Americans was so powerful that the idea had to be quashed. "My point was that the Black Panther Party had to be destroyed because of the idea that it represented. Black assertiveness and Black self-defense, that this should be achieved by any means necessary, in fact by the same means, if necessary, that white people would employ to defend themselves. And the system couldn't tolerate that." See his essay "War Within," in *Still Black Still Strong: Survivors of the US War Against Black Revolutionaries*, edited by Jim Fletcher, Tanaquil Jones and Sylvere Lotringer (New York: Semiotext(e), 1993), p. 26.
12. Charles Patterson describes a series of events that have stayed executioners' hands in his book *Eternal Treblinka*. He describes both slaughterhouse workers and Nazis whose killing was paused for a moment when the face of compassion shines through the system of oppression. In these small windows of solace, we can argue that the transformation of agents of evil is possible. The actions of the ALF and Holocaust resistance fighters can expose killers to the ethical face of the animals and people they are killing and possibly stay their hand (118–120).
13. Patterson, p. 199.
14. There are certainly activists who have put their lives at risk for a variety of social causes; I do not claim that the ALF are unique in this regard. Rather, the ALF are the first to put their lives at risk to agitate for the rights of *animals*. The level of commitment calls upon the audience to re-interpret their own value system in regards to animals. Some might argue that the public perception of the ALF is primarily negative. This claim is irrelevant to the argument I am making. I am arguing that the ALF's actions encourage a momentary pause or reflection. Because ALF activists are willing to destroy property, liberate animals, and steal records, the public perception will likely be negative. But along with that dislike of the tactics will be a moment of curious reflection where people wonder what might make a person do this kind of thing. Another good comparison might be John Brown, the American abolitionist who attacked Harpers Ferry military outpost to gain weapons in preparation for a large-scale slave revolt. Brown's actions were universally ridiculed, but the meaning of his actions reframed the conversation about slavery long before the issue was seriously addressed in the traditional political realm. The ALF may make new meaning about animals by perhaps moving the audience into a moment of reflection.
15. Dave Foreman, *Confessions of an Eco-Warrior* (New York: Harmony Books, 1991), p. 119.
16. Ron Eyerman and Andrew Jamieson, *Cognitive Approach to Social Movements* (University Park, PA: Pennsylvania State University Press, 1991).
17. Adrian Morrison, a prominent animal researcher, describes his reaction when his lab was destroyed in 1990: "I was shocked but not surprised . . . animal rightists had good reason to be angry with me so I knew I was vulnerable. . . ." See his "Personal Reflections on the 'Animal Rights Phenomenon.' " *Perspectives in Biology and Medicine* (Winter 2001), p. 62. Morrison's public defense of Edward Taub (the primary researcher in the Silver Spring monkey experiments which were exposed by direct activists and publicized by PETA) and his willingness to defend animal experimentation made him a primary target (not to mention his own animal experimentation). The vital thing is that he was well aware of the risk he was taking. The ALF had successfully communicated what their reaction to his work and politics would be.
18. Perhaps the best example of this kind of campaigning is the Huntingdon Life Sciences

campaign, which has put significant pressure (primarily using direct action) on investors of the infamous animal research laboratory. The actions of this campaign have been incredibly successful in getting industries to abandon Huntingdon Life Sciences when the pressure from animal rights activists has gotten to be too much.

19. Gina Lynn, "Direct Action: Time Tested . . . and Effective," in *No Compromise* (March–April 1996), p. 4.

20. Carla McClain, "ALF: A Secret Interview With A Compassionate Commando," in *No Compromise*, March–April 1996 p. 12.

21. Dave Foreman points out the potential of direct action to change the investments of those who might cause damage to the earth. He writes: "Some contractors nowadays refuse to bid on Forest Service road projects or timber sales in roadless areas because of the likelihood of damaged equipment and resulting cost overruns. Companies bidding on road construction for the Mount Graham Astronomical Observatory complex in Arizona doubled their bids because of fears of monkey wrenching and the need for round-the-clock security on site" (135).

22. Remember that people benefit from animal and human oppression. The Nazi regime used Jews as slave labor, and as testing subjects for medical experiments. Humans use animals as "beasts of burden" and as subjects for biomedical experiments. Both of these institutions have a concerted financial benefit in not questioning these systems.

23. Patterson, p. 110.

24. For more on this, see "Memories of Freedom," a pamphlet by the Western Wildlife Unit of the ALF, available at http://www.cala-online.org/Academic/mof_us2.html, in which the authors describe the particular meaning of the graffiti left at the UC-Davis. "The circle 'A' anarchy symbol was affixed to the 'A' of the ALF's signature. To those who bothered to look beneath the carefully controlled media coverage of ALF actions this was a sign that the ALF was no longer simply just an 'animal' group but one that also was opposed to the entire system which perpetuated animal abuse" (4). This argument can be made for Jewish Holocaust resistance units—many of the first to be persecuted were outspoken activists, anarchists, and communists. In fact, the original role of Auschwitz was to house political prisoners; only later was it used as a death camp. When it was found to be insufficient for the job, Birkenau was built.

25. Werner, p. 161.

26. Werner, p. 164.

27. Shmuel Krakowski, *The War of the Doomed: Jewish Armed Resistance in Poland, 1942–1944*, translated by Orah Blaustein (New York: Holmes and Meier Publishers Inc., 1984), p. 92. Krakowski also describes partisan groups in Zelechow who, in the summer of 1943, focused their sabotage actions on bridges and railway lines, including destroying a train bound for Auschwitz (128).

28. Western Wildlife Unit, p. 22.

29. Anonymous, "Inside an ALF Cell," in *No Compromise* magazine, Summer 1999, p. 18.

30. This approach can certainly be applied to the Earth Liberation Front as well. See "A History of the ELF" in *Resistance: Journal of Grassroots Direct Action*, 2000, p. 5. The newspaper outlined a series of ELF attacks and included a quote from a biotech researcher who claimed to have "lost basically my entire professional life. I've lost every paper I've ever wrote that analyzed the benefits and risks of this technology" (5).

31. Robin D.G. Kelley, *Race Rebels: Culture, Politics, and the Black Working Class* (New York: The Free Press, 1994).
32. This notion of self-affirmation can be seen in the grimmest of uprisings, the resistance in the death camps during the Holocaust. Krakowski describes the terrible conditions and the inspiring yet overwhelmed acts of rebellion that emerged in the concentration camps in *The War of the Doomed*.
33. I am not the only person to have this realization. Charles Patterson describes artist Judy Chicago's similar experience in *Eternal Treblinka* (48–50).
34. Birkenau housed up to 100,000 inmates and at the height of the Holocaust exterminated 25,000 people in a single day.

Also Consulted

Bauman, Zygmunt. *Postmodernity and its Discontents*. New York: New York University Press, 1997.

Coronado, Rod. "Strategic Nonviolence in Perspective." *No Compromise* (Winter 1998–9): 12–13.

Finsen, Lawrence and Susan Finsen. *The Animal Rights Movement in America: From Compassion to Respect*. New York: Twaine Publishers, 1994.

Foreman, Dave and Bill Haywood. *Ecodefense: A Field Guide to Monkeywrenching*. Chico California: Abbzug Press, 1993.

Foucault, Michel. *The Archaeology of Knowledge and the Discourse on Language*. Translated by A.M. Sheridan Smith. New York: Pantheon Books, 1972.

——. *Power/Knowledge: Selected Interviews and Other Writings 1972–1977*. Edited by Colin Gordon. New York: Pantheon Books, 1980.

Guither, Harold D. *Animal Rights: History and Scope of a Radical Social Movement*. Carbondale, IL: Southern Illinois State University Press, 1998.

Jasper, James M. and Dorothy Nelkin. *The Animal Rights Crusade: The Growth of a Moral Protest*. New York: The Free Press, 1992.

Smith, Paul. *Millennial Dreams: Contemporary Culture and Capital in the North*. London: Verso Publishing, 1997.

Wicklund, Freeman. *Strategic Nonviolence for Animal Liberation*. Minneapolis: Animal Liberation League. ca4a.org/literature/snv.

Abolition, Liberation, Freedom: Coming to a Fur Farm Near You

Gary Yourofsky

For weeks after the events of 9/11, I was transfixed by the news media. CNN, MSNBC, Fox News, Peter Jennings, Dan Rather, Brian Williams. Report after report. Image after image. The collision. The fireball. The smoke. The collapse. The rubble. The debris. Ground zero. The panic. The response.

As a national lecturer on animal rights, and one of the country's most outspoken animal liberationists, I believe I speak for the entire movement in saying that animal rights activists have the utmost empathy for every innocent victim of the World Trade Center and Pentagon attacks. We mourn human tragedy as much as animal tragedy. The notion that animal rights activists are somehow anti-human is untrue. Rather, we choose to be activists for other species because billions of innocent animals are murdered each year, without even a twinge of guilt. We are vegans because we realize that violence and hatred must be destroyed at the root, in our everyday habits of consumption. We embrace Alice Walker's words of wisdom: "The animals of the world exist for their own reasons. They were not made for humans any more than black people were made for whites or women for men."

Missed Opportunities

Shortly after the 9/11 attacks, the outpouring of love, empathy, compassion, and community inspired faith in humanity. The world was condemning evil and the taking of innocent lives. As we united to find the perpetrators, I wondered if we would realize that murdering any living being was wrong. I hoped that, by a collective awakening to compassion, the terror that humans inflict upon innocent animals for food, clothing, sport, entertainment, and research would end or at least abate.

In a moment of optimistic speculation, I pondered whether the camouflaged hunters—lurking on American soil, skulking in the distance with guns and bows, waiting to terrorize and kill more than 200 million innocent animals annually—might throw their weapons to the ground.

Would the animal researchers who terrorize 50 million dogs, cats, primates, and mice annually in vivisection procedures have a revelation? The March of Dimes experimenters who sew shut the eyes of kittens and ferrets to see if blindness affects their brains would surely stop their barbaric acts of terrorism. The researchers at the Oregon Regional Primate Research Center—who electro-ejaculate primates in order to obtain sperm for their breeding colonies—would make the connection now. Surely, the animal research community was going to be arrested and charged with acts of terrorism.

Would fur farmers and trappers be sent to prison for breaking the necks of mink, anally electrocuting foxes, genitally electrocuting chinchillas and catching wild animals in steel jaw leghold traps?

Would humankind realize that animals do not want to be our food, clothing, entertainment, and research specimens? Would we finally hear and accept the words of British Bishop William Inge—"If animals ever formulated an organized religion, the devil would be depicted in human form"—and would we finally seek to change that image? Would Gandhi's immortal words of peace—"The life of a lamb is no less precious than that of a human"—be recited at every school across America?

No. Nothing changed in human attitudes toward fellow animal species. The routine violence of human custom was swept even further under the rug. Hypocritically, deceitfully, people talked of revolting against evil, and it sickened me.

It seems, to our shame, that human hatred for nonhumans is so vicious, bitter and entrenched that millions of wishes for peace could not eradicate it. When reporters, civilians and government officials vowed to "destroy the evil," they were only referring to the evil people who disrupt the rest of society in the performance of its own evil deeds.

Each human carnivore is responsible for the death and dismemberment of more than 3,000 animals throughout his or her lifetime. Annually, in the US alone, over 10 billion cows, pigs, chickens, turkeys and other animals live in concentration camps. Within the first year of their pathetic lives, they're sent to killing houses where knife-wielding terrorists slit their throats, drain their blood and dismember their bodies, all too often while the animals are still conscious and aware. Sadly, I realized that any lesson learned in the wake of 9/11 was not going to change that.

Path to Liberation

If people truly want to end terrorism, then they should discard animal flesh from refrigerators, toss bows and bullets into the trash, insist that universities close down their vivisection laboratories, demand that department stores close their fur salons, drop animal acts from circuses, abolish the rodeo once and for all, and support the courageous ALF activists who liberate animals from places of terror. People who yearn for a compassionate world should have nothing but praise for these amazing altruists. Otherwise, any talk of peace, civilization and justice will only be hypocritical rhetoric.

Remember, outlawing an act does not make that act morally wrong. And legal avenues are not necessarily the best ones for facilitating substantive change. Laws have always been broken by freethinking, radical individuals who realize that it is impossible to make progressive changes within a corrupt, discriminatory system.

Nelson Mandela, Rosa Parks, Martin Luther King, Jr., Mohandas Gandhi, Henry David Thoreau and Jesus, to name a few, were routine, radical lawbreakers who went to jail for disobeying unjust laws. We see them as heroes today, but in their time they were considered by many to be villains and radicals. The word "radical" has a negative connotation in society today; however, it is simply the Latin word meaning "root," and what radicals do is to bypass pseudo-solutions and get to the root of a problem. Everyone should realize that all social justice activists were considered radical in their time. It is only after social justice activists die and society begins to evolve and comprehend their actions that the "radical" is placed on a pedestal and embraced.

Without question, ALF liberations are akin to Harriet Tubman and the Underground Railroad, which assisted in the liberation of blacks from white slave-owners. One must understand that ALF raids have two goals: giving enslaved animals a chance at freedom and causing major economic damage. As a movement, we must let go of the fantasy that those directly involved in torturing and murdering animals, and profiting handsomely from it, will listen to reason, common sense, and moral truth. The vast majority will not. If they did, there wouldn't be an animal liberation movement, because they would have understood the cruelty of their ways by now and adopted a vegan lifestyle.

I am aware that some activists like Howard Lyman and Don Barnes were former abusers of animals who had epiphanies and changed. But in the vast majority of cases, it is just a fantasy to believe that direct abusers collectively will change. What those involved in animal exploitation will listen to, however, is damage to their profits and livelihood. Only if we make their blood businesses unprofitable will they cease the violence against the animal kingdom.

Remember, since the inception of the animal liberation movement, no human has ever been injured or killed during a liberation or an act of economic sabotage. We need to stop accepting the lies propagated by the media and the corporations who murder animals for a living. ALF activists are not terrorists; those who abuse animals for a living are. ALF activists are not criminals; those who enslave, torture, mutilate, dismember, and murder animals for a living are. Activists who liberate animals should not go to prison; animal exploiters should. It should never be viewed as a crime to try to forcibly stop hatred and discrimination and terrorism; it is an act of compassion and courage.

All animals are simply disenfranchised nations in search of the one thing that every sentient being demands: FREEDOM. They are not property. They are not objects. And they are not commodities. Humans place an inordinate amount of value on property such as buildings and machines. But the earth and its inhabitants do not belong to humans, and the property of animal killers should never be placed ahead of an animal's inherent right to be free.

Let Them Read Lies

I believe one main reason the ALF does not yet have broad public support is the lies spewed by animal exploiters and the distortions reported and perpetuated by the mass media. Sadly, animal killers and their supporters will go to any lengths to deceive and mislead the public into believing that they, and not the animals, are the victims. Having inside knowledge of what animal liberation entails, let me give an example of how the propaganda machines work.

On April 31, 1997, I was part of a mink liberation effort at the Eberts Fur Farm in Blenheim, Ontario. We released 1,542 mink from their cages but were apprehended shortly thereafter. The media reported four lies that are typically issued by the fur industry after liberations: (1) the mink froze to death after freedom; (2) the mink starved to death overnight after freedom; (3) the mink suffered from stress and pneumonia after freedom; (4) the mink were run over by cars on rural roads at three in the morning after freedom.

Let's look at the facts. (1) Mink are clothed in natural fur coats that make it impossible for them to freeze to death; also note that the Ontario raid took place not in the dead of winter, but in April. (2) It takes several weeks for mink to starve to death. It cannot happen overnight. In fact, authorities involved in the Ontario mink liberation stated that the liberated mink raided a nearby chicken farm for food, incontrovertibly exposing the starvation lie. As for the chickens, my heart goes out to them. But my enmity is still enflamed by the almost 300 million Americans who kill and eat billions of chickens each year to satisfy their meat addictions. If humans didn't enslave chickens, mink wouldn't raid chicken farms. If humans didn't enslave mink, the ALF wouldn't raid mink farms.

On rare occasions, some people claim that mink attack companion dogs or cats; however, I have never seen proof of this happening. Rather, I believe it is another ploy to divert attention from the real victims: the mink. Even if the mink did attack a dog or a cat, dogs do from time to time attack cats, cats attack birds, and so on. Neither the domestication of companion animals nor the farming of wild animals has changed this fact.

It should be noted that in the late 1990s after the Frye Fur Farm in Illinois was raided—and thousands of mink were given a chance to escape—the fur industry issued a press release professing the Fryes' love and affection for their mink. The release stated that the Fryes routinely picked up and played with the mink. Yet, across the waters in England that same year, a liberation of 10,000 mink took place. That release stated that everyone should hide their dogs and cats and children, because the mink were vicious animals who would attack and eat everything in sight. Isn't it remarkable that Illinois mink are sweet and cuddly, yet English mink are rapacious and vicious?

The fur industry's public relations people are masters of doublespeak, which they use to hide their atrocities from public view. It is obvious that the fur industry can't even get their lies straight. And that's because one lie leads to another.

(3) Mink do not spontaneously contract pneumonia or stress when they are not in cages. Being kept in a cage for your entire life causes stress and neurosis. Freedom is the cure for caged-induced stress and neurosis. (4) There are no cars on rural roads at three in the morning except for those of fur farmers and police who are trying to recapture

the liberated mink. If they backed off and let the mink go, mink–car casualties would be rare.

The fur industry knows that if people were aware of the five methods they use to kill mink, foxes and chinchillas, virtually no one would buy a fur coat. The anal electrocutions, genital electrocutions, gassings, neck breakings and toxic chemical injections are purely evil. So the fur industry's spin doctors have devised some glittering propaganda in order to divert attention from the heinous methods of killing, and the prejudiced media are all too happy to report them uncritically. The industry and media conspire in an attempt to make animal liberations appear foolish and describe the actions as creating more harm than good.

Any wildlife biologist or veterinarian who is not associated with the fur industry and does not own a fur coat will admit that mink and foxes are wild animals who will undoubtedly survive after being set free. They also will admit that no amount of genetic breeding can take away animals' innate, instinctive survival mechanisms. And let me be perfectly clear: Freedom does not cause death. Hunters, meat eaters, fur wearers, leather lovers, and animal experimenters cause death.

According to the fur industry, 400 mink instantly died after my Easter Sunday raid. Yet, on my request, the lawyers asked them to provide proof of the purported 400 dead mink. They were asked to do so by either bringing in photos, dead bodies or testifying under oath. They declined all offers.

Not surprisingly, the death toll quickly descended from 400 to 300 to 200 to 100 to 12. Subsequently, during my three-day trial, when I was convicted and sentenced to six months in prison, the furriers brought in photographs of two dead mink who had allegedly died the night of the raid.

Now, I did not believe in the authenticity of the photos, but for argument's sake, let's say that two mink were run over by the cars of the fur farmers who were trying to recapture the freed mink. Those two deaths are unfortunate. But every mink in the concentration camp was going to die. Opening the cages was the only chance any of them had. The act was justified.

The job of an ALF activist is not to guarantee safety and freedom, but to give incarcerated animals an opportunity to live in freedom. Unfortunately, 1,000 mink were recaptured because they never found the holes in the fence that would have allowed them to make it across the street to the fields on the other side. (According to some authorities who spoke on the condition of anonymity, the official numbers of the Ontario raid were 1,542 released, 1,000 recaptured, 540 escaped and two dead.) However, of the 1,000 recaptured mink who never made it off the grounds through the cut fence-holes, the best news was that 70 to 80 percent of the pregnant ones miscarried their fetuses. The animal rights community does not want animals bred into enslavement. A miscarriage is infinitely more humane than a lifetime of imprisonment, horror, and eventual murder.

It's truly disheartening when the media and much of society get so upset when enslaved, tortured and soon-to-be-murdered animals are liberated. Yet these same individuals don't get upset when enslaved, tortured, and soon-to-be-murdered animals—who spend their pathetic lives inhaling the fumes of their own excrement—are gassed, anally electrocuted, genitally electrocuted or injected with toxins, or have their necks broken manually. In reporting on liberation stories, journalists rely on the words of the police, who are experts at manipulation, and furriers, who collectively murder 40 million animals a year for profit. If reporters would think rationally instead of trying to fit into the sleazy world of media hype, they could actually produce a brilliant story on ALF humanitarians and the current paradoxes in our society.

People who put their lives on the line for a cause should be commended, not condemned. Dr. Martin Luther King, Jr., once stated, "There are some things so dear—some things so precious—some things so eternally true—that they are worth dying for. And if a person has not discovered something that he or she is willing to die for—then that person isn't fit to live."

I wholeheartedly concur!

The Aftermath

For my random act of kindness and compassion on behalf of the tortured and doomed mink, I spent 77 days in prison. (Hilma Ruby, my lone, upstanding compatriot out of the five who were accused, spent 60 days in prison.) Canadian Judge A. Cusinato sentenced me to six months in the Elgin Middlesex Detention Center in London, Ontario. A deportation parole was issued, though, and I returned to Michigan after serving 77 days at the maximum-security lockup.

Before being carted off to prison, I was able to address the judge:

I stand before this court without trepidation and without timidity because the truth cannot be suppressed today and the truth will not be compromised.

Mohandas Gandhi, one of the most benevolent people to ever grace this earth, once said, "Even if you are only one person the truth is still the truth."

The dilemma we face today is whether this court chooses to acknowledge the truth. The following statement is for everyone's edification.

One day every enslaved animal will obtain their freedom and the animal rights movement will succeed because Gandhi also proclaimed, "All throughout history the way of truth and love has always won. There have been murderers and tyrants and at times they have seemed invincible, but in the end they always fall. Always!"

The true devoted humanitarians who are working towards the magnanimous goal of achieving freedom for animals cannot be stopped by unjust laws.

As long as humans are placed on a pedestal above nonhumans, injustice to animals will fester, because without universal equality, one type of equality will always create another type of inequality. There will be no compromise here today because the truth cannot be compromised.

My presence in this courtroom today is paradoxical. I ask this court: If it is not a crime to torture, enslave and murder animals, then how can it be a crime to free tortured, enslaved and soon-to-be-murdered animals?

Humankind must climb out of its abyss of callousness, apathy, and greed. Enslaving and killing animals for human satisfaction can never be justified. And the fur industry must understand that the millions of manual neck-breakings, anal and genital electrocutions, mass gassings, drownings, and toxic chemical injections can never be justified.

The snaring of millions of free-roaming animals in steel jaw leghold traps, where they die slow, horrific deaths, is unjustifiable as well.

There will be no compromise, for the truth cannot be compromised. The schism that this court has created among the five co-accused has been sealed.

Now that I have been convicted, through my volition and in a symbolic protest of the unjust conditions that animals endure, a hunger strike will begin tomorrow at 7:30 A.M.

For every mink who ever languished in a tiny cage and was savagely murdered at the Eberts Fur Farm, I will go hungry. And for the 40 million other animals worldwide who have the skin ripped off their backs in a disgusting display of barbarity, in the name of vanity, I will go hungry.

And if this court expects me to experience an apostasy, meaning an abandoning of my beliefs, it is sadly mistaken. In April of '97, when I was incarcerated for 10 days in a Chatham jail, I briefly experienced, vicariously, what a caged animal goes through. And, thanks to that 10-day bail hearing, my empathy for every mistreated animal intensified.

Whatever I go through during my incarceration and hunger strike will be nothing compared to the everlasting torture that innocent animals endure on a daily basis.

And if this court is alarmed by my honesty, let me close with a quote from slave abolitionist William Lloyd Garrison: "I will be as harsh as the truth and as uncompromising as justice. On this subject, I do not wish to think or speak or write with moderation. I am in earnest. I will not equivocate. I will not excuse. I will not retreat a single inch. And I will be heard. The apathy of the people is enough to make every statue leap from its pedestal and hasten the resurrection of the dead. My influence shall be felt in coming years, not perniciously but beneficially, not as a curse but as a blessing, and posterity will bear testimony that I was right."

There will be no compromise here today because the truth cannot be compromised.

Mothers with Monkeywrenches: Feminist Imperatives and the ALF

PATTRICE JONES

Its necessity is its excuse for existence.—Elizabeth Gurley Flynn, Sabotage, 1916[1]

I

The black cat glances back before springing ahead. It was she who inspired the Yellow Turban Rebellion and the Boston Tea Party. She gives breath to the Shakers and Quakers and Sufis who even now weave their bodies in dances of defiance. She sat down with Rosa Parks and stood shoulder to shoulder with Wobblies on wildcat strikes. The tunnels of the Underground Railroad still echo her name.[2]

Call her Krazy, but she knows that direct action brings satisfaction. Call her Mehitabel because she is always hopeful, *toujours gai*, despite the horrors she confronts every day. Call her Felix because she's never without her bag of tricks.[3]

Today the black cat rides on the backs of the women and men who sabotage animal research labs, delivering very real kittens from death. She graces the shoulders of tree huggers, road blockers, and the black-clad "night gardeners" who uproot test plots of genetically modified monstrosities.[4]

Along with the sabot and the monkeywrench, the black cat has long been a symbol of direct action. Direct action is often misused as a synonym for civil disobedience or flamboyant protest. But, in fact, mass arrests and dramatic street theatre may or may not add up to direct action, depending on the context. Direct action includes only activist tactics that, like boycotts and sabotage, are intended to have an immediate impact on a problem or its causes. In contrast, indirect action aims for future change through more circuitous routes, such as education, legislation, and symbolic demonstrations of opinion. Actions may include both direct and indirect elements. Ideally, direct action will illustrate or illuminate the problem at the same time as it interferes with its causes or effects. The very best direct action contributes to a long-term strategy for future change even as it offers tangible results in the here and now.

Direct action is best understood by example. People who have integrated segregated lunch counters, put their bodies in the paths of troop transport trains, distributed illegal clean needles or birth control devices, boycotted chocolate or Coca-Cola, staged rent strikes, or built "tent cities" for the homeless have all taken direct action against one or another form of oppression. Direct action for animals is similarly diverse. People who interfere with hunts, deface fur coats or egg cartons, stage open or covert rescues, provide sanctuary to escaped and rescued animals, block the entrances of slaughterhouses, destroy the laboratory equipment of vivisectors, or simply stop buying animal products all immediately impact the lives of actual animals.

Specific examples may help to clarify the distinction between direct and indirect action. When the Berrigan brothers destroyed draft records during the Vietnam War, that was direct action, because they went straight to a target and the destruction of the records actually impeded the conduct of the draft. More recently, when massive crowds protested the attacks on Afghanistan and Iraq by marching through the empty streets of the District of Columbia, that was indirect action aimed at changing the hearts and minds of citizens in the hopes that they would, in turn, influence or replace their elected officials.[5]

Symbolic demonstrations can be designed to be direct action as well. When the Field of Dreams Hunting Club went out in a huge yellow rubber ducky, shooting into the air in order to scare the birds away from the real hunters, they took both direct and symbolic action because they saved bird lives while mocking hunters. In contrast, trying to pass legislation to ban certain types of hunting is indirect action, since there are very many steps between the activists, who may or may not succeed in convincing enough legislators, and the wildlife officials, who may or may not effectively enforce any new regulations.

Direct action for animals may be legal or illegal, overt or covert, sardonic or sober. The one thing all forms of direct action have in common is that they without doubt relieve the suffering of animals or obstruct the activities that cause that suffering. This is in contrast to the more speculative nature of indirect action, wherein success depends on both an accurate theory of social change and an effective implementation of that theory. Harriet Tubman may well have had a theory of social change concerning how her actions might lead to abolition but did not need such a theory to know that leading specific slaves to free-dom would result in liberation for them. In contrast, when Sojourner Truth made abolitionist speeches, she was working according to the theory that rhetoric can change people's minds, which in turn can change their behavior. Tubman's actions were certain to bring the desired results as long as she didn't get caught. In contrast, success for Truth depended upon both the accuracy of her theories about relation-ship between beliefs and behavior and the effective enactment of her theories about rhetoric.

In direct action, one often risks physical injury or loss of freedom; in indirect action, one wagers time and energy on strategies that may or may not bear fruit. Thus, direct action tends to require more courage while indirect action tends to require more faith. Both require skill and dedication. Neither is entirely effective without the other. Analysis of other social movements in history suggests that our best bet will be a strategy that includes a diversity of direct action tactics in coordination with a diversity of other types of tactics.

The black cat of direct action is usually presumed to be female, per-haps because of the association with witchcraft and the left-handed, or feminine, nature of transgressive activity. The black cat usually symbol-izes the most secret and subversive forms of direct action, such as those utilized by the ALF. The kitten in the laboratory is the captured kin of the black cat. It is her ongoing and inescapable pain that makes direct action against vivisection necessary. We must remember that kitten, and the cow crying for her calf, and the hen driven mad by the battery cage, whenever we assess the allegedly extreme tactics used by the ALF to free animals and interfere with the industries that abuse them.

II

Like the black cat, feminism doesn't ask whether ALF actions adhere to the law or conform to abstract philosophical principles. Like the black cat, feminism asks: Do ALF actions contribute to the aboli-tion or relief of animal suffering?

Why should we care what feminism asks of the ALF? Because ani-mal liberation is a feminist project. Speciesism and sexism are so close-ly related that one might say that they are the same thing under differ-ent guises. Women and animals, along with land and children, have historically been seen as the property of male heads of households. Patriarchy (male control of political and family life) and pastoralism (animal herding as a way of life) appeared on the historical stage

together and cannot be separated, because they are justified and perpetuated by the same ideologies and practices.[6]

Both women and animals are seen as less rational and more con-
strained by biology than men. Both suffer by being reduced to their
bodies or, worse, their body parts. As Simone de Beauvoir wrote in *The
Second Sex*: "Woman? Very simple, say the fanciers of simple formula-
tions: she is a womb, an ovary; she is a female—this word is sufficient
to define her. In the mouth of the man the epithet *female* has the sound
of an insult."[7]

The word *animal* also has the sound of an insult. Women are derid-
ed as "fat cows" and condemned for "cattiness." Meanwhile, as Karen
Davis has pointed out, even people who claim to venerate "wild and
free" animals display only contempt for the farmed animals "whose
lives appear too slavishly, too boringly, too stupidly female."[8] Tactics
such as objectification, ridicule, and control of reproduction have been
and continue to be used to oppress and exploit both women and animals.

This can be seen more easily by looking at specific issues generally
assumed to be within the sphere of either feminism or animal liberation. . . .

Milk is a feminist issue. Milk may be defined as the exploitation of
the reproductive capacities of the cow in order to produce profits for
the dairy industry. Cows are forcibly and repeatedly impregnated so
that their bodies will produce the milk intended to sustain their calves.
People then steal both the milk and the calves. The cows suffer painful
physical ailments, such as mastitis, as well as the emotional distress of
having their children and their own freedom torn away from them.
Meanwhile, milk products are responsible for an unhealthy accelera-
tion in the onset of menses in girls and are also correlated with breast
cancer in women. Thus the mammary glands of cows are exploited in
order to produce a product that harms the mammary glands of
women.

Rape is an animal issue. One out of every three women is sexually
assaulted in her lifetime—one in four before the age of 18. Experts
agree that rape is about power, not sex. Rape puts into action the idea
that women and children are objects that can be used for pleasure
without regard for their own wishes or subjective experiences. The
same attitude underlies a host of abusive practices toward animals,
ranging from circuses to factory farming. Animals are raped too, sometimes for the pleasure of the male human rapist (as in so-called "bes-
tiality") but more often to control their reproduction so that corpora-

tions can have the pleasure of profits (as when bulls are electro-ejaculated and cows forcibly impregnated on what dairy farmers sometimes call "rape racks").

Cockfighting is a feminist issue. Sex role stereotypes hurt both human and nonhuman animals. In cockfighting, the natural behavior of roosters is perverted in order to force them to act out human ideas about masculinity. The birds are traumatized and then deliberately placed in harm's way so that their handlers can feel like big men. They die in stylized spectacles of masculinity that have nothing to do with natural bird behavior and everything to do with human ideas about gender. Meanwhile, human boys are also traumatized in order to make them conform to cultural ideas of masculinity. Those who do not distort themselves into stereotypes of "masculinity" may find themselves "gay bashed" to death.

Domestic violence is an animal issue. Domestic violence is one way that men maintain control of the women, children, and animals in their households. The World Health Organization has identified domestic violence against women as a global public health emergency of the highest order. Here in the United States, partner violence is the number one reason women visit the emergency room, and at least two out of every 10 pregnant women are beaten by their male partners. Very often, domestic violence includes abuse of companion animals as a way to frighten, traumatize, or control women. Many women remain in dangerous households because battered women's shelters do not accept animals and they are afraid of what will happen to their animal companions if they leave them alone with the abuser. No one knows how many companion animals have been killed by domestic abusers or how many women are dead because they stayed to protect a companion animal.

And the list goes on and on.[9] Eggs, sex tourism, Premarin, lack of many legal rights enjoyed by adult males—all of these and other problems have both sexist and speciesist components.[10] This is why so many of us insist that neither women nor animals can truly be free until both speciesism and sexism are abolished.

The ALF seeks the abolition of animal enslavement and exploitation. Hence it is legitimate to ask whether it is consistent with feminist theory and practice. That's not so easy to do, because there are so many varieties of feminism, each of which is a matter of ongoing debate. Below, I examine the ALF from the perspectives of ecofeminism, anarcha~feminism, radical feminism, and feminist ethics *as I understand them*. Some may disagree with my demarcations or descriptions of these feminisms, but I trust that no one will fail to agree that all of the ideas and principles I discuss fall somewhere within feminism.

ALF and Ecofeminism

The world is round. Everything that happens on it happens in it. Mystics have intuited it and scientists have proved it: everything is connected to everything else. That means that the old anarchist slogan—"no one is free while others are oppressed"—is literally true.

Ecofeminism understands that the exploitation of ecosystems, animals, and women is connected and that the solution to these problems resides in the resituation of people within, rather than outside or above, the web of life. From tree huggers in India to tree sitters in the US, from oil refinery occupiers in Nigeria to road blockers in the UK, ecofeminists express their kinship with people, plants, and animals by using their own bodies to block the bulldozers and chainsaws coming to kill their relatives.[11]

Abstraction is the antithesis of ecofeminism, which is all about embeddedness, embodiment, and embrace. "Theoretical ecofeminism" is a contradiction in terms. This does not mean that theory is useless, only that it is impossible to be an ecofeminist only in theory—one can only *be* an ecofeminist in practice. The best ecofeminist theory arises from and interacts with practical experience.[12]

Ecofeminist principles must be *lived* to be meaningful. Thus, just as the Declaration of Independence asserts the right *and the duty* to rebel against illegitimate authority, the credo of ecofeminism might be said to mandate sabotage and other forms of direct action.

The ALF is also all about action. Anyone who liberates animals and/or interferes with animal abusers in accordance with the ALF principle of nonviolence can consider herself a member. Absent such action, one cannot claim membership in the ALF, no matter how pretty one's political opinions or how earnest one's intentions.

Thus, the ALF is the antithesis of an abstraction. It coincides precisely with a group of people engaged in the difficult and dangerous work of actually liberating animals. In this existentialism, the ALF is entirely consistent with ecofeminism.

Being based in an awareness of the intrinsic and practical value of biodiversity, ecofeminists understand that both beauty and survival require a balance of diverse elements. Scattered everywhere like seeds, flowering individually within agreed-upon parameters, ALF "cells" are diverse in comparison with each other while also offering a necessary balance to the more conservative aims and tactics of other animal activists.

Deeply rooted in natural reality, as well as analysis and spirituality, ecofeminism agrees with abolitionist and suffragist Frederick Douglass that it's not possible to have "rain without thunder" or "the ocean without the awful roar of its many waters." ALFers are always ready to "bring the thunder," consequently facing not only the risk of arrest but also the hostility of allies who do not understand the role of the ALF in the natural order of the animal liberation movement. Ecofeminists do, or at least ought to, recognize the ALF as an agent of change that may, in retrospect, prove to have been as vital as carbon dioxide to photosynthesis.

ALF and Anarcha~Feminism

Just as the ALF is often viewed with annoyance by both mainstream animal advocates and the left, anarcha~feminism has been angering male anarchists and mainstream feminists since the early 1970s. Anarcha~feminists insist on actually putting into practice the principles that spring from feminist and anarchist analyses of the dynamics of oppression. Thus, anarcha~feminists believe that liberation movements and organizations must be non-hierarchical and unselfish in order to overturn an oppressive social order that is based on private property and an algebra of hierarchical dualisms (e.g., men over women, people over animals, culture over nature, etc.).

The ALF is non-hierarchical and unselfish. No one runs the ALF, and no one who is truly ALF tries to take credit for it. Unselfish action intended to undermine the people-over-animals paradigm is its reason for its existence.

Most anarcha~feminists do their work in other movements, and few bother to explicitly identify themselves as such. Nonetheless, anarcha~feminist principles have been elaborated by women working within anarcha~feminist collectives. Peggy Kornegger notes that anarcha~feminists work to dissolve power rather than to seize it, value both collectivity and individuality, and favor both spontaneous and organized action.[13]

Anarcha~feminists believe, as one manifesto put it, that "the world obviously cannot survive many more decades of rule by gangs of armed males calling themselves governments." Thus, anarcha~feminists seek to destabilize and replace, rather than join and reform, governments. The ALF is anarchistic in both aims and means. The goal is abolition of illegitimate authority. Actions are aimed at undoing, rather than revising, power over animals. ALF activists take matters into their own hands, rather than waiting for governments to get around to liberating the animals.

Anarcha~feminists believe in individuality within collectivity, valuing both the creativity of the individual and the power of the group. Similarly, anarcha~feminists value spontaneity within the context of a set strategy. In its cell structure, the ALF embodies the principle of individuality within collectivity. Individual cells are free to be as creative as they please within the guidelines of the limits set by the minimal ALF principles.

Thus, the ALF appears to be consistent with both ecofeminism and anarcha~feminism. That is not surprising, since it also turns out to be consistent with radical feminism in general.

ALF and Radical Feminism

Radical feminists and radical lesbian feminists of the 1960s and 1970s took direct and often flamboyant action concerning many of the problems that have since been addressed more moderately by mainstream feminists. It was radical feminists who first established safe houses for battered women and brought previously unspeakable topics like rape and child sexual abuse into the public discourse. Radical feminist activism persists to this day, but the dominant tone of the feminist movement is now determined by quieter and less troublesome women.

Radical feminism aims to identify and undermine the very roots of sexism, understanding that the original subjugation of women under patriarchy has served as the template for all subsequent intra-species oppression. Thus, radical feminists also do the intellectual, cultural, and educational work of undoing the often unconscious categorical thoughts that pattern our perceptions about sex and gender.

Any investigation into the roots of sexism has to go back to the origins of patriarchy, which turn out to be entirely entangled with the emergence of pastoralism. Again and again, enslavement and exploitation of women and animals appear together in the historical record, and it is impossible to say whether one preceded the other or they arose contemporaneously.[14] Thus, the radical feminist project of exposing and uprooting the sources of sexism will necessarily require uncovering and dislocating the roots of speciesism.

The distinction between radical and mainstream feminists is not unlike that of animal liberationists and animal welfarists and may best be understood by example. Radical feminists talk about women's liberation rather than women's rights. Seeing the police as the muscular arm of the patriarchal state, the radical feminist works to directly protect and empower girls and women rather than asking for more police protection against rape and domestic violence. Radical feminists write the names of date-rapists on bathroom walls and subvert the billboards of companies that exploit women's bodies for profit. They shout and stomp and don't think its a crime to feel and express anger. They have a history of physically protecting women from batterers and rapists just as ALFers protect animals from farmers and vivisectors. They do not implore or compromise. They set limits, impose consequences, and do whatever they can to make the bad behavior stop immediately. You probably want a mainstream feminist to argue for you in court or Congress, when what you need is credibility and persuasive ability. But you hope that a radical feminist will be around when you need action because the fundamentalists are menacing your picket line or the cops are banging on your head.

Who do you hope will be around if you are ever confined in a cage or about to be forcibly impregnated?

Both animal liberationists and radical feminists take what are seen as extreme positions on fundamental questions and are often willing to use what are seen as extreme means to achieve their aims. Quiet as it's kept, many of the so-called Suffragettes were radical rock throwers and fire starters who ended up in prison—where they more often than not asked for vegetarian meals. Like many radical lesbian feminists of the 1970s, many of the most radical women's advocates in Edwardian England found that their feminism led them naturally to vegetarianism.[15]

Radical feminists of more modern times coined the phrase "the personal is the political." The implications are often uncomfortable and go well beyond the prescription of veganism for those who believe that animals are not property. Every time you walk past a dog on a chain, the radical feminist or ALF activist might remind you, you are making the political choice to allow that animal to spend his or her days in lonely anguish. These kinds of difficult political choices face us every day, making us all complicit to some degree in the ongoing abuse of animals. Radical feminists demand that we learn to live with the feelings that awareness of such realities brings and take appropriate action. Only in so doing can we make our ethical choices with necessary modesty, honesty and empathy.

ALF and Feminist Ethics

The ALF is the metaphorical mother of all animal activism. Like a mother, the ALF rushes to the rescue of endangered youngsters. Like a mother, the ALF labors behind the scenes, rarely getting credit for the results of its productivity. Like a mother, the ALF says, "Eat your vegetables," and, "Just because everybody does it doesn't mean it's right."

It's not an accident that women were the actual mothers of the early antivivisection and animal welfare movements, or that women continue to far outnumber men in virtually all animal advocacy and liberation organizations, including, so far as we know, the ALF. Carol Gilligan's groundbreaking research demonstrated that, for a complex constellation of reasons, women tend to make their ethical decisions on different bases than men. While there are always individual departures from the norm, boys and men tend to make their decisions on the basis of laws or abstract principles while girls and women tend to make their decisions on what is best characterized as an *ethos of care*.[16]

When asked if it is justifiable to steal medicine to save the life of someone who cannot afford to purchase it, boys and men will tend to talk about the illegality of stealing versus the principle that life must be valued above all else. In contrast, girls and women will tend to talk about who gets hurt and who needs care. They may reach the same conclusion by different routes—a boy concluding that the value of life trumps the value of private property while a girl concludes that the harm suffered by the shopkeeper if the medicine is stolen is less than the harm suffered by the sick person if it is not. Feminist ethics assert that this ethos of care is at least as valid a method of moral reasoning as the rule-based method preferred by men.

The ethos of care is pragmatic rather than theoretical, and particular rather than abstract. The ethos of care infuses the activities of ALF activists, who exercise actual care for actual animals who would otherwise suffer almost unimaginable harm.

"But," one might ask, "what if ALF activities slow down or hinder efforts to improve the conditions for animals in general? Wouldn't that contradict the ethos of care?" That seems a reasonable objection until one realizes that there is no evidence whatsoever that ALF activities on behalf of specific animals will in any way inhibit the efforts of other activists to free or improve the welfare of animals in general.

"But," the argument often goes, "they make us look bad, and that makes us less effective." Another common argument is that ALF activities make our opponents angry and thus unwilling to compromise with us. These are understandable but baseless concerns. As other liberation movements have learned through hard experience, it doesn't matter how "good" you are—they will always find someone to mock or condemn in an effort to discredit your movement. It's no good telling gay boys to stop swinging their hips or women to stop showing their emotions; those who benefit from the oppression are always going to find some person or organization to point to with derision or censure.

People enjoy their privileges and don't give them up without a struggle. It's trying to take away their privileges that makes them mad, by whatever manner or means you try to do it. People enjoy the material and emotional benefits of owning and feeling superior to animals; corporations enjoy the profits they obtain through animal exploitation. That means that ALF efforts on behalf of specific animals, by interfering with the process of extracting profits from animals, may make the ultimate liberation of all animals more rather than less likely. Just as the pig farmer may switch to organic vegetables if the costs of complying with new environmental regulations make pork less profitable, so corporations have scaled back animal exploitative operations due to real or imagined ALF-related costs. In this way, the ethos of care for particular animals furthers the cause of caring for animals in general.

III

If ALF principles and practices are consistent with ecofeminism, anarcha-feminism, radical feminism, and feminist ethics, are there any critiques feminism might offer the ALF? Since feminism never lets anybody get away without some sort of challenge, the answer to that is, of course, yes.

Like speciesism, sexism is inherently violent, requiring constant force (or threat of force) to maintain itself. While men like Mohandas Gandhi and Martin Luther King, Jr. have tended to get the credit for the theory of nonviolent social change, it has been women who have most consistently deployed nonviolent tactics against violence throughout recorded history. From the Sumerian priestess who wrote the first war protest poem circa 2300 BCE to the women who set up the Greenham Common peace encampment in opposition to nuclear weapons in the 1980s, women have used creative and nonviolent means to contest violence against themselves and others.[17]

Hence, the primary feminist challenge to the ALF is to find ways to ensure that individuals and cells considering themselves ALF do, indeed, act in accordance with the ALF principle of nonviolence. It's not good enough to simply disclaim any actions that are violent by using the circular reasoning that "the ALF is nonviolent, hence any violent actions are not ALF." If, indeed, violent actions are taken by persons inspired by or believing themselves to be ALF, then the ALF bears some responsibility.

Maintaining disciplined adherence to principles across widely distributed secret cells is difficult but not impossible. One must learn, as feminists have done concerning issues like domestic violence, to be able to quite firmly say, "That's not okay," and be willing to back up that assessment with action.

This means that it will be necessary for ALF cells to immediately disclaim any alleged spokesperson who implicitly threatens or condones violence, as one self-proclaimed ALF spokesman recently has done when answering media inquiries about a non-ALF action. Spokespersons who cannot be trusted to voice the collective position of the ALF without straying into the realm of personal opinion must be jettisoned in favor of spokespeople with the discipline and reserve required to place the needs of the group above their own wish to give voice to heroic fantasies of violent resistance.

This might more easily be done by setting aside the practice of the single, stable spokesperson altogether. Allowing a single person to call him or herself the voice for the ALF gives that person more power than anyone should have in a non-hierarchical organization. Furthermore, there's simply no way to ensure that this person does, in fact, speak for all of the widely distributed and secret cells of the ALF. Better for individual cells or sets of cells to call upon a rotating set of spokespeople who can be trusted to say only what they have been given explicit permission to say and to make clear that they are speaking for only a subset of the ALF. This would bring the ALF's method of communication with the outside world into better agreement with both ALF and anarcha-feminist principles concerning distribution of power and individuality within collectivity.

The ethos of care requires one to actively prevent foreseeable harm. This raises the question of arson as a means of property destruction. I would argue that fire always involves an inherent risk of harm to firefighters and ecosystems and thus is not consistent with either ALF principles or the ethos of care. More creative effort must be expended to discover alternative methods by which to interfere with or raise the costs of exploitative operations. Remembering the proverbial monkeywrench in the machine, it may be possible to identify the point in a complex system where a simple intervention can have a profoundly destabilizing effect.

Just as people may disagree when interpreting abstract rules, differences may arise when invoking the ethos of care. For example, some feminists have argued that the tactic of picketing the houses of vivisectors should not be permitted when there are children in the home, because the children might be frightened or traumatized by the idea that their parents are not able to make home a safe place. Others argue that it does children no favor to collude with the deceptions of violent parents and that therefore, so long as the picket lines are peaceful and no invective is hurled at the children, such demonstrations are not only permissible as direct action against vivisection but also may have the side benefit of encouraging the children of animal abusers to help pressure their parents to change or to look outside of their families for role models.

It takes discipline and self-restraint to maintain the proper attitude during actions in which care must be taken to avoid harming people or other animals. An uncomfortable issue that cannot be avoided is the potential for disaffected and potentially violent young men to use the ALF as an excuse to vent their anger in inappropriate ways. Studies of the violent racist right have established that, prior to recruitment, the young men involved could have gone either way—right or left. Filled with pain and rage and desperate for a feeling of belonging, these young men are drawn to any extreme movement that will help them feel less powerless and alone.[18] It stands to reason that the ALF, which offers the opportunity to defend the powerless in a powerful manner, would be attractive to young men fitting this profile. The animal liberation movement can offer such young men the opportunity to develop the discipline and maturity needed to channel their emotional energy into productive activism. But the combination of macho posturing by ALF spokesmen, the unstructured nature of the ALF cell system, and the essential lawlessness of the ALF itself makes it equally if not more likely that such young men will use the ALF as an excuse for destructive behavior.

One way to mitigate this potentially very serious problem would be to put a feminine face on the ALF. What mental image comes to mind in response to the phrase "Animal Liberation Front"? Probably a black-clad young man. What happens when you change that mental image to a young woman or a gray-haired grandmother? One thing that happens is that the ALF suddenly becomes much less attractive to young men motivated more by macho ego than by compassion. Such a paradigm shift easily could be accomplished by deliberately choosing female spokespersons and using images of women on t-shirts and other promotional materials.

Putting a feminine face on the ALF would be accurate, since the US ALF was founded by a woman and we have no reason to believe that the gender balance of the ALF is any different from the rest of the animal liberation movement. Such a shift might help the ALF to accomplish the other feminist challenge facing it, which is to ensure that the ALF does not in any way hamper total animal liberation by contributing to the oppression of human animals.

Obviously, since people are animals, total animal liberation will not be achieved until both human and nonhuman animals are free. That explains why all animal liberationists must, at minimum, avoid contributing to the ongoing oppression and exploitation of women and other persecuted groups. At best, animal liberation activists will forge alliances with social justice activists and sometimes structure their actions so as to illustrate one of the many connections among speciesism and sexism, racism, militarism and economic exploitation.

For the ALF, this means that, in the selection of targets and tactics, care must be taken to ensure that ALF actions are never used as an excuse to express sexist or racist aggression. In addition, ALF cells must consciously attend to gender dynamics so that certain common problems do not occur. Thanks to sex role socialization in childhood, it's very easy for women and men to slip into unequal relationships without realizing that they have done so. In group discussions men may interrupt and dominate while women wait politely before giving up and giving in. This can lead to an illusion of consensus. In allegedly non-hierarchical groups, an unofficial leader often arises and often just happens to be the most masculine person in the group. Sexual harassment or sexual assault may be perpetrated by one member on another. Partner violence might be an issue when two group members are dating. Such problems are always difficult for groups to process, even more so when the group is underground and group members may feel that it would be disloyal to confront the rapist or batterer.

In confronting these often unconscious dynamics, it's important to remember that, just as we were all taught to think about animals in certain ways, we were all taught to think about men and women in certain ways. It takes just as much conscious work to undo sexist socialization as it does to undo speciesist socialization. In neither instance is the job ever done. Ongoing unlearning and relearning is necessary.

Thinking through such issues might aid ALF activists in framing actions and communiqués that illuminate the connections between exploitation of animals and exploitation of women. In this way, and by helping cells to become more equitable and effective, confrontation of sexism can increase the ALF's contribution toward total animal liberation. For example, ALF cells might elect to challenge sexism by questioning what Marti Kheel has called a "heroic ethic" in which the natural world and nonhuman animals are reduced to "damsels in distress" awaiting rescue by the muscular hero.[19] Of course, many captive animals are, indeed, powerless to effect their own escape and thus in need of rescue. Our cultural conditioning makes it very easy for us to slide from that fact into the fantasy of the helpless feminine victim who is entirely dependent on the powerful masculine hero. This, in turn, can lead us to fail to take the animals' own agency and opinions into account when planning our actions on their behalf. Seeing ourselves as their voice, we can forget to listen to them.

Thus, the feminist challenge to the heroic ethic leads us to a renewed appreciation of the animals' participation in their own liberation. How this might be put into action will vary according to circumstance. For example, ALF cells in relevant regions might seek to understand the patterns of and put themselves into alliance with the recent upsurge in elephant escapes and attacks on property. In the United States, sanctuaries and those who staff them offer opportunities to get to know individual animals, so that plans can be grounded in their hopes and experiences rather than our fantasies and theories. This, of course, is a prescription that applies to all animal advocates, not just those associated with ALF.

IV

Feminism also offers challenges to all animal activists—ALF and non-ALF alike—concerning cooperation, coordination, coalition, and communication. Because social change struggles have always been most effective when diverse tactics have been deployed within the context of a coordinated strategy, these principles of feminist practice can help us to build a more effective animal liberation movement.

Cooperation means, at minimum, not impeding the actions of one's allies and, at best, facilitating their work. The rest of the animal liberation movement must recognize ALF activists as allies and vice versa. Mainstream animal advocates need not jump to distance themselves from the ALF and certainly should not find reasons to criticize the ALF in public. Similarly, ALF activists ought not harshly condemn liberationists who include within their work efforts to improve the lives of animals until such time as freedom is achieved. There's simply no evidence to support the idea that either ALF actions or welfare reforms in any way inhibit the long-term struggle for animal liberation. Both ALF actions and welfare reforms seek to improve the lives of actual animals right now, and the animals have not given us any indication that they believe we should cease such efforts on their behalf.

Cooperation beyond mutual respect extends to coordination of efforts. Coordination need not involve discussions across the aboveground/underground divide. For example, if news of an ALF raid on an egg factory appears in the media, aboveground groups might strike while the iron is hot by immediately staging events, lobbying lawmakers, or publishing educational material or letters to editors about battery cages. Or, if an ALF cell were to notice that an aboveground organization in its region was mounting a campaign about eggs, that might be the time to gather and release some footage revealing what goes on behind closed doors at the local egg factory.

Coalition goes a step beyond coordination and does require some communication, if only through a trusted third party. The potential benefits are worth the effort. If, for example, a diverse array of organizations were to agree to focus for a set period of time on milk—with each tackling the topic from its own perspective and with its own favored tactics—then the public and the government would encounter different aspects of the problem at every turn, as they did when both the Black Panthers and the Southern Christian Leadership Conference were among the diverse groups fighting segregation.

Honest and responsible communication is another important principle of feminist practice. This could go a long way toward bridging the divide between the ALF and mainstream animal advocates. In the context of communication, responsibility and honesty mean owning one's feelings, being willing to back up opinions with fact, and ruthlessly examining one's own assumptions. Thus, in debate with an ally, one doesn't say, "You're making it hard for the rest of us," or, "You don't really believe in liberation," but rather, "I believe your tactics are counterproductive because. . . ," or, "I feel uncomfortable with your approach because. . . ," offering evidence to support any assertions of fact. You can even say, "It's not okay with me that you . . . because . . . ," as long as you stick to talking about behavior and refrain from making assumptions about the feelings or motivations of others. Feminist practice requires assuming that the other person (or group) is acting in good faith unless you have solid evidence to the contrary. That means refraining from calling ALF activists "reckless" or "destructive," as if they were not pursuing a viable, if debatable, strategy for social change. That also means taking people at their word when they say that they believe working for welfare reforms can eventually lead to liberation. Open debate is great as long as we all admit that there's no way to say for sure what will work to achieve total animal liberation until we have done so. But the confrontation of thesis with antithesis will never lead to synthesis in an atmosphere of name-calling and character assassination.

It bears repeating that one's circle of communication ought not be confined to human animals. Debates about animal liberation tactics quickly become sterile in the absence of the viewpoints of actual animals. The challenge to all of us is to improve our ability to listen to the animals for whom we purport to speak and act.[20] Only then can we trust ourselves to be the allies they so desperately need.

V

The need for animal liberation remains as urgent as ever. Despite arguments and pleas for vegetarianism dating back to antiquity, per capita meat production and consumption is at an all-time high in the US and around the world.[21] Meanwhile, genetic engineers are designing ever more perverse methods of vivisection, factory farming, and other modes of exploitation. While significant gains have been made against a few specific forms of animal exploitation, such as veal and fur, we must admit that our efforts on behalf of animals cannot yet be described as successful.

More of the same is not enough. All of us—ALF and non-ALF alike—must be more creative and cooperative. Feminist analyses and practices can help to guide us. The ALF is implicitly feminist but often not explicitly so. While the ALF must remain underground, its inherent feminism need not stay under cover. More conscious use of the principles of ecofeminism, anarcha-feminism, radical feminism, and feminist ethics will make the ALF an even more effective component in the multi-faceted struggle for total animal liberation.

The black cat stalks the slaughterhouses and haunts the dreams of vivisectors. Strong and stealthy, fierce and fearless, she taunts and tricks the rapists and the child abusers, too. Sometimes, in quiet moments, you can feel her watching you. The ALF should follow her, because she knows what to do.

Thanks to Karen Davis, Karen Dawn, Miriam Jones, Marti Kheel, and editor Steve Best for insightful and practical comments on earlier versions of this chapter.

Notes

1. Elizabeth Gurley Flynn (1890–1961) was an organizer for the Industrial Workers of the World (IWW) and a founding member of the American Civil Liberties Union. Her essay on sabotage is online at digital.library.arizona.edu/bisbee/docs/128.php.

2. The Yellow Turban Uprising of 184 CE was a peasant uprising staged by Taoists. The Boston Tea Party was a night of property destruction staged by American colonists protesting British rule. Shakers, Quakers, and Sufis all have been condemned as heretics, and all use motion in pursuit of spiritual goals. Contrary to popular belief, Rosa Parks sat down in the white section of a segregated bus as part of a deliberate strategy for change, rather than just because her feet hurt. IWW members are called Wobblies. Wildcat strikes are staged by workers without the sanction of a union recognized by the employer. Harriet Tubman and others used the Underground Railroad as an avenue of freedom for enslaved people of African descent.

3. Krazy Kat was the black cat of indeterminate sex who appeared in the George Herriman comic strip of the same name. Poet e.e. cummings wrote that Krazy's "ambiguous gender doesn't disguise the good news that here comes our heroine." Mehitabel appears in *archy and mehitabel* by Don Marquis, which is a novel in verse about a roach and a black cat. Mehitabel the cat has an "extensive past," proclaims herself to be "toujours gai" [always happy] in the face of deprivation, and says that "the things that i had not ought to/ i do because i ve gotto." Felix the cat is a more modern cartoon prankster known for his bag of tricks. For historic and modern examples of images of black cats used as symbols of sabotage and other forms of direct action, visit the IWW online graphics library at www.iww.org/graphics and click on the *Sabocats* link.

4. For many years, women in the *Chipko Andolan* (the hugging movement) in India have blocked bulldozers by wrapping their bodies around trees. See Ynestra King, "Healing the Wounds: Feminism, Ecology, and the Nature/Culture Dualism," in Irene Diamond and Gloria Feman Orenstein, eds., *Reweaving the World: The Emergence of Ecofeminism* (Sierra Club Books, 1990). Many of the activists who block environmentally destructive road development in Britain are "eco-pagans" who blend an appreciation of fairy mythology with the hard-core realities of direct action. See Andy Letcher, "The Scouring of the Shire: Trolls and Pixies in Eco-Protest Culture," *Folklore*, October 2001. Night gardeners uproot and otherwise interfere with plantings of genetically modified plants.

5. For more on the distance between purely symbolic demonstrations and effective direct action, see my "Marching in Circles: The Tactics of Dizziness and Despair" in *Freezerbox Magazine* at www.freezerbox.com/archive/article.asp?id=264.

6. For the latest scientific evidence concerning the link between pastoralism and patriarchy, see "Cattle Ownership Makes It a Man's World" in the 01 October 2003 issue of *New Scientist* magazine (available online at www.newscientist.com), which summarizes Holden and Mace (2003), "Spread of cattle led to the loss of matrilineal descent in Africa: A coevolutionary analysis," *Proceedings of the Royal Society: Biological Sciences*, DOI 10.1098/rspb.2003.2535 (available at www.pubs.royalsoc.ac.uk).

7. Simone de Beauvoir's 1952 *The Second Sex* (Knopf) helped to launch the modern feminist movement. Her 1948 *Ethics of Ambiguity* (Philosophical Library) provides an easy-to-understand explanation of the ethical implications of the existential principle that existence precedes essence. I would argue that this principle means, for example, that one *becomes* an environmentalist by making environmentally sustain-

able choices and that one cannot *be* an environmentalist if one's choices run counter to the best interests of the ecosystem.

8. "Thinking Like a Chicken: Farm Animals and the Feminine Connection" by Karen Davis is one of several important essays in Carol J. Adams and Josephine Donovan, eds., *Animals and Women: Feminist Theoretical Explorations* (Durham, NC: Duke University Press, 1995). This essay is also online at www.upc-online.org/thinking_like_a_chicken.html.

9. For more examples of links between sexism and speciesism see Carol Adams's *The Sexual Politics of Meat* (New York: Continuum, 1990) and *The Pornography of Meat* (New York: Continuum, 2003).

10. Premarin is a hormone replacement medication made from the urine of cruelly confined pregnant horses and given to women who have been led to believe that the natural life cycle of menopause should be treated like a disease. The Women's Health and Ethics Coalition is an innovative international alliance of feminists and animal advocates using a multifaceted strategy against Premarin and its derivatives. Visit www.stoppremarin.org for more information.

11. Tree sitters such as Julia Butterfly Hill live in the branches of trees that have been marked for felling, protecting the trees with their bodies. In Nigeria, women have challenged the environmental and economic practices of Chevron-Texaco by occupying a major facility and stopping production.

12. We all think about and come up with theories to make sense of our lives and the world. In his *Prison Notebooks* (New York: International Publishers, 1971), Antonio Gramsci identified the "organic intellectual" as someone who conceives and articulates ideas that are rooted in experience rather than education. Organic intellectuals exist in all classes and can play key roles in liberation struggles. The slaughterhouse worker who perceives and articulates a connection between her company's inhumane treatment of animals and its disregard for the safety of workers is fulfilling the function of an organic intellectual. Her observations will be more accurate and persuasive than the speculations of a theorist who has never seen the blood of butchered animals mingling with the blood of injured workers on the floor.

13. For more on anarcha-feminism, see *Quiet Rumours: An Anarcha-Feminist Anthology*, published by Dark Star Rebel Press (UK) and available online at www.cluefactory.org.uk/ace/rumours.

14. Although deeply flawed by its reliance on Reichian assumptions, James DeMeo's "The origins and diffusion of patrism in Saharasia c. 4000 BCE: Evidence for a worldwide, climate-linked geographical pattern in human behavior" (*World Futures*, 30, 247–271) gives a thorough presentation and thought-provoking analysis of key facts concerning the origins of patriarchal societies in various regions. While he does not stress this fact, all of the original patriarchal cultures he discusses were also pastoral (animal herding) cultures.

15. For more on radical vegetarian women in Edwardian England, see Leah Leneman, "The Awakened Instinct: Vegetarianism and the Women's Suffrage Movement in Britain," *Women's History Review*, Vol. 6 No. 2, 1997.

16. Carol Gilligan's findings concerning moral reasoning can be found in most textbooks of introductory psychology as well as in her book *In a Different Voice* (Cambridge, Massachusetts: Harvard University Press, 1977).

17. For further information on women and nonviolent social change, see Pam McAllister, ed., *Reweaving the Web of Life: Feminism and Nonviolence* (Gabriola Island, British Columbia: New Society Publishers, 1982). For further information on

past and present women's activism against war, see Daniela Gioseffi, *Women on War* (New York: The Feminist Press, 2003).

18. For an insightful analysis of violent young men drawn to extreme organizations, see Rafe Ezekiel's *The Racist Mind: Portraits of Neo-Nazis and Klansmen* (New York: Viking, 1995).

19. Marti Kheel's "From Heroic to Holistic Ethics: The Ecofeminist Challenge" is but one of many illuminating essays in Greta Gaard, ed., *Ecofeminism: Women, Animals, Nature* (Philadelphia: Temple University Press, 1993). This essay is also online at www2.pfeiffer.edu/~lridener/courses/ECOFEM2.HTML.

20. If you have no idea how you might go about taking the opinions of animals into account, that's a sign that you have not paid enough attention to the problem of how to listen to the animals before attempting to be their voice. Given the limitations of cross-species communication, one must take particular care to learn whatever it is possible to learn about the hopes and fears of the nonhuman animals one hopes to help. There are two intersecting avenues of approach: empathy and observation. Getting to know animals—either by spending time with them or by learning from trustworthy people who have spent time with them—allows one to use empathy accurately. That means asking not "What would I want if I were in a battery cage?" but "What would I want *if I were a chicken* in a battery cage?" Careful observation—either directly or via the factual reports of trustworthy people—allows one to make inferences about animal preferences based on the actions they have taken on their own behalf. That means asking not "What do the experts believe that these animals want?" but "What do the actions of these animals tell anybody willing to listen about what they want?"

21. Up-to-date statistics concerning US and worldwide per capita meat production and consumption may be retrieved from the US Department of Agriculture and the UN Food and Agriculture Organization.

Motivation

To know what is right and not to do it is the worst form of cowardice.—Confucius

The only thing necessary for the triumph of evil is for good men to do nothing.—Edmund Burke

The world is too dangerous to live in—not because of the people who do evil but because of the people who sit and let it happen.—Albert Einstein

Aquinas's Account of Anger Applied to the ALF

Judith Barad, PhD

When I moved from Chicago to Terre Haute, Indiana to accept a university position in 1985, I began personally encountering cruelty to cats and dogs on a regular basis. For instance, one four-month-old kitten I found and subsequently brought home was crippled by four BB gun pellets in her leg and back. Another cat I took in had a flea collar embedded in her neck that had been placed there when she was a kitten. She belonged to a neighbor who let her run loose and eat out of garbage cans. An extremely emaciated dog I fed was so eager to eat anything at all that he ate the plastic spoon as I was attempting to scoop food onto a paper plate. Like a lot of dogs in the area, he lived outside on a short chain, with no shelter, and no visible food or water. Neglected cats and dogs ran loose on the city streets or were dumped in the country to fend for themselves. This continual barrage of cruelty enraged me. What could I do? I couldn't take them all home, yet I couldn't take them to the humane shelter, which would probably kill them. After attempting to change the animal control ordinance, I decided to build the first no-kill shelter for stray and abused cats and dogs in West Central Indiana. Whenever I became discouraged during the next eight years, my anger at past and current experiences of local animal abuse and neglect spurred me to continue my efforts. The shelter, a 5,000-square-foot, state-of-the-art building, opened on July 3, 2001. Not only did I fulfill a dream project, but, through the publicity the no-kill shelter generated, I found satisfaction in trying to publicly shame irresponsible animal guardians. In retrospect, if I had merely been sad about the plight of cats and dogs in this area, I would not have accomplished anything. It was my anger, controlled by reason, that made me persist in my efforts.

Many people who witness atrocities committed against animals become very angry. Some become sufficiently angry to take action aimed

159

at preventing these atrocities. According to a communiqué sent by the "Pirates for Animal Liberation" to a news information service, "20 holes were drilled in the right side" of a 30-foot yacht belonging to the President of Capital Markets, and "one 6" x 6" hole was sawed through the right hull. Various workings of the boat were also tampered with" until it took on water and was pushed out to sea. This was done to protest the Bank's financial services to a notorious animal testing laboratory that tests agrochemical and pharmaceutical products on puppies, cats, monkeys, rabbits, and a number of other animals, killing approximately 180,000 a year. While some people may understand the anger that triggers such actions, other people say that some of the animal rights groups formed to address these abuses take their anger too far.

St. Thomas Aquinas provides an account of anger that could help elucidate how it functions in such associations as the Animal Liberation Front and how their anger can be harnessed constructively. At first, however, it may seem that anger as Aquinas describes it would support the public image of the ALF as embittered fanatics or terrorists, or encourage animal activists to give up anger altogether. Consider Aquinas's definition of anger as a "desire to punish another by way of just revenge."[1] He maintains that when we feel anger we want to punish the offender and feel pleasure in doing so. Thus, in avenging animal suffering by punishing an offender, an ALF member would experience pleasure. This idea may make us uncomfortable, because it sounds vindictive and therefore reprehensible. Nonetheless, Aquinas insists that anger has a role to play in facilitating justice. Now, how can a potentially vindictive emotion help animal protectors to achieve justice? If Aquinas's description of anger is correct, shouldn't ALF members attempt to avoid anger and its incumbent desire for revenge when they seek justice for animals?

After discussing the distinction between retribution and revenge, I will explain Aquinas's general account of the nature of anger. The various features of anger I examine in the early sections of the essay will be revisited in its later sections. I will then analyze the conundrums posed by anger and conclude by suggesting how the complex nature of anger may in some cases impede and in others promote the cause of animal liberation.

The Pleasure of Revenge

As mentioned above, Aquinas holds not only that anger facilitates justice, but also that once the angry person achieves justice, he or she feels pleasure.[2] As soon as vengeance is present, pleasure ensues. In fact according to Aquinas, even before we avenge ourselves on an offender, vengeance gives us pleasure:

> Before vengeance is really present, it becomes present to the angry man in two ways: in one way by hope; because none is angry except he hopes for vengeance . . . in another way, by thinking of it continually, for to everyone that desires a thing it is pleasant to dwell on the thought of what he desires.[3]

Revenge gives us hope and pleasure, both very positive feelings. Don't most of us enjoy the feelings of hope and pleasure? However, shouldn't a truly just person recoil at the notion of feeling pleasure in revenge?

Nowadays, it may disturb us to think of taking pleasure in revenge. Louis Pojman, writing about theories of capital punishment, advocates a retributive position, contrasting it with a position based on revenge.[4] The difference between the two, according to him, is that retribution is impersonal, implying fairness, whereas revenge is personal, involving bias. Moreover, he claims that seeking justice based on revenge is also unfair, since it may lead to "more suffering from the offender than the offense warrants." While Pojman does not discuss the motivation for this excessive zeal, it is reasonable to assume that it is based on anger, since it is our anger that motivates us to seek revenge. Further, revenge is usually viewed as a primitive goal, unworthy of enlightened people. Advocates of this position are disturbed by Aquinas's claim that taking revenge on someone who acts unjustly should bring us pleasure.

Is Aquinas's position on this issue obsolete? Can any philosophical or practical insight be derived from it? Consider Aquinas's observation that "by means of punishment the equality of justice is restored."[5] Now if justice is something that pleases us, shouldn't its restoration likewise give us pleasure? If we believe that punishment is a means to restore justice, then we may appreciate how an animal liberationist may take pleasure in punishing an animal abuser. If you have ever fumed inwardly, uttered retaliatory retorts, or raised your clenched fists to strike, you have probably thought, "I'm giving him what he deserves." "Let's give them a taste of their own medicine." "That should teach her!" These ordinary expressions suggest that we implicitly link pleasure and revenge on a regular basis, even though the issues may vary.

The Expressions and Effects of Anger

Aware of this human tendency, Aquinas discusses three ways we express anger: in the heart, in speech, and in action.[6] Anger that is present in the heart occurs when we internalize our anger. We sometimes withhold our feelings and become indignant.[7] For instance, someone may read a newspaper account of a horrific experiment on animals and feel an inner anger that results in indignation. Anger present in the heart can also take the form of a "swelling in the mind," that is, when we savor planning various ways to take vengeance. When anger erupts into speech, "clamor, inordinate and jumbled utterance" may result. Frequently, an angry person is not able to articulate an immediate response and becomes "tongue-tied." Alternately, anger in speech may be expressed by calling the offender names or swearing at him or her, an approach often heard in traffic jams. Finally, when anger "proceeds to action, quarreling arises, under which are included all its consequences, for instance, wounds, murders and the like."[8] Naturally one need not express anger in only one of these ways.

Anger is expressed when someone acts in a way judged to be unjust. The judgmental nature of anger is the most manifest of all the emotions, with oneself as the court in which indictment, argument, verdict, and sentence are all carried out. The judgmental component in anger evaluates the degree to which the offense received is unjust. Thus anger is related to justice, either actually or at least in the eyes of the offended person.

But judgment is not the only component of anger. Defining anger as a judgment of personal offense, Robert Solomon emphasizes the judgmental character of all the emotions.[9] Since emotions are judgments, they can be rational in the same sense in which judgments can be rational. We choose our emotions and can be held responsible for them. Stressing their cognitive role and sharply minimizing the physiological aspect, Solomon explicitly denies that emotions are feelings.

Yet Solomon's view runs counter to our experience. The command "Control yourself" makes sense only when applied to one's emotions and not to one's judgments. Emotions do not always reflect conscious choices, for weakness of will (a familiar state to most of us) typically occurs when our avowed judgments are in conflict with our emotions. Additionally, while physical changes may occur in the absence of emotion, when a strong emotion is present they are never lacking. The physical changes that occur in every strong emotion include changes in blood pressure, respiration, and pulse rate.

In contrast to such intellectualist theories of emotion as Solomon's, Aquinas maintains that emotions are sensory reactions of attraction or repulsion accompanied by physiological change. They are more directly attributed to the physical powers than to the rational.[10] It is a matter of common experience that attraction and repulsion affect our physical desires more than they affect our knowledge. The physical changes induced by attraction and repulsion are an integral part of the emotional process, for the emotions are deeply rooted in biology.

Moreover, Aquinas believes, it is essential to justice that judgment be accompanied by a strong feeling. It is inappropriate to judge merely dispassionately that some horrific crime has been perpetrated against an innocent individual. While correct rational judgment is an important criterion of when we should become angry, the desire to inflict just punishment for suffering should accompany this judgment. Justice is demanded by an angry, morally indignant person, who seeks to relieve anger by injuring the cause of his or her pain. The purpose of revenge is to relieve that anger and thereby promote justice. To revenge ourselves for an egregious offense, to seek revenge against evil, may be the root of our sense of justice.

Besides judgment and feeling, anger, like the other emotions, also has a physiological component. Aquinas notes that the bodily effects of anger are among the most dramatic of any emotion. His description, borrowed from St. Gregory the Great, illustrates this:

> The movement of anger produces fervor of the blood and vital spirits around the heart, which is the instrument of the soul's passions. And hence it is that, on account of the heart being so disturbed by anger, those chiefly who are angry betray signs thereof in their outer members. For, as Gregory says (*Moralia* v. 30), the heat that is inflamed with the stings of its own anger beats quick, the body trembles, the tongue stammers, the countenance takes fire, the eyes grow fierce, they that are well known are not recognized. With the mouth indeed he shapes a sound, but the understanding knows not what it says.[11]

Many of our ordinary expressions mirror Aquinas's description of anger's bodily effects, as when we speak of someone being "hot under the collar," "red with anger," or "giving a look that could kill," or when we experience our own "blood boiling." Considering its intense bodily effects, it is understandable that anger can manifest itself as an explosion.

Kinds of Anger

There are also three kinds of anger, distinguished by the different things that stimulate them. Aquinas, following St. John Damascene and Gregory of Nyasa, uses Greek terms to name the three species of anger. The first kind of anger, distinguished by its quick arousal, is called *cholos* (bile). Nowadays we would call a person prone to this kind of anger "hot-tempered." The hot-tempered person not only becomes angry too quickly, but also finds his anger triggered by any slight cause. He often becomes angry "with the wrong people, at the wrong things, and more than he should."[12] A hot-tempered person might be aroused to anger merely by the way someone looks at him. While such people are hard to get along with, one of their redeeming features is that they do not allow their anger to fester. Their anger flares up quickly, but they soon return to a tranquil state.[13]

The second type of anger, termed *menis* (ill will), is caused by grief.[14] Aquinas uses a fanciful etymology to explain this term, supposing (wrongly) that this type of anger gets its name from the Greek *menein*, meaning "to dwell."[15] He adds that ill will causes a lasting displeasure, making a person "grievous" and "sullen" to himself.[16] Such a person harbors whatever makes him angry, replaying the insult over and over again in his memory. Aquinas says, "In this case time is needed to absorb the anger. Such persons are burdensome to themselves and especially to their friends."[17] It is not surprising that this lingering anger replayed over and over again would produce a dour personality that few people would be willing to endure.

The third type of anger "pertains to *kotos* (rancor), which never rests until it is avenged."[18] Ill will and rancor are similar in that they both last a long time. But they differ in that ill will wears away with time, whereas rancor can be quelled only by revenge.[19] Aquinas further describes the person who feels rancor as "stern," not giving up his anger until he has inflicted punishment.[20] However, the desire for vengeance leads to ill temper or a stern state only when anger is excessive.

Excessive Anger

But how do we know whether anger is excessive? Since anger lacks an internal system of controls, it can become a destructive force within us if it is permitted to run rampant, without rational restraint. Having spontaneously experienced anger, there are appropriate and inappropriate ways in which one can respond to its object. In order for us to respond morally in a given situation, reason must determine whether the object of our anger is really good or bad and whether our anger is appropriate to the situation. It is reason that informs us whether we are "angry over the right things, with the right persons, and moreover in the right way, at the right time."[21] Employing the Aristotelian theory of the mean, Aquinas holds that our emotional balance can be found between poles of excess and deficiency. For instance, a person who feels only minor irritation upon witnessing a kitten being kicked responds deficiently, and a person who feels great anger over a dog barking once responds excessively.

Anger is excessive if a person is angry over the wrong things, with the wrong persons, in the wrong way, or at the wrong time. Anger is also excessive if we "desire the punishment of one who has not deserved it, or beyond his deserts, or again contrary to the order prescribed by law, or not for the . . . maintaining of justice and the correction of defaults.[22] The desire to punish a person who does not deserve it is not intended to avenge a particular offense, but to hurt that person. The same is true of a desire to punish a person beyond what he deserves. Thus Aquinas would agree with Pojman that *if* revenge leads us to exact more suffering from the offender than the offense warrants, it is excessive. On the other hand, he differs from Pojman, since he does not hold that revenge necessarily leads to an excessive response.

For Aquinas, anger can be excessive not only in terms of its effects on the victim, but also due to its effects on the angry person:

> In the matter of vengeance, we must consider the mind of the avenger. For if his intention is directed chiefly to the evil of the person on whom he takes vengeance and rests there, then his vengeance is altogether unlawful: because to take pleasure in another's evil belongs to hatred, which is contrary to the charity whereby we are bound to love all men. Nor is it an excuse that he intends the evil of one who has unjustly inflicted evil on him, as neither is a man excused for hating one that hates him: for a man may not sin against another just because the latter has already sinned against him, since this is to be overcome by evil.[23]

Aquinas warns us that if we allow hatred against a person in our hearts, it will have a negative impact on our characters. In short, he maintains that anger against a sin is virtuous, whereas anger against the sinner is sinful.[24]

The expression of anger in an excessive manner can be so sinful that is it counted among the capital vices. Because these vices are more popularly known as the "seven deadly sins," some people may misconceive them as purely evil.[25] However, for Aquinas, while it is true that capital vices are never good considered in themselves, they are not necessarily evil, since they may be sources of action in virtue of good.

Antecedent and Consequent Anger

Moreover, our expression of anger can be good or bad "either from being commanded by the will, or from not being checked by the will."[26] To experience anger in itself is morally neutral: I may not be able to control whether or not I feel angry; anger may well up in me before I have time to reflect on it. But anger loses its moral neutrality when I fail to keep my expression of it within rational bounds. For Aquinas, failing to restrain my expression of anger is just as blameworthy as having intentionally "worked myself up" into a violent rage.

Suppose you were present during the following actual experiment. You watch as dogs are deliberately burned to test the usefulness of an anti-infection vaccine when given after severe burn injuries. Forty beagle puppies are clipped of hair from the neck to the base of their tails. Then the researchers mark with indelible ink the parts of the puppies' bodies to be burned. They inflict burns over a third of the anaesthetized puppies' body surface using kerosene-soaked gauze which is ignited, allowed to burn for 60 seconds, and then extinguished. For 18 hours following the burning, the puppies receive "light anesthesia." You are then told that 90 days later, only 16 percent of the control puppies had survived, compared with 48 percent of those given the vaccine.[27] As you watch the experiment, and later, as you hear the results, you may feel an abrupt surge of anger prior to reflecting on what you saw or willing yourself to feel the anger. Since emotions are spontaneous feeling states, it is natural for you to have little control over your immediate feeling of anger. You are responsible for controlling the expression of your anger, but you are not responsible for the onset of anger in the first place. The difference between the immediate presence of anger in you and the subsequent expression of anger is captured in Aquinas's distinction between anger experienced antecedent to a rational judgment and anger consequent to a rational judgment:

> Anger . . . can be related in two ways to the judgment of reason: in one way antecedently, and thus of necessity anger . . .

always impedes the judgment of reason, because the soul can best judge truth in a certain tranquillity of mind. . . . In another way anger can be related to the judgment of reason consequently, namely inasmuch as after reason has judged and determined the manner of vengeance, then the passion arises to carry it out, and thus anger and other such passions do not impede the judgment of reason which has already preceded, but rather help to execute the judgment of reason more promptly, and in this way the passions are useful to virtue.[28]

Antecedent anger, the anger experienced prior to judgment, arises from a bodily disposition or from the operations of the senses and the imagination. It heightens the imagination and hinders our power of judgment. Sometimes antecedent anger may be so strong as to prevent the intellect from deliberating about alternative courses of action. If anger becomes the sole motive for an act, the act is no longer voluntary and forfeits its moral value. If my desire for vengeance is so strong that it obscures my rational judgment, then the anger is wrong, even if it was provoked. Since antecedent anger precedes rational judgment, it may easily become excessive and thus a capital vice. Following Gregory, Aquinas calls this kind of excessive anger "vicious anger," describing it as a "desire of vengeance that appears just but is not really just."[29]

Consequent anger, which we experience following a judgment, may increase the goodness of a moral act in two ways: "First, by way of redundance; because . . . when the higher part of the soul is intensely moved to anything, the lower part also follows that movement: and thus the passion that results in consequence, in the sensitive appetite, is a sign of the intensity of the will."[30] For example, having rationally judged that animals should be treated with respect, I feel anger when I think about the way they are treated in laboratories or factory farms. The second way a consequent emotion may increase the value of an act is by "way of choice, when a person, by the judgment of his reason, chooses to be affected by an emotion in order to work more promptly with the cooperation of the sensitive appetite."[31] I may choose to pay special attention to news stories about animal cruelty, thereby arousing my anger in order to take action. In both cases, the emotions are voluntary since they follow a judgment.

In addition to adding to the moral value of an action, consequent anger enables an individual to perform an action "more promptly and easily" than if the anger were absent. Since anger "is closely connected with a change in the body," physical movement is naturally elicited when the anger corresponds to the choice of the will.[32] Referring to consequent anger, Aquinas explains, "When a person is virtuous with the virtue of courage, the emotion of anger following upon the choice of virtue makes for greater alacrity in the act."[33] Anger is a strong motivator, stirring up activity and arousing us to energetic action. The increased adrenaline generated by a person's anger can give her the physical boost she needs to deal more efficaciously with a perceived wrong. A person who is not only rationally but also emotionally committed to a moral act is more resolved to accomplish it. Thus Aquinas praises consequent anger, since it increases the moral value of a good act and intensifies our commitment to it.

In contrast to "vicious anger," consequent anger is called "zealous anger" if it is a desire for vengeance insofar as the anger is truly just. Aquinas says that if consequent anger "is directed against vice and in accordance with reason, this anger is good, and is called zealous anger."[34] Zealous anger originates in the recognition that people are responsible for their actions, and thus should be held accountable for what they do.

The Cause of Anger

In order to understand the relationship between justice and anger more deeply, we must understand the cause of anger. Aquinas holds that "All the causes of anger are reduced to slight."[35] People slight us when they neglect us, do not hesitate to say painful things to us, express glee about our bad luck, act indifferently toward us, or frustrate our efforts to accomplish something.[36] All slights belittle some particular characteristic of the victim. Our anger is caused partly by the pain of this belittlement. We desire vengeance with the intention of reestablishing the just relationship that was disrupted by the slight against us.

Aquinas claims that "whatever injury is inflicted on us, in so far as it is derogatory to our excellence, seems to savor of a slight."[37] Feeling that we excel in some way, we want to be recognized for it. If, instead, someone acts contemptuously toward that which we believe we excel in, we become angry. *Excellentia*, according to Aquinas, refers to any positive asset. Our excellence is our self-worth. Aquinas recognizes that people assess their self-worth in different ways. Some may be concerned with their outward excellence, such as power and position. Others find self-worth in their knowledge and virtue.[38] Aquinas is aware, however, that the common people, the masses, "acknowledge none but outward excellence."[39] This is probably just as true today as it was in his time.

Discussing Aquinas's concept of excellence, Diana Fritz Cates writes that the powerful have a tendency "to identify their economic, political, and social privileges as excellences that compose an objective scale of value against which all people are to be measured."[40] She notes in passing that Aquinas also includes virtue as an excellence, but adds that he easily "assimilates social, political, and economic goods to the good of virtue."[41] Nonetheless, Aquinas not only separates the excellence of virtue from the external excellences, as noted in the passage cited above, but he deems the former to be more deserving of honor. In numerous passages, Aquinas makes it clear that the excellence we should be honored for is moral virtue. For instance, he observes, "Private individuals are sometimes honored by kings, not because they are above them in the order of dignity, but on account of some excellence of their virtue,"[42] and he clearly notes that excellence belongs to virtue more than to external goods, writing that "Honor denotes attention to someone's excellence, especially the excellence which is according to virtue."[43] In short, Aquinas admits that economic, political, and social excellences are those that the masses acknowledge, but the excellences worthiest of honor are those associated with virtue.

Since our excellence is our self-worth, it is when people slight *us*, have contempt for *us*, that anger arises. Anger is usually direct and overt in its projection of our personal values onto the world. Expressing our anger makes people realize that we are serious, and so they pay attention to us. Even if our anger is not expressed, it is our insistence upon our own ideals. It records our disapproval that the world does not live up to our expectations, and shows our desire to punish those who would not comply with our deeply held beliefs. Aquinas very clearly argues that we are angry only about personal offenses:

> Nor does any injury provoke one to vengeance, but only that which is done to the person who seeks vengeance: for just as everything naturally seeks its own good, so does it naturally repel its own evil. But injury done by anyone does not affect a man unless in some way it be something done against him. Consequently the motive of a man's anger is always something done against him.[44]

Anger defends the self. Consider that a person will not get angry if she says to herself, "It is none of my business."

Identification with Others

Just as clearly as Aquinas argues that we are angry only about offenses to our own selves, he insists that injustice is concerned about our dealings with others.[45] But then how can justice, with its concern for others, be reconciled with anger, a concern for injury to self?

Aquinas was not unaware of the seeming incompatibility between anger as a response to a personal offense and justice as a concern for what is due others. In reply to an objection that it is not always harm done to us that makes us angry, he says, "When we take a very great interest in a thing we look upon it as our own good, so that if anyone despises it, it seems as though we ourselves were despised and injured."[46] Recognizing that we are able to identify with others and will their good as another self, he writes, "For when we love a thing, by desiring it, we apprehend it as belonging to our well being."[47] Love denotes the principle of the movement by which our desire tends toward the object we love. Desire urges that a union with the object loved is good for us. Aquinas tells us that what is loved is in our "will as the term or a movement arising from the conformity it has with the lover."[48] Through love our will is conformed to the object, causing the object to be effectively present in us. Consequently, love seeks an intimate union with the object loved—a union so strong that it amounts to an identification.

This means that we take personally not only our physical and psychological characteristics, but also what happens to other individuals whom we identify with. These identifications break down the barrier between subject and object, creating an expanded self. According to Aquinas, each person is this expanded self, comprised of other things and individuals we love and thereby with which we identify. By punishing a person who has injured those with whom we identify, we demonstrate that we are not simply isolated individuals, each pursuing his or her own egoistic concerns. In contrast to Pojman, Aquinas insists that revenge is and *should* be personal. While we think that observing the injustice done to others causes our anger, the political is always personal. Our anger is always about ourselves, even if it about our expanded self.

The anger directed at those who have harmed those whom we identify with can be better understood by returning to the concept of "zealous anger." Recall that zealous anger is a desire of vengeance insofar as it is really just. If we identify with something we love, zeal may become aroused when that thing is harmed. Aquinas elucidates this relationship:

> Zeal . . . arises from the intensity of love. For it is evident that the more intensely a power tends to anything, the more vigorously it withstands opposition or resistance. Since therefore love is a movement towards the object loved . . . an intense love seeks to remove anything that opposes it.[49]

Accordingly, zealous anger has its source in love, wanting good for someone else. If someone opposes that which we love, we will seek to remove the opposition. One motivated by zealous anger will demand that the offender stop expressing his contemptuous attitude to those with whom she identifies. If the demand is ignored, zealous anger will issue in action. Ingrid Newkirk, co-founder of People for the Ethical Treatment of Animals, writes:

> How many of us would be content writing letters to the editor and politely talking about the situation if our very own loved ones had been snatched away from us and were being imprisoned and tortured? Would we sit back if our sisters were being force-fed bleach? Well, someone's sister is being force-fed bleach. . . . We know about it, but we continue sitting here. Should we blame the ALF for getting up and trying to stop it?[50]

The zealous anger an ALF member experiences "arises from the intensity of love." She may identify with the dog being force-fed bleach as her own relative or her own self. The more she identifies with the animal victim, the more "vigorously" she will seek to remove the oppressor.

Anger and Animal Rights Activism

Much of Aquinas's account of anger has great significance for those engaged in animal liberation efforts. The aim of animal rights activists is to improve the lives of oppressed animals, thereby restoring justice. Moreover, animal rights activists identify with these animal victims and become angry at their unjust treatment. Offenses against animals and slights against their particular cause commonly elicit their anger. And many do seek revenge against those they perceive as oppressors. Since Aquinas's description of anger and its cause seems applicable to those activists, his account may be able to help them understand how their anger may be used constructively.

First, however, let us examine how anger can counteract the activist's efforts to help the oppressed. Recall that a person feeling anger undergoes physiological changes. The physiological factors of anger result in increased activity and intensified strength, facilitating an immediate response to the offender. But the angry person may seek revenge, not as a reasonable response to a circumspectly calculated injustice, but as a physically incited, impetuous reaction to an immediately perceived attack. In some instances, the bodily changes that normally accompany anger may become so turbulent as to short-circuit reason. Thus an activist can become consumed with anger. Such a condition should be avoided, for it can lead to extreme or unsuitable behavior, such as "wounds, murders, and the like." We need only think of the anger that led one "pro-life" activist to murder a physician who performed abortions. Clearly, anger is always a dangerous impulse, and needs observant management.

In the heat of a confrontation, an activist whose reasoning process is diminished can lose sight of his or her constructive objective. Aquinas reminds us that a tranquil state of mind is necessary for planned anger and effective revenge. The difference between anger as an impetuous reaction and planned anger is embodied in Aquinas's distinction between anger experienced prior to rational judgment and anger experienced consequent to rational judgment. For example, Alex Pacheco, an animal-rights activist, worked undercover at the Institute for Behavioral Research in Silver Springs, Maryland. In this laboratory primates were crippled through surgery and then tormented in attempts to make them use their deadened limbs. For Pacheco, the vivisector's ridicule, neglect, and torture of the animals was certainly an unmerited slight. The sorrow and pain he felt upon seeing the primates' plight was naturally followed by anger. Had Pacheco acted on his antecedent emotion of anger, he might have uttered hostile, threatening words at the laboratory technicians or even physically assaulted one of them. But if he had acted in this way, his attempted revenge would have turned against both him and his cause. Instead, he used his consequent anger and waited four months to build a case sufficiently strong to initiate the first-ever police raid on an experimental laboratory—a raid that also led to closing the laboratory and resulted in the first criminal conviction of an experimenter on charges of cruelty to animals in the

United States. Acting on his consequent anger, Pacheco must have taken pleasure in exposing and halting the blatant cruelty of the vivisector. Moreover, in line with Aquinas's exhortation, Pacheco accomplished all of this without focusing on the character of the vivisector, but on his action.

Activists should also pay heed to Aquinas's description of hot-tempered anger and ill will. When we continually dwell on what makes us angry without showing "outward signs of anger," this internalized anger can easily lead to depression. When we become angry quickly and for relatively trivial reasons, activist burnout can occur. "Burnout" is a state of fatigue or frustration brought about by a devotion to a relationship, a way of life, or a cause that fails to produce the expected results. Excessive anger may deplete an activist's energy and cause her to lose touch with herself and her movement. In extreme cases, the person who once cared very deeply about a cause may insulate herself to the point that she no longer cares at all. As time elapses, her enthusiasm dies and she becomes continually angry, or angry over almost everything. The anger may erupt continually or may be bottled up within her, but if she allows it to continue unchecked, the result is burnout. In these cases, anger can be a whirlpool: overwhelming, frustrating, leaving a person feeling helpless or incapable of acting.

Not knowing how to channel anger may lead to an unhealthy condition. If we combine Aquinas's account of hot-tempered anger and ill will with his recognition of anger's bodily effects, it should not surprise us that the hormonal changes associated with these types of anger have been directly linked to cardiovascular and gastric disease. And studies show that the stress associated with a quick temper and with continually dwelling on offenses can cause severe anxiety and depression, and indirectly contributes to diabetes, hypertension, and asthma. Clearly, anger can be a counterproductive force, socially, biologically, and psychologically.

On the other hand, anger can be a positive force, an impetus for social change. The physical changes of anger can facilitate virtuous action against a person who has either actually harmed or potentially could harm those for whom we care. Anger can serve as energy for action, increasing our internal strength and resolve. Recurrent surges of anger can provide a continual source of energy for our social commitments. Our zeal to avenge an offense can make us take up the gauntlet of activism. As an outlet for anger, activism can overcome one's sense of isolation in that one joins with a group of like-minded people. A group identity not only creates a culture of support and solidarity for anger, but can also have a much broader impact than our revenge as isolated individuals.

In his discussion of how we express anger, Aquinas has warned us that anger residing solely in the heart may lead to unfulfilled indignation. In speech, it may lead to vitriolic words spewed out in haste. Commonly, novice activists charge angrily into the fray without stopping first to reason what action may constitute the most effective approach to the perceived injustice. They risk triggering anger in others, either against the individual activist, against the cause that is represented, or both.

Using a rational approach, our anger is not eliminated. Instead our anger becomes the kind of moderate anger that Aquinas praises. We still feel anger, but in a moderate, less intense way, when we take action governed by reason. At this point we can more effectively focus on resolving our grievances. The excess anger that we no longer feel has become the energy, the fuel to help us keep actively involved in the animal rights movement. Think of anger as a fire within us. When we nourish anger excessively, we add fuel to the fire. Naturally, this may lead to an unfortunate explosion. However, when we moderate our anger by allowing reason to control it, the fire still burns, but the fuel is channeled into constructive action impelling us forward rather than adding to the fire. Using anger as a catalyst for constructive growth and change can be liberating for activists themselves, as well as for the animals they seek to benefit.

Aquinas's analysis of anger provides a further insight into this passion that may help animal rights activists. In fact, their very activism can expose the root of anger that Aquinas identifies, namely, love, inspiring love to work in partnership with justice. We want animal abusers to acknowledge the excellences of our movement and of the animals we love. We want these animals to be treated as valuable, worthwhile individuals by the people who have slighted them. The acknowledgment we hope for and the treatment we desire shows, as John Giles Milhaven observes, that anger is not only love of the victims, but also love of the offender. He says that one who does not take others seriously is lacking (in human goodness). Thus when we compel an animal abuser to take animals seriously, it is "a way of loving her."[51] By making her confront the unjust way she has treated animals, we provide her with the opportunity to restore her human goodness. Our belief that the abuser can be better than she is and our desire to make her so can be considered a type of love. The activist who is aware of the love for both victim and offender that underlies her anger will be more inclined to moderate her passion and seek constructive ways to express it. And knowing that anger is grounded in love can help us to better accept it than if we perceive it as a raw, hostile passion we should expunge from our lives.

Finally, activists can learn from Aquinas's observation that anger is caused by a slight against our excellence. Identifying their excellence with justice, animal liberators may come to understand why a slight against their movement arouses their ire. They may feel vindicated by Aquinas's claim that their excellence is more deserving of honor than the excellence of those concerned with outward trappings. The fact that the masses acknowledge only the excellences of wealth, power, and position may help us to understand why more people may not appreciate liberators' efforts on behalf of animals. This is especially true when activists represent an oppressed group with which the masses do not identify. For instance, the masses may take the sinking of an animal testing laboratory executive's yacht more seriously than they take the fact that their laboratory kills 500 animals on a daily basis. So they will not recognize the justice of the ALF's action. Not valuing the activists' identification with the animals and not seeing any property, wealth, or power that the activists stand to lose, the majority may become suspicious of animal rights activism. Moreover, if the property, wealth, or power of animal abusers is threatened by animal rights activists, the majority may be expected to side with the offenders.

No wonder animal rights activists feel anger so frequently! Yet rather than approaching justice through an impersonal retributive standpoint, the personal quality of anger and the revenge it seeks, if moderated, can provide a greater motivation for accomplishing the activist's goals pertaining to justice. Aquinas's account of anger, due to its intense association with justice, can help those involved in animal rights activism to better understand their own anger, the most salutary expression of it, and its usefulness as a tool to enhance the effectiveness of their cause.

Notes

1. St. Thomas Aquinas, *Summa Theologiae* I-II (New York: McGraw-Hill, 1944), 47, 1. Further references to this work will be noted as *S. T.*
2. "The movement of anger arises from a wrong done that causes sorrow, for which sorrow vengeance is sought as a remedy. Consequently, as soon as vengeance is present, pleasure ensues, and so much the greater according as the sorrow was greater." Ibid., I-II 48, 1.
3. Ibid.

4. Louis Pojman, "Yes, the Death Penalty is Morally Permissible," in *Philosophy: The Quest for Truth*, edited by Louis Pojman (Belmont, CA: Wadsworth Publishing, 1996), 547.

5. *S. T.* I-II 108, 4.

6. Aquinas, *De Malo*, 12, 5. Cf. Aquinas, *Commentary on Saint Paul's Epistle to the Ephesians*, Chapter 4, Lecture 10.

7. In the process of becoming indignant we are first sorrowful, then immediately desire revenge, and finally imagine that whatever offends us is an insult. If the insult goes unpunished, we feel indignant.

8. *De Malo*, 12, 5.

9. Robert Solomon, *The Passions* (Notre Dame, IN: University of Notre Dame Press, 1983), 184.

10. *S. T.* I-II 22, 3.

11. Aquinas, *Commentary on the Nichomachean Ethics*, Book 4, Lecture 13.

12. Ibid.

13. *S. T.* I-II 46, 8.

14. According to Pierre Chantraine's *Dictionaire Etymologique de la Langue Grecque* (Paris: Editions Klincksieck, 1974), the origin of *menis* is unknown, although Chantraine does observe that the ancients commonly regarded the term to be derived from *menein*.

15. *S. T.*, II-II 158, 5.

16. *Commentary on the Nichomachean Ethics*, Book 4.

17. Ibid.

18. *S. T.* I-II 46, 8.

19. Ibid., II-II 158, 5, ad 2.

20. Ibid., II-II 158, 5.

21. *Commentary on the Nichomachean Ethics*, Book 4, Lecture 13, 346.

22. *S. T.* II-II 158, 2.

23. Ibid., II-II 108, 1.

24. *De Malo* 12, 1.

25. Solomon Schimmel comments, "The terms *vice* and *sin* are often interchanged in medieval writings, but they are not identical. Vices and virtues were the concepts and terms of the Greek and Roman philosophers; sins of the Hebrew Bible and New Testament. Vices are character traits. Sins are specific acts of commission or omission. Once Judaism and Christianity adopted the concepts of vice and virtue from the Greek and Roman moralists, vices were often called sins and the sins vices. The seven deadly 'sins' are also called the deadly 'vices,' which is more accurate. They are basic, perhaps universal human tendencies from which sins result." *The Seven Deadly Sins* (Oxford: Oxford University Press, 1997), 14.

26. *S. T.* I-II 24, 1.

27. Dr. Richard Sharpe, *The Cruel Deception* (Wellingborough, England: Thorsons Publishing Group), 271.

28. *De Malo*, 12, 1. Cf. *S. T.* II-II 158, 1 ad 2.

29. Ibid., 12, 2.

30. *S. T.* I-II 24, 3 ad 1.

31. Ibid. On the other hand, Aquinas observes that consequent emotions may also increase the malice of an act if used to serve a morally bad judgment. For instance, if I judge that animals may be treated cruelly, my emotion of anger toward animals increases the malice of my acts of cruelty toward them.

32. Ibid., I-II 59. 2 ad 3.

33. Thomas Aquinas, *On Truth* 26, 7. Cf. *De Malo* 12, 1 reply 4.

34. *S. T.* II-II 59, 2 ad 4.

35. *Decendum quod omnes causae irae reducuntur ad parvipensionem. S. T.* I-II 47, 2.

36. Neglect is a form of slighting; we take the trouble to remember things that are important to us. Again, it is a mark of slight regard for another if one does not hesitate to hurt him in bringing bad news. One who expresses glee in the midst of another's bad luck seems to be indifferent to his good fortune or bad. So, also, one who frustrates another's effort to accomplish something, without himself deriving any benefit, does not care a great deal about his friendship. Thus all of these provoke anger because they indicate contempt. Ibid., II-II 47, 2 ad 3. See John Giles Milhaven's detailed illustrations of different kinds of slights in *Good Anger* (Kansas City, MO: Sheed and Ward, 1989), 130–31.

37. *Ex omnibus autem bonis nostris aliquam excellentiam quaerimus. Et ideo quodcumque nocumentum nobis inferatur, inquantum excellentiae derogat, videtur ad parvipensionem pertinere. S. T.* I-II 47, 2.

38. Ibid., II-II 102, 1 ad 2.

39. Ibid., II-II 186, 7 ad 4.

40. Diana Fritz Cates, "Taking Women's Experience Seriously: Thomas Aquinas and Audre Lorde on Anger," in *Aquinas and Empowerment* by G. Simon Harak, S. J. (Washington, DC: Georgetown University Press, 1996), 64–65.

41. Ibid., 86 fn. 91. Cates quotes *S. T.* II-II 63, 3 in support of her contention.

42. Ibid., II-II 2 ad 4. Elsewhere Aquinas says, "Since the magnanimous man pursues great aims, he must strive chiefly for those which involve some excellence, and avoid those which involve defect. Now noble action, generosity, and the return of more than one receives are marks of excellence. He therefore applies himself eagerly to those acts, on the grounds of their excellence. . . . It is a defect to exaggerate the importance of certain external goods or evils to the extent of abandoning justice or some other virtue." *Quia magnanimus tendit ad magna, consequens est quod ad illa praecipue tendat quae important alquam excellentiam, et illa fugiat que pertinet ad defectum. Pertinet autem ad quamdam excellentiam quod aliqua benefaciat, et quod sit communicativus et plurium retributivus. Et ideo ad ista promptum se exhibet, inquantum habent rationem cujusdam excellentiae. . . . Ad defectam autem pertinet quod aliquis intantum magnipendat aliua exteriora bona vel mala, quod pro eis a justitia vel quaecumque virtute declinet. S. T.* II-II 129, 4 ad 2. Aquinas connects "excellence" and "virtue" in 78 different places in his various texts.

43. Ibid., I-II 47, 2.

44. Ibid., II-II 58, 2.

45. Ibid., I-II 47, 1 ad 3.

46. Ibid., I-II 28, 1

47. Ibid.

48. Aquinas, *Summa Contra Gentiles* IV, 19.

49. *S. T.* I-II 28, 4.

50. See Newkirk in this volume.

51. Milhaven, *Good Anger*, 138.

Direct Actions Speak Louder than Words

ROD CORONADO

From 1985 to 1995 I was a member of the Animal Liberation Front. In 1999 I completed a 57-month prison sentence for my partic-ipation in a 1992 raid on Michigan State University's Furbearer Research Facility, where 32 years of research intended to benefit the fur farm industry was destroyed by fire and two mink from an experimen-tal fur farm were rescued. As a former participant and continuing sup-porter of the ALF's campaign of nonviolent direct action, I would like to respond to accusations that the ALF is a violent terrorist organiza-tion.

Some critics within the animal rights movement argue that actions by the ALF set back our struggle rather than propel it forward. This claim is made despite the fact that after 19 years of direct action the ALF has rescued tens of thousands of animals that would have certain-ly being slaughtered and cost their abusers tens of millions of dollars through the destruction of property such as computers and lab equip-ment. In 1984 the ALF's raid on the University of Pennsylvania's Head Injury Laboratory began a series of events that led to its closure. In 1991 I led an ALF attack on Oregon State University's Experimental Fur Farm, a facility that had served the fur industry for over 60 years. In addition to setbacks to ongoing research, the facility, unable to recover from the incursion, was forced to close. In 1997 an ALF foray into the Cavel West horse slaughterhouse led to its permanent closure. Another clear example of the ALF's ability to reduce animal suffering is Operation Bite Back. Between 1995 and 1999, after over 50 raids on fur farms, illegal releases led to the closure of at least a dozen targeted mink and fox farms. In 2001 the ALF demonstrated the effectiveness of a campaign of economic sabotage when it targeted the Coulston Foundation, the single largest chimpanzee research laboratory in the country. Already in dire financial straits, the ALF's September arson attack caused $1 million in non-recoverable damages and helped push the already troubled lab one step closer to shutdown.

Even targeted vivisectors themselves—such as those at the University of Arizona, where a 1989 ALF raid torched two research laboratories and rescued 1,200 animals—admit to the effectiveness of direct action. Following the action, animal research at the university fell under greater scrutiny. Vivisectors reduced the number of animals sacrificed in redundant experiments and were forced to address charges of animal abuse claimed by the ALF. All of these achievements were accomplished without harm. And we're supposed to believe these concrete victories to be counterproductive to the goals of animal liberation?

In all struggles for liberation from oppression there are segments that will accept compromises that leave the oppressed behind. These are often the same people who condemn those who engage in sabotage and are unwilling to compromise for crumbs from the oppressor's table. The ALF is forced through the ineffectiveness of the means of change offered by our allies and the animal exploiters alike to engage in a campaign that subverts the law yet adheres to the ALF's principles of nonviolence. While some in the animal rights movement may still believe that passive resistance and Gandhian tactics will reverse the lack of morality among the world's most powerful industries and governments, the ALF abandons this naiveté. The escalation of institutional animal exploitation in this last century continues, as abusers are guided by profit, not moral imperatives. The laws of capitalism dictate that as long as there is money to be made through the continued destruction of the animal world and earth, industry and government will conspire to allow this, despite legitimate protests and with total disregard for the consequences for future generations.

The ALF thereby is forced to operate in the real world; it is not extremist but rather pragmatic. If the abusers and destroyers of the earth's future care only about money, and cannot be swayed by mass protests or legal pressure, then we must drive a stake through their economic heart. In a campaign of economic sabotage, pressure must be levied against the oppressor until continued exploitation and abuse is no longer profitable. For the billions of animals held captive still, this remains our greatest weapon. Property destruction and sabotage are bludgeons that do not target living sentient beings, but rather the very machinery and tools used to destroy their lives.

The ALF, as the underground army of the animal rights movement, has for years fought to end war, not perpetuate it. With great pain, we have looked into the eyes of our animal relations in the laboratories and fur farms. We are the few from our side who have seen firsthand the torture inflicted on beings who were once our friends and companions. We have been the ones who, while rescuing a few, have had to leave thousands more behind. Once you have witnessed the callousness of animal exploiters, all arguments rationalizing a less aggressive strategy in the hopes of far-off victory remain a betrayal of those we claim to love and represent. To those animals suffering today as we debate the many ways in which our movement helps them, surely we should be able to agree that immediate liberation and a reduction in suffering whenever possible is a good thing to support and even encourage.

Many critics argue that the ALF should replace illegal direct action with more "moderate" political means. Yet the fact remains, as evidenced by almost all human liberation struggles, that both strategies—methods that work inside and outside the system—not one in exclusion of the other, are capable of coexisting for the greater good. We need not eliminate any of the diverse methods that bring about victory for animals. No one tactic alone in our nonviolent arsenal is adequate, and no one strategy stands to suffer because of the existence of the other. Greater harm is done to our movement, and to the animals, when we resist the positive benefits that come from a harmony of all tactics in our common strategy towards animal liberation.

In questioning ALF strategies as "extreme" measures, we suggest that the animals the ALF saves are not valuable enough to warrant extra-legal means of alleviating their pain. Thus we demonstrate a unique form of speciesism. The ALF instead recognizes a worldview that sees a brother- and sisterhood with all life and in doing so answers the calls on our hearts to protect those we are honored to represent. When a moral people embrace the belief that all life is sacred and deserving of worth unto itself, the laws of society historically will contradict and criminalize the moral obligations and actions of such people. Bound not by the laws of society and capitalism, but by the laws of nature and morality, the ALF remains an easy target for those eager to assign the labels of "criminal" and "terrorist." When we as co-inhabitants of earth are against such odds, it becomes impossible to turn away from the guerrilla tactics that have brought about victory here and now for our nonhuman constituents.

The question the animal rights movement should ask itself is: What course of action would we justify and engage in if it was our own mothers, fathers, sisters, brothers and children in the torture chambers and not nameless, unfamiliar animals? And also: Is the ALF justifiable in its own moderate choice of tactics? Once we answer these questions honestly we might better appreciate that in over 19 years of operation in the US, the ALF has yet to cause physical injury or loss of life in a campaign that has achieved liberty for tens of thousands of the voiceless victims of humanity's war against the animal nations. Meanwhile, corporate, governmental, military and private animal abusers remain committed to their own code of real violence and terror, as evidenced by their contemptuous disregard for all other life on earth.

Still, the ALF is not only a freedom-fighting force for animals, but also a voice for the larger animal rights movement. Without the support of countless individuals who help find homes for rescued animals and finance the ALF's campaign, we would cease to exist. When the majority of those in the animal rights movement who provide such support deem ALF actions no longer necessary or counterproductive to the goals of animal liberation, our actions will end. This is the flaw in the thinking of the law enforcement agencies whose mandate it is to destroy us. No underground struggle can survive without aboveground support. It remains difficult if not impossible to believe that animals and our movement would be better off without the ALF. Without question, more animals are alive and living in peace today because of the ALF's campaign.

In fairness to those who accuse the ALF of terrorism, let us ask what constitutes violence, and whether defense against violence is ever justified. Does the decommissioning of weapons of mass destruction constitute the same level of violence as their use against innocent victims? The Nuremberg Trials accused those aware of Nazi atrocities with gross apathy and inaction. Will our generation one day be questioned as to why we did not take greater action to stop the violence that engulfs the world of animals on earth? Do we who are aware of the danger and consequences facing life on earth bear any of the moral responsibility for failing to prevent it, our only excuse being that to act differently would violate the laws of rich men and jeopardize our own freedom?

The animal rights movement has long explained our moral obligation to prevent the suffering of animalkind with words, while being quick to judge the ALF, who demonstrate that commitment with action. These actions may be illegal from the vantage point of an ecocidal and genocidal property system, but they most certainly are not immoral or unjustified according to the register of higher ethical norms. Adherence to the principles of nonviolence practiced by the ALF requires that our actions be less passive and more aggressive. ALF

tactics are applied when all other avenues of change have proven ineffective. Such a strategy is in accordance with Gandhi's principles of
satyagraha or truth-action, which never condemned the destruction of
property. In 1942 India's Independent Congress, of which Gandhi was
a founder, openly advocated acts of sabotage to British railways.
According to Gandhi himself and his biographer Yogesh Chadra, during World War II Gandhi thought of forming a national militia as well
as resorting to guerrilla warfare to combat Japanese aggression. "It is
better to fight than be afraid. It is better to indulge in violence than to
run away," responded Gandhi when questioned about his own participation in the Boer War and WWII.[1]

Gandhi's principles of nonviolence formed merely one strategy
employed by India's independence struggle, yet they are often cited as
a successful example of the power of nonviolence. Only someone unfamiliar with India's history would believe passive nonviolence to be
solely responsible for India's independence. Such arguments fail to recognize the value illegal direct action plays in a liberation struggle. They
also perpetuate the myth that as long as we adhere to our moral and
ethical principles, we will be rewarded. In doing so, proponents of passive nonviolence exercise a choice of tactics that is the product of privilege and only available to those in the First World. This privilege itself
is the product of the violence committed to create the so-called "liberties" the United States government promotes. The ALF was not created as a matter of choice, but of necessity. Only because of the lack of
a truly democratic society that reflects the public's support for humane
treatment of animals is the ALF forced to illegal means. In his autobiography, Nelson Mandela aptly states, "It is not the oppressed who
determine the means of resistance, but the oppressor."[2]

Our opponents should remain grateful that the ALF is committed
only to the destruction of property and rescue of prisoners and refrains
from directing physical violence toward them, however morally justifiable it might be when preventing a greater act of violence. Reflecting
Gandhi's own strategic understanding of the necessity of remaining
flexible in determining a movement's tactics, the ALF believes its
actions to be a contemporary incarnation of *satyagraha*, a response to
the ever-growing institutional violence in our dominant society. Only
when there is disregard for the issues raised through passive nonviolent
civil disobedience does aggressive nonviolent uncivil disobedience
become justified as it now is.

Another strategic mistake for which the ALF often is criticized is the
apparent disregard for the consequence of negative publicity that fol-

lows some ALF actions. Unlike those elements of the animal rights movement whose strategy is dependent on media publicity, the ALF's is determined by one thing alone: how to cause as much disruption as possible to systems of animal abuse and rescue as many of the prisoners as possible without the slightest risk of harm to life itself. ALF actions are most effective when greater attention is given to their impact on the abuser rather than the media those actions will generate.

The ALF believes today's mainstream media corporations to be an extension of the animal abuse industries they represent through advertising and ownership. If truth and morality were the driving forces behind mainstream journalism, then the violent actions of industry and government would be reported as the real terrorism that they so often are. Instead, the corporate media establishment maintains a general condemnation of illegal forms of resistance in the hopes that the public will also label such acts terrorism. Protecting the economic interests of their advertisers and owners helps maintain the status quo, in which animals and the earth are private property, not entities unto themselves. The formulation of our movement's methods of resistance should not be determined by any perception the public or media has of the ALF, but rather by the ability to deliver concrete results that bring us closer to animal liberation. Pursuing a strategy that hopes to appeal to the morality of those who rarely demonstrate any is noble, but it should not be at the expense of tactics that for years have brought victory for animals.

The ALF has never endorsed or participated in physical violence and never will. Our 19-year record of no injuries or deaths is no coincidence. It is the product of a determined nonviolent underground movement sincerely committed to alleviating physical violence—not rationalizing it, as our opponents regularly do. The ALF has always been grounded in such a reverence and respect for life that in the course of every ALF action that I participated in, our members were ready to sacrifice their own freedom and even life in the hopes of protecting the lives and liberty of those animal nations we represent.

Far from compromising the principles of nonviolence, the ALF's actions have and always will be those of a highly moral and disciplined group of compassionate individuals whose efforts would be hypocritical if they ever sanctioned physical violence as our opposition does. Those in industry and government can rest assured that in the coming years the ALF will continue to exist to provide an avenue of freedom for those innocent victims the animal rights movement is unable to rescue legally. The ALF brings hope when others feel hopeless. For the peaceful warriors of the ALF, nonviolent direct action to save lives remains not a choice, but the obligation of every enlightened human being.

Notes

1. Gandhi, Mohandas K. *An Autobiography: The Story of My Experiments with Truth* (Boston: Beacon Press, 1957).
2. Mandela, Nelson. *Long Walk To Freedom: The Autobiography of Nelson Mandela* (Boston: Little, Brown and Company, 1994).

Touch the Earth

Lawrence Sampson

The Animal Liberation Front should be commended. After all, it's easier to think than to act. It's more convenient to have a belief than to act on that belief. It's simpler to talk about what is right than to act righteously. And in this day and age, where any sort of non-mainstream, secular, or divergent thought or ideology gets you branded a "terrorist," it is a courageous thing indeed to take action toward the implementation of what a person thinks is right or just. It is perhaps the saddest statement on the mindset of society that acting on your beliefs is so unusual, indeed so rare, that it can be easily demonized. Questioning the status quo is as close to becoming illegal in America as it has ever been. In the annals of human experience, every despotic government that implemented this sort of stifling of the conscience has eventually met with revolution. It is the natural progression of our humanity.

America's corporate elite have become legal criminals. Our courts have declared corporations as having all the rights of a human being, without any of the human accountability we all accept as necessary to maintain a society worth living in. Their agendas, their profit projections, their needs in relation to profit, too often translate into the laws that govern the do's and don'ts we are bound to live by. Too often, however, human laws enacted to benefit the corporate rapist and polluter conflict with another set of laws—the laws that we must live by, sooner or later, no matter what spreadsheets and greed prompt some of us to do. These are the laws of nature. Natural laws, sooner or later, always govern the actions of those who live on Earth; ultimately, we have little choice as to whether to live by these laws. And what are we, the human beings, who must live by natural laws first, and societal laws second, to do when these two are diametrically opposed? Do we complain, or protest? Do we contact our representative leaders, and demand changes within the legal confines provided us? Yes, we do all of these, and more. It goes without saying, however, that corporate millions tilt the scale against the voices of balanced and sustainable living. A politician doesn't have a very long shelf life if he or she doesn't kowtow to the corporate mob. Perhaps this is the greatest weakness of democracy—so much so that the market economics that have become the underpinnings of democracy may very well be its undoing.

It is when morality rages against the machine of corporate-induced illegalities that the new "terrorist" is born. When the common voice is not heard, when right becomes wrong in a world contaminated by the waste of corporate excess, the humanist, the passionate lover of life, becomes a criminal. We currently exist in such an environment. It is in this morass that the ALF and other organizations engage in illegal, but humanely defensible, campaigns.

I am not a member of the ALF. I am not a vegetarian. I am a human being, indigenous to the Western Hemisphere. As such I find myself agreeing with and even admiring the ALF's principles, motivations, and courage, while having a different view on the world as a whole, and how to live as a part of it. It is in our traditional outlook that these differences arise.

When people think of Indians, they think of people who live "with nature." But this is a poetic notion that for most does not encompass an understanding of what living with nature truly means. It means living within an ecosystem. It means living in rhythms and cycles. We believe in being a part of our surroundings, not superior to them, and not merely an observer of them. Being an observer is akin to attending a zoo. Admiring nature and wildlife from a sterile distance keeps you separate from nature and from the world. It is in this separation from the rest of the world's creatures, and therefore many of the laws of nature, that problems arise. Separation, no matter how well intentioned, creates walls of ignorance, and a lack of understanding that inevitably leads to conflict.

I believe it is when society distances itself from nature that it begins to lose its own sense of a place in the world. When one no longer sees the self as an equal and integral part, but as superior and separate, then dysfunction inevitably results. Separation from the earth does not give rise to a spiritual resolve to protect that earth, as one protects one's home. Separation does not instill in one a sense that sustainable life, for the welfare of seven generations to come, is a must. When the earth ceases to be seen as a living entity and instead becomes something to be profited from, the road to hell is paved. Deforesting becomes easier.

Strip mining becomes easier. Polluting becomes easier. It becomes easier to abandon faith in a natural order of things in favor of faith in the human ability to contain damage through technology. The rape of the earth, also known as "progress" and "development," has long been rationalized by the claim that Indian people did nothing to or with the land we lived on, and therefore we were "wasting" it. These terms alone, when studied closely, illuminate the differences in our way of life.

When killing a buffalo, an elk, or a deer, the Indian apologizes to the animal for having to do so, and thanks the animal for its sacrifice. The Indian understands that our lives are intertwined, neither superior to the other. Our coexistence is a balance that must be maintained. Prayer is involved in every aspect of the kill. And to show our thanks for the life-giving sacrifice, the Indian uses all parts of the animal. Nothing is wasted.

Indigenous people do not sit back and admire their surroundings, but there is a love and sense of admiration for the powers of nature. This is expressed time and time again in our spirituality, which is part and parcel of our daily life. There is nothing more exemplary of our love of life than our participation in life, and death, in balance. This is what many non-indigenous people do not understand. The sense of separation that fostered the extinction and endangerment of many animals and of the earth itself still causes misunderstanding of our methods and motivations of preservation to this day. Case in point: the recent tension surrounding the Makah nation and their assertion of their sovereign and natural right to hunt whales. To the Makah, the whale represents sustenance. The whale represents tradition. The whale represents an understanding of one's place in the world. Yet the Makah voluntarily suspended their hunts over 70 years ago, due to non-indigenous hunting practices, which endangered the species.

Without the whale, the Makah were lost as Indigenous people. Their stories and teachings revolve around the whale. When the numbers of the whales rebounded, the Makah resumed their hunting, which was protected by treaty agreements. The Makah suspended whale hunting in order to save the whale, and they resumed hunting in order to save the Makah. Yet these two goals do not conflict with one another. The belief in being a part of an ecosystem is exemplified in both the suspension and the resumption of the hunts. Yet many "environmental" and "animal rights" groups opposed the Makah hunts, to the point of threatening the Makah people and advocating violence against them.

We have seen a similar situation with the last wild buffalo herd in North America, which lives on and near Yellowstone National Park. While the buffalo are protected, to a degree, this protection was not given as an effort to protect an ecosystem, of which the bison are a very integral part. It was done so that people could observe them. Once people lived with the buffalo, practicing a sustenance lifestyle. But what happens when a buffalo's existence conflicts with commerce? Take a look at Montana, where the buffalo are massacred whenever they roam off of parkland to forage for food. The irony is, they are still on public land, which is supposed to be our land, citizens' land. But in reality, it is the ranching industry's land. Ranchers are the driving force behind the murder of these magnificent, sacred, life-giving animals.

Time and time again, the separation of "society" and "nature" has led to dysfunction. It happens time and again. It is only when humans not only intellectualize what it means to live with nature, but incorporate this into a lifestyle, that we live as the creator intended us to. This is the only long-term way to live. Anything else is shortsighted, self-serving, and results in entropy. As Chief Seattle said, "This is the end of living, and the beginning of survival." Non-indigenous people need to learn to understand our outlook, in order to have a place truly worth living in. Otherwise, all that will be accomplished, at best, is the division of our world into two: a greed- and technology-driven world that dominates the other, which exists only in small refuges where some sense of wildlife has been preserved so that it may be observed, as in a museum. This is only marginally better than a world where everything is sacrificed for profit, and nothing natural is respected. And the end result is the same: human beings lost, with no place in the world, where all is lost.

Take No Prisoners

WESTERN WILDLIFE UNIT

This article has been reprinted from the "Memories of Freedom" booklet.[1]

Sitting around the campfire one night, some of us warriors of the Animal Liberation Front decided it was time we said a few words about our deeds, as continually we are labeled by those outside of our circle as everything except what we really are. Since few people ever see our communiqués except the corporate-controlled media, few would understand that our concerns go way beyond animal abuse. In our view from the shore, we see animal abuse as just one symptom of a much larger disease complex that also brings us racism, sexism, militarism, environmental destruction, alcoholism, drug abuse, domestic violence, male domination and a downright bad attitude toward our fellow creation, just to name a few. What has caused us to be plagued with these diseases when the world we are given could be such a beautiful place? That's not for us to discuss. We're warriors, not philosophers. Whatever it is, we see that disease slowly creeping into our various struggles and it makes us want to cry. Rumors, back-biting, inflated egos, trying to get laid, trying to raise funds by appearing "respectable"—we've all seen it and it's causing our movement to self-destruct, just as we begin to become the catalyst for real change. Now, we're far from perfect ourselves; we have made our mistakes, hurt each other; but from where we stand we are far from giving up. We don't want to see others make the same mistakes we have made, hence this 'zine.

This is the story of a handful of people who cared enough to risk their lives and freedom for what they believe: for Earth and for the release of the prisoners of the war on Nature. It hasn't been without its costs. Though we are all here tonight, one of us is sitting in an 11' x 7' cell in a federal prison for the next four years. He isn't the first and he sure as hell won't be the last. In this story there are many chapters. We are but one. The rest is up to you. We are here to tell you about our moments of victory and defeat. Our moments of tremendous joy at being alive on this beautiful planet Earth as we fought proudly in her defense, and our moments of great despair when the whole world seemed against us. Mostly this 'zine is about a struggle that began before our great-grandparents were alive. It's about a spirit. The spirit of freedom and the spirit of the wild that refuses to be tamed. It's about a struggle that began long before the term "animal rights" was ever spoken. When Earth First! wasn't a slogan, but a way of life . . . and death. It's about remembering the past and remembering that those of us who choose to represent the Earth Mother and her Animal Nations now inherit a responsibility that others have been killed fulfilling and which we must put before anything else in our lives, including our own freedom if necessary. It's about power. Not man-made power, but the power that only the spirit of Earth can give us. The power we receive when we awaken to the sounds of the coyote's song and the howling wind through the last ancient old-growth trees. Power that no man can give us and power that no man can take away. Power that can lift us above our enemies to become the type of warriors we only hear about in myths and legends. Power that is just waiting for us to rediscover and unleash it. It is about breaking the chains wrapped around us beginning on that first day of school, the first day of work. Chains that slowly wrap around us until we are ready to be considered responsible adults, but because of those chains we have forgotten how to move, how to be free, how to live in harmony with all of life, with the four-leggeds, the winged ones and all the animal people as our brothers and sisters.

Let's face it—many of us are afraid. Afraid of being wrong. Afraid of being alone. Afraid of spending years in prison. Afraid of being shot or incinerated, like 60 adults and 24 children in Waco, Texas at the bloody hands of the US government. Fear is our enemy's greatest weapon, because, unlike having to place a police officer in every home, it is already there, waiting to be unleashed with carefully orchestrated images on corporate-controlled TV and newspapers. Prison cells with their iron doors slamming shut, police beatings by baton-wielding Nazis, "terrorists" being led away in orange suits and chains, images that keep our fear at being different alive and strong.

The Plains Indians have a saying they would yell going into battle, "Hoka Hey!"—It is a good day to die! To us, that means they had overcome that most common of fears, the fear of death. Unleashed from their fear of death, they would charge forward into battle against people who were very much afraid to die, and as a result those warriors won the only victory in history in which an unconditional surrender was signed by the US government: Red Cloud's War of the 1860s. Much like those of us who would rather die than live in a world without wilderness and animals, those brave warriors overcame their fears of imprisonment and death because they knew the power of the earth was very real. Not just a belief, but a reality. Much more real than anything the US government had to offer. A reality where all animals were messengers and every mountain a cathedral.

The stories we read about those tribes and their relationship with the earth, animals and their spirits were not myth or folklore; they were and are real. Real enough to drive humans to sacrifice all in their world for the hope that future generations might share in that same power that lies within the spirit of every living being and flows through every wild creation. For the hope that you, the children of Earth, might awake to the screams of our tortured earth and her Animal People. It is over a hundred years since the true warriors of the Earth gave their lives on this continent for the Earth Spirits and Animal People. Through the years, often the spirits of resistance have arisen, always to be beaten back by prisons and bullets, lies and deceit. Now it is your turn. Whether you realize it or not, the spirits of those fallen warriors are watching. Watching to see if you will rediscover the power that the Animal People and their wilderness homes can give us. The power that breaks our chains and awakens our spirit to the realization that you represent possibly the last hope for this planet we all call home.

There are those who can see the horrors of vivisection and fur farming, the oil-covered shorelines and the clearcut mountainsides, and plod forward through the muck of lobbying, petitioning, letter writing, politicking and protesting. This 'zine is not for them. This 'zine is for every young man and woman who has cried for the blood of the earth, stood in shock, open-mouthed at the callousness and cruelty some can inflict on the most peaceful of our fellow creations, the Animal People. For all who have ever felt helpless against an enemy a thousand times larger than themselves. For those who cannot live with the pain of knowing that every morning the laboratory lights are turned on, the chainsaws are oiled and sharpened, the gas chambers are wheeled out to the pelting barns, and the slaughter is continuing—this is for you, so that you may never feel alone again, so that you may see that though we may never achieve total victory in our lifetimes, sometimes victory and freedom is ours simply by fighting, by breaking our own chains before we can break the chains of others.

For you we speak out and tell the story of what a handful of warriors can do, what a handful of warriors must do. A handful of people just like you.

Notes

1. cala-online.org/Academic/mof_us2.html

Perception

There comes a time when a moral man can't obey a law which his conscience tells him is unjust. It is important to see that there are times when a manmade law is out of harmony with the moral law of the universe. There is nothing that expressed massive civil disobedience any more than the Boston Tea Party, and yet we give this to our young people and our students as a part of the great tradition of our nation. So I think we are in good company when we break unjust laws, and I think those who are willing to do it and accept the penalty are those who are part of the saving of the nation.—Rev. Dr. Martin Luther King, Jr.

It's a matter of taking the side of the weak against the strong, something that the best people have always done.—Harriet Beecher Stowe

The whole history of the progress of human liberty shows that all concessions yet made to her august claims, have been born of earnest struggle. The conflict has been exciting, agitating, all-absorbing, and for the time being, putting all other tumults to silence. It must do this or it does nothing. If there is no struggle there is no progress. Those who profess to favor freedom and yet depreciate agitation, are men who want crops without plowing up the ground, they want rain without thunder and lightening. They want the ocean without the awful roar of its many waters.—Frederick Douglass

Understanding the ALF: From Critical Analysis to Critical Pedagogy

Anthony J. Nocella II

Many in the animal liberation movement are frustrated at the lack of diverse public support for the ALF. The most common image of the group's advocates may be that of the "punk rocker"—chain wallet, baggy pants, a black shirt, and colored spiked hair—or other rebellious types. Yet no group or individual that endorses the ALF has presented the public with a credible alternative image. This, however, is beginning to change as the ALF gains a more professional look, better forums of communication, and, indeed, serious academic support as a bona fide liberation movement. *No Compromise*, a militant above-ground grassroots magazine defending animal liberation, recently has revamped itself from an inky newspaper into a professionally produced magazine. *Bite Back* has emerged as another appealing magazine for supporting animal liberation, and *Arkangel* magazine, founded by Ronnie Lee (the originator of the Animal Liberation Front), is a well-designed international magazine on militant underground and above-ground animal liberation. In 2001 the Center on Animal Liberation Affairs (CALA) opened the door for serious discourse on the ALF in the academic community.[1] With new and improved magazines, better reporting and analysis, and an academic "think tank," dialogue around and support for the ALF expands and diversifies.

Saul D. Alinsky, author of *Rules for Radicals*, emphasizes that a diverse support network for a radical cause is important because power lies in diversity and numbers.[2] It is for this reason that the Student Nonviolent Coordinating Committee (SNCC), for example, invited high-school and college students to join their "Freedom Summer" organizing drive to advance voting registration and civil rights in the American South. It is the reason Subcommandante Marcos has on numerous occasions allowed radical academics such as Dr. Peter

McLaren to conduct field research on the Zapatistas in Chiapas, Mexico, so that a sympathetic writer could deepen understanding of their movement and help legitimate it through substantive historical, political, and philosophical analysis. And, to complement the external contextualizing by academics, socio-political movements have internal mechanisms to develop legitimacy and foundation, as when charismatic leaders such as Malcolm X or Dr. Martin Luther King Jr. eloquently and incisively dissect the logic of poverty and racism in their writings and speeches. While there is a need for eloquence and motivational speaking, there also is a need for leaders and organization members to be able to articulate a coherent strategy for their movement.

Solidarity and interaction with sympathetic academics helps to give political movements a more diverse base and increased legitimacy through what many may view as respectable viewpoints and voices. After an articulate and sound theoretical and political foundation is developed, it needs to be promoted and popularized by the movement. At that point other important figures should be targeted for support, such as musicians (e.g., Rage Against the Machine in solidarity with the Zapatistas), politicians (e.g., President Bill Clinton meeting with Gerry Adams of Sinn Fein), and religious affiliation (e.g., Subcommandante Marcos's popular story about Votán Zapata, a mythological figure he created to develop a spiritual connection with the Mexican working-class on behalf of revolution). A diverse and sympathetic network increases the possibility of popularizing a movement and thereby diversifies and strengthens it.

But, before even the development of relations to the academic community is possible, there needs to be set in place a method that academics and others can use to understand a complex political movement. To understand a native culture foreign to her, anthropologist Margaret Mead took an ethnological approach, living among the people, learning its language and customs, and adopt them as her own. Along the same lines, Brazilian professor and educator Paulo Freire believed that to comprehend a particular people or culture, one must submerge oneself in their everyday activity, culture, and rituals. The researcher, argued Mead and Freire, needs to develop the ability to see life not from a detached, external perspective, but through the lens of the group or culture being studied. It is this particular interpretative approach that I ask all to adopt when trying to understand the ALF, or any other radical or oppositional group challenging standard ethics or ways of thinking.[3]

Unfortunately, many people believe that the ALF is a violent organization that grew out of anger and hate. In order to understand the ALF, one must sidestep this and other stereotypes, generalizations, and preconceived mindsets that for the most part have been developed and re-enforced by mass media, capitalist ideologues, and legal authorities. Through a more open and informed approach, one will find that the ALF grew out of love for all life, a perspective strongly supported by the "ALF Guidelines," which state that it is crucial ". . .to take all necessary precautions against harming any animal, human and nonhuman."[4] The misconception that the ALF is a "violent" group can be avoided by understanding the group's origins and the reasons and motivations for their actions. In this essay, I suggest a process the public can use to better understand the ALF and their actions.

In order to understand an issue, we can approach it from "outside the box," i.e., from a detached standpoint (critical analysis), or from "inside the box," i.e., from a participatory standpoint (critical pedagogy). While critical pedagogy strives to experience issues through empathy or by living among the subjects studied, critical analysis strives to dissect an issue or object, much like a scientist categorizing, labeling, and defining living processes, thereby removing himself or herself from the object of study or field of experience.

Whereas critical analysis maintains the distance of "objectivity," critical pedagogy breaks down the distinction between subject and object. In the case of anthropology, for instance, critical pedagogy is willing to live among indigenous people in order to acquire knowledge and help preserve their culture. Critical pedagogy argues that the theorist is not dominant over or separate from an issue or subject, but rather strives to understand it by being part of it. A perfect example would be Jane Goodall, whose groundbreaking research was attained only by living among—and often acting like—the chimpanzees in Gombe, Tanzania. Her work revolutionized our understanding of our closest ancestors. A juxtaposition of both of the contrasting approaches I have described can be seen in the film *Instinct*. Anthony Hopkins plays Dr. Ethan Powell, an anthropologist engaged in becoming part of a gorilla "family." He has a run-in with the law and is imprisoned. Dr. Powell explains to psychiatrist Dr. Theo Caulder (Cuba Gooding Jr.), why Caulder cannot understand him. It is the same reason why Powell for some time could not understand the apes—he did not dissolve the subject-object dichotomy to live among the apes and gain true insight phenomenologically.

Because understanding cannot always be achieved through the rigid barrier of "objectivity," a critical pedagogy approach is often useful. In

Pedagogy of the Oppressed[5], Paulo Freire demonstrates the importance of striving for an intimate educational experience in the classroom, in Freire's case through a dissolution of formal boundaries between "teacher" and "student," requiring a give-and-take relationship between them. In critical pedagogy, the institutional roles are loosened or dissolved and replaced by the "syllabus of experience." "Critical pedagogy," writes social scientist Margaret Ledwith, "is that form of education which emerges from critical compassion; a transcendence of the emotional and the intellectual; the heart and mind learn to see and know in new ways."[6]

To examine something critically, one must become aware of one's own interpretative position. This will include being aware of one's response to such aspects of the research as economic class, race, gender, physical or mental characteristics, culture, and religion. The more one is aware of one's own position on an issue, the more easily one can see through a variety of lenses and perspectives. One cannot properly understand any subject when one begins an examination from a highly biased position. In addition, it is not enough to physically experience the "subject"; it also is important to have one's mind and spirit involved in the experience. bell hooks notes that Vietnamese Buddhist monk Thich Nhat Hanh approaches this kind of pedagogy by emphasizing the union of mind, body, and spirit.[7] An infiltrator of the ALF might be in a cell for a number of years and feel that he or she understands the ALF, but the essence of critical pedagogy is what Hanh explains as the necessity of the union of the mind, body, and soul, which all have to be engaged in the experience of understanding. One can begin to understand and appreciate ALF actions either through an intellectual understanding of justice, an emotional understanding of animals' suffering, or a spiritual understanding of the unity of all life. When all of these powers are engaged, critical pedagogy becomes possible.

Dr. Martin Luther King Jr. suggested that the crucial element for activism is to engage in one's community in a loving manner.[8] This is much like critical pedagogy. King talked about three kinds of love: eros, "a sort of aesthetic or romantic love"; philia, "affection between friends"; and agape, an "understanding, redeeming goodwill for all . . . [an] overflowing love which is purely spontaneous, unmotivated, groundless and creative . . . the love of God operating in the human heart." He stated, "Agape does not begin by discriminating between worthy and unworthy people. . . . It begins by loving others for their sakes." It "makes no distinction between a friend and enemy; it is directed toward both. . . . Agape is love seeking to preserve and create community."⁹ Dr. King believed that agape could be expressed as involving justice for all. The key to understanding the motivations of the ALF lies in the view that "justice for all" applies to all nonhuman and human animals.

Paulo Freire seems to suggest that critical pedagogy leads to the researcher's own liberation through an experiential form of education that strives for enlightenment or what Gandhi might refer to as the state of seeking the truth. Gandhi believes that the search for truth is the ideal purpose of life. He explains that the struggle to free India was in fact the search for truth on a mass level—and suggests that it is only possible to be in a state of truth if one is willing to give up one's own freedom to stand up to an unjust act or law, or to save or free another being. Such people as St. Francis of Assisi, Henry David Thoreau, and Martin Luther King Jr. would also favor this perspective. Dr. King stated it best: "I became convinced that non-cooperation with evil is as much a moral obligation as is cooperation with good." When the oppressed animals—to whom the ALF member is connected in a holistic and emotional manner—are freed, then part of the body and spirit of the ALF member is freed as well. For example, after a liberation by an ALF member or cell, not only do the animals experience freedom, but the ALF member experiences emancipation—*from* fear, alienation, and perhaps guilt (at not doing enough), and *for* spiritual development. That is why it is common for a member of the ALF to cry with happiness after liberating an animal. The liberated animals and the ALF member all achieve a piece of the truth of wholeness and union.

The essence of performing an act in the name of the ALF is that love must be present in one's heart. This love allows one to act with respect for all life (even those who exploit animals) and to use one's intellect to its fullest potential. Have acts been committed in the name of the ALF by people in a negative or hostile state? Yes. Should activists in the wrong frame of mind be questioned by animal liberation and rights advocates? Yes. How would one prevent such acts? One should never let go of the true meaning of the ALF, which is to respect all life (the fundamental principle of the animal rights movement as a whole), to the extent that one feels oppressed due to another's oppression. While many say that activists should use their anger and hate toward the enemy, I say it is better to emulate individuals like Jesus, Gandhi, Cesar Chavez or other great peacemakers, and redirect anger and hatred into a state of love.

But one should never confuse nonviolence with weakness. King and Gandhi, though promoters of nonviolence, did not favor cowardice or walking away from conflict. The ALF acts with strength and daring, yet stops at violence, because it acts from love. Its actions are revolutionary and sometimes "extreme" in resorting to property destruction and breaking the law, but to the right-thinking person these acts should pale in comparison to the truly extreme actions that involve not damaging things but injuring and taking life and profiting from killing and death—the routine actions of animal exploitation industries such as vivisection laboratories, zoos, circuses, factory farms, and slaughterhouses. It is only when all people understand that love will create love, and hate will only create hate, that all will be liberated. As the Quakers, Martin Luther King, Jr., Mohandas Gandhi, and the ALF believe, love will light the path to liberation.

Thus, if one wants to understand the ALF, one must transcend the false rhetoric of "terrorism" and approach the real purpose of its struggle—animal liberation—through the method of critical pedagogy. One can thereby strive to understand the liberators' motivations as rooted in a concern for the suffering of nonhuman animals and for peace. For when you engage in understanding the ALF, you will understand the need for the liberation of all life.

Notes

1. See "The History and Philosophy of the Center on Animal Liberation Affairs" *Journal of Animal Liberation Affairs* 1 (2001), www.cala-online.org/Journal/journal_articles.html#8.
2. Saul Alinsky, *Rules for Radicals* (New York: Vintage Books, 1971).
3. Peter McLaren, *Che Guevara, Paulo Freire, and the Pedagogy of Revolution* (Lanham, MD: Rowman & Littlefield, 2000).
4. See the ALF Primer, www.animalliberation.net.
5. Paulo Freire, *Pedagogy of the Oppressed* (New York: Continuum, 1997).
6. M. Ledwith, "Community work as critical pedagogy: re-envisioning Freire and Gramsci," *Community Development Journal* 36 (3), July 2001, 171–182.
7. bell hooks, *Teaching to transgress: Education as the practice of freedom* (New York: Routledge, 1994).
8. "Dialogue cannot exist, however, in the absence of a profound love for the world and for people. The naming of the world, which is an act of creation and re-creation, is not possible if it is not infused with love. Love is at the same time the foundation of dialogue and dialogue itself. It is thus necessarily the task of responsible Subjects and cannot exist in a relation of domination. Domination reveals the pathology of love: sadism in the dominator and masochism in the dominated. Because love is an act of courage, not of fear, love is commitment to others. No matter where the oppressed are found, the act of love is commitment to their cause—the cause of liberation. And this commitment, because it is loving, is dialogical. As an act of bravery, love cannot be sentimental; as an act of freedom, it must not serve as a pretext for manipulation. It must generate other acts of freedom; otherwise, it is not love.

Only by abolishing the situation of oppression it is possible to restore the love which that situation made impossible. If I do not love the world—if I do not love life—if I do not love people—I cannot enter into dialogue" (Freire, *Pedagogy of the Oppressed*, 70–71).

9. Martin Luther King, Jr. "Pilgrimage to Nonviolence," in *Stride Toward Freedom: The Montgomery Story* (New York: Harper & Row, 1958).

Open Rescues: Putting a Face on the Rescuers and on the Rescued

Karen Davis, PhD

Using darkness as a cover and compassion as their guide, five members of Mercy for Animals (MFA) covertly entered sheds at Ohio's two largest egg producers . . . following criteria for a recently documented technique known as open rescue.
—Rachelle Detweiler, "Missions of Mercy," *The Animals' Agenda*[1]

When I first started writing this essay I thought I would discuss the ALF practice of concealment versus disclosure of personal identity as a strategy for achieving animal liberation through appeals to public perception and public conscience. But as I sifted through my files looking at the faces of animal liberators both masked and unmasked, as well as at undercover rescue scenes in both video format and verbal evocation, I decided that, important as the mask question may be from the standpoint of public perception, of equal and perhaps more fundamental importance is that of the rescuers' overall body language and the expression of their hands in a videotaped rescue intended for general audiences. When it comes to faces, it seems that the most important ones to be shown in a rescue operation taped for public viewing are the faces of the animals themselves. But those faces and the suffering they express have become increasingly hidden and disguised.

The "Disappearance" of Animals in Western Culture

Attention to the plight of animals raised for food is still relatively new in the United States. In 1987, when the first ALF action at the Beltsville (Maryland) Agricultural Research Center was conceived and carried out, even ALF activists who used the term "animal rights," according to Ingrid Newkirk in *Free the Animals*, "had not yet incorporated the systematized abuse of 'farm animals' into their agendas, couldn't 'see' an attack on the farm industry at all."² One reason they couldn't envision such an attack was that they didn't yet "see" the animals entombed within the industry. In his essay "Why Look at Animals?" John Berger discusses the disappearance of nonhuman animals into institutionalized anonymity in Western society, a process that he says began in the nineteenth century and was completed in the twentieth century as an enterprise of corporate capitalism.³ Berger's observations about animals in zoos, which to him symbolizes what our culture has done to animals as part of our overall rupture of the natural world, are equally applicable to factory-farmed animals. By extension, he includes them in his analysis of the cultural marginalization and disappearance of animal life, with the difference that nobody is expected even to pretend to look even at a factory-farmed animal, or to remember that factory-farmed animals were ever "wild" and free, and could be again. "The space which modern, institutionalized animals inhabit," Berger states in speaking of zoos, "is artificial":

> In some cages the light is equally artificial. In all cases the environment is illusory. Nothing surrounds them except their own lethargy or hyperactivity. They have nothing to act upon—except, briefly, supplied food and—very occasionally—a supplied mate. (Hence their perennial actions become marginal actions without an object.) Lastly, their dependence and isolation have so conditioned their responses that they treat any event which takes place around them—usually it is in front of them, where the public is—as marginal. (Hence their assumption of an otherwise exclusively human attitude—indifference.) . . . At the most, the animal's gaze flickers and passes on. They look sideways. They look blindly beyond. They scan mechanically. They have been immunized to encounter, because nothing can any more occupy a *central* place in their attention.⁴

This condition—of blind, and blinding, encounters between a potential human audience and the animals involved in a rescue operation—is what the ALF and open rescue teams, insofar as their purpose is winning public sympathy, have to overcome, because as Berger says about animals at the zoo, they "disappoint" the public, especially the children—"Where is he? Why doesn't he move? Is he dead?" As for the adults, "One is so accustomed to this that one scarcely notices it any more."[5]

The human onlookers adjust. After all, it isn't their own fate they are seeing, even if, in some essential way, that's what they're looking at. They go to the zoo almost in the same way that they go out to eat—to entertain themselves and their children, like a trip to Disneyland, which succeeds where zoos fail, because, like hamburgers and chicken nuggets, "animated" creatures are more prized by our culture than living animals are. As for the animals, they are imprisoned in an impoverished world imposed on them which their psyches did not emanate and which they do not understand. Factory-farmed animals are imprisoned in total confinement buildings within global systems of confinement, and thus they are separated from the natural world in which they evolved, including their family life. They are imprisoned in alien bodies manipulated for food traits alone, bodies that in many cases have been surgically mutilated as well, creating a disfigured appearance—they are debeaked, detoed, dehorned, ear-cropped, tail-docked, and so on. Factory-farmed animals are imprisoned in a belittling concept of who they are.[6] Outside the animal rights community, and the intimate confines of their own lives, these animals are unreal to almost everyone. They are not only prisoners but, in a real sense, they are the living dead. The entire life of these animals is a series of overlapping burials.[7]

Factory-farmed animals go from being in wombs and eggs in factory hatcheries and breeding facilities to being locked up (until they go to slaughter, unless they die first) in CAFOs—Concentrated Animal Feeding Operations. They are thus buried in a rhetoric of exploitation equivalent to the layers of material coverup in which their "silent" suffering goes on. The purpose of their existence is to be buried in the gastrointestinal tract of a human being. In the United States, hens deemed no longer fit for commercial egg production are literally buried alive in landfills after being entombed for a year or more in metal cages inside the walls of windowless buildings.[8] According to Australian activist Patty Mark, when the manure pits are bulldozed at the end of a laying cycle, "any live and/or debilitated hens still stuck in the manure are simply scooped up with the waste and buried alive on the trucks."[9]

The Role of the ALF

The ALF seeks to expose our society's enormous cruelty to nonhuman animals. The ALF is set up to rescue individual animals from specific situations of abuse, with a view to ending all of the abuse, and to wreak economic havoc on animal exploiters with the goal of making it hard, and ultimately impossible, for the exploiters to continue doing business. The ALF also supports property damage on moral grounds: "[W]hen certain buildings, tools and other property are being used to commit violence," ALF spokesperson David Barbarash explains, "the ALF believes that the destruction of property is justified."[10] In considering these goals I am reminded of what Aristotle said in the *Poetics* about the goals of tragic drama with respect to audience response. He said that tragic drama should arouse pity and fear in the audience: pity and compassion for the victims, fear and horror directed at the causes of the victims' suffering. Similarly, the ALF seeks to arouse pity and compassion for the animal victims (the audience in this case is the general public, including the news media and the exploiters themselves), and to instill fear of economic destruction—loss of livelihood, funding, business, and credibility—in those who profit from institutionalized animal abuse. "[I]n the end, make sure it's the animal abusers who really pay," says the ALF.[11]

Since the public at large is the ultimate cause of all of the animal abuse being exposed, in laboratories, on factory farms and elsewhere, it is morally and strategically appropriate, necessary in fact, to instill a "fear of oneself" in all audiences for having passively or actively contributed to the suffering and abuse taking place behind the scenes. All of us, in our conscience at least, should have to "really pay" more than a mere token of regret. In the brief discussion that follows, I shall concentrate only on the "pity" aspect of what many of us regard as the greatest tragedy on earth—our species' smug and evil treatment of the other animals who share this planet, including their homes and families—and on how to get audiences to identify compassionately with the animal victims and their rescuers. My illustrations are drawn mainly from recent battery-hen farm investigations, in which all of those involved were, in one way or another, "unmasked."[12]

United Poultry Concerns Forum On Direct Action for Animals

At a small conference on direct action in 1999, Australian activist Patty Mark introduced many US activists to the concept of open rescues. Most participants in the conference were accustomed to the "traditional" notion that people who rescue animals ought to act clandestinely so they can avoid detection and arrest and continue to free as many animals as possible. So when confronted with the idea that people can freely admit to

rescuing animals, many—if not most—of the conference participants seemed somewhat skeptical.—Paul Shapiro, "The US
Open," *The Animals' Agenda*[13]

On June 26–27, 1999 United Poultry Concerns held a historic—the
first ever—forum on direct action for animals. Speakers included: Katie
Fedor, founder of the Animal Liberation Front Press Office in
Minneapolis, Minnesota; Freeman Wicklund, an outspoken ALF advocate and founder of the ALF advocacy magazine *No Compromise*, who
in 1997 renounced his support for the ALF in favor of strategic nonviolence based on Gandhian principles;[14] and Patty Mark, founder of
Animal Liberation Victoria, editor of *Action Magazine*, and
Coordinator of the Action Animal Rescue Team, which conducts nonviolent rescues inside Australian factory farms.[15] The forum, which I
conceived and organized, was inspired in part by a statement by
philosopher Tom Regan concerning ALF activities in his essay on
"Civil Disobedience" in *The Struggle for Animal Rights*. Instead of
concealment, Regan wrote, "[W]hat I think is right strategy and right
psychology is for the people who liberate animals to come forth and
identify themselves as the people who did it."[16]

During the forum, the question of concealment versus open
acknowledgment of one's identity in conducting illegal direct actions
for animals expanded into a wider range of issues surrounding this
question. This larger focus resulted from the showing of two different
videos of recent animal rescues: an ALF raid at the University of
Minnesota and a battery-caged hen rescue at an egg facility in
Australia.[17] The Australian video shows the Action Animal Rescue
Team's well-planned rescue of several hens. It documents the conditions in which the hens live inside the battery shed. We see the hens'
suffering faces up close. We watch and hear a hen scream as she is
being lifted out of the molasses-like manure in which she is trapped in
the pits beneath the cages. The video captures not only the terrible suffering of the hens being rescued, but the gentleness and firmness of the
rescue team (as expressed, for example, by their hands), who, as an
integral part of their videotaped operations, contact the police, get
arrested, and explain their mission with the intention of putting
battery-hen farming visibly on trial before the public and in the courtroom during their own trial for trespassing and theft.

By contrast, the video of the ALF break-in and rescue of animals at
the University of Minnesota shows rescuers dressed in black, Batman-
like outfits wearing black masks. All rescues are shot at a long-distance

angle. The rescuers look and act like remote, stylized figures rather than flesh-and-blood people, and the animals, including birds and fish, are so far away that it is difficult to be sure what kinds of birds, for example, are being taken out of the cages.[18] Where the Australian direct action shows suffering, compassion, a trained team, and the highly skilled use of a camera, the ALF video shows a posturing, self-centered rescue—despite the anonymity of the rescuers—in which empathy for the victims, however *felt*, is *visibly* lacking. Significantly, there is no involvement between the ALF rescuers and the animals they are liberating, as there is between the rescuers and the hens in the Australian video. The body language of the ALF rescuers is "choreographed" to resemble swordplay, in the style of Zorro or Batman.

The forum overwhelmingly chose the Australian operation and style of direct action over the characteristics depicted in this particular ALF operation. Attendees felt that the Australian video was a model for the kind of activism that, when aired, would move and educate the public, whereas the ALF video we looked at (part of which had recently been televised in Minneapolis-St. Paul), with its focus on the masked and posturing rescuers rather than on the animals and without any show of sensitivity toward them, would have a negative effect, or no effect, on most viewers. Another critical difference was in the settings: on the one hand you see the obviously filthy and inhumane battery-cage facility; on the other hand you see an antiseptic-looking laboratory at the University of Minnesota in which the suffering and cruelty are harder to convey.

Undercover Investigations of Battery-Caged Hen Facilities

Inspired by the Australian model, three undercover investigations of battery-caged hen facilities, including hen rescues, were conducted in the United States in 2001: In January, members of Compassionate Action for Animals (CAA) openly rescued 11 hens from a Michael Foods egg complex in Minnesota;[19] in May, members of Compassion Over Killing (COK) openly rescued eight hens from ISE-America in Maryland;[20] and in August and September, Mercy for Animals (MFA) openly rescued 34 hens from DayLay and Buckeye egg farms in Ohio.[21] All three groups took powerful documentary photographs that can be found on their Websites. In addition, Compassion Over Killing and Mercy for Animals produced high-quality videos of what went on inside the houses: COK's *Hope for the Hopeless* and MFA's *Silent Suffering*.[22] Both groups published explanatory news releases, provided press packets, and held well-attended press conferences that resulted in significant news coverage by the *Washington Post, United Press International*, statenews.org: The Ohio Public Radio and Television Statehouse News Bureau, and more. Because Compassion Over Killing held their press conference first, and, in doing so, set the standard for the equally impressive investigation conducted by Mercy for Animals, I will cite COK's investigation to illustrate the characteristics of what I and many others regard as a well-organized open rescue operation with charismatic effects.

On June 6, 2001, Compassion Over Killing (COK) announced that the group would hold a press conference that day to "present findings of a recent investigation into animal treatment at an International Standard of Excellence (ISE) egg facility in Cecilton, Md."[23] According to the news release,

> COK's month-long investigation began after the organization was denied a tour of the facility. ISE's Cecilton facility is "home" to 800,000 laying hens, all of whom live in "battery cages" (long rows of wire cages holding up to 10 birds per cage).
>
> The investigators documented in videos and photographs numerous acts of animal cruelty at ISE, including immobilized hens with no access to food or water, hens living in overcrowded cages with the decomposing corpses of deceased hens, and sick and injured hens suffering without veterinary care.
>
> After making repeated nighttime visits to the facility to document abuses, COK investigators requested that the Cecilton authorities prosecute ISE for animal cruelty. But, no action was taken. So, on May 23, 2001, COK investigators rescued eight sick and injured hens in dire need of immediate veterinary care.
>
> On June 6, 2001, the details of the investigation and rescue will be on line at www.ISECruelty.com. Also, COK's new 18-minute documentary on the investigation and rescue, *Hope for the Hopeless*, will be aired and distributed to media at the press conference.
>
> According to COK investigator Miyun Park, "The animals at ISE are suffering miserably. If consumers knew how animals are abused by the egg industry, they would never eat eggs."
>
> Expert veterinarian Eric Dunayer, VMD, viewed footage

taken from ISE's Cecilton facility and stated, "[T]he videotape shows hens subjected to extremely inhumane conditions that inflict severe deprivation and injury. I have no doubt that these hens suffer terribly under such conditions."

ISE is an international animal agribusiness based in Japan. Its US affiliate, ISE-America, holds captive 5.6 million egg-laying hens: 2.3 million in South Carolina; 1.5 million in Maryland; 1.3 million in New Jersey; and 500,000 in Pennsylvania.

COK's recent investigation is not ISE's first run-in with animal advocates. On October 17, 2000, ISE was found guilty on two counts of animal cruelty in New Jersey. The case involved two live hens who were found tossed in a garbage can filled with dead hens.

The Drama of Open Rescue

Mirroring the group's investigative procedure, COK's news release is very thorough. It explains the cause, process, and nature of the investigation, while placing it within a context of information about the company, ISE-America. The group did their homework. They provided veterinary validation of their animal cruelty charges (their press packet contains several letters from veterinarians), and they produced a dramatic video documenting their claims. *Hope for the Hopeless* combines the professionalism of the rescue team with the pathos of the hens. It overcomes a fundamental difficulty in drawing public attention to the plight of factory-farmed animals: the lack of drama. However, when the rescue is visually crafted and deftly narrated, as COK's is, then you have the drama, the dramatis personae, the tension, a storyline, and a "resolution," in what must otherwise appear to be, as in reality it is, a limitless expanse of animal suffering and horror—an eternal Treblinka, in the words of the Nobel Prize–winning writer, Isaac Bashevis Singer, concerning the plight of all other animal species in relation to our own.[24] *Hope for the Hopeless* shows the helpless victims and their heroic rescuers deep in the pit and under the shadow of the "enemy." These elements, skillfully combined, should elicit public sympathy and outrage.

Otherwise, except for the "veal" calf, whose solitary confinement stall and large, sad mammalian eyes draw attention to him- or herself as a desolate individual, all that most of the public sees in animal factories are endless rows of battery-caged hens, wall-to-wall turkeys, and thousands of chickens or pigs. What they hear is deathly silence or indistinguishable "noise." They see a brownish sea of bodies without conflict, plot or endpoint. There is no "one on one"—no man beating a dog, say, on which to focus one's outrage. To the public eye, the sheer number and expanse of animals surrounded by metal, wires, dung, dander, and dust renders all of them invisible and unpersonable. There are no "individuals." Instead there is a scene of pure suffering—worse, suffering that isn't even grasped by most viewers, who are more or less consensually programmed not to perceive "food" animals as individuals with feelings, let alone as creatures with projects of their own of which they have been stripped.

Open the Cages

> Each individual life we save means the world to us and to them. Pure bliss is watching a withered, featherless, debilitated, and naked little hen look up at the sky for the first time in her life, stretch her frail limbs, and then do what all hens adore: take a dust bath!—Patty Mark, "To Free a Hen," *The Animals' Agenda*[25]

Revealing the faces of these birds and other animals as they are being compassionately lifted from the dead piles onto which they were thrown, the cages upon cages surrounding them, or the manure pits into which they fell, showing them responding to a little cup of water in a close-up shot after all they have been through—this is what the animal liberation movement as a whole and the ALF and open rescuers, whether masked or otherwise, must try to accomplish. Regardless of what else is involved, as Ingrid Newkirk says in *Free the Animals*, the emphasis of the story must remain on the animals—getting them out safe and getting them seen.[26] The moment of rescue is their moment. It is their "role," and their right, at that moment to be in the spotlight, and thus also to shed a light on all of their brothers and sisters who, together with them, deserved and would have chosen to be freed, and to be free.

Notes

1. Rachelle Detweiler, "Missions of Mercy," *The Animals' Agenda*, Vol. 22, No. 1 (January–February 2002), 11.

2. Ingrid Newkirk, *Free the Animals* (Chicago: The Noble Press, 1992), 336.
3. John Berger, "Why Look at Animals?" in David M. Guss, ed., *The Language of the Birds: Tales, Texts, and Poems of Interspecies Communication* (San Francisco: North Point Press, 1985), 275–287.
4. Berger, 286–287.
5. Berger, 285.
6. I examine the cultural practice of belittling nonhuman animals, especially farmed animals, in my book *More Than a Meal: The Turkey in History, Myth, Ritual, and Reality* (New York: Lantern Books, 2001).
7. For a Marxist look at the "alienation" of factory farmed chickens (and by extension all factory-farmed animals), see especially pp. 21–24 of my book *Prisoned Chickens, Poisoned Eggs: An Inside Look at the Modern Poultry Industry* (Summertown, TN: The Book Publishing Company, 1996).
8. "The simplest method of disposal is to pack the birds, alive, into containers, and bulldoze them into the ground. Euphemistically called 'composting,' it still amounts to being buried alive," according to Canadian Farm Animal Care Trust President Tom Hughes, quoted in Merritt Clifton, "Starving the hens is 'standard,'" *Animal People: News For People Who Care About Animals*, Vol. 9, No. 4 (May 2000), 1, 8. See also Chris Miller, "Cooped up: Animal rights activists say the transportation of chickens to slaughterhouses remains cruel and inhumane despite an increase in [Canadian] government regulations," *The Vancouver Courier*, Vol. 11, No. 29 (July 27, 2001), 1, 3, 17.
9. See Patty Mark, "To Free a Hen," *The Animals' Agenda*, Vol. 21, No. 4 (July–August 2001), 25–26.
10. Claudette Vaughan, "The ALF Unmasked," *Vegan Voice*, No. 8 (December–February 2002), 9–10.
11. "The Secret Life of Cells: From the Website of the Animal Liberation Front," *Harper's Magazine*, Vol. 304, No. 1821 (February 2002), 20–21.
12. The masks worn by open rescuers of battery-caged hens are gas masks, used as a protection against the poisonous excretory ammonia fumes that permeate factory-farm poultry houses.
13. Paul Shapiro, "The US 'Open,' " *The Animals' Agenda*, Vol. 21, No. 4 (July–August 2001), 27.
14. See Freeman Wicklund, "Direct Action: Progress, Peril, or Both?" in this volume.
15. Mark, 25–26. Contact Animal Liberation Victoria/Action Animal Rescue Team at amag@ihug.com.au, or call 03-9531-4367.
16. Tom Regan, *The Struggle for Animal Rights* (Clarks Summit, PA: International Society for Animal Rights, 1987), 182.
17. The ALF raid took place in the pre-dawn hours of April 5, 1999. See Erin Geoghegan, "Minnesota ALF Raid Stirs Debate," *The Animals' Agenda*, Vol. 19, No. 3 (May–June 1999), 12, 18. The Action Animal Rescue Team video was a 37-minute segment edited from a compilation tape called *Pigs, Broiler Chickens, & Battery Hens—1995-1999*.
18. More than 100 rats, mice, pigeons, and salamanders were freed. See Geoghegan.
19. See Shapiro, n. 13 above. Michael Foods is the third largest egg company in the US and the world's largest producer of "value-added egg products," according to *Egg Industry*, January 2001, pp. 2, 16. Visit CAA's Website at www.ca4a.org. Also visit www.banbatterycages.org, or call CAA at (612) 922-6312.
20. See Shapiro, n. 13 above. ISE-America is the tenth largest egg company in the US, according to *Egg Industry* magazine, 16. Visit COK's Website at www.COK-online.org; also visit www.ISECruelty.com, or call 301-891-2458.

21. See Detweiler, n. 1 above. According to *Egg Industry*, January 2001, Buckeye Egg Farm ranks no. 5 and Daylay Egg Farm ranks no. 22 among the largest US egg producers. Visit MFA's Website at www.mercyforanimals.org; also visit www.EggCruelty.com, or call (937) 652-8258.

22. Both videos can be purchased from United Poultry Concerns, PO Box 150, Machipongo, VA 23405, for $10 each including shipping. Visit www.UPC-online.org. To order these videos directly from COK and MFA, see notes 20 and 21 above.

23. This investigation goes back ultimately to a phone call from a volunteer fireman to United Poultry Concerns in December 1993. His crew had been called in to put out a fire at one of the ISE-America complexes in Maryland. He said he had no idea such a horrible place existed, and he would never eat another egg. In the winter of 1995 my then office assistant, Jim Sicard, and I paid a midnight visit to ISE-America, where we took photos and removed 10 hens. When COK codirector Paul Shapiro asked me in 2001 about battery-hen complexes near Washington, DC, I told him about ISE-America and how to get there. For the story of Jim Sicard's and my rescue at ISE-America, see Jim Sicard, "Take the Chickens and Run! How 10 battery-caged hens came to live at UPC," *PoultryPress*, Vol. 6, No. 2 (Summer 1996), 1–2.

24. "In his thoughts, Herman spoke a eulogy for the mouse who had shared a portion of her life with him and who, because of him, had left this earth. 'What do they know—all these scholars, all these philosophers, all the leaders of the world—about such as you? They have convinced themselves that man, the worst transgressor of all the species, is the crown of creation. All other creatures were created merely to provide him with food, pelts, to be tormented, exterminated. In relation to them, all people are Nazis; for the animals it is an eternal Treblinka.' " This passage appears in Isaac Bashevis Singer, "The Letter Writer," *The Collected Stories* (New York: Farrar, Straus and Giroux, 1982). For a comprehensive look at human Nazism towards nonhuman animals, see Charles Patterson, *Eternal Treblinka: Our Treatment of Animals and the Holocaust* (New York: Lantern Books, 2002).

25. Mark, op. cit., 26.

26. Newkirk, op. cit., 350.

From the Front Line to the Front Page—An Analysis of ALF Media Coverage

KAREN DAWN

Every social movement has factions that use different tactics while aiming at the same goal. In the animal rights movement there are those who lobby on Capitol Hill and those who vandalize animal exploitation industries. There are those who will do anything to get any press, those who want only "good" press, and those who disdain the press.

Increasingly, those factions have been attacking and criticizing each other. Stuck in their own trenches—too often shooting at each other—they are dismissing the front line media reports of the war, and missing vital opportunities to help shape the reports and reach the public.

Our Little Civil War

In February 2003 during an interview on the KPFT Pacifica radio station in Houston, ALF spokesperson Rod Coronado described the Animal Liberation Front as employing "the most effective means" in our movement. He said that all of the major groups should come out in full public support of the ALF. Though he sought their support, he disparaged their work, referring to their successes as "winning a few crumbs from the oppressor's table." He implied that they distance themselves from the ALF in order to win victories to help raise funds for salaries. And he scorned their fear of bringing repression down on themselves—as if repression of these groups would not adversely affect our movement's ability to help the animals. He noted PETA's support of the ALF and expressed no regret about the resulting challenge to that organization's tax-free status. I was one of the hosts interviewing him. I asked him if it were realistic to expect those lobbying on Capitol Hill to come out in public support of the ALF. He replied, "Their not publicly supporting us is leaving us twisting in the wind."

In that interview Coronado did not acknowledge the value of the work of the mainstream groups, let alone admit the need for some of them to maintain a law-abiding image. I understand he qualifies that view in this volume. We may have caught him on a particularly bad day, a day on which his disdainful tone was unlikely to win allies in the movement mainstream. I found it alienating. I recognized the ALF as freedom fighters for the animals, but I thought the suggestion that the underground arm of our movement should be publicly embraced by every animal protection organization indicated a lack of strategic thinking, perhaps indicating combat fatigue. Should the ALF really be the face of our movement—a face with a mask?

As the 2003 national animal rights conferences approached, I heard that the Humane Society of the United States had cancelled plans to participate. In previous years it had been a sponsor of the conference and was the group that focused most on training activists to lobby in the legislative field. But Senior Vice President Wayne Pacelle felt that the rhetoric of Rod Coronado and Stop Huntington Animal Cruelty (SHAC)'s Kevin Jonas had become so inflammatory that participation in a conference where they spoke would damage HSUS's mainstream image (which translates into millions of much-needed mainstream dollars in donations) and subvert HSUS's standing in the legislative arena. I respected Pacelle's position but would have preferred he use the platform at the conference to argue against the tactics that he felt were counterproductive and that I presumed brought largely negative press coverage. I suggested that by excusing himself he was handing the conference over to the ALF and SHAC.

Indeed, throughout the conferences, the most vocal positive reaction from the attendees was in response to ALF and SHAC calls for direct action. A video montage played on the last night of the AR East conference that featured photos of most of our movement's leaders included over half a dozen shots of masked ALF rescuers; the ALF pictures got the loudest cheers. I did not find that surprising. The ALF is sexy. It represents the breaking of laws that shield unjust institutions, and the appearance of power in defense of the powerless. As we get discouraged with slow progress and doubt the impact of our movement, the ALF at least appears to be active, to be achieving something.

Good Press, Bad Press?

As one focused on the media, a force disdained by some ALF spokespersons, I found myself often taking an anti-ALF stance in informal debates at the conferences. I compared ALF activity unfavorably with open rescues. Open rescues also save animals, but do so without masks and with minimal destruction. They concentrate on getting "good" press, and they succeed. Media stories on ALF actions had often turned the animal oppressors into victims. They focused on activists rather than on animal suffering, whereas open rescues had received some superb press in recent months, mostly focused on the animals. By superb, I mean both sympathetic and educational. Thanks to the undercover work of Mercy for Animals, the *Cleveland Plain Dealer* gave front-page placement to a series on egg farming packed with information on animal suffering, including an article headed, "How hens live." After a chicken rescue in Maryland, the Washington DC–based group Compassion Over Killing got a full-page story in the *New York Times* (December 2002) detailing the suffering on egg farms, and has since had a huge story on the front page of the Style section (September 2003) focusing, sympathetically, on the activists but including information on farmed animal suffering.

The positive press following open rescues is no accident. Open rescue groups concentrate on getting the good press that the current spokespersons for the ALF shun. On accepting the Animal Rights Hall of Fame award at the 2003 animal rights conference in Los Angeles, Rod Coronado said that when you save 50 dogs from a laboratory, saving their lives is all that matters. But one might note that people will make money from catching or breeding 50 dogs who will replace those saved. What do we say to the replacements—"Sorry, the lives of those we rescued mattered more than yours"?

However, if an action gets "good" press, it can influence public opinion and therefore save far more animals in the long run; it can lead to changes in the system such that the animals are never replaced. Sadly, in the United States, industries that financially support political parties have more power than the public in influencing policy. But the effect on tuna fishing practices due to public outcry over mass dolphin deaths indicates that public opinion can override the power of industry. And media influences public opinion.

How can the ALF disdain the media? Those who doubt the power of the media should consider the American public's response to those dolphin deaths; the reaction is inconsistent with the US public's attitude towards other animals and differs from attitudes towards dolphins in other nations. Why do Americans care so much about dolphins? We all know one obvious factor: His name is Flipper. The current generation of parents buying tuna for their children's sandwiches grew up with him.

Immediately after the AR West 2003 conference, I picked up Ingrid Newkirk's *Free the Animals*, a book written like an adventure story, which gives terrific information about the ALF raids of the 1980s. I began to see how the ALF could contend that it uses the "most effective means" in our movement; much of the footage that led to early successful campaigns was obtained illegally.

But I learned that the early ALFers had pursued the media, making sure that raids were followed by press conferences. The conferences were held by those not directly involved in illegal activity but willing to accept evidence of animal abuse and share it with the press. Thus the actions generally got great press, as compared to recent ALF activity, which has resulted in largely unsympathetic coverage.

Then, just weeks after the AR West conference, in the space of 10 days in late August 2003, three different actions got so much press that I was driven to reassess my presumption that ALF press was necessarily bad. Certainly, it was not the universally favorable press of open rescues. But, for one thing, it was much *more* press than those rescues achieve.

Was it good press or bad press? I found myself starting to question the idea of good press and bad press, and beginning to side with the PETA philosophy that, at this stage of our movement, almost any press is good press—or it can be turned into good press. The animals could not be doing much worse than they are. If a story focuses on our movement's bad behavior but at least mentions the suffering of the animals, isn't that better than silence?

Some say no. They assume that unsympathetic press slows our progress. They say it furthers the public view of animal rights activists as crazy radicals with a cause that cannot be taken seriously. They say that violence, even against property, damages the reputation of our movement and will alienate those who might otherwise have been attracted to it. They don't go so far as to suggest that vegetarians are likely to start eating meat again because they don't like animal rights activists, but they say that those who might have been likely to become vegetarian will be less likely to give up meat if our movement is alienating.

Those are not theories that should be swallowed without question. Each ethical vegetarian or activist I know gave up meat upon becoming vividly aware of animal suffering, through footage or literature; his or her impression of animal rights activists was not a factor. And though the vast majority of the population eats meat, I have never met a person who said she was concerned about the suffering of animals but kept eating meat because she didn't find animal rights activists appealing. The change to vegetarianism is made for the sake of the animals, not the sake of the activists.

I have presented (and challenged) the view that an unattractive activist image will hurt the animals; respected activists hold it. Those activists sound alarm sirens when the ALF gets unsympathetic press. But I will now discuss the press achieved by the string of ALF actions on the West Coast in August 2003 and posit that it is difficult to pinpoint the harm in such press—for one thing, to assume harm, one would have to believe that anger at activists translates into anger at animals. What the recent media response to ALF activity has definitely achieved is to move animal rights issues more strongly into the limelight and public awareness. Only with awareness will there be discussion. With no discussion there will be no change.

I am going to focus on three August 2003 actions because they are diverse and wonderfully exemplary. One involves vandalism against property and threats to its owner, the second involves the release of animals, and the third moves into an area almost universally condemned: the use of explosives.

Foie Gras: In the News, Off the Menus

On Tuesday, August 19, the following story broke on the front page of the *San Francisco Chronicle:* "Animal-rights vandals hit chef's home, shop; Activists call French-style foie gras cruel to birds." In this front-page article, San Franciscans learned that "animal rights vandals" had done about $50,000 worth of damage to a store/restaurant soon to be opened that would specialize in foie gras. The vandals had splashed acid on the chef/owner's car, spray-painted his house, and sent him threatening letters along with a videotape of him and his family at home.

The article covered the suffering of the chef to a greater degree than the suffering of the animals. However, the torture of the birds whose livers become foie gras was not entirely ignored and thus made the front page of a major newspaper. Readers learned of the controversy: "Foie gras—fattened goose or duck liver—has become controversial because of the way it is produced, which involves force-feeding fowl. How much the animals suffer—or whether they suffer at all—has been the subject of much debate."

They read: "It is created when ducks or geese are force-fed grain through tubes that are put down the birds' throats." Readers were treated to a quote from a PETA spokesperson, saying that foie gras is "one of the most egregiously cruel food products out there."

Over the next 10 days, the *Chronicle* opinion page printed nine letters about foie gras, including one from Ingrid Newkirk noting, "A civilization is indeed judged by how it treats its animals." Five of the letters took the animal rights position. The first printed objected to the use of the word "terrorism" to describe actions necessary to stop "institutionalized violence" and included the John F. Kennedy quote: "Those who make peaceful revolution impossible will make violent revolution inevitable." One letter complained of the lack of media coverage to educate the public about "the horrific treatment of ducks being processed for foie gras." The writer took it upon herself to provide some reader education: "We only need to imagine a tube stuck down our throat while large amounts of food are pumped through to have a clue as to what these animals go through." Another letter plugged the PETA Website. And one letter summed up a point I will be making in this essay: "The animal-rights groups are wrong to vandalize or threaten chefs but, unfortunately, it seems to have worked—front page of *The Chronicle*. It is too bad that the simple truth about factory farms isn't enough to get a front-page story. . . ."

The foie gras action got some national and even international press. A story in London's *The Times* opened with, "Chefs in California's foodie capital of San Francisco are at war with each other—and animal activists—over the ethics of selling duck or goose foie gras." How wonderful to see an ethical issue about animal consumption take the lead line in an article in this prestigious UK paper.

Then on Friday, August 22, the *Chronicle* printed an article headed, "Some rethink menu after violence over controversial fare." Kim Severson reported, "Elite Bay Area chefs, stunned by the vandalism directed at one of their San Francisco colleagues who serves foie gras, are taking a serious look at what's on the menu." San Franciscans read that for some chefs "the furor over foie gras has rekindled concerns about the way some animals are raised for the table." Others said they were less concerned about the animals than afraid of the activists, but either reaction had the same effect: "Whether fearful or angry, Manrique's professional colleagues say the situation has made it clear that writing a menu is becoming a political act."

The article included an interesting quote from Jardiniere's Traci Des Jardins, who said she plans to discontinue her signature foie gras. She said she did have some concern about being the next target, but her decision was based not on fear but on having visited a foie gras farm in 1995 and having been "haunted by the image of those ducks." That is a wonderful quote to have in a major paper. But since it took her eight years to stop serving the dish, it is hard to deny that something other than those haunting images had just given her the push she needed to do what she knew was right.

Which leads us back to the question, is bad press necessarily bad? I notice that the bulk of our movement's leadership condemns fear tactics that turn the oppressors into victims. But in San Francisco, fear could be helping to phase out foie gras.

That first front-page foie gras story, which some might have seen as bad press for the movement, inspired more than fear. Television news generally takes its cues from the press—particularly from the front pages. In San Francisco, the Channel 7 "I-Team" took up the story (September 16) but shifted the focus onto the suffering of the animals. The reporter made no attempt to hide that the vandalism inspired the story. He said, "Few people have seen how foie gras is made, and that's the motive behind this recent spree of vandalism."

He warned viewers they were about to see disturbing images, then delivered those images as he reported, "At least three times a day, a worker grabs each duck, shoves a long, thick metal tube down its throat and an air pump shoots up to a pound of corn into the duck. . . . The tube sometimes perforates the side of the duck's throat, causing scarring and other damage. And, the large amount of food has an impact. . . . The activists found barrels of ducks that died before their livers could be harvested, others still barely alive. They also watched ducks too weak or overweight to defend themselves against the rats at Sonoma Foie Gras. Rats were eating these two ducks alive and you can see evidence of similar battles on several other ducks."

An open rescue of ducks destined for foie gras was covered, soon afterwards, by the *Los Angeles Times* (September 18) and *Time* Magazine (September 29). The coverage was clearly positive and sympathetic, as is typical of open rescue coverage. But *Time* does not usually cover open rescues. The short *Time* article noted, "The effort, the fourth attack against the foie gras business in California since July, represents the latest campaign by animal-rights activists." One has to ask whether the open rescue effort would have been covered by *Time* if not for its eye-catching precursors.

On September 24 the *New York Times* ran a huge piece on the front page of the Dining section, headed "Foie Gras Fracas: Haute Cuisine Meets the Duck Liberators." The reporter opened with the recent attacks on the California restaurant. She noted, "Animal rights activists who claimed responsibility for the destruction—and for an earlier attack on the homes of the cafe's chef and his partner—call foie gras the 'delicacy of despair,' born of cruelty to animals." I have heard from those in the open rescue field that a completely sympathetic article in the works was pulled in favor of this one thanks to the spate of vandalism. However, the topic is now so hot that more articles about the foie gras controversy are likely to run. And, following the Dining story, the *Times* printed at least the equivalent of a sympathetic article—an extraordinary page of letters to the editor, universally condemning foie gras and giving more details on the brutality involved in its production. The first letter called for vegetarianism; others expressed disgust that the FBI had labeled those trying to save lives terrorists, when the real terrorists are those who torture animals.

As this book goes to press the foie gras controversy continues to make the news. *The New York Times* has run an anti-foie gras op-ed headed: "Honk if you hate foie gras" (September 27, 2003). It focused on the personality of geese. *The Chicago Tribune* ran a shorter version of the *New York Times* Dining section story (September 29, 2003). *The San Francisco Chronicle* still pursues the foie gras story, with the focus now on poor conditions at a Sonoma duck farm. And the cover of the Metro section of the Saturday, November 29, *Los Angeles Times* tells us of a petition presented to the Sonoma City Council, requesting a ban on the sale of foie gras! It is clear that the ALF attacks and the resulting front-page coverage got the ball rolling. Therefore, the mainstream of our movement should not deny that this ALF action has had a positive effect. And the ALF should not deny that the coverage mattered. Because of the media, the attacks on the chef had an effect greater than interference with the targeted store: Chefs throughout San Francisco, such as Traci Des Jardins, are now wary of foie gras. That is because they know what happened to Manrique, because there was press. And the press led to mass education on the cruelty of foie gras thanks to an unprecedented, highly informative, and sympathetic exposé on San Francisco's evening news. All factions of our movement must see the value in that.

Mink: To Free or Not to Free?

On August 25 a week after the foie gras store attacks in San Francisco, an ALF raid of a Seattle fur farm released 10,000 mink into the surrounding environment. That is the sort of action I have not supported in the past. Mink are carnivores, which makes their release into the environment ethically questionable. Moreover, most of the mink were recaptured within a day, many were run over, and many soon died of starvation or dehydration. Neighbors shot many of them because they attacked and killed cats and dogs, exotic birds, ducks, and chickens. The press therefore suggested that the release was cruel to the mink. That argument is weak. Why is life in a tiny cage till certain death by asphyxiation or anal electrocution better for a wild animal than freedom and death elsewhere? Further, it is reasonable to assume that at least a few of the mink have survived and are happy to be free.

But the animals they will eat as they live out their lives in the wild are presumably not so happy they are free. And since the fur farm is still in business and other mink waiting to be skinned will fill their cages, there is perhaps no overall benefit for the animals—except that in this second major August 2003 ALF action, there was again extraordinary press.

The story was on the front page of the Tuesday, August 26 *Seattle Times*, on local Seattle TV that night, and covered extensively on CNN the following Monday and Saturday. None of that coverage could be considered positive in the traditional sense. It focused on the suffering of the fur farmer, the neighbors, and the released minks rather than the suffering on fur farms. It included no graphic fur farm footage. Yet, again, I must question whether there is really such a thing as negative press on animal rights issues at this stage of our movement. The fur industry is doing well; many see the anti-fur movement as over. But the huge amount of coverage the mink liberation garnered sends a clear signal that it is not.

And some of the press coverage was clearly positive—it discussed the issue. The Sunday, August 31, *Los Angeles Times* ran a half page story, including a close-up photo of a mink, in its front section (page A19). The story was headed "Freed Mink Unleash a Debate on Cruelty to Animals." It was sub-headed "In a Washington town, activists release 10,000 farm-raised animals into the wild." (The same article on the Web was sub-headed "Extremists set loose 10,000 animals, raising havoc and tempers in a Washington town." What a difference an editor can make!)

The article did describe the havoc created by the loose mink. But then it noted that the release had led, among residents, to "a renewed discussion on the nature of cruelty, the issue at the heart of the debate over fur farming." It asked, "What is more cruel to the mink: being raised and killed in a cage, or being freed and possibly killed in the wild?"

A neighbor, who lost companion animals to the mink and was furious about the release, nevertheless gave this valuable quote: "I mean, c'mon, it's 2003. No one needs to wear fur coats." And another neighbor was quoted saying that the worst thing you can do to wild animals is put them in a small cage. She shuddered at the thought of how they are killed.

Theresa Platt, executive director of Fur Commission USA was quoted saying that the state's fur farms are on "pins and needles" since such attacks usually happen in strings.

The *Los Angeles Times* article ended with a superb quote from Mitchell Fox, an animal rights advocate in Seattle: "What those ALFers did was goofily, amateurishly, well-meaningly dumb. What the farmers do is calculatedly, professionally, unremittingly cruel."

The last line of an article plants the impression with which people are left. So when an action leads to a prominent *Los Angeles Times* piece that ends with a quote noting the cruelty of fur farming, one has to admit to some uncertainty as to how dumb the action really was. Perhaps few mink from the release survived in the wild, or each one taken from a cage was replaced. But what if some readers of the *Los Angeles Times* article, reminded of the cruelty of fur farming, declined the mink trim jackets for sale on Rodeo Drive? Then the action might have saved some animals. If those readers included trend-setting Los Angeles celebrities, it might have saved many animals.

Did the press on this action make animal rights activists look bad? Dumb, perhaps. But I doubt that a view of animal rights activists as dumb will cause people to wear fur. Overall, did the action hurt or help animals? It hurt the animals the mink ate in the wild. But the press may have discouraged people from buying fur coats. The action clearly started discussion in the town where the release occurred, and the press spread the discussion elsewhere. Discussion of animal rights issues will no doubt help the animals.

Should We "Stop Worrying and Learn to Love the Bomb"?

Do coverage and impact change significantly with the use of explosives? Two small bombs exploded early Thursday, August 28, 2003, at the Chiron Corp compound in Emeryville, California. Chiron had been a SHAC target, due to its past use of Huntingdon Life Sciences to test products and its refusal to rule out future dealings with the company.

Days after the attack, a group called the Revolutionary Cells Animal Liberation Brigade took responsibility. It is not a group with which leaders of SHAC or spokespersons for the ALF appear to be familiar.

Some activists have posited that the bombs were actually the work of agents provocateurs who hope to give animal rights activists bad press and would like to encourage an FBI crackdown on SHAC in order to allay the harassment of Chiron. However Rod Coronado told a *San Francisco Chronicle* reporter that the increased use of explosives is likely, as there is a new crop of radical activists who think classic ALF tactics have been too lightweight. Such a statement from somebody who is presumably familiar with the current tenets of the ALF makes it seem less likely that the blasts were the work of agents provocateurs.

The story made the front page of the *San Francisco Chronicle* on three different days and has been in over 100 papers nationally and internationally. In this way millions of people have been reminded that there are those who vehemently, even violently, oppose animal testing. Many of the articles mentioned SHAC or *Bite Back* magazine, so interested readers could find out more. The press made it clear that the FBI was treating the incident as domestic terrorism. But every major article included quotes from ALF or SHAC spokespersons saying that though they supported economic sabotage, violence against humans or members of other species is unacceptable.

Perhaps the most interesting article, because of its timing, less than two weeks after the blasts, appeared in the *San Francisco Chronicle* on Sunday, September 7. It is hard to deny that the blasts probably inspired the article. It opened with the line, "New technology and the drive to cut research costs could do as much to reduce animal testing in the United States as the intense animal-rights protests that hit Chiron this summer." Note that it gave at least some credit to the intense animal rights protests. The article discussed a gradual trend towards reduced animal use, "partly out of concern for animal well-being, but also from a practical need to trim expenses." Since SHAC's tactics have been aimed at making animal experimentation not just expensive but economically unfeasible, the article could suggest that the tactics are on the right track.

If Somebody Dies, Does Our Movement?

SHAC was not responsible for the bombs. Yet it did not condemn the action, since nobody got hurt. The fear that when arson or explosives are used, somebody eventually will get hurt, is realistic. Some would not care if that somebody were a vivisector. But in such a case, there is little doubt that the press coverage would be entirely unfavorable; we could lose much public sympathy. There is a general assumption that it would set back our cause.

For argument's sake I am going to present a radical view: Some say fear is the strongest motivator and that the death of some vivisectors would send the strongest possible signal that vivisection is a bad investment and certainly not a good choice for a promising long-term and lucrative career.

Would the "bad" press around a human death necessarily be bad? Or might it be good for the movement to have a new image—to trade ineffectual virtue for the threat of justice brought by force? Might it announce that the movement must be taken seriously or there will be dire consequences?

I asked feminist icon Gloria Steinem about the effect of violence, and even murder, on the pro-life movement. While she is strongly opposed to all violence and feels in the long run it will harm the pro-life movement, she wrote, "Yes, the murder of doctors and other personnel working in clinics—plus a terrorist attack on a clinic on the average of once a month—have been effective in the short-term. Landlords, insurance companies and even neighbors are now reluctant to accept clinics, and most doctors who perform abortions are the older and more idealistic ones who remember the bad old days of illegal abortion."

The threat of violence from the animal rights movement appears to be having a similar effect. Frankie Trull, from the Foundation for Biomedical Research (quoted by conservative columnist Debra Saunders in the *San Francisco Chronicle* on September 30, 2003) has noted that medical researchers are forced out of business all the time since "People are afraid to step up and help because they don't want to draw attention to themselves."

Would violent action from our movement turn the public away from the animals? Or, having been given a sure message that animal rights issues can't be ignored, might people run towards the more mainstream groups such as HSUS that publicly and vehemently condemn ALF activity? The HSUS is now anti-circus, anti-rodeo, recommends eating less meat as the first line of attack on the cruelty of factory farming, and encourages the use of alternatives to animal testing. Would it be such a bad thing if violent animal rights activity made the HSUS look very mainstream and if that organization therefore became the public darling, the savior, rather than the well-regarded but less influential group it is now?

I am against any action that could reasonably be expected to result in the death of humans, including vivisectors and other animal abusers. I experimented on rats in college and believe that almost anybody can be shown the light. Indeed, an interesting phenomenon in our movement is the prominence of those whose careers or leisure pursuits involved egregious abuse. They make superb spokespersons. They have knowledge in the fields of abuse, plus an ability to see the issue from both sides, making their choice of sides more compelling. Regret over the suffering they have caused in the past seems to add an extra dose of passion and commitment to their work. Not all abusers will choose to change, but we must find ways other than murder to put them out of business.

Moreover, if an innocent janitor, or one who risks her life to help others, such as a paramedic or firefighter, were killed, most activists would be heartbroken and feel that our movement had surrendered the high ground. We would be distressed, ashamed, and dispirited.

But still, I ask the question at the head of this section, in an attempt not to let my own views on what is right and wrong cloud my analysis of what the impact of the "bad press" might be. We don't know. Rejecting violence against people on moral grounds is not the same as categorically stating that it would set our movement back. I cannot pretend to be able to predict the entirety of the press that would follow a human death, and the long-term impact on our movement.

Recently, in the Netherlands, an animal rights activist killed a right-wing candidate for prime minister who intended to reintroduce fur farming. Though the connection between the assassination and animal rights activism is disputed by some, the press focused on the connection in early reports. Dutch activists have, of course, almost universally condemned the murder, and some have said it set the movement back. But I have asked many Dutch activists to point to direct negative effects and have yet to be given evidence of significant, let alone long-term, effects on progress. Those who aver that such an action must have only negative consequences forget that President Garfield's assassination in 1881, by a disappointed job applicant, spurred Congress to pass the Civil Service Act of 1883.

I personally cannot condone the use of explosives, since they can endanger innocent lives. I am similarly uncomfortable with the setting of fires. They could kill humans and must often kill members of other species living in roofs and under floorboards. But I understand that reasonable people might differ, some feeling that force, even violence, can be appropriate in the defense of the innocent. Looking at the polls taken after 9/11, one can see that most Americans feel that way. So I will focus on the press, and must admit that the Chiron bombing has not led to notable anti-animal press. Further, the press they received has reminded millions of people that animal testing is violently opposed; it has no doubt generated some discussion. We can't know what direction all of that discussion has taken. But, as millions of animals continue to die torturous deaths in laboratories, can we really think that silence is preferable?

ALF and Ronnie Go to Hollywood

Every year Genesis Awards are given to members of the major media who shine the spotlight on animal cruelty. The HSUS Hollywood office now runs the show, which is ironic in the face of the plot line I am about to discuss, since HSUS has such a mainstream image; it seems as far from the ALF as an animal activist can get. Two years ago, however, the dramatic TV series *Law and Order* won an award for what I think is the strongest animal rights piece ever to appear on prime time television.

The premise is as follows: monkeys are rescued from a vivisection lab; one escapes the cage, can't be quickly caught, and is left behind. In the morning, he bites the vivisector who tries to re-cage him and the man dies. Since the show tries to be as realistic as possible, and occurs in current times when other primates still have no rights, and given that the possibility of the doctor's death might have been foreseeable, the activist is charged with and convicted of murder. What made the show so groundbreaking was the beautifully scripted presentation of the animal rights argument, the highlight of which came in the defense lawyer's speech.

The lawyer presented the activist's act as one of conscience, motivated by compassion. He noted how unusual it is in our society to worry about "suffering other than human suffering." He argued, "We think nothing of killing animals to mount their heads over our mantels or to test hairspray" because animals are viewed as property, like lumps of wood or coal or hammers or nails. Then, in the most daring pro–animal rights argument I have ever seen presented on television, he drew the analogy with which we are familiar from books such as Marjorie Spiegel's *The Dreaded Comparison*. He said, "I'd like to remind you of a time in the not-too-distant past when that same distinction was drawn based on the color of one's skin—when Africans were packed into ships like cordwood and brought to this continent as property of their owners, and they had no rights, and their suffering did not matter, and anyone who objected was a kook and outside the mainstream."

When the writer, William Finkelstein, received his Genesis Award, he gave an enlightening acceptance speech. He told us that his intention, when starting work on the project, was indeed to present animal rights activists as "kooks, hopelessly outside the mainstream." But he had to do some reading on the subject in order to write a good script, and the reading opened his eyes and shifted the story's direction. That Finkelstein became well-acquainted with our movement is clear, not only from his having penned a speech that many of our leaders would have been proud to write, but also from a delicious "inside joke"—he named the dead scientist Ronald Lee. So the defense speech includes a line in which the jury is asked not to criminalize the defendant's intent just because it "brought about the unanticipated tragedy in the death of Ronald Lee." One suspects Finkelstein's jab might be a way of asking if the ALF would be willing to engage in actions that risk human life if the lives at risk were their own.

On the one hand, Finkelstein's original intention, to paint animal rights activists as kooks, indicates the general public's reaction to the ALF. On the other, as noted in an article cited above about the mink raid, ALF action generates discussion. And when animal rights issues are discussed, there are opportunities for people to learn. Here, ALF activity caught the imagination of a major television writer who took the discussion to prime time television. Though we wish the simple fact of animal suffering would have the same effect, without lawbreaking or heroes, it is hard to deny that most major media is interested in sex and violence. Therefore, illegal, even violent activity is highly likely to get media coverage and therefore to generate discussion. Prime time, top-rated television drama in which animal rights theory is presented in a gripping manner is about as good as media coverage can get.

Arming the Forces for the Media Ambush

Press generates discussion, and each of the three actions I cite above, and the host of actions that led to the fictionalized *Law and Order* incident, generated much press. Whether unsympathetic press sets our movement back, moves it forward, or does neither is hard to document. But almost all activists agree that sympathetic press takes us forward.

During the ALF raids of the 1980s, the underground arm worked with those aboveground so that press conferences followed raids. Videos of abuse were provided to the press and aired on television.

One wonders how much more educational the TV coverage of the Washington mink release might have been if a press conference had been organized, or if the day after the release the local stations had received video evidence of the appalling conditions on mink farms. What if the attacks on the foie gras restaurant had coincided with the delivery to every major media outlet of photos and film of force-feeding, or of geese who had died when their livers burst? Or if the Chiron bomb blasts had happened in the early hours of a day on which the press received the Huntingdon Life Sciences video of the beagle being punched for misbehaving during his torture? Perhaps that video finally would have made the US news.

Some of the current spokespersons for the ALF have voiced disdain for the media. And some of the leaders of our movement mainstream, in love with the press but disdaining the ALF, won't take advantage of the media inroads made by the underground. Yet ALF action has still managed to inspire loads of press, some of it sympathetic. If that can happen with plain dumb luck, imagine what might be achieved with a real battle plan!

TACTICS

Cowardice asks the question, Is it safe? Expediency asks the question, Is it politic? Vanity asks the question, Is it popular? But conscience asks the question, Is it right? And there comes a time when one must take a position that is neither safe, nor politic, nor popular, but he must take it because his conscience tells him that it is right.—Martin Luther King, Jr.

It is not the oppressed who determine the means of resistance, but the oppressor.—Nelson Mandela

The '60s are over and the animals don't have time for their hippy dreams.—*Bite Back* magazine

How to Justify Violence

Tom Regan, PhD

Mahatma Gandhi has had a profound influence on my life. I think it is fair to say that I would never have become an animal rights advocate if I had not read his autobiography.[1] Learning about his life changed mine. Gandhi helped me see that cows and pigs, not just cats and dogs, are unique somebodies, not disposable somethings. Voiceless somebodies. Vulnerable somebodies. Innocent somebodies. Gandhi made me feel deeply responsible for how we humans treat other creatures. If I did not assert their rights, if I remained neutral, who would speak for them? For the past 30 years and more, speaking for them has been a large part of my being in the world.

Pacifism is one place Gandhi went where I never have been able to go. He teaches that the use of violence is always wrong, even in defense of those who have done no wrong, those who are innocent. I think I understand this way of thinking. It is at least as old as Jesus' injunction to "turn the other cheek" if someone smites thee.

Maybe it's my blue-collar background, but I have always believed that anyone who smites me (or my wife or our children, for example) is looking for trouble. Depending on the circumstances (the attacker is not carrying a gun, for example) I hope I would have the courage to do some serious smiting back.

If my experience has taught me anything, it is that I am not the exception. I am the rule. Throughout my life I have met very few people (I could count them all with the fingers on one hand) who think differently. *Sometimes*, in *some* circumstances, violence is justified. That's what the rest of us believe. Where we sometimes part company is over the question, "In what circumstances?"

My answer sets forth three conditions.[2] First, the violence employed is used to defend the innocent. Second, nonviolent alternatives have been exhausted, as time and circumstances permit. Third, the violence used is not excessive; in other words, the amount or kind of violence employed is not more than is needed to achieve the desired objective: the defense of the innocent. Here is an example that illustrates how things can go wrong.

Suppose an estranged father kidnaps his children and threatens to kill them if the police try to rescue them. Clearly, the children are innocent, so one of the conditions is satisfied. However, if the police shoot the father before negotiating with him, their use of violence would be unjustified in my view. In their haste, they did not take the time to exhaust nonviolent alternatives. Further, if the police used lethal force when another method would have sufficed (tear gas, say), that would be wrong, too. The amount of violence used was excessive.

My judgment is different, given different circumstances. If the police have every reason to believe that the father intends to kill his children, if they patiently negotiated in good faith, and if no less violent means would succeed in rescuing the children, then, in my view, the police would be justified in using lethal force.

Is my view "crazy," "weird," "irrational," "extreme"? I don't think so. Except for Gandhian pacifists, I think the rest of humanity is on my side. None of us endorses the use of violence for frivolous reasons. Or a policy of shooting first and asking questions later. Or using more violence when less will do. We all understand that we can justify using violence some of the time without believing that its use is justified all of the time.

My view (our view, I dare say) is directly relevant to the central question at the heart of some forms of animal rights advocacy. This question asks, "Is the use of violence in defense of animals ever justified?"

Some animal rights advocates (ARAs) dismiss this question because of how they understand the meaning of "violence." In their perspective, violence is restricted to causing physical harm to a sentient being, human or otherwise. Given this usage, the police used violence when they shot the estranged father. The same is true when rapists assault their victims or when bombs are dropped on people during a war. But if no harm is caused to anyone, then, no matter what people do, no violence is done.[3]

I personally disagree with ARAs who think this way, and I am not alone. Ask any member of the general public whether firebombing an empty synagogue involves violence. Ask any lawyer whether arson is a violent crime (whether or not anyone is hurt). The response is overwhelmingly likely to be, "Am I missing something? *Of course* these acts are violent." The plain fact is, our language is not tortured or stretched when we speak of the "violent destruction of property." The plain fact is, we do not need to hurt someone in order to do violence to some thing.

Gandhi agrees. "Sabotage [destroying property for political purposes, without hurting anyone in the process] is a form of violence," he writes, adding, "People have realized the futility of physical violence but some people apparently think it [that is, violence] may be successfully practiced in its modified form as sabotage."[4] Gandhi does not count himself among those who think this way.

Martin Luther King, Jr. sees things the same way. Among the many relevant examples: In March of 1968, shortly before his death, King was leading a march in Memphis on behalf of the city's sanitation workers. "At the back of the line," King's biographer, Stephen B. Oates, observes, "black teenagers were smashing windows and looting stores. . . . King signaled to [James] Lawson [the local march coordinator] . . . 'I will never lead a violent march,' King said, 'so please call it off.' While Lawson yelled in his bullhorn for everybody to return to the church, King . . . climbed into a car [and sped away]."[5] No one was hurt that day in Memphis, but some serious violence was done.

ARAs who think that arson and other forms of destruction of property are forms of "nonviolent direct action" are free to think what they will. Certainly nothing I say can make them change their minds. I will only observe that, in my opinion, unless or until these advocates accept the fact that some ARAs use violence in the name of animal rights (for example, when they firebomb empty research labs), the general public will turn a deaf ear when their spokespersons attempt to justify such actions.

So the real question, I believe, is not whether some ARAs use violence. The real question is whether they are justified in doing so. Here are the main outlines of a possible justification.

1. Animals are innocent.
2. Violence is used only when it is necessary to rescue them so that they are spared terrible harms.
3. Excessive violence is never used.
4. Violence is used only after nonviolent alternatives have been exhausted, as time and circumstances permit.
5. Therefore, in these cases, the use of violence is justified.

What should we say in response to this line of reasoning? If all the premises (1 through 4) are true, how can we avoid agreeing with the conclusion (5)? True, Gandhian pacifists can avoid the conclusion; they do not accept any violence, even in defense of the innocent. However, most of us are not Gandhian pacifists; for us, the plot thickens.

Personally, I don't think the second premise is true of all or even most of the violence done in the name of animal rights. Why not? Because the vast majority of this violence does not involve animal rescue. The vast majority (I estimate 98 percent) is property destruction, pure and simple. In cases like these, the defense we are considering contributes nothing by way of justification.

What of the remaining two percent of cases, cases where violence is used and animals are rescued? For example, suppose a multi-million dollar lab is burnt to the ground *after* the animals in it have been liberated. Would this kind of violence be justified, given the argument sketched above?

Again, I don't think so. And the reason I don't think so is that I don't think the requirement set forth in premise 4 has been satisfied. Personally, I do not think that ARAs in general, members of the ALF in particular, have done nearly enough when it comes to exhausting nonviolent alternatives. Granted, to do this will take time and will require great patience coupled with hard, dedicated work. Granted, the results of these labors are uncertain. And granted, animals will be suffering and dying every hour of every day that ARAs struggle to free them using nonviolent means. Nevertheless, unless or until ARAs have done the demanding nonviolent work that needs to be done, the use of violence, in my judgment, is not morally justified. (It is also a tactical disaster. Even when animals are rescued, the story the media tells is about the "terrorist" acts of ARAs, not the terrible things that were being done to animals. The one thing ARA violence never fails to produce is more grist for the mills run by spokespersons for the major animal user industries.)

ARAs who disagree with me are certainly free to argue that violence is justified under different conditions than those I have given. For example, they could argue that violence is justified when the damage caused is so extensive that it puts an animal abuser out of business. In this case, no animals are rescued but (so it may be argued) some animals are spared the horrors of vivisection in a lab or a lifetime of deprivation on a fur farm, for example. However, to consider such an argument is premature. Before it merits consideration, ARAs who support such actions need to acknowledge that these are violent acts, something that, as we have seen, these supporters are loath to admit.

The role of violence in social justice movements raises complicated questions that always have and always will divide activists on matters of substance, ethics, and strategy in particular. It need not divide ARAs when it comes to assessments of character. I know ARAs who have spent years in jail because they have broken the law, having used violence as I understand this idea. To a person, these activists believe ARAs already have exhausted nonviolent alternatives. To a person, they believe the time for talking has passed. To a person, they believe the time for acting has arrived.

I have never doubted the sincerity and commitment—or the courage—these activists embody. I am reminded of an observation (I cannot find the source) Gandhi once made, to the effect that he had more admiration for people who have the courage to use violence than he had for people who embraced nonviolence out of cowardice. So, yes, ARAs who use violence are courageous in their acts, and sincere in their commitment. And yes, perhaps some of us who reject the violence they employ do so out of cowardice. Nevertheless, violence done by ARAs, in my judgment, not only is wrong but hurts, rather than helps, the animal rights movement.

Before concluding, it is important to take note of how the story of "animal rights violence" gets told by the media. On the one side, we have the law-abiding people who work for the major animal user industries. On the other side, we have violent, law-breaking ARAs. Paragons of nonviolence versus beady-eyed flamethrowers. Not only is this absurdly unfair to ARAs, 99+ percent of whom do not participate in violent forms of activism, it is nothing less than a cover-up of the truth when it comes to what the major animal user industries do. The treatment animals receive in the name of scientific research illustrates my meaning.

Animals are drowned, suffocated, and starved to death; they have their limbs severed and their organs crushed; they are burned, exposed to radiation, and used in experimental surgeries; they are shocked, raised in isolation, exposed to weapons of mass destruction, and rendered blind or paralyzed; they are given heart attacks, ulcers, paralysis, and seizures; they are forced to inhale tobacco smoke, drink alcohol, and ingest various drugs, such as heroine and cocaine.

And they say ARAs are violent. The bitter truth would be laughable if it were not so tragic. The violence done to things by some ARAs (by which I mean the violent destruction of insensate property) is nothing compared to the violence done to feeling creatures by the major animal user industries. A raindrop compared to an ocean. On a day-to-day basis, by far the greatest amount of violence done in the "civilized" world occurs because of what humans do to other animals. That the violence is legally protected, that in some cases (for example, vivisection) it is socially esteemed, only serves to make matters worse.

Finally, and lamentably, one thing seems certain. Unless the massive amount of violence done to animals is acknowledged by those who do it, and until meaningful steps are taken to end it, as certain as night follows day, some ARAs, somewhere, somehow, will use violence against animal abusers themselves to defend the rights of animals.[6]

Notes

1. Mohandas K. Gandhi, *Autobiography: The Story of my Experiments with Truth* (Boston: Beacon Press, 1965).

2. As I understand the issues, these three conditions represent the paradigm case of the justification for the use of violence. Additional conditions may be possible. My discussion of violence here is adapted from my discussion in *Empty Cages: Facing the Challenge of Animal Rights* (Lanham, MD: Rowman & Littlefield, 2004).

3. Thus do we find the Animal Liberation Front described as being involved in "a nonviolent campaign, activists taking all precautions not to harm any animals (human or otherwise)." See www.hedweb.com/alfaq.htm.

4. Thomas Merton, ed., *Gandhi on Nonviolence* (New York: New Directions, 1965), 39.

5. Stephen B. Oates, *Let the Trumpet Sound: The Life of Martin Luther King, Jr.* (New York: Harper & Row, 1982), 477.

6. For further elaboration on the future of violence by ARAs, see my "Understanding Animal Rights Violence," in *Defending Animal Rights* (Champaign, IL: University of Illinois Press, 2001).

Direct Action: Progress, Peril, or Both?

Freeman Wicklund

This article was published in the July–August 1998 issue of
The Animals' Agenda. *Some people no longer hold the positions and titles that they did when the article was first published, and more recent direct actions are not taken into consideration.*

Direct action—placing oneself in harm's way for a cause more important than oneself—may prove a formidable challenge to injustice and bolster positive social change. It may be nonviolent as in Dr. Martin Luther King, Jr.'s civil disobedience campaigns against segregation in the 1960s, or it may be violent as in fugitive "slave" Nat Turner's 1831 armed rebellion, which killed 60 people. Direct action may wield psychological and persuasive force as did Mohandas Gandhi's 1930s civil disobedience campaign for an independent India, or it may wield physical and coercive force as does the Irish Republican Army's assassinations and bombings. The United States has a long tradition of direct action: the American Revolution and the movements for civil rights, women's suffrage, temperance, and the abolition of slavery all had a direct action component. The present struggle for animal liberation is no exception.

This article seeks to evaluate the effectiveness of direct action for animals.[1] To do this, we must first know what we want. Before you read on, try visualizing an ideal society where animal liberation has already been achieved. What would the people be wearing and eating in this society? How would they treat the animals in their lives? And what is their motivation for behaving in this way?

In your visualization, did you see a society where an unwilling majority is forced by a tiny minority to adhere to a vegan lifestyle? Such a society would require a loyal force of animal rights troops and probably martial law. The troops would be needed to accompany campers and hikers into the woods to ensure that they are not hunting, trapping, or fishing. They would also be responsible for finding and eliminating the inevitable black market trade in illegal animal products; raiding the homes of non-believers in search of contraband animal flesh, milk, eggs, and skins; and busting the illegal speakeasy-style burger bars. The troops would basically do all they could try to force an unwilling public to live vegan lives.

Creating such a society would be impractical. Animal rights supporters lack the money, material resources, authority, people, skills, and will to implement this kind of society. More importantly, such a society is undesirable. In the same way that back-alley abortions were conducted prior to abortion's legalization, and speakeasy bars violated Prohibition, violence toward animals will continue as long as there is a demand for the products of exploitation.

If you are like most animal advocates, the society you envisioned did not have martial law, but was rather a respectful society where people did not eat, wear, vivisect, or otherwise use animals or animal products because to do so would be morally repugnant, unconscionable, and wrong. In other words, the majority of people in an animal rights society have *voluntarily* adopted an animal rights philosophy.

Although all social justice struggles achieve their victories through a combination of coercion and persuasion, to effectively strategize, we must choose which mechanism will be the primary mechanism best suited for achieving our objectives. Harry Emerson Fosdick wrote, "He who chooses the beginning of the road chooses the place it leads to. It is the means that determines the ends." The road of coercion leads toward the society of martial law. The road of persuasion leads to the respectful society where the majority of people voluntarily choose a vegan lifestyle.

Understanding these distinctions allows us to better evaluate direct action by determining when, and under what circumstances, it moves us closer to—or further away from—our ultimate objective of a society where most people live vegan lives because they believe in animal rights.

Direct Action for Animals

Coordinated direct action for animals began in Britain in the early 1960s with the formation of the Hunt Saboteurs Association (HSA). Its members prevented the killing of wildlife by confusing the hunters' hounds with false scents and signals, and by placing themselves between the hunters and the hunted. In 1972 some HSA members formed an underground organization called the Band of Mercy and conducted nighttime raids to damage vehicles used to transport hounds to the hunting grounds. In 1973 the Band of Mercy diversified its targets by attempting to burn down an unfinished vivisection laboratory in Milton Keynes, and by burning a sealing boat in East Anglia. In 1975 the Band of Mercy changed its name to the Animal Liberation Front (ALF) and continued to conduct clandestine raids against industries that use animals.

In the United States, ALF actions started in 1977 when two dolphins were released from a research facility in Honolulu, Hawaii. In the 1980s, the American ALF conducted a handful of expertly planned, high-profile, and well-orchestrated raids on research laboratories to rescue animals and obtain evidence of abuse. The 1994 raids at the City of Hope medical center in Duarte, California and the University of Pennsylvania's head injury clinic resulted in an $11,000 fine against the former and helped obtain a suspension of grant money to the latter. At some raids the ALF damaged equipment and used fire to destroy vacated labs. Labs responded by increasing security and pressuring government officials to take stronger action, which they did.

In 1987 the first Federal grand jury was convened in Sacramento, California to investigate the $4.5 million arson that had destroyed a research lab under construction earlier that year. Historically, the government uses grand juries to intimidate activists and destroy the solidarity and trust within political movements. Grand juries targeting animal activists in California, Michigan, Oregon, Washington, and Utah did just that. The US ALF's last high profile lab raid was the Texas Tech raid in July of 1989.

Recently, the ALF have been focusing their attention on fur farms. According to J. P. Goodwin, who was arrested for ALF activity in 1992 and is currently the executive director of the Coalition to Abolish the Fur Trade, the ALF have raided more than 45 fur farms and released 80,000 animals since the fall of 1995. Although many of these animals were recaptured or died soon after release, Goodwin defends the raids by claiming, "At least now the animals have a fighting chance at life, instead of a certain death from neck-breaking, gassing, or anal electrocution." He also says that at least two raided farms went out of business, and others may have closed rather than invest in security measures to protect their farms from raids. Although he admits it is impossible to know how many mink farms have closed because of ALF actions, Goodwin says the US Department of Agriculture's National Agriculture Statistics Service shows that between 1995 and 1996, the number of US mink farms dropped from 450 to 415.

Pros and Cons of the ALF

According to Katie Fedor, founder of the North American ALF Press Office, the ALF consists of anonymous activists who work individually or in groups called "cells" to conduct clandestine commando raids that rescue animals, destroy the opposition's property, and obtain evidence of animal cruelty, while taking all precautions to avoid injuring human or nonhuman animals. Fedor claims that besides saving animals and reducing the opposition's profits, ALF actions generate media coverage and help shed light on the atrocities committed against animals.

But do ALF actions further the attainment of our ultimate goal—the creation of a society where the masses voluntarily adopt a belief in animal rights? Goodwin believes so. "I think [ALF actions] lead to controversy, which leads to education, which leads to the removal of demand for the product," he says. For the most part, Fedor, Direct Action Defense Fund co-founder Catherine Rice, and People for the Ethical Treatment of Animals chairperson Ingrid Newkirk agree with Goodwin. As Newkirk explains, "Sometimes a direct action angers people, annoys them, and causes them to deride our cause. . . . [W]e have to find ways that may not be popular and may not be appealing and may not be initially persuasive to grab headlines, put animal issues on the front page, and keep the debate alive. Out of those debates changes come whether people like what got them talking in the first place or they don't."

However, not all activists agree. Courtney Dillard, who has a master's degree in rhetoric and has extensively researched the animal rights movement's use of direct action and media coverage, says, "If there has been one downfall of this movement, it is our subjugation of the message to gain media coverage at the expense of our argument. The message is lost to image, and that image is typically negative, which decreases our numbers. People steer away from extremely controversial images. They steer away from things that are easily ridiculed, and a lot of the images that have come out of this movement taint us as being violent or ludicrous."

Dillard believes the public's typical response to hostile, threatening, or disrespectful actions could be summed up by the words of author Ralph Waldo Emerson: "What you do speaks so loud that I cannot hear what you say." Instead of discussing animal exploitation, the focus shifts to critique the activists' negative characteristics. This is evidenced by the fact that after ALF actions in Minneapolis, Salt Lake City, Norfolk, Syracuse, and other cities, editorials by local media representatives vocally condemned the ALF and animal rights.

ALF actions create other outcomes we must also consider when evaluating their overall worth. Four US ALF activists are currently serving sentences ranging from 12 to 57 months. Joshua Ellerman, who used pipe bombs to cause $1 million in damage to the Fur Breeders Agricultural Co-op in Sandy, Utah, faces a 35-year jail sentence. Since June of 1995 grand juries, accompanied with increased governmental surveillance and harassment towards activists, have convened in New York, Utah, and Oregon under the guise of investigating ALF activity. As a result, many activists have left the movement and some of the targeted animal organizations have been crippled. Time and energy is diverted away from direct animal rights work and into justifying ALF actions, training activists in security, challenging grand juries, and coping with increased government repression. Financial resources are diverted away from animals and into paying bail and providing lawyers for ALF activists, and maintaining movement support throughout their sentences. Considering these realities, we should ask ourselves how much of our limited resources we are willing to divert away from promoting animal rights in order to sustain the ALF and endure the movement-wide and publicly sanctioned repression it creates? At what point do these actions cost more than they are worth?

The Nonviolent Path

In order to create the ideal society we visualized, we must convince society of the justness of our cause and mobilize them to take action. Both Gandhi's struggle for an independent India and King's struggle for civil rights successfully used direct action to change their societies' views and mobilize the masses. Considering our similar aims, we should analyze their direct action strategies to see if we may learn from them.

In his book *Why We Can't Wait*, King wrote that people engaged in direct action "must do so openly, lovingly, and with a willingness to accept the penalty."[2] By openly revealing their plans beforehand, treating their opponents with goodwill, and courageously bearing violent repression without hitting back, members of the US Civil Rights Movement maintained the moral high ground, exposed the tyrannical nature of their rivals, mobilized public sympathy, and ultimately won the support of enough people to gain their demand for equal legal rights.

King viewed direct action as the final part of a natural progression. He said, "In any nonviolent campaign there are four basic steps: collection of the facts to determine whether injustices exist, negotiation, self-purification, and direct action." In all of King's campaigns, diverse arrays of tactics were used, such as public speeches, literature distribution, boycotts, marches, sit-ins, kneel-ins, freedom rides, etc. However, these tactics were only used if negotiations did not secure their demands. King's sincere attempts to gain justice through negotiations and extensive public education efforts helped justify to the public his eventual escalation to the use of direct action.

But before engaging in direct action, King required activists to undergo "self-purification." This refers to the training and screening conducted to ensure that all direct action participants would remain calm, dignified, and respectful regardless of the violence they might endure. Potential civil rights demonstrators were required to sign a pledge agreeing to "sacrifice personal wishes in order that all [people] might be free" and to "refrain from violence of fist, tongue, or heart." During workshops, they were asked if they could endure jail time and beatings without retaliating. Trainers assumed the role of hostile and abusive police officers to test the courage, nerves, and discipline of the activists, and to ensure that they would follow the nonviolent creed "to resist without bitterness; to be cursed and not reply; to be beaten and not hit back." Not everyone who volunteered could pass these rigorous tests.

The self-purification stage prepared civil rights activists to courageously endure violent repression without retaliating or surrendering. In May of 1963 Birmingham activists seeking integration were beaten with clubs, attacked by police dogs, and blasted down streets with high-pressure water hoses, yet they remained nonviolent in word and deed. King firmly believed that this blatantly unjust repression helped positively transform the values of the nation. He felt that because of these incidents, "the moral conscience of the nation was deeply stirred and, all over the country, our fight became the fight of decent Americans of all races and creeds."

It seems the attitudes of the entire country were shifting in a positive direction—including those of white segregationists and police. During the campaign, King noticed the unusual neutrality of white citizens who previously would have violently resisted them. He was also aware of one incident in which police forces violated direct orders from their superior officer by refusing to attack peaceful marchers with fire hoses and dogs.

At the peak of this direct action campaign, an estimated 2,500 protesters were in jail, but their heroic self-sacrifice had galvanized to action thousands more who saturated the streets of Birmingham until finally local businesses agreed to the protesters' demands of integrated facilities and nondiscriminatory hiring practices.

As it turns out, self-sacrifice is a major component of King's—and his mentor, Gandhi's—direct action strategy. Gandhi explains it this way, "I have found that mere appeal to reason does not answer where prejudices are age-long and based on supposed religious authority. Reason has to be strengthened by suffering and suffering opens the eyes to understanding."

Contemporary nonviolent strategist Gene Sharp, author of the book *The Politics of Nonviolent Action*, names this technique of courageously and respectfully bearing violent repression to gain active support for your cause "political jujitsu." Political jujitsu allows activists to turn their opponent's repression into an asset. The more their opponent represses them, the stronger their movement becomes. However, in order to use this technique activists must be willing to endure the repression without retaliating with violence or hostility.

Some question animal activists' ability to use this technique because we are not fighting for our own rights, as black people and Indians were for theirs. Thankfully, irrespective of the victim of violent repression, political jujitsu undermines the opposition's authority while bolstering the authority of the courageous activists who endure the repression. Sympathy for activists translates into sympathy for the cause they represent. If people respect you, they will want to emulate you. The fact that we fight for others does not invalidate this strategy. However, it does mean we must conduct our actions in such a way that it maintains the focus on the animals, while avoiding the temptation to change the focus to issues of police brutality or our own suffering.

Lessons at Hegins

The protests surrounding the annual pigeon shoot in Hegins, Pennsylvania, reveal the different forms that direct action for animals can take. Every Labor Day since 1934, over 5,000 pigeons are used as live targets for shooters. Seventy percent of the birds shot are only wounded. Local children catch the wounded birds and kill them by breaking their necks, stepping on them, or throwing them into piles to suffocate on each other.

Since 1990, the Fund for Animals has spearheaded the campaign to end the shoot. They have initiated petition drives, "Action Alerts" to mobilize local residents, cruelty complaints, legislation, and advertising, and produced an educational video to affect change. The group has also tried a diverse array of direct action, some of which included openly violating the law.

In 1992 the Fund encouraged people from all over the country to attend the protest at Hegins. According to Heidi Prescott, the Fund's national director, more than 1,500 people came and the tone of the protest was extremely hostile. Shooters and their supporters entered the park through an intimidating gantlet of activists who shouted insults and spit on them. A crew of activists calling themselves the "Black Berets" dressed in military fatigues and picked fights with shoot supporters. Amidst loud chanting and yelling, some activists rushed the field in an attempt to disrupt activities or free birds from their cages. In all, 114 arrests were made (mostly of protesters but including shoot supporters) on charges including disorderly conduct, criminal trespass, theft (for releasing the birds), and harassment.

The following year, after reconsidering the tactics of the previous protest, the Fund sought to avoid confrontation and law-breaking. They encouraged people to not attend the event unless they could fill a volunteer role in the group's organized efforts, and they trained volunteers not to engage shoot supporters in verbal confrontations or respond to their caustic remarks and behaviors. The Fund set up mobile veterinary units where volunteers brought wounded birds for treatment. The action was calm, disciplined, focused, and non-threatening.

According to Prescott, Fund organizers made a conscious decision to change their tactics because the hostile approach was not working: "The media focused on the yelling match between the people, and the birds got lost." She says it wasn't until protesters adopted a respectful, non-threatening approach that the media focus returned to the birds: "When we changed our role at the shoot to that of rescuers, caretakers, and abuse documenters, there was no clash for the media to focus on, and instead they focused on the wounded birds and their treatment. The cameras would be inside the vet van filming the veterinarians taking care of these poor wounded animals. Consequently, the more nonviolent our behavior became, the more violent the shoot supporters became, and that's when they started to bite the birds' heads off and attack the rescuers. This allowed the media to clearly see who was violent."

The demonstrators' actions were so compelling that even locals, who until then had been extremely hostile, became more sympathetic to the Fund. More and more, local newspaper's editorial boards spoke out against the shoot as did state legislators. State Representative Sara Steelman helped the Fund document killed and wounded birds at the 1995 and 1996 shoots. One hunter even offered to write a letter to the legislature asking for a ban on all live bird shoots after witnessing the 1996 civil disobedience action in which activists, who occupied the killing field to halt the shoot, calmly and quietly endured the angry taunts of shooters before being arrested.

Although the shoot continues, the Fund's respectful and selfless actions keep the focus on the birds' suffering and has started generating the sympathy and support from all areas that is moving them closer to their goal of ending the shoot.[3]

Comparing Movement Strategies

When we compare some forms of current animal rights direct action to King and Gandhi's mandates that they be conducted in a respectful, open, and self-sacrificial manner, we see some striking differences. Few animal rights groups have formal nonviolence codes, and those that do often allow verbal hostility, threats, clandestine property destruction, and/or arson—none of which meets the standards of respect promoted by King and Gandhi. Likewise, most law-breaking activists do not openly reveal their plans to the opposition in an attempt to remove the opposition's fears as Gandhi and King did. Instead, ALF raids depend on secrecy for their success. Furthermore, the ALF seeks to avoid punishment. Even aboveground activists who break the law for animals typically try to avoid jail by accepting deals or using hunger strikes in an attempt to shorten their sentence after being convicted.

There are also differences in the natural progression of direct action campaigns. Most animal rights direct action activists assume negotiations will fail, and skip this stage of the campaign. However, King and Gandhi saw even unsuccessful negotiations as strategically important for helping justify the escalation of their direct action tactics, correcting any of the opposition's misconceptions, and showing the sincerity of their beliefs. Besides skipping negotiations, animal activists also tend to skip the campaign stage of self-purification—which helps activists' foster the courage, discipline, and self-sacrifice that enables them to conduct respectful direct action despite violent repression.

These differences between our direct action and those of Gandhi and King explain the difference in results we receive, and show a fundamental difference to our strategies. The animal rights movement predominantly uses direct action as a physical force to save animals, destroy property, disrupt the opposition's business through blockades and occupations, and to harass and intimidate. King and Gandhi on the other hand used direct action predominantly as a psychological force to persuade, empower, and mobilize the masses. Only after gaining the support of the majority of the public or opposition did their direct action take on more of a coercive, yet still nonviolent, nature.

In the End

Given our ultimate objective of achieving a cooperative and respectful society that voluntarily avoids animal exploitation, we should seriously consider adopting Gandhian direct action to gain the psychological force needed to rally support and mobilize the masses. Certainly ALF direct action has rescued thousands of animals, closed abusive establishments, exposed animal exploitation, and generated much media coverage. But have these actions decreased the demand for the products of animal exploitation, or have the rescued animals just been replaced? Have the abusive establishments closed only to be replaced by others that are better suited to provide for the demand? Has the media coverage helped persuade people to adopt a belief in animal rights or urged them to deride us as irrational and violent? And most importantly, are we sacrificing a lasting liberation for animals at the altar of short-term gains? Let me draw an analogy to explain this further.

Imagine a gigantic tree of oppression that represents all animal exploitation. Each of its thousands of branches represents a different manifestation of animal abuse. The ALF's current attacks against the industries would be represented by attempting to trim the tree's branches. Certainly they have their victories—thousands of mink released, the closure of a fur store, the destruction of a slaughterhouse—and a branch or two fall to the ground. However, as a societal minority, our movement has few tree trimmers. Our numbers are so small that we can only cut down a few branches. Meanwhile, as we cut a few of the easier branches off, the tree continues to sink its roots deeper into the soil, growing larger, and sprouting even more branches so that overall, despite our victories, we are even worse off than when we started.

Conversely, Gandhian direct action recognizes the best way to permanently remove all of the tree's branches is by starving its roots—or removing the public's demand for the products of animal exploitation. Despite the tree trimmers' efforts, the branches of animal exploitation will continue to flourish as long as the tree continues to feed from the soil. At first the process of digging up the roots seems slow and tedious, and results may seem unclear as the branches continue to thrive. But as we continue to dig out the roots, the tree's growth is stunted. With more persistence, the tree of oppression with all of its thousands of branches will be completely starved and die a permanent death.

Words can't describe the depth of tragedy of the fact that millions of animals suffer imprisonment and slaughter on a daily basis, but our task as animal activists is to minimize their casualties and suffering. Considering this analogy, we can see that non-Gandhian actions divert our resources away from attacking the roots of the problem, and thereby prolong the struggle. ALF advocates speak of the thousands of animals freed to show how ALF actions bring about desired results in the shortest amount of time. But given this new understanding of the situation, we must ask ourselves, "Are we sacrificing millions of animals to save thousands?"

As a movement, we need to rethink our current direct action strategy: Do we want to engage in a battle of physical force with our government that has nearly an unlimited ability to repress us? Do we really want to portray the opposition as the victim by attacking their businesses? Do we sincerely believe the media will reward our anti-social actions by portraying animal issues in a favorable light, or that society will encourage our threatening behavior by adopting a *belief* in animal rights? Most importantly, will our current form of direct action move us closer to our ultimate goal of a respectful society that voluntarily recognizes the inherent value of all animal life, or will it only ensure that we never attain it?

It is my sincere hope that by honestly evaluating these questions and engaging in respectful dialogue we can start to build a growing, sustainable, and strong animal rights movement that—united in nonviolence—will be able to unearth the roots of oppression as quickly as possible, and establish in its place our ideal society. Please do all you can to help make this dream a reality.

Afterword: Where We Go From Here

Although I believe strongly in a Gandhian approach to animal activism, I also believe animal activists need to let our shared commitment to the animals be stronger than any disagreements we may have on strategy or other issues. Maintaining solidarity within the movement is paramount. The way to do this is by respecting other activists and seeking to understand their thoughts and ideas. We do not all need to agree with each other, as this will never happen. But our diversity of opinions and free exchange of ideas in an environment of mutual respect will help keep our movement strong. There is much that animal advocates can learn from one another.

For example, Gandhian nonviolence proponents need to feel the same sense of urgency as the ALF activists and supporters do. In the US and its surrounding waters, an average of 47,000 animals are killed every minute for food alone. The animals' need for immediate action cannot be denied. Although strategic nonviolence proponents keep their "eyes on the prize" and seek long-term results, they must at the same time feel this urgency, so they continue making daily contributions to achieving those long-term aims and never become complacent.

Moreover, strategic nonviolence supporters need to have the same courage and willingness to make sacrifices that ALF members do. The open rescues conducted by Compassionate Action for Animals, Compassion Over Killing, Mercy for Animals, and United Animal Rights Coalition are excellent examples of courageous, Gandhi-style direct action. Open rescues not only save sick, injured, and neglected individuals now, but also effectively expose the horrors of factory farming in a compelling manner that creates public awareness and moves people to action. More groups around the country need to actively organize open rescues and investigations.

Besides open rescues, humane education is another powerful, yet under-utilized Gandhian tactic within our movement. Not all courage and sacrifice need involve risking jail sentences. More activists need to sacrifice their time and money to develop the courage and skills to teach social justice issues like animal rights in a respectful, non-judgmental manner so that students may develop their critical thinking skills, become informed on the issues, and learn about the compassionate choices they can make. Humane education is a powerful way to attack the root problem of people's demand for animal products and swell the number of activists in our movement. It would be worthwhile for animal organizations to devote some of their resources toward local humane education efforts.

Of course, ALF members and supporters who do not adopt a Gandhian approach may still want to acknowledge the importance of gaining public sympathy and support for our cause. Simple refinements of ALF actions could go a long way toward minimizing public backlash and promoting education on the issues.

For example, instead of short ALF communiqués that sometimes read as threatening, angry, and fanatical, there could be respectful letters that explain in a reasonable manner the facts about the animal exploitation targeted and the compassionate motives that compelled the activists to action. Mass media outlets often use quotes from these communiqués, and animal rights media often reprint them in their entirety. The quotes will be more persuasive to the general public if they contain information on animal abuse, cogent arguments in support of animal rights, and solutions for how to end animal exploitation rather than hateful words directed at the abusers.

Similarly, the ALF's spray-painted messages could be less threatening, and more compassionate and issue-focused. I recall the ALF spray-painting fur stores with the slogans, "Fur scum your time has come," and "Fur is dead and you're next." Threats and name-calling only conform to the public's stereotype of the ALF being angry, misanthropic terrorists. The action itself shows the determination and commitment of the activists; any slogans left behind should reveal the love that drives them and their compassionate message. Slogans like "Animals need you to stop buying fur" or "Please go vegan," keep the attention focused on the issue and help defy negative stereotypes. After all, how many "terrorist" groups use the word "please"? Maybe even spray-painting pro-animal bible verses like "Proverbs 12:10" and "Genesis 1:29"[4] would also challenge stereotypes and court discussion on the issues.

ALF members may also want to revive a tactic used in vivisection lab raids during the '80s: leaving behind an animal rights book, like Peter Singer's *Animal Liberation*. Such a gesture demonstrates that the ALF sees its opponents as potential allies and not enemies. It shows a respect and hope that the vivisectors and other animal abusers may change their ways and join our cause. At the very least, it helps promote the book and make people aware of it if mentioned in the media coverage.

In essence, the more the ALF shows that they are reasonable, respectful, and loving toward both human and nonhuman animals, the fewer negative consequences will result from their missions of mercy.

Regardless of the tactics we employ, we will face repression by those who have a stake in maintaining the status quo. Repression comes in many forms—from our co-workers and family members ridiculing our vegan diet to the police arresting and jailing us for rescuing abused and injured animals. Because repression is a given, it makes sense that we adopt an attitude where we are thankful and honored for the sacrifices we are called to make for the noble and worthy cause of animal rights. We need not fear these sacrifices. Rather, we should embrace them as the stones that pave the road to total and lasting animal liberation.

Moreover, since each and every one of us is expected to endure repression for the cause, let us all respect and support each other as human beings, even when we do not support each other's actions. It is our solidarity that will help us survive the rough times and steel ourselves for the continued struggle.

In conclusion, listen to your conscience and your experiences. Think for yourself. Take whatever actions you believe to be the most effective. Have all of your actions for animals be motivated by love. And, most importantly, never give up. We will achieve animal liberation.

Notes

1. For a much fuller statement of my position, see *Strategic Nonviolence for Animal Liberation*. This strategy guide includes 29 chapters with practical information on implementing Gandhian nonviolence for more potent campaigns. It may be found on the Web at articles.animalconcerns.org/snv/ or requested from Eco-Animal Allies, 3010 Hennepin Ave. S. #579, Minneapolis, MN 55044; Info@EcoAnimalAllies.org; www.EcoAnimalAllies.org.

2. Martin Luther King, Jr., *Why We Can't Wait* (New York: Penguin Books, 2000). This is King's classic exploration of the events and forces behind the Civil Rights Movement.

3. The Hegins Pigeon Shoot ended in 1999. According to the Fund for Animals' National Director, Heidi Prescott, "The actual victory was in the courts," referring to the State Supreme Court Chief Justice Flaherty's ruling that humane officers could file cruelty charges and bring the case against the pigeon shoot. The ruling also described the myriad cruelties at the shoot. "What I think turned public opinion in our favor, was us turning into the 'good guys' with the rescue effort and turning them back into the violent 'bad guys' while focusing the attention back on the birds and their suffering," said Prescott. However, there is still no statewide ban on pigeon shoots in Pennsylvania. A substantial amount of legislative support the Fund had evaporated after some anonymous animal activist(s) broke the windows at the pigeon shoot coordinator's house in 1997. "I had to work really hard to turn 25

State Representatives back around and there were a couple I couldn't turn around. It took a year to undo the damage that was done by that action," said Prescott.

4. Proverbs 12:10: "A righteous man has regard for the lives of his beast, but the mercy of the wicked is cruel." Genesis 1:29: "And God said, 'Behold, I have given you every plant yielding seed which is upon the face of all the earth, and every tree with seed in its fruit; you shall have them for food.' "

Defending Agitation and the ALF

Bruce G. Friedrich

Some activists in the animal rights movement argue that only "non-violent" activities in the tradition of Martin Luther King, Jr. and Mahatma Gandhi are acceptable in the struggle for animal liberation (for the purposes of this essay, I will refer to this sort of activity as "strategic nonviolence"). These activists have disparaged, and even labeled as counterproductive, direct action tactics that involve secrecy and/or property destruction. The animal rights movement calls the people who carry out such actions, subject to some other guidelines, of course, the "Animal Liberation Front," or ALF, and refers to their acts as "ALF actions."

Those who uphold strategic nonviolence as the sole acceptable tactic for the animal rights movement suggest, for example, that burning down a veal slaughterhouse or freeing dogs under the cover of night from their cages in vivisection laboratories to find them good homes serves only to alienate people who might otherwise agree with us, while draining our movement of resources (both mental and physical/monetary). They further argue that using the tactics of the oppressors (i.e., secrecy, sabotage, and so on) lowers us to their level ethically. They suggest that all actions for social justice, whether justice for animals or justice for people, must, both for reasons of morality and practicality, adhere to some basic standards, including complete openness among all participants.

In one of the more widely circulated examples of this view, one long-time activist and former ALF-advocate, Freeman Wicklund, wrote in *The Animals' Agenda*, July–August 1998, "I believe non-Gandhian actions jeopardize the movement's sustainability, solidarity, and ultimate effectiveness to such a degree that I [now] speak out against them" (see Wicklund in this volume).

To be clear, these activist theorists support education, demonstrations, leafleting, tabling, speaking, and civil disobedience that is done openly. They support, then, the vast majority of activities in which activists engage. The one activity they oppose is direct action where activists do not take responsibility for their actions, or direct action that uses tactics of duplicity.

So, for example, this philosophy would not oppose the hen liberations of 2001, which found activists from Compassion Over Killing (Washington, DC), Compassionate Action for Animals (Minneapolis, Minnesota), and Mercy for Animals (Dayton, Ohio) documenting the extremely abusive conditions of egg-laying facilities, rescuing hens from battery cages, producing videos, and taking full responsibility for their actions. This sort of direct action would be deemed acceptable, but not property destruction and other tactics that are secretive.

Drawing Lines and Making Choices: Which Side Are You On?

Just to let you know which side I'm on and how I got there: I wrote my college honors thesis on the continuum in thought from Leo Tolstoy to Mohandas Gandhi to Martin Luther King, Jr., distilling the essentials of each of their political programs, and discussing how they overlap and how they differ. After college, I spent more than six years working full time in a Catholic Worker shelter for homeless families and a soup kitchen in Washington, DC without pay (part of Gandhi's nonviolent program). I've been an animal rights activist since 1987, but have dedicated the bulk of my post-college years to nonviolent activism on behalf of peace and justice. This activism has been framed in the tradition of *strategic nonviolence*, as discussed earlier.

As someone who has read extensively in the nonviolent tradition and who has been arrested repeatedly for acts of nonviolent civil disobedience, I would like to address some of the arguments that are made in opposition to more subversive direct action tactics such as those engaged in by the ALF.

I do want to be clear: I wholeheartedly support strategic nonviolence, and I even think that actions in this mode may be, as the outlet for most of our energy, more effective in most respects (although clearly not for the specific animals involved in the case of liberations) than ALF activities, especially for our historical situation. I fully believe in education, leafleting, open demonstrations, and so on.

My disagreement is not, at all, with activists who use exclusively strategic nonviolence; this is the route I've chosen for my life. My issue is with activists who claim that this is the only route, and that ALF-style direct action is counterproductive and/or inherently indefensible. For the reasons discussed below, I have a strong sense that their analysis is wanting. That is, my strong sense is that ALF actions are helpful in the long-term struggle, and I am totally convinced that they are a reasonable response to the level of violence inflicted against animals today.

Looking for Cues from Other Movements

There seems to be an assumption among some who feel that only strategic nonviolence is acceptable in a social justice movement that Gandhi and King were solely responsible for the transformations that took place in India and then in the southern United States, that the actions and agenda of Gandhi and King were the only methods of social change being practiced. They seem to look to Gandhi and King as the sole liberators of their people and to say, "Hey, if it worked there, it can work here."

In actuality, as I examine the history, it seems undeniable that strategic nonviolence played a role, but was only one of many tactics—and not necessarily the most important or effective one. A more thorough analysis indicates that a significant portion of the impetus for change has come from the Nat Turners, John Browns, and Malcolm Xs. And, in one of history's more vivid examples, the United States gained freedom from the British by fighting a war—and one of the first actions of liberation was the Boston Tea Party. The perpetrators were never apprehended.

It is worth recalling that the assassinations of both King and Gandhi, the avatars of the nonviolent path, caused violent rioting on the part of their supporters, and that disinterested histories of the abolition of slavery or civil rights in the US, or independence in India, indicate that constant social unrest and riots were essential to the success of those movements.

Going further, I would suggest that including ALF activity in our movement has both practical and moral value. Practically speaking, ALF activity is more challenging than strategic nonviolence and will inevitably be more effective in some situations than strategic nonviolence alone. Even if strategic nonviolence were the best thing for India and civil rights in the United States (which, as I've indicated, is less than clear), there are still many aspects of historical reality that indicate that lessons from these movements may not be transferable to our efforts for animal liberation.

Limitations in Extrapolating from Gandhi and King to Animal Rights

As one rather serious, if obvious, example, Gandhi and King had massive numbers of followers who were fighting for their own liberation. Their movements involved and required hundreds of thousands of people, marching and sacrificing—all of them hoping to get something back for themselves or their ancestors, all of them responding to oppression against them personally. Gandhi was so beloved by the masses that he was able to convince people to stop rioting by conducting a fast. At the present time, a very small portion of the US population is willing to make these sorts of sacrifices for animal rights. Does it seem reasonable to wait until we have the mass movement required for this program to enact animal liberation? Do the animals have the time to spare?

As another example of how these past human rights movements do not lend themselves to easy replication by the animal liberation movement, Gandhi and King stressed that strategic nonviolence requires that the oppressors see the suffering of the *satyagrahis* (nonviolent activists) and say, "That person is like me, despite being [Indian, black, etc.]." Gandhi and King talked about looking into the eyes of the oppressor as he (it was always a *he* then) hit you with a club or doused you with a fire hose, to connect to him on a deep and human level. It is hard to fathom the animals doing any more suffering than they already have, but public empathy has yet to develop. Billions of animals have been tortured in myriad ways, without the oppressors, so far, feeling the empathy required for societal change. There is just no way to replicate this concept, which is essential to strategic nonviolence, in the animal movement.

Gandhi and King also stressed the power of global opinion to win their liberty. What gave them the limited power they possessed was *massive global popular opinion on their behalf*. Almost the entire world in the 1930s and '40s was awed by Gandhi and supported Indian independence. Support for civil rights in the US was so strong that King won the Nobel Peace Prize in 1964, years before most of the reforms actually took hold. The world was able to look at India, to look at the US, and say, "*We* don't do that *here*. Look at how *that* country is treating its people." Unfortunately, it seems unlikely that we will be able to generate massive global outrage over animal abuse any time soon.

Gandhi and King also both spoke and wrote eloquently about the need for *satyagrahis* to "fill the jails," to "enter the prisons as the bridegroom enters the bridal chamber," with joy. However much I wish we had enough animal liberationists to "fill the jails," at this moment in history, we don't. Again and unfortunately, animal liberation is a unique movement that does not compare easily to any past social movement.

And, just to be clear, despite these liberation movements having the numbers, having the benefit of being the same species as the oppressors, having people willing to go to jail, and so on, the oppressors still fought, hard, to retain control. And a look at history indicates, as mentioned previously, that the violent revolutionaries were probably as essential to change as the nonviolent ones.

So, if we can't apply the experiences of Gandhi and King to the animal movement, what past social justice movements do apply? The movement for the abolition of slavery and the Nazi resistance throughout Europe seem to me closer approximations to where we are with the animal rights movement, because they involved people advocating for and acting on behalf of others (though even these movements generated supportive global opinion and had exponentially more supporters than animal liberation today, among other differences). In fact, I have on many occasions responded to those who are incredulous that I would suggest that destroying instruments of oppression is okay by pointing out that if these were Nazi gas ovens or slave ships, everyone today, through the lens of history, would support their destruction. I have no doubt that the lens of history will one day focus on the fact that items of torture and oppression against animals are in the same class as items used for human torture and oppression, and deserve to be destroyed.

Regarding ALF activities, I would agree with the proponents of strategic nonviolence who note that we're not in a historical space where we can mobilize enough people to make such tactics as effective as they would be were they occurring on a widespread scale. However, simply granting that they would be justified were they happening on a routine basis does destroy the underpinnings of the argument that says they're inherently counterproductive.

With so much economic pressure against the animal movement (think about advertising, just for starters), so little support, no voices from the oppressed themselves (at least not in the streets, getting arrested and demanding justice), nothing like the international support commanded by Gandhi or King, few willing to go to jail involuntarily (let alone voluntarily), etc., strategic nonviolence (proposed as the best or only alternative) seems naïve and misguided.

The Value of the ALF

Far from alienating our likely allies, I have found that ALF activities speak to people, regardless of their belief in animal rights. They provide an opportunity to discuss the gravity of the situation, the fact that animals suffer and die like we do, the fact that they are not less important than we are, the fact that when animals are liberated, there is cause for celebration, not shame. People grasp these concepts, even if they don't agree. That activists would go to such lengths, risking their own freedom for the cause, taking steps that hark back to the Underground Railroad and anti-Nazi activities, speaks to the public in ways that passing out leaflets can't.

The second way in which ALF activities are, practically speaking, useful to the movement is that they shift the debate. In the same way that John Brown made William Jennings Bryan respectable, ALF activities make the rest of the movement respectable. John Kennedy said, "Those who make peaceful revolution impossible make violent revolution inevitable." I think it's equally true that those who work on the radical fringe push that fringe outward and make others, formerly radical from society's vantage, seem far more mainstream. And that, of course, is our goal: to alert society to the fact that animal liberation is every bit as reasonable, as a movement and philosophy, as was the abolition of slavery and suffrage for women. This psychology of "good cop, bad cop" is used in a million different ways, and I think it can be applied both analytically to past social justice movements and tactically to the current movement for animal liberation.

Blow It Up

At an animal rights conference in July 2001 I stated that "if we believe that animals have an equal right to be free from pain and suffering as do human beings, then of course we're going to be blowing stuff up and smashing windows. For the record, I don't do this stuff, but I do advocate it. I think it's a great way to bring about animal liberation. And considering the level of the atrocity and the level of the suffering, I think it would be a great thing if all these fast food outlets, and these slaughterhouses, and these vivisection laboratories, and the banks that fund them, were to explode tomorrow. I think it's perfectly appropriate for people to take bricks and toss them through windows and everything else along those lines."

In the wake of the awful tragedies of September 11, some anti-

258 / TERRORISTS OR FREEDOM FIGHTERS?

animal groups publicized my statements, placing the sound file online, taking out anti-PETA ads using an excerpt from this quote as the centerpiece, and attempting to use my statements to attack both PETA—despite the fact that my comments were not on behalf of PETA—and the animal rights movement generally. It was another red herring, but it did give us an opportunity to explain why anyone would feel so strongly about the abuse of animals inherent in raising them for food or "research."

Let me offer a parenthetical reflection: Although the anti-animal forces try to paint these as "terrorist" activities, no human being has ever been harmed in an ALF action. The ALF has always required that all reasonable steps be taken to ensure this. However, as we all were, I was shaken by the events of September 11, and now, along with many other activists, I question the ability to ensure that burning down a building can be done without putting human beings, especially firefighters, at risk. Based on my time living with rats and mice in Washington, DC, I have always assumed that animals will escape such fires, since their senses of smell, wariness of such dangers, and ability to move through almost invisible holes is so impressive, but I think that we should not dismiss the possibility that they, also, will be harmed. These reflections do not, of course, rule out burning meat trucks. And they don't mean that when the next slaughterhouse or vivisection lab burns down, I will denounce those who carried out the burning, or that I will feel anything other than joy in my heart for the loss of the torture dungeons.

I've been interviewed repeatedly regarding my July 2001 statements. In every instance, I was able to describe the awful abuse of animals involved in the farmed animal and vivisection industries, the complete waste and horrible abuse involved, and so on. I was able to paint a vivid picture, pointing out that if these were human beings in laboratories, slaughterhouses, or factory farms, everyone would support burning down the implements of their torture. In fact, if these were dogs and cats, most of the general public would be supportive of such actions. These arguments resonate with people. From a public relations standpoint, the anti-animal groups seem to me to have made a big mistake.

Again, I want to be clear that these are not tactics that PETA uses or suggests, and they're not tactics to which I personally resort. All I am saying is that, in my view, they have their place in our movement and should not be actively opposed by people who support animal rights, even if they're not what we consider to be the best use of our own energy.

Taking Responsibility: Reflections on the Pragmatism of "Doing Time"

The one "escape clause" offered by those who suggest that only strategic nonviolence is acceptable is that ALF-type activity is okay as long as one does it aboveboard and claims responsibility. It seems obvious to me that this sort of action, if it lands us in jail, is more likely to alienate us from people than ALF activities. It confuses people. I speak from experience, as a member of a peace and justice community that routinely engages in civil disobedience in broad daylight, and then goes to jail, refusing bail, refusing to do community service as penance for our "wrongdoing," and so on.

Although I find this a deeply powerful witness and would not trade my jail and prison experiences for anything, I can say with complete certainty that these sorts of actions do not resonate with people. I can't even count the number of people (fellow prisoners and guards while I was in prison; relatives, church groups, and others outside of prison) who said to me, basically (and sometimes explicitly), "You went to jail voluntarily? If the cause is so important, why go to jail when you can keep acting for your cause on the outside? Why on earth don't you keep acting until you're caught?" And so on.

If we believe that animals have as much right to be free from pain and suffering as human beings do, and if we understand the degree of the animals' suffering, how can we disdain actions that liberate them, actions that treat their suffering as important? In the *Agenda* article referred to above, it was put this way: "Certainly ALF direct action has rescued thousands of animals, closed abusive establishments, exposed animal exploitation, and generated much media coverage. But are we sacrificing long-term liberation on the altar of short-term goals?"

I can't understand how one could argue, if one believes that other animals have as much right to be free from suffering as humans do, that such consequences are not enough to justify ALF activity. In addition to totally disagreeing with the argument that ALF activities alienate people (certainly, they shake people up, and some people will claim to be alienated), I can't imagine arguing, even if it were true: "Well, yes, animals were saved, but you know, some people are now alienated from our message." Imagine applying similar logic to some movement for human liberation.

Furthermore, the oppressors claimed (and their apologists still claim) that Gandhi's and King's more radical tactics were alienating and set back their overall cause for liberation. King's "Letter from a

Birmingham Jail" addresses these arguments, suggesting that people need to understand the seriousness of the situation. His arguments are equally valid in defending his strategic nonviolence, which unsettled people, or in defending ALF or Underground Railroad styles of nonco-operation with evil. The naysayers were—and are—wrong in both cases.

Freedom Cannot Wait

Ask yourself: Is strategic nonviolence always the best tactic, as its adherents claim? For example, there is the story of the man who "stole" a mistreated rabbit from an abusive "owner's" yard and placed her in a good home. He contends that ALF activity worked wonders for that rabbit overnight. Would you have forced that rabbit to remain in those conditions? I doubt that many of us would. At the very least, this anecdote should lay to rest the idea that strategic nonviolence is the only tactic worth supporting. Surely the small ethical compromise, if you feel there is one, in this man's unwillingness to leave a note claiming responsibility for taking the rabbit (even though some might argue he should have; we're evaluating the action as it happened), is far outweighed by the rabbit's ability to live a normal rabbit life and be spared the suffering to which she had been subjected.

There are similar cases where abused animals, especially dogs on chains in back yards or cats in feces-ridden households, have been taken away, without their "owner's" consent, and placed in good homes. Surely these actions are justified.

And, although direct action methods involving secrecy and/or property destruction have comprised a tiny fraction of activist work in the realm of animal protection, certain of these actions are milestones in tracing the progress of the modern animal rights movement. For example, in 1985, members of the ALF broke into animal labs at the University of Pennsylvania, where an insider had leaked disturbing information of cruel experiments being conducted on baboons. During the laboratory raid, the ALF stole videotapes, taken by the vivisectors themselves, of the "research" being carried out in the lab. While the actual perpetrators of the break-in and theft disappeared underground, general release of the stolen videotapes resulted in a public uproar. On the videotapes, we see the vivisectors strapping baboons to operating tables, cementing a helmet harness to an animal's shaved skull, and propelling the baboon's head forward into the cement, all in the presence of other baboons and to the accompaniment of loud rock music, joking and smoking. The vivisectors describe the force of the crash as "1,000 Gs" (a 15-force "G" can kill a human being). After the blow, the experimenters strike the helmet repeatedly with a hammer, using their full force in attempts to dislodge it from the injured head. As a result of public outcry, the lab was eventually shut down by order of former Department of Health and Human Services Secretary Margaret Heckler.

Similarly, in 1987, members of "True Friends" broke into SEMA Laboratories in Rockville, Maryland, where chimpanzees were kept in barren isolation cages. Video footage taken by True Friends documents the animals' isolation and expressions of insanity. Four chimpanzees were taken in the raid and delivered to sanctuary homes. As a result of the True Friends investigation, world-renowned chimpanzee experts Jane Goodall and Roger Fouts demanded a tour of the SEMA facilities. Disturbed by what they saw, Goodall and Fouts ignited a fresh debate on the use of nonhuman primates in research, radically altering the discourse on the subject.

Indeed, how can those who suggest that strategic nonviolence is the only acceptable means of social change so discount the many animals who have been saved by ALF activities? And how can they disdain the many undercover investigations carried out (and photos/videos taken) by PETA, Farm Sanctuary, Viva!USA, SHARK, and others, followed by powerful exposés that have saved countless animal lives, brought the issue of animal suffering into the public sphere, mobilized public opinion, led to lawsuits against animal abusers, led to labs shutting down, and been so valuable and important for our movement?

All Roads Lead to Liberation: Maintaining a United Front

We are all working toward the same goal, and we should support one another—as long as basic humane principles are not violated. I have heard that some who adhere to the "strategic nonviolence is the only way" camp claim that ALF activities are the moral equivalent of vivisection. This is completely antithetical to the philosophies of King and Gandhi, who understood that "We are all in this struggle together."

Beyond the need to unify, I find most people's adherence to "strategic nonviolence" as a moral principle to be questionable. How many proponents of strategic nonviolence as the sole acceptable tactic in animal liberation were opposed to the US bombing missions in Bosnia, Afghanistan, or Nazi Germany? Why is it sometimes okay to kill people as a means to an end, but not okay to engage in ALF activities?

Even Gandhi said repeatedly that violence was preferable to apathy or cowardice, stating explicitly, "When my eldest son asked me what he should have done, had he been present when I was almost fatally assaulted in 1908, whether he should have run away and seen me killed or whether he should have used his physical force which he could and wanted to use, and defended me, I told him that it was his duty to defend me even by using violence. . . . I would rather have India resort to arms in order to defend her honour than that she should in a cowardly manner become or remain a helpless witness to her own dishonour." And when England was defending itself against the Nazis, although Gandhi felt that nonviolent defense would be better, he agreed that armed defense was preferable to acquiescence, and even assisted in the war effort, as he had in previous wars.

I am convinced that it is our innate speciesism, deeply ingrained in most of us, that allows this discussion to even occur. When I'm wondering about my actions, or the actions of others in the movement, I attempt to relocate the scenario and ask myself, "What if there were people in these cages, people in these slaughterhouses?" When I start to feel uncomfortable, when I evaluate ALF actions, I strive to break out of my need to be accepted or respected, and I try to think about how I would react if this were happening to a dear friend or relative— because these animals have every bit as much right not to be in these conditions as you do, as I do, as anyone does.

In the end, it seems to me that the most important thing is that those of us who take the animals' side simply stop the internecine fighting and name calling, which does not help animals *at all*, and get back to the essential work of animal liberation.

Bricks and Bullhorns

Kevin Jonas

By means of a well-thought-out strategy, and extremely effective campaigning methods, SHAC has decimated a once powerful vivisection company and trepidation has been spread through the vivisection industry as a whole.—Ronnie Lee, founder of the Animal Liberation Front

The One-Two Punch

The debate over the use of animals in laboratory research has been taken to an uncomfortably personal level for those involved in this barbaric industry. The Stop Huntingdon Animal Cruelty (SHAC) campaign, currently battling to close down the notorious Huntingdon Life Sciences (HLS) in 15 different countries, consistently pushes the middle ground of protest activity by engaging in unexpected home demonstrations, property destruction, liberations of animals, office disruptions, and electronic attacks. While controversy surrounds this campaign at every step and target, SHAC proudly proclaims that it is not your grandparents' Humane Society or ASPCA, but rather a radical abolitionist effort that will not compromise, will not apologize, and will never relent.

Since 1999 the SHAC campaign has laid siege to Huntingdon Life Sciences—a contract research organization that kills roughly 500 animals a day testing household and industrial products—by means of a strategic combination of lawful campaign tactics and illegal direct action. This combination has targeted HLS employees, clients, investors, and laboratory suppliers by day (as hordes of emails, phone calls, and sign-wielding demonstrators obstruct the business), while breaking windows at homes, sinking private yachts, and disseminating personal credit card information throughout cyberspace by night. The combined impact of both types of action, legal and illegal, carries far more weight than either approach alone. Complete siege mentality has set in for those targeted; scores have capitulated to the SHAC bark, and even more to the SHAC bite.

Demonstrations on their own often seem benign and manageable to those on the receiving end. Likewise, ALF attacks have traditionally been random, and those targeted with liberations and economic sabotage could reasonably expect no further concerted efforts directed against them. The seemingly logical marriage of both forms of social activism has demonstrated that the grass roots can assemble an effective and cohesive fighting unit, independent of forces such as the mainstream press and political processes.

When Harry Met Sally

The SHAC campaign, and its unique blend of activism, has its origins in the UK in the mid-1990s.[1] For over 25 years, the ALF in England had been hammering away at businesses that exploit animals. Thousands of animals were liberated from vivisection labs and millions of pounds in damage were inflicted. A few concerted efforts by direct action advocates at specific targets had met with success; for example, a series of arson attacks convinced all the major department stores to discontinue the sale of fur garments (especially after one major store, Dingles, completely burned to the ground), and Boots, a widely known drugstore chain, had its windows smashed so many times that it ceased testing its products on animals. By and large, however, the actions of the ALF were scattershot; accessibility and opportunity seemed to determine the targets of such direct actions.

At the same time, numerous aboveground campaigns were in progress. It seemed as though every weekend activists would hold a different placard at a different demonstration. One weekend you were demonstrating against the live export of animals, the next fur, and the next fox hunting. As public exposure to cruelty issues grew, positive change for the animals was slowly taking place, but the tangible accomplishments seemed stiflingly slow. Lacking strategy and cohesion, the movement was unable to curb the increasing number of animals killed.

In 1996 a husband-and-wife team decided, after years of this sort of protest campaigning, that they were going to try to infuse more strategy into the struggle and give the grass roots a much-needed victory. They decided to concentrate all their efforts on a breeder of beagles used for vivisection called Consort Kennels, a target that was winnable and whose demise would be significant. For 10 months the campaign to close Consort brought in hundreds from the grassroots animal movement to stage daily pickets, nightly home protests, and large riotous national demonstrations. At every turn those who owned and worked at Consort were greeted by screaming protestors. Meanwhile, the ALF went where protestors could not—liberating puppies from the facility, trashing the homes of the employees, and painting their cars. After 10 months of aggressive, nonstop pressure, the employee turnover rate and security costs became so great that it was no longer profitable to breed beagles for misery and death, and Consort closed, releasing its last 200 dogs to animal welfare advocates.

This victory was a much-needed shot in the arm for the British animal rights movement. It galvanized the grass roots into a formidable force. More importantly, it empowered these activists, demonstrating that the grass roots need not wait for the media to champion our cause, for the politicians to answer to us (rather than the corporate sector they are wedded to), and for the national groups to do our bidding for us. We can achieve animal liberation on our own. If all activists pool their resources and skills—deploying tactics ranging from letter writing to brick throwing—and concentrate on one target, the opposition does not stand a chance.

After Consort closed, the activists who had united against it turned to a new target, one that would become a legend in animal rights history. Hillgrove Cat Farm was one of the last commercial cat breeders for the vivisection industry and, as such, a significant component of the English animal research infrastructure. The all-out, high-pressure "Save the Hillgrove Cats" campaign ran for 18 months. Again, daily pickets, followed by nighttime home protests, and large-scale national demonstrations destroyed the morale of the owner and the employees. Christopher Brown, who owned the breeding facility, also lived on the premises. Over the course of the campaign he became so vilified that the *Sunday Express* dubbed him "the most evil man in Britain." Brown also became the center of many ALF attacks. Not only were kittens rescued from the facility on several occasions, but Brown's cars were fire-bombed, his windows were smashed, and a telephone pole was actually tipped over onto his home. The animal rights movement had never seen such intensity directed at one target, and, despite countless arrests and eventually a court injunction banning all demonstrations within five miles of the farm, the pressure in the end became too much and

Brown closed the farm. Over 800 cats were released to the RSPCA for a chance at a better life.

This same recipe for success—the coupling of intense lawful protest activity with direct action focused on one target—has been repeated over and over again in England. A handful of fur stores have shut, a primate importer and breeder has closed permanently, and, in perhaps the truest testament to this strategy, rabbit breeder Regal Rabbits was closed in just one week. The campaign to close Regal was inspired by an ALF raid in which some 20 rabbits were saved. Only one week of intense action was needed, because the owner of the facility had seen what had happened at the other campaign targets and realized that he didn't stand a chance. He released the remaining 1,300 lives to the very people who were trying to shut him down. He is now a mushroom farmer.

"SHAC Attack"

SHAC was born from these victories and strategic foundations in 1999. The idea of using every tool in the toolbox took form and was set into motion. Across the UK, then America, Europe, and the rest of the world, animal rights campaigners set about making HLS a name synonymous with animal cruelty. Preying upon the fiduciary vulnerabilities of the beleaguered lab, the SHAC campaign protested and aimed direct action against any company that financially or otherwise supported the lab. Unlike the breeders that had been singled out previously, HLS is a multinational corporation—with major investors and over 1,200 employees—that depends largely upon relationships with other companies for its operation. Simple daily pickets will not close this company down. Instead, SHAC directs activists' anger, passion, and disgust at companies that HLS needs to survive—companies that don't need HLS.

Over the past three years a laundry list of the world's most significant financial institutions have withdrawn their investments from the lab. Scores of major pharmaceutical, agrochemical, and household product companies have canceled their contracts. Even the lab's janitors, laundry service, and cafeteria suppliers have come under fire. These companies have found it obnoxious and disruptive to have protestors on the phone lines, in their email systems, occupying their boardrooms, and visiting the executives at night. The result has been that HLS has declined in value by 90 percent and teeters on the brink of collapse.

The SHAC campaign has widened the circle of targets more than any other animal rights group. Banks, insurance companies, auditors, and private investors have found themselves receiving the same sort of vitriolic attention as those who actually test on animals. SHAC has made it clear that anyone who touches HLS is fair game. This approach has made the idea of sponsoring, investing in, or providing services to the vivisection industry in any way far less palatable; whole new forms of personal accountability have been brought into play. Although focusing on one target, HLS, the reach of SHAC extends far beyond it.

Direct action in the SHAC campaign has also risen to new levels of intensity and frequency. Since 1999 nearly 80 percent of the ALF attacks that have taken place in the US and the UK have been aimed at closing down HLS. Hundreds upon hundreds of windows have been broken, red paint has been thrown on cars, stink and smoke bombs have cleared office towers (and several city blocks on one occasion), bomb hoaxes have ended business days early, buildings and cars in several countries have been torched, and bombs have been detonated outside some facilities. Never before has the ALF been so active towards the same goals as aboveground groups lawfully protesting.

Just as with Hillgrove, Consort, and the others, the effect has been overwhelming. HLS remains open at the time of this printing only because the British government has interceded twice to prevent the closure of the lab by offering both bank and insurance services when no other commercial company in the US or the UK would. This is unprecedented, and its historical significance cannot be overestimated; volunteer and grassroots activists, joined by the faceless men and women of the ALF, have forced the government of a major western power to show its hand in support of a single failing company.

The battle over HLS has become more than just the battle to close down one rather heinous animal testing lab. A line has been drawn in the sand between animal rights and animal research, and the battleground is Huntingdon Life Sciences. It is a winner-take-all scenario. The politicians, law enforcement agencies, and corporate overlords that pull the state's puppet strings all recognize that when the SHAC campaign succeeds in closing HLS, any company could be next. Once activists get that taste for victory and understand the power that is theirs through direct action, they will not retreat. SHAC, and the campaigns that preceded it, are a menace to established forms of traditional activism in that they prove conclusively that not only does direct action work, but it can be compatible with lawful campaigns.

You Scratch My Back, I'll Scratch Yours

It must be said that the SHAC campaign does not run the ALF or have any sort of authority or control over their actions. SHAC has never solicited or funded a liberation or an act of economic sabotage. The relationship between a grassroots campaign approach and underground action developed organically, with both adhering to an unspoken but pragmatic utilization of each other's efforts to maximize their own impact.

For SHAC, there has been no question as to how the campaign has benefited from the hard and fast actions of the underground. Companies under protest fire have made their decisions to sever ties with HLS that much more quickly when faced with underground action. One of the most frightening aspects of a demonstration or home protest is the question, "What if this is not where the action stops?" The presence of ALF activity in the campaign has caused a great deal of trepidation for anyone who lands on the SHAC radar screen.

The ALF have exploited the benefits of incorporating their actions within the confines of a large national campaign. Their actions carry far more weight when taken in conjunction with other protest activity than in isolation against random targets. Significantly, the ALF can count on SHAC to publicize and defend their actions. In SHAC, and typically in the grass roots of the movement, the ALF finds sympathetic advocates who are willing to step forward and help with jail and legal costs for those caught in illegal activities. SHAC has helped create this culture of direct action support by selling ALF T-shirts, posters, magazines, and pins. It has hosted ex-ALF activists as speakers and sponsored a cross-country speaking tour for a legendary UK ALF Press Officer.

The various ways that SHAC and the ALF play off each other are mutually beneficial to the cause of animal liberation. The uninvited, but not unwelcome, addition of ALF activity to SHAC's efforts saw a mutually beneficial relationship develop. Both groups saw positive qualities in the other and used them in complementary ways to benefit the cause.

The Dreaded "T" Word

Does the combination of direct action by the ALF and unrelenting protest pressure from SHAC amount to "terrorism"? Yes and no. The campaign to close HLS is without question a concerted effort to strike fear into the hearts of those who criminally abuse animals. SHAC warns that those who support HLS in any way will be called to account for their actions. It warns that those who work at HLS should fear the loss of their jobs, humiliation within their community, and having any semblance of a comfortable life they have made for themselves off the backs of suffering animals callously stripped away.

The SHAC campaign seeks to recognize that this fight to close HLS is encompassed in a war for animal liberation, a battle in which the death toll on the side of the animals and their defenders grows daily. The SHAC campaign drives home the message that the animal rights movement is called a struggle for a reason, because it is a long, hard fight. It will take hard work, sacrifice, and sometimes doing things we are not comfortable doing in any other context. Whatever anxiety the animal abusers experience as a result of the campaign pales in comparison with the pain and horror the animals in Huntingdon suffer daily.

While the targets of direct action may be harassed and even traumatized, the actions are not terrorism in that innocents are not being targeted, only those "combatants" who are involved in the suffering of animals. Should those targeted not enjoy this personalized attention, it is their decision to end it whenever they wish by surrendering their violent profession. The ALF and SHAC are not flying planes into buildings or committing suicide bombings on crowded city buses, and it is an insult to those who have lost loved ones in real acts of terrorism to diminish cataclysmic events like 9/11 with comparisons to liberated dogs and paint-covered doorsteps. Far from being a terrorist attack, political direct action carried out by the ALF or SHAC follows in a noble tradition of social rebellion against prejudice and injustice.

History teaches us that all successful social justice movements have incorporated some aspects of direct action and tactics that seem unsavory and controversial. The animal rights movement cannot be locked away in a vacuum from the rest of this social justice history if we are to be successful. If protest and potlucks alone could win our cause then, by all means, these would be the avenues we should pursue. Reality teaches us a different lesson. Education, winning the hearts and minds of the general public, is of paramount importance, but in many circumstances, public opinion is difficult to organize and inform. For example, in the fight against pharmaceutical and university research on animals, public access to information is limited, and boycott campaigns have no main street products to target. In addition, a chief vulnerability of our opposition is their fear of personalized attention. In such circumstances, such as the case of Huntingdon Life Sciences, the immediate impact of direct action is not only appropriate, but essential.

Friend or Foe?

The "gloves off" approach to animal advocacy, championed by the ALF and campaigns like SHAC, has ruffled the feathers of many compatriots within the animal advocacy movement. Activists debate the "appropriateness" of certain tactics, and many fear losing the moral high ground in seeking to intimidate the opposition.

Such criticism of direct action and controversial ventures like SHAC is a speciesist insult to those animals who depend on humans to advocate on their behalf. If those opposed to direct action are really honest with themselves, they will have to admit that they do not believe the goal of animal liberation justifies the tactics they claim to oppose but would support in other contexts. Most people do support property destruction, violence, and murder for certain causes. If people in Liberia were being rendered for food, it would be a safe bet that most would support a war to end such an atrocity. If critics of the ALF and SHAC honestly faced the internalized prejudices that they harbor, and imagined that it was white, middle-class kindergartners from Kansas being pumped full of bleach or anally electrocuted, most would be ready to take up arms themselves. It is not children who are suffering and dying by the billions, however, but rather nonhuman animals, and only for that speciesist reason are certain tactics condemned as "terrorist" or taken off the table of discussion.

Those who may ethically support the ALF and the use of controversial means, but see it as a strategic mistake because of the negative impact on public opinion, have only themselves to blame. It is the failure of movement organizations and speakers to reframe the debate away from the tactic to the more substantive issues of animal exploitation. It is a tragic mistake and a setback for the animal rights movement to let the media determine our tactical agenda because of a fear of negative coverage. The actions of the ALF and SHAC play a crucial role in this movement and will not be stopped anytime soon, and if there does exist a problem with media portrayal it is well worth the effort of national groups to invest in becoming more media-savvy organizations.

Direct action has a crucial role to play in the animal advocacy movement, and when the mainstream can look past its fundraising worries, comfort levels, and personal speciesist biases, the opportunity to use the power of the ALF has great potential. The early campaigns of PETA working with the ALF direct action efforts against university vivisection labs proved this masterfully, as have the persistent Sea Shepherd campaigns against whaling and seal clubbing that combined lawful campaigning and illegal direct action. Today, SHAC is the intelligent and strategic continuation of such a rounded attack, effectively coupling both legal and illegal tactics.

When history is written about the animal rights movement, the notable exceptions that will stand out for their achievements will be those efforts that dared to risk scorn and controversy by embracing and/or spearheading cutting edge and radical activism.

Notes

1. The "SHAC campaign" has come to mean any endeavor aimed at contributing to the legal SHAC efforts, whether it be legal or not. In various legal proceedings we have distinguished SHAC the incorporated group as a news/information clearing house, and the "SHAC campaign" as all other protest activities.

Revolutionary Process and the ALF

NICOLAS ATWOOD

This article originally appeared in No Compromise *magazine.*

One day an "animal lover," out of curiosity, stops at a frozen pond to investigate bright flags sticking out of muskrat mounds and finds leghold traps stuck deep in the nest of reeds and mud. Fortunately, the traps are empty, but she can't help but think of the potential victims. She pulls up the stakes, holding the traps secure, and takes home as many as she can carry. She feels a mixture of fear and excitement, but overall she's happy knowing that at least the traps in her garbage will never kill an animal.

This, in the simplest terms, is an ALF action—destroying the physical property of an individual or business to benefit an animal, either directly or indirectly. The "animal lover" may become an activist, and as an activist, she'll protest and work to educate others, but in her mind remains the memory of destroying the traps, the small victory.

There is a theory that the use of "violence" by political groups has not caught on in the US to the extent it has in other countries because most Americans believe that there are agencies and institutions that exist to peacefully resolve conflicts, and that this belief is a barrier against participating in political violence. Perhaps in relation to animals this theory collapses, and it is here that the existence of the ALF can be explained. Crimes of enormous proportion against animals are commonly ignored by the legal system. Battery cages and veal crates are accepted as "normal agricultural practice." Billions of chickens and turkeys are denied even the illusion of humane slaughter. Birds, mice and fish in laboratories are denied the most basic of legal protections. In some states, animals in farms are specifically written out of laws against cruelty.

Of course, opposition—the desire to make a fundamental change in society by throwing oneself against the atrocity of animal abuse—is the right course. The debate over the ALF has never been a question of what is morally justified. How to best bring about change, though, is open to debate. Everyone involved in the animal liberation movement has doubts about the effectiveness of their actions and is searching for the best way to fight animal abuse and exploitation. Most people find that different tactics and strategies fit different contexts and that one way to defend animals does not have to replace other types of activism. Perhaps the biggest debate is over so-called violence versus nonviolence. There are no arguments for or against either approach that prove it universally superior or inferior to the other, or that one will inevitably have really good or really bad effects.

In defense of the ALF, it is certain that the ALF has rescued animals. Well-thought-out releases from fur farms and liberations from research labs have saved animal lives that you can count. Destroying a slaughterhouse or a fur farm–feed wholesaler does not save animals in an easily quantifiable manner, but may save animals nonetheless through monetary loss, inconvenience, fear, etc., that may dissuade a breeder from one last season or spur an exploiter's early retirement. "Violence" and "terrorism" are terms that have long been applied to the most important social, religious and historical forces in this country and in others around the world.

To be fair, much of the criticism of the ALF is justified. The ALF is not revolutionary. It will not bring about fundamental change in society to benefit animals by itself. But ALF actions can be a part of a revolutionary process and can have very important and necessary effects for animals who are suffering.

The ALF has not been proven ineffective. What has been pointed out is that acts born out of frustration, impatience, and impulse do not bring results. In "Making Our Actions Count," in the #9 issue of *No Compromise*, Dari Fullmer wrote that "direct action without strategy is useless." Although random actions may not be entirely useless, the point of choosing targets strategically is important. Direct action activists have to set priorities and be careful to make each effort count. Realistically, we are all limited in the time and energy we can commit to activism (of any kind). We only have a few chances; actions should be more than just symbolic. Don't sit in jail for breaking a window at your local McDonald's.

Research and planning are essential to be effective. This should mean fewer actions, but bigger, more focused actions intended to weaken or remove a vital link in an animal abuse industry. Activists must get to know their local animal industry and the role it plays at the national and local levels. An industry is made up of many different levels, from the farmers, the animal transporters, and the slaughterhouses to the processors and down to the retail end. Also included are industry research centers, promotional groups, industry publications, advertising agencies, etc. Every larger community in this country has at least one company that plays an important role in the larger industry, making the abuse and exploitation of animals profitable.

The Western Wildlife Unit of the ALF in the early 1990s, as well as some recent actions targeting the fur industry, showed us the way. By targeting the research that kept the fur industry prosperous and the fur feed co-ops that provide assistance to farmers, they attacked a weak link in the industry, making an enormous impact. If they had chosen to target the retail end and instead destroyed fur stores, they would have made the evening TV news, but insurance would likely have rebuilt the stores, leaving the industry little the worse. For the most part, the results of attacking retail outlets are not worth the risk.

What industry should the ALF target? Is it better to target a greater evil (such as the meat industry) or plan for a greater impact (by hitting the weakened fur industry)? Huge companies like IBP, ConAgra, National Beef Packing and Perdue Farms kill billions of animals every year. There are approximately 5,000 commercial poultry and livestock farms in the US, approximately 300 large meat-packing plants nationwide and another 6,000 small and medium-sized meat-packing facilities. Internationally, the US is the world's largest exporter of bird carcasses and other animal "products." Companies like Tyson and Hormel aggressively target overseas markets. Fighting the meat industry statewide or regionally is the only realistic option. The livestock haulers, the auction yards, the slaughterhouses and farm supply companies are examples of vulnerable links at this level.

What are the weak industries? We're familiar with fur, but there's also horse slaughter, the veal industry, foie gras, dog racing and circuses with animals, among others. For example, circuses remain extremely vulnerable to sabotage. The few dozen circuses that remain in this country are dependent on their means of transportation. A few (empty!) destroyed trucks can stop a circus in its tracks, literally. Many of these circuses survive performance by performance (season by season), and the loss of revenue due to canceled performances could seal their end.

ALF actions are dynamic and inspirational. The ALF can interrupt the dreariness of everyday campaigning with drama that reveals the animal rights struggle at its most essential level, if only for a short time. ALF actions can be a symbol of the revolutionary potential of our movement. The anonymous activist who destroyed muskrat traps acted out of moral duty without thinking of educating the public or hoping for media attention, and, if only temporarily, refused to accept the confines of the law. This ALF has great potential.

TERROR

There is one source, O Athenians, of all your defeats. It is that your citizens have ceased to be soldiers.—Demosthenes

One man's terrorist is another man's freedom fighter.
—Anonymous

There is nothing more difficult to take in hand, more perilous to conduct, or more uncertain in its success and more dangerous to carry through, than to take the lead in the introduction of a new order of things. Because the innovator has against him those who benefited from the old system; while those who should benefit from the new are only lukewarm friends, being suspicious, as men generally are, of something new and not yet experienced. In speaking of innovations, it is first necessary to establish whether the innovators depend upon the strength of others or their own . . . in the first case, things always go badly for them, in the second, they almost always succeed. From this comes the fact that all armed prophets were victorious and the unarmed came to ruin.—Niccolo Machiavelli

ALF and ELF—Terrorism Is as Terrorism Does

Paul Watson

Can the Animal Liberation Front and the Earth Liberation Front accurately be called terrorist organizations?

It depends on who is judging the actions. Accusations of terrorism are usually very subjective. There seems to be no objective adjudicator on the subject of terrorism. In fact, in the post-9/11 United States the label has been thrown about with such carelessness in the media that the very word is in danger of losing its significance. It is rapidly becoming the most commonly, carelessly, thoughtlessly and irresponsibly used word in the English language.

Terrorism can be objectively defined as any act of violence that utilizes tactics and strategies that involve non-combatants. Is the hijacking of two jumbo jets filled with innocent passengers and the crashing of these aircraft into the World Trade Center an act of terrorism? Of course it is. Was the attack on the USS Cole in Yemen an act of terrorism? The answer must be no. Only combatants were involved. The target was military. It was a violent act, but it was not a terrorist attack. Similarly, the Japanese attack on Pearl Harbor was a military attack and not an act of terrorism. In contrast, the US bombing of Hiroshima and Nagasaki would qualify as terrorist attacks because the targets were civilians. Was the hijacking of a jumbo jet and crashing it into the Pentagon an act of terrorism? Yes, because although the target was unarguably military, the hijacking of the plane involved innocent civilians.

Terrorism thus defined is not a recent media invention. Terrorism has been an occupation of human cultures since the dawn of recorded history. Of course, it is not always viewed as such by those who are doing the recording. For example, during the Native American and US government conflicts, massacres of Indian villages were called battles, whereas the Battle of the Little Big Horn went down in American history as a massacre, although it was a clash of combatants. In Nicaragua, the *contras* were certainly seen as terrorists; the Reagan administration, however, saw them as freedom fighters. The British government certainly did not see the Boston Tea Party as a legitimate legal action, and all of George Washington's men were considered traitors and terrorists. Nathan Hale was hanged for terrorism, and Washington would have met the same fate if he had been captured.

It should be a simple matter to designate an attack as a terrorist attack or a military attack by identifying the target. All violent attacks on civilians by military, criminal, political, or religious groups can be legitimately labeled as terrorist attacks. But of course it is not so simple.

For example, one common definition of terrorism is the utilization of low-tech or no-tech weapons in the hands of civilians against high-tech weapons systems under the control of a government. Throw a Molotov cocktail onto a tank and you're a terrorist. Drop a napalm bomb on a school bus from a $100 million aircraft and you're striking a military target. It's all about the price of the hardware.

As I am writing this, I have just seen two back-to-back news stories on the television news. One story described how environmental "terrorists" released 10,000 mink from a mink farm. No one was hurt. Property was not damaged and 10,000 animals were spared a gruesome death by anal electrocution. The story that preceded it told how an Israeli military "strike" against Hamas killed six bystanders. Innocent people died, yet the media described it as a military strike.

When is terrorism not terrorism? The answer is when it is sanctioned by government, established institutions or religions—or when the media says so. The more dominant and powerful the governments, religions and institutions are, the more justified is the rationale for utilizing terror as an instrument of social or political change or as an instrument to defend the status quo.

We forget that Adolf Hitler was a democratically elected leader and thus any opposition in the thirties to his government by Germans or foreigners was a legitimate crime. Interference with the internment of Jews was a crime, and those who assassinated Nazi persecutors of Jews were in fact breaking the laws of a legitimate state and thus could be accused of terrorism. Although it was clearly illegal to oppose Jewish internment, it was still morally right, and sometimes the law had to be broken before the law broke those who were forced to break it for self-defense or to protect a life from the legal tyranny of the state. And that is what we have with the environmental and animal rights movements today. People are forced to disobey the law to protect life from the legal tyranny of the state.

How is this different from other movements or individuals who have taken the law into their own hands—for example, the anti-abortion activists who violate laws to protect unborn babies from the policies of the government? There is in fact no difference in basic principle, but there are differences in degrees of violence. Christian anti-abortion activists have deliberately murdered doctors and bombed civilians. Animal rights activists and environmentalists have not been implicated in a single murder or a conspiracy to commit a murder. Anti-abortionists argue that the doctors are killers and deserve to die. This argument is ridiculous coming from a group that describes itself as right-to-lifers. (And most right-to-lifers are also pro-capital punishment.) I was once forced to evacuate a radio studio after a person called in a bomb threat to protest my violence in shutting down a whaling operation. The hypocrisy is amazing and even amusing. However, animal rights and environmental activists who disagree with the philosophy of the anti-abortionists would be also hypocritical to condemn their tactics and strategies based simply on philosophical differences. They are, however, free to condemn their acts of murder and violence as morally unacceptable in themselves.

A terrorist is also not a terrorist if the acts of terror succeed in elevating the terrorist to the status of statesman. Michael Collins ceased to be a terrorist once the nation of Ireland was granted independence by Britain. The Irish employed terrorism as a weapon against the British, and they succeeded in achieving their military objective because of terrorism. Without tactics of terror, Ireland would not exist as an independent nation today.

One of the best examples of the legitimization of terrorism is postwar, British-ruled Palestine. There were a number of Jewish terrorist groups, the most famous being the Stern Gang, founded by Avraham Stern as a splinter group from the anti-British activist organization Irgun. The operations commander of the Stern Gang was Yitzhak Shamir, later to become Israeli foreign minister for the Likud Party. And this was a stepping-stone to holding the esteemed office of prime minister of Israel. When he appointed Shamir as Foreign Minister, Prime Minister Menachem Begin selected a man that he knew was responsible for two famous and violent political assassinations. Shamir had personally ordered and organized the killing of Lord Moyne, the British minister representative in the Middle East in 1944, and Swedish Count Folke Bernadotte, the United Nation's special mediator on

Palestine in 1948. But this was not unexpected or surprising from Menachem Begin, a former member of the Jewish terrorist group Irgun. It was Begin himself who had planted the bomb at the British headquarters in the King David Hotel in 1946, leaving 90 dead and 45 wounded. And this man was actually awarded the Nobel Peace Prize 32 years later in 1978.

After Israeli independence, Prime Minister David Ben-Gurion banned and condemned both the Stern Gang and Irgun, although there was never any attempt to bring the terrorists to justice. On the contrary, streets were named after the assassins of Lord Moyne and Count Bernadotte, and Israel under Begin issued a commemorative postage stamp with the picture of Avraham Stern. Today, in its righteous condemnation of Palestinian terrorism, Israel has conveniently forgotten that it was violent terrorism in the form of assassinations and bombs that gave birth to the nation of Israel.

There is a word in Hebrew, *mekhabbel*, meaning a person who uses political violence, that Yitzhak Shamir and his colleagues used to proudly describe themselves in their armed struggle against the British. The word translated to "saboteur" in the forties, although the Stern Gang did considerably more than commit sabotage. The word has now changed in meaning to the more negative "terrorist," as in "Palestinian" terrorist. In other words, once the objective had been achieved, the objective, i.e., the State of Israel, had to be protected from those who would take it away using the same means by which it was achieved.

Governments set the framework for the opinions and actions of their citizens. When Timothy McVeigh was asked how he could dismiss the children who died in the Oklahoma City bombing as collateral damage, he answered that it was a word he had learned from his government. "They told us that the children we killed in the Gulf War were collateral damage and they said that the children who were killed at Waco were collateral damage. What is the difference?"

When asked why he believed that violence was the answer to solving problems, McVeigh answered that his government had taught him that also, and that the government solved all problems through violence—including the problem of Timothy McVeigh, who was put to death by a government that pretended to oppose violence. The government did not disagree with McVeigh's tactics; they disagreed with his choice of targets.

In a violent society, we should not be surprised that people utilize violent solutions. Our media culture in fact indoctrinates each generation with years of exposure to films, magazines, books, and music that glorify violence and emphasize the achievements of violence. And all violence is justified by the perpetrators and their supporters, and condemned by those who disagree. In other words, all humans support violence when they agree with the philosophy of the perpetrators and condemn violence when they disagree with that philosophy.

Social change is a violent enterprise and always has been. There has never been a successful nonviolent social or political revolution in the history of humankind. Gandhi, of course, will always be trotted out as an example of nonviolent revolution. Unfortunately, it was not a nonviolent struggle. Gandhi utilized nonviolence as a strategy against the British. It was their Achilles heel. Gandhian tactics would never have worked against a Hitler or a Stalin. And his tactics did not work completely with the British, either. The Indian Revolution was a multifronted struggle. There was violent resistance, one example being Subhas Chandra Bose and his organized armed opposition against the British Raj. Gandhi's followers were killed. Gandhi himself was assassinated.

The Civil Rights Movement in the United States was won through the martyrdom of the freedom riders, including Dr. Martin Luther King, Jr. Although King and his followers are to be admired for their nonviolent tactics, the achievements were still won because of violence. Lives had to be sacrificed to force the government to change the status quo.

The activists of the Earth Liberation Front and the Animal Liberation Front are merely emulating the strategies and tactics of every other social and political movement that has ever existed but with one distinct difference—they have not killed anyone. Yet environmentalists and animal rights activists have been murdered, and the media is reluctant to portray the deaths as terrorism.

In 1985 agents of the government of France sank the Rainbow Warrior in New Zealand and killed a photographer. Not one leader of any nation described the attack as terrorism. Yet when the Sea Shepherd Conservation Society sinks illegally operated whaling ships without injuring anyone, they are described as an eco-terrorist organization in some media, even though no legal charges have been brought. Fishing corporations eradicate entire species without a murmur from the media or governments, yet when Earth Island Institute calls for a boycott of tuna to protect dolphins, they are accused of advocating economic eco-terrorism.

There are indeed eco-terrorists. Exxon committed eco-terrorism in Alaska. Union Carbide committed acts of eco-terrorism at Bhopal,

India. The forest industries commit eco-terrorism each day. These corporations will not be found on any federal list of "terrorist" organizations, because they have money, and money calls the shots in what Mark Twain once described as the "Parliament of Whores" in Washington, DC.

The wholesale destruction of our oceans and forests and the incredible assault on biodiversity is terrorism of the highest order—terrorism that is accepted by anthropocentric culture as normal. The fact is that we will lose more species of plants and animals between 1980 and 2040 than have gone extinct over the last 65 million years. This mass extinction is of greater significance and will have a far greater consequence than the present hominid on hominid terrorist attacks by all sides upon each other.

Where are groups like the ALF and the ELF heading? The answer is, wherever the participants wish to take them. These groups are not under the control of any government or organization. There is no central authority. They are completely unpredictable and as such practically unstoppable. They are simply reactions to a cruel culture that does not offer any legal form of redress and thus spawns the frustration and the anger that fuels activist organizations. People will be jailed and harassed within the entire movement, but this cannot be helped, because there is absolutely nothing that mainstream organizations can do to stifle the actions of underground organizations.

In fact, the entire world is now being divided into visible establishments at war with invisible resistance groups representing a host of issues, many of which are in conflict with each other. Some are good and some are bad, depending on the eye of the beholder. All are good in the eyes of their members and participants. Such is to be expected in a world with six and a half billion competing primate egos. As the populations increase further there will be more oppressive laws created to contain all these chaotic conflicts.

The challenge that the animal rights and environmental movements have is how to survive in systems where both movements are being marginalized by the establishment—global governments, media and financial institutions. Human nature being what it is, the movements will adapt to the more repressive measures, and the safest way to adapt is to go underground with operations through cell structures. In fact, it is repression that motivates underground resistance, and the greater the repression, the more resourcefulness is demonstrated by the resistance movements.

The best example of this is the fact that as lethally repressive as the Nazi regime was in Germany and Austria, the underground resistance was never neutralized. The French resistance never comprised more than two percent of French citizens, yet they practiced "terrorist" tactics against the Germans and helped to defeat the Nazis despite many losses. The majority of French citizens did nothing as the extremist groups fought and died for them. It was extremism as a reaction against an extreme action—the occupation of France.

The ELF and the ALF have already proven themselves to be highly adaptable and very resourceful. Very few of them have been arrested and convicted, and very few of their attacks have been successfully prosecuted—this from a movement that is relatively undisciplined compared to the resistance movements in other more traditional causes. By all accounts the ELF and the ALF are growing in strength, and this makes sense as both the animal rights movement and the environmental movements are also growing in strength every year. If the radical underground of these two movements represents only a fraction of one percent of all adherents to both causes, it still adds up to continued growth of the underground, because that small fraction is continually supplied from the ranks of the more mainstream of these groups, especially if it is seen that these mainstream groups are not accomplishing much. The irony, however, is that because of the extremist groups, the more mainstream groups are given legitimacy and a credibility that they would not otherwise have. The Sierra Club and the Humane Society of the United States both benefit, like it or not, from the actions of the ELF and the ALF. Because of extremism, moderates can make progress. The underground groups are simply the shock troops for the movement armies of supporters.

Just as Israel would not now exist if not for the actions of the Stern Gang and Irgun, the animal rights and environmental movements may not succeed without the ALF and ELF. The Civil Rights Movement had Dr. Martin Luther King, Jr., but it also had the Black Panthers. The Indian Revolution had Gandhi, but it also had Bose. The animal rights movement has Peter Singer, but it also has Rod Coronado. Movements are incomplete without diversity.

In fact, it is only through diversity that any movement can survive, and this diversity demands tolerance of all participating groups within the spectrum of action for each other. It makes little sense for a mainstream group to waste resources and time attacking the ALF or the ELF. There is nothing that a mainstream group can do to prevent actions by covert activist groups or individuals. Agreement to disagree is the only solution. When challenged to justify an action by a covert group, a mainstream group should reply by saying that it is unfortunate that the problem or the threat is so extreme that some people have been moved to take extreme measures to address it.

The bottom line is that, like them or hate them, the ELF and the ALF are here to stay for as long as the environmental and animal rights movements exist. They are both decentralized, diversely widespread, unknown and unpredictable, and their membership is so fluid and transient that it is virtually impossible to shut them down. In fact, they don't exist in any real sense as tangible entities. Both the ELF and the ALF are decentralized organizations of shadows. Arrest an activist, and that activist will be completely unable to betray more than a small group that would have no connection to any other group. The ELF and the ALF only exist as two sets of triple letters, sometimes scrawled on a wall in red paint, sometimes photocopied on a communiqué, sometimes shouted from the crowd.

A movement is simply a device to convey an idea into the hearts and minds of humanity. Ideas flow like water, over barriers and through obstacles, taking the path of least resistance and striking with the lethal force of a pounding surf, only to dwindle into puddles and drops that simply evaporate and disappear. Like a tidal wave, the water is gone before it is fully realized what has happened. Behind it, however, is a trail of destruction. The establishment may just as well attempt to stop the surf from crashing as try to stop covert activism. But ideas can simply crash on the rocks of culture without impact unless a movement focuses those ideas and delivers them with stunning results. The freeing of Nelson Mandela was an idea that gained momentum throughout the 1960s, the '70s and the '80s until it broke like a wave upon the dike of apartheid, overwhelmed it, and simply washed it away. No one in 1970 could have ever conceived of Nelson Mandela becoming president of South Africa. It was impossible. And the impossible happened, because of a movement that was both mainstream and covert, nonviolent and violent, but most importantly a movement whose time had come.

Can humanity learn to live in harmony within the bounds of the laws of nature? Will humanity put an end to the mass exploitation of other species? It sounds impossible now, but it is an idea whose time has not yet come. But the stream is moving and picking up speed, and this planet and all its nonhuman inhabitants may one day receive the miracle that they deserve—the miracle of living on a planet without fear of the species Homo sapiens.

The mainstream movement should accept the presence of the ELF and ALF and carry on doing mainstream work. The future will see escalation of covert tactics, and ALF and ELF attacks will increase. There is a large pool of anger and frustration to draw upon, and the more the movements are persecuted, the stronger they will become.

But there is one way to stop the ELF and the ALF. It's simple, really. All society needs to do is to eradicate its own violence against other humans, species, and ecosystems. The raison d'être must be removed and, after all, what are these movements demanding?

An end to cruelty, destruction and death and the right of all species to live in dignity.

Not such a bad objective, really. Why would anyone want to disagree with that?

Once this goal is achieved, the ELF and the ALF will fade away as mysteriously as they arose—as shadows into the mists of history.

The Rhetorical "Terrorist": Implications of the USA Patriot Act on Animal Liberation

Jason Black and Jennifer Black

The United States has witnessed, in the wake of the September 11, 2001 tragedy, a heightened state of emergency and, consequently, an increase in national security measures. At the time of this writing, the US Senate and House remain tangled in a debate over the creation of a Department of Homeland Security. Additionally, the Department of Transportation and the National Transportation Safety Board continue making attempts to bolster airport safety measures, including enhanced luggage inspections, detailed body searches, and what civil libertarians deem unnecessary acts of profiling. These contemporaneous measures, while original in scope, find their roots in the passage of the USA Patriot Act, a legislative device passed on October 26, 2001, designed to curb terrorism and quell national outrage over the attacks on the World Trade Center and Pentagon.

The Patriot Act proposes "to deter and punish terrorist acts in the United States and around the world, (and) to enhance law enforcement investigatory tools."[1] The Act seeks to modify and build upon prior discussions of terrorism located in Title 18 of the United States Code. Title 18, in sum, encapsulates America's criminal codes, including acts against property, person, and nation. The Act, however, crafts an overly broad definition of what constitutes, and thus what can be punished as, an act of terrorism. The American Civil Liberties Union and other libertarian watchdogs have worked to alert the American public to the negative implications of the Patriot Act. They have warned, "Congress is about to pass a law that drastically expands government's power to invade our privacy, to imprison people without due process, and to punish dissent. More disturbing is the fact that this power grab over our freedom and civil liberties is in fact not necessary to fight terrorism."[2] The ACLU's worry resonates particularly clearly with movements in the vanguard of social change. That is, "imprisoning without due process" for mere "dissent" violates the basic tenets of protest and activism.³ When a "dissenting" group—whether established or underground—can attract the label of "terrorist," activism is squelched, and individual liberties are at stake. When that activism takes the form of animal liberation, which society views as an "extreme" act, threats to personal freedoms are increased exponentially.

One group that will undoubtedly be disadvantaged by the broad definition of "terrorist" in the Patriot Act is the Animal Liberation Front (ALF) and similar cells of animal liberators in the United States. The ALF "is an international organization that seeks the total elimination of animal abuse and suffering at the hands of humans."⁴ The group contains cells all around the world, including pockets of activists in the United States. The way in which the ALF seeks to fulfill its purpose is "by performing nonviolent direct actions and liberations."⁵ Animal liberation first received institutional threats in the United States with the Animal Enterprise Protection Act of 1992, which directed a joint study between the attorney general and the secretary of agriculture "on the extent and effects of domestic and international terrorism on enterprises using animals for food or fiber production, agriculture, research, or testing.⁶ The result, a 1993 Department of Justice report, forever linked liberation with the rhetorical notion of "terrorism," and moreover tied animal liberators with the label of "terrorist." The Patriot Act extends the bond between the ALF and terrorist activity first established in 1992 by expanding the definition of what constitutes terrorism in the wake of the September 11 tragedy.⁷

The present essay strives to uncover the rhetorical "terrorist" of the USA Patriot Act, the new institutional definition of terrorism that may, in the future, present dire consequences for both animal liberators and those who support animal liberation action. We argue first that the Patriot Act presents a spurious, broad characterization of terrorism that constructs animal liberation as a "terrorist" act. Second, we contend that the ALF and miscellaneous liberation cells should not fall under the precepts of the Patriot Act. Throughout both arguments, we will critique the Act as potentially dangerous for the animal liberation and animal rights movements in the United States, in that the movement faces a number of legal repercussions for their actions.

The Patriot Act, Title 18, and Animal Liberation

In the past, Title 18 referred to acts committed by internationals as the primary category of terrorism. The Patriot Act adds that "an act of terrorism means an act of domestic or international terrorism."[8] This new rhetorical construction henceforth employs three criteria in determining the classification of an act as domestic terrorism. First, an act must be dangerous to human life and violate any state's criminal laws. Second, the act must appear to be intended to perform at least one of the following tasks: "to intimidate or coerce a civilian population; to influence the policy of a government by intimidation or coercion; or to affect the conduct of a government by mass destruction, assassination, or kidnapping."[9] Third, the terrorist act must occur primarily within the United States' territorial jurisdiction.

The second criterion exerts enormous consequences for animal liberation. According to Harold Guither, the ALF intends not violent or injurious measures, but rather actions designed to intimidate animal users and pressure decision-makers and governmental agencies. These aims are achieved through:

> Break-ins and destruction of laboratory equipment; damage to vehicles owned by research institutions; trespassing and blocking of entrances to research facilities; bomb threats; threat or destruction of research data and audio and video tapes; taking employment in research facilities to spy on the operations and taking illegal photos of the operations; and vandalism and attempted arson to offices and animal and poultry production facilities.[10]

The strategy of the ALF, then, is to damage physical property and cause economic hardship in order to undermine the heinous animal producing industries. These actions, however, are purely surface representations of a far deeper goal, the abolition of animal use. The ALF holds that such abolition can only be achieved through forms of symbolic coercion and persuasive measures directed at policy-makers and elite audiences, i.e., industry leaders, mainstream media. If this is the case, then animal liberation unfortunately fits under the new institutional definition of domestic terrorism. Statements such as "Arson has always been a valuable asset; it makes animal use unprofitable, it is the ultimate pressure point. Fire removes the apparatus . . . adding to the overall financial burden"[11] place the ALF under the Patriot Act's aegis.

The United States government has not only amended its definition of terrorism, it has also modified the potential punishment for such actions. Perhaps the most important amendment dealing with punishment regards the removal of a statute of limitations for certain terrorist offenses.[12] These offenses include those that result in—or create a foreseeable risk of—death or serious bodily injury to another person. By adding the caveat of a "foreseeable risk" as a possible cause for eradicating statutes of limitation, almost any activist action—whether liberation-oriented or not—could qualify as terrorism. Most social "extremism," because it threatens the dominant public in more radical rather than conciliatory ways, contains some sort of potential risk of hazard. So, for example, the 1987 destruction of a veterinary diagnostic center under construction at the University of California-Davis could conceivably have created a risk of human death or injury.[13] The assumption that an unfinished building would be empty would not hold weight. The chance that a rogue worker might still be in the building at, say, 3 A.M. would constitute enough circumstantial evidence to charge an animal liberator with terrorism, regardless of whether the action was committed 10 years ago or 10 days ago.

Before we move the focus of our analysis from the individuals who commit supposed "terrorist" actions to those who harbor and/or conspire with them, it is important to briefly discuss the act of animal "theft." Animal liberation is obviously one of the primary tactics utilized by the ALF, since one of its goals remains "to liberate animals from places of abuse and place them in good homes where they can live out their natural lives free from suffering."[14] Liberation of animals could easily be viewed as "theft" of animals, and could thus be seen as criminal. The portion of Title 18 that deals with theft, however, has not been affected by the changes brought about through the Patriot Act. In other words, the theft of a living being alone does not classify one as a "terrorist" according to the Patriot Act. The legislation offers no new categories of theft qua theft as an act of terrorism. Instead, the theft of animals (or "property" as the Act deems them), *combined with* breaking into, setting fire to, or destroying an animal industry facility, classifies one as a "terrorist." Since, however, one cannot liberate an animal without at least "breaking and entering," the liberating of an animal will ultimately pull an activist into the Act's definition of "terrorist" by implication of the break and enter criterion.

Other amendments involve particular actions and their corresponding punishments. For instance, Title 18 previously designated as the maximum penalty for a crime of arson "not more than 20 years." The Patriot Act amends this punishment to read: "for any term of years or for life."[15] Hence, in addition to being labeled "terrorist," a suspected animal liberator may face punishment commensurate with the charge of terrorism. Rather than the three and a half years' incarceration served by Melanie Arnold, an animal liberator arrested in England for firebombing a dairy, liberators could be sentenced to life imprisonment. So, Arnold's "firebomb attack against 36 large milk tankers which caused £2 million worth of damage" would, in the United States, possibly result in a sentence ranging from a few years to life.[16] The Act similarly modifies the punishment for other so-called terrorist acts, as well, ranging from sabotage to mass destruction.[17]

Animal liberators are not the only individuals susceptible to the Patriot's Act's rhetorical terrorist label. In fact, the Act states explicitly the dangers for people aiding so-called acts of terrorism, or even conspiring to aid a liberator.[18] So, for instance, if an animal rights organization were to provide "material" support to a cell of liberators—recalling that animal liberation is akin to terrorism according to the Patriot Act—its leadership could be punished with a prison sentence of up to 15 years. Before the Patriot Act, the maximum sentence for those providing support to alleged terrorists was up to 10 years' incarceration. Additionally, if a death results from an aided action, the leadership—or anyone extending corporeal sustenance—could suffer a life sentence in prison. The court is left to decide a suitable punishment. Given the United States' current state of emergency and obvious bias against those associated with any semblance of "terrorism," the prospect of the court's decision is both frightening and threatening.

As with the act of providing material support, the act of harboring or concealing terrorists has been modified. This section of the Patriot Act was added to USC Title 18, Section 113B, and thus arises as a new indictment of so-called terrorism. Acts relating to "arson and bombing of property, risking or causing injury or death" are hit especially hard within this segment. Now, anyone thought to harbor or conceal a terrorist—in the case of animal liberation, a safe house or facility that receives liberated animals from laboratories, factory farms, or fur farms—can receive upwards of 15 years imprisonment, an increase of five years from the previous version of Title 18. In addition, if human harm or death occurs, a life prison sentence could be imposed on those alleged to hide or harbor a "terrorist" under the Patriot Act.

Finally, the scariest amendment—and similarly the most violative of civil liberties—involves penalties for conspiring to (a) commit a terrorist act, (b) provide material aid to a suspected terrorist, or (c) harbor or conceal a suspected terrorist.[19] This portion of the Patriot Act should signal red flags for any individual even remotely associated with, or interested in, animal liberation. President George W. Bush, Attorney

General John Ashcroft, Secretary of Homeland Security Tom Ridge, the Federal Bureau of Investigation, the radical-to-moderate right, and other architects of the Patriot Act have designed this loophole to give them the power to, veritably, charge anyone with "terrorism." If monied and influential politicians can name Arab peoples terrorist simply because of religious affiliation or skin tone, imagine what the animal industry and its well-paid lobbyists and politicians can do to a "conspiring" animal liberator.[20] Is the writing of this essay, or the publishing of this volume, considered a conspiratorial act? Under the Patriot Act, there exists no barricade to the contrary; for, even "talking" about someone else's participation in animal liberation might spark a McCarthyite investigation into one's motives for such talk. This final amendment presents the most danger for the simple reason that there are few rules that apply. Similar to America's red scare in the 1950s, all an institutional accuser need do is point the finger.

One group of so-called Animal Liberation Front conspirators that could face significant danger from this portion of the Act is People for the Ethical Treatment of Animals (PETA). Many, particularly the US Department of Justice, have questioned PETA's connections to animal liberators. For instance, the organization is cited as "publicizing the Animal Liberation Front's statements" following various animal liberations and acts of ecotage, or economic sabotage.[21] Animal welfarists, who often find themselves at odds with animal rights advocates, argue that PETA president Ingrid Newkirk's books (e.g., *Free the Animals*) demonstrate a connection between the nation's leading animal rights organization and "terrorist" tactics such as animal liberation.[22]

It seems possible that PETA's real—or imagined—connections to animal liberators could mean the organization will find itself a target of the Patriot Act. Take, for instance, the 1989 arrest of ALF raider Roger Troen, who was convicted of theft, burglary, and conspiracy. PETA helped pay Troen's legal tab, and even publicly announced its participation to members and the press. Also, PETA has also been under attack by consumer groups like the Center for Consumer Freedom for providing material support to liberators such as Rod Coronado (convicted of arson), Gary Yourofsky (charged with mink liberation), and Josh Harper (convicted of striking a law enforcement officer). If these scenarios were unfolding in the present, PETA could be held liable as a "terrorist" based on the Patriot Act. That is, PETA's material support of Troen, Coronado, Yourofsky, and Harper—not to mention the suspicion of conspiring with these activists to commit animal liberations—would place PETA under the Act's aegis.

Similarly, PETA often supports undercover investigations, wherein animal rights activists gain employment at various laboratories and factory farms to document abusive conditions. These operations often precede break-ins and liberations at these locations. Under the Patriot Act, PETA's humane motives in sponsoring undercover investigations could be seen as conspiracies to commit acts of "terrorism." With the unchallenged methods and unbridled power that Attorney General John Ashcroft presently exerts, he no doubt might query whether PETA engages in investigations to document animal brutality or to "case out" the venue in question.

ALF and the Misnomer of "Terrorist"

The fundamental principle of the Patriot Act is to punish those individuals committing acts of terrorism that *intend* to harm or injure the American public, the United States government, or American industries. We argue that the Animal Liberation Front, and additional cells of liberators, does not fit into this construction primarily because of the lack of intention to harm or injure inherent in their actions. Let us not forget that animal liberation argues from a pro-animal stance, not an anti-institutional standpoint. That is, the ALF and others *intend* to save animals from human use and abuse. As the ALF exhorts, it exists "to reveal the horror and atrocities committed against animals behind locked doors, by performing nonviolent, direct actions and liberations . . . (and) to take all necessary precautions against any animal, human and nonhuman, harm."[23] Thus, the ALF aims to exact a positive effect for animal welfare, not to create a negative impact on human welfare. Moreover, the actions taken to reach these goals employ nonviolence as a method—a sure sign that the ALF means no harm to humans. Even when an action such as arson is undertaken, it is done so under extreme care to ensure that no human (or animal) life is imperiled beyond the economic damage intended.

In contrast, let us examine the quintessential terrorist act, the actual instance of inhumane malice that gave birth to the Patriot Act in the first place. The following discourse is excerpted from Osama bin Laden's October 7, 2001 address outlining the rationale behind the World Trade Center and Pentagon attacks:

God Almighty hit the United States at its most vulnerable spot. He destroyed its greatest buildings. Praise be to God. Here is the United States. It was filled with terror from its north to its south and from its east to its west. Praise be to God. What the United States tastes today is a very small thing compared to what we have tasted for tens of years. Our nation has been tasting this humiliation and contempt for more than 80 years. Its sons are being killed, its blood is being shed, its holy places are being attacked, and it is not being ruled according to what God has decreed. . . . When Almighty God rendered successful a convoy of Muslims, the vanguards of Islam, He allowed them to destroy the United States.[24]

The motive behind bin Laden's attack was the wholesale destruction of the American system. His *intended* method employed to achieve this goal was the extermination of the American public. The several thousand who perished stand as a symbol for the populace of the United States. Compare bin Laden's motive and method to the Patriot Act's stated purpose, "to deter and punish terrorist acts in the United States and around the world," and to the Act's characterization of terrorism as "acts dangerous to human life."[25] Undeniably, the events of September 11 constituted the purest definition of terrorism in accordance with the Patriot Act. Here we find individuals who agitate for no reason *other than* to harm others.

Appraising Rod Coronado's February 1992 raid on an animal research facility at Michigan State University, we find that his motives and methods are quite different from those of the terrorists whom the Patriot Act seeks to punish. Coronado represented the goals of animal liberators—to save animals—with his break-in and arson. He achieved this goal through inflicting economic damage. The ALF Primer explains the connection between liberation as a motive and material sabotage as a method: "ethical vandalism and sabotage does help liberate animals. It makes animal abusers pay for repairs and increased insurance with money they would reap from their blood trades. People will stop abusing animals when they lose money doing it."[26] Coronado's harm was not meant to damage for the *sake of damage*. Bin Laden's "damage," if you will, was undoubtedly meant to cause harm. Coronado acted with a positive goal of *saving* life, not the destructive intent of harming life.

Viewing these contradictory examples, we conclude that true terrorists take as their goal the indiscriminate destruction of (for the US-focused purposes of this discussion) the United States government, capitalistic industries, and/or the American public. These true terrorists are not opposed to sacrificing human life to achieve their goals. In fact, their motives and methods are circular. That is, terrorists annihilate people to devastate the United States, and they achieve this national devastation through the taking of human life.

The ALF and other animal liberators should *not* be considered terrorist. When taken at its root, liberation is not primarily anti-institutional; rather, it is pro-animal life; it is not primarily about breaking the law, but about ending suffering. In practice, illegality may occur, but it is always performed with human safety and ethical responsibilities in mind. In theory, then, animal liberation is nonviolent and law-abiding. It is horrible enough that efforts at preserving animal life and the environment are punishable under Title 18 as it was originally designed. To then link compassionate and benevolent actions to "terrorism" represents the true capricious, unscrupulous, and evil nature of the USA Patriot Act.

Implications of the Patriot Act

The present essay does not seek to suggest ways that individuals and groups interested in animal liberation should undertake direct action in the age of the Patriot Act. We have sought instead to highlight the changes that the creation of the Patriot Act made to Title 18, and to stimulate a discussion of what consequences these additions may have on those individuals who participate in animal liberation actions. Although the question of "what next" retains vital importance to the future of animal liberators everywhere, it is not one that has been addressed in this analysis. Certainly, though, our analysis uncovers, for those who theorize about methods of liberation, that there are new challenges in the wake of the Patriot Act.

The most profound implication generated from this essay involves forewarning animal liberators (including the ALF) about the potential effects the Patriot Act could have on their efforts and individual liberties. As we have indicated, the term "terrorist" can apply to almost any person or group agitating against the dominant public, particularly the United States government and its according industries. With this in mind, anyone can retain the label of "terrorist," if from nowhere else than the Act's open definition of "conspirator." One intention of this essay, then, is informing animal rights circles and animal welfare organizations, not to mention underground liberators, of the danger implicit in their actions. The Patriot Act could impress a challenge far stronger than that of the 1993 US Department of Justice report to the liberation causes and personal freedoms of activists. Recall that even tenuous association with the ALF might satisfy the Patriot Act's definition of harboring, concealing, or supporting an alleged terrorist.

Animal liberators and those who support them should take note that the United States government is fully aware of extremist activities, and now possesses a necessary tool—the Patriot Act—to surveil, infiltrate, and prosecute liberation cells. But this tool is sharpest and best used when liberators provide rhetorical fodder that the establishment can use against groups like the ALF. With this in mind—and as communication scholars—the ALF would probably do well to "cool" its rhetoric and reduce the amount of attention it draws from Attorney General Ashcroft and the rest of the Patriot Act backers. As Stewart, Smith, and Denton note, there are "rhetorical" movements and those agitative groups that "speak" through action.[27] Liberators' sentiments may be better voiced through clandestine actions than through media-driven campaigns or careless sound bites calling attention to operations that the Patriot Act labels "terrorism."

Animal liberators should also take care to monitor for the proverbial "mole" or "plant" in their underground cells. Just as Alex Pacheco was able to infiltrate the Silver Spring primate lab in order to expose and prosecute its leadership, so too can the government and its monitoring bodies turn the tables on animal liberators and rightists. Care should be taken to work with participants who can demonstrate continued involvement in animal rights activities, and who boast a long-term track record of reform and abolition. Proven experience in animal rights circles is something government "moles" often cannot fake, especially given the close network of rights organizations and liberation cells. If an individual's contacts or past activities seem "off," it is advisable to do some more digging into the person's reason for getting involved. Of course, maintaining masked and nameless relationships with other members of cells is still vital. Remember, the Patriot Act cannot label "terrorist" whom it cannot find.

Second, the identity of "terrorist" requires a clearer definition. The Patriot Act needs to specify its "terrorist" in more accurate terms, namely as an individual, group of individuals, or socio-political enclave committing acts against America's landscape and institutions for the purposes of harming the touchstones of the United States: capitalism, democracy, free markets, and representation. Animal liberators are *not* out to end democracy, attack any religion, or promote a fanatical nationalism. Liberators seek, instead, a fair existence for animals—one that involves neither injury nor death perpetrated by superfluous human exploitations of animals for their skins, their flesh, their milk or eggs, their entertainment value, or as test subjects.[28] If a "patriot" is one committed to life, liberty, and the pursuit of happiness—as goes the American standard—then liberators should be placed alongside American revolutionaries, abolitionists, civil rights activists, and human rights champions as the highest echelon of "patriot."

Unfortunately, it appears that America's knee-jerk reaction to the September 11 tragedy was to create standards that apply to nearly any scenario involving even slight disagreement with United States policy. Understandably, the American public was scared. The response to such fear, however, should not undercut the tenets of our freedoms. Given the far-reaching power granted to American authorities via the Patriot Act, any form of protest may soon come under fire. Will PETA's famous tofu-cream pie slinging soon be viewed in the same vein as flying a jumbo jet into a skyscraper or a symbol of America's military-industrial complex? After all, says the Patriot Act, any action against government or industry that could potentially cause harm characterizes an actor as a prospective terrorist. The National Dairy Council, whose executives PETA has targeted, represents an industry, and a pie to the face could, we suppose, injure or blind the intended recipient. This scenario seems far-fetched, but if the Patriot Act remains in effect—and garners the support and corroboration of contemporaneous measures such as the Department of Homeland Security bill—the reality of such minor acts of protest is possible association with the term "terrorism." Starting with animal liberation and moving to animal rights, activism on the part of nonhuman beings might suffer its strongest opposition ever with the advent of the Patriot Act and its oppressive impact.

Notes

1. *Uniting and Strengthening America by Providing Appropriate Tools Required to Intercept and Obstruct Terrorism (USA PATRIOT ACT) Act of 2001*, 107th Cong., 1st sess., 2001.
2. American Civil Liberties Union, "Letter to the House Urging them to Vote 'No' on the Patriot Act," October 12, 2001, www.aclu.org.
3. See Charles J. Stewart, Craig Allen Smith and Robert E. Denton, Jr., *Persuasion and Social Movements*, 3d edition (Prospect Heights, IL: Waveland Press, 1994).
4. "The ALF Primer," www.animalliberationfront.com/ALFront/ALFPrime.htm.
5. Ibid.
6. United States Department of Justice, *Report to Congress on the Extent and Effects of Domestic and International Terrorism on Animal Enterprises*. Washington, DC, August 1993.
7. The USA Patriot Act, a 342-page bill, includes a number of revisions to Title 18 and

various sections of the United States Codes that the present essay does not address. The forthcoming analysis focuses only on the sections of the Patriot Act dealing specifically with definitions of terrorism. For a more detailed account of the Act, refer to House Resolution 3162, in the public record. For an online version of the Act, see www.eff.org or www.aclu.org.

8. USA Patriot Act, Sec. 802.
9. Ibid.
10. Harold D. Guither, *Animal Rights: History and Scope of a Radical Social Movement* (Carbondale: Southern Illinois University Press, 1998), p. 156.
11. Rod Coronado, "The Flames of Victory: An Interview with Convicted ALF Activist Melanie Arnold," *No Compromise*, March 7, 2000, www.nocompromise.org/alf/mel.html.
12. USC Title 18, Sec. 3286; USA Patriot Act, Sec. 809.
13. Rod and Patti Strand, *The Hijacking of the Humane Movement* (Wilsonville, OR: Doral Publishing, 1993), p. 178.
14. Guither, p. 155.
15. USA Patriot Act, Section 810.
16. Coronado, p. 3.
17. See USC Title 18, Sec. 810 of the USC; USA Patriot Act, Sec. 810.
18. USC Title 18, Sec. 2339A[a]; USA Patriot Act, Sec. 810.
19. USC Title 18, Sec. 811; USA Patriot Act, Sec. 811.
20. See ACLU "Letter."
21. United States Department of Justice report, p. 23.
22. See Daniel T. Oliver, *Animal Rights: The Inhumane Crusade* (Bellevue, WA: Merrill Press, 1999), Strand and Strand, and Guither.
23. "The ALF Primer."
24. Osama Bin Laden, "Bin Laden's Warning: Full Text," British Broadcast Corporation News, October 7, 2001, news.bbc.co.uk/1/hi/world/south_asia.
25. USA Patriot Act, Sec. 802.
26. "The ALF Primer."
27. Stewart, Smith and Denton, p. 125.
28. "The ALF Primer."

It's War! The Escalating Battle Between Activists and the Corporate-State Complex

Steven Best, PhD

Many activists do not understand the revolutionary nature of this movement. We are fighting a major war, defending animals and our very planet from human greed and destruction.—David Barbarash, former ALF Press Officer

We have given all of the collaborators a chance to withdraw from their relations [with Huntingdon Life Sciences]. We will now be doubling the size of every device we make. Today it is 10 lbs, tomorrow 20 . . . until your buildings are nothing more than rubble. It is time for this war to truly have two sides. No more will all of the killing be done by the oppressors, now the oppressed will strike back. We will be nonviolent when these people are nonviolent to the animal nations.—Communiqué from the Revolutionary Cells Animal Liberation Brigade after the 2003 bombings of Chiron and Shaklee Corporations

Right now we're in the early stages of World War III. It's the war to save the planet. [Direct] action will be getting stronger. Eventually there will be open war.—Paul Watson

The time has come for [animal] abusers to have but a taste of the fear and anguish their victims suffer on a daily basis.
—Justice Department Manifesto

Is it my imagination, or is all hell breaking loose? Through increasingly militant and globalized actions, vegan, animal rights, and environmental activists have caught the attention of government and the animal and earth exploitation industries. The struggle has escalated to intense battles in the countryside, the streets, urban centers, suburbs, courtrooms, boardrooms, classrooms, mass media, and major political forums such as the US Congress. The level of conflict suggests a new social war that has been long in coming. As stated earlier in this volume by British ALF press officer Robin Webb, "Animal liberation is not a campaign, not just a hobby to put aside when it becomes tiresome or a new interest catches your eye. It's a war. A long, hard, bloody war in which all the countless millions of its victims have been on one side only, have been defenseless and innocent, whose tragedy was to be born nonhuman."

"War" entails violence, hatred, bloodshed, and an escalation of conflict when dialogue fails. In the insightful words of General Karl von Clausewitz, "War is the continuation of politics by other means." He might just as well have stated the converse—"Politics is the continuation of war by other means"—for in our uncivil global village the distinction between war and politics is meaningless. War is the intensification of the conflicts inherent in politics, and politics is the waging of war through nonmilitary means such as class warfare or economic policies that are as devastating to people as dropping bombs (as the World Bank and International Monetary Fund wreak havoc on underdeveloped countries by enforcing harsh austerity policies, or as the US blockade of Iraq before the 2003 war killed over one million people, half of them infants and small children).[1]

In the battle over animal rights, negotiations are breaking down and boundaries are being erased on both sides. Government and industry thugs unleash violence on activists, while groups such as the Animal Rights Militia, the Justice Department, the Hunt Retribution Squad, and the Revolutionary Cells openly advocate violence against animal abusers. More and more activists grow tired of adhering to a nonviolent code of ethics while violence from the enemy increases. Realizing that nonviolence against animal exploiters in fact is a pro-violence stance that tolerates their blood-spilling without taking adequate measures to stop it, a new breed of freedom fighters has ditched Gandhi for Machiavelli and switched principled nonviolence with the amoral (not to be confused with immoral) pragmatism that embraces animal liberation "by any means necessary."

A new civil war is unfolding—one between forces hell-bent on exploiting animals and the earth for profit whatever the toll, and activists steeled to resist this omnicide tooth and nail. We are witnessing not only the long-standing corporate war against nature, but also a new social war *about* nature.

A Specter Haunts Society: Animal and Earth Liberation

If the animals could fight for themselves, there would already be a lot of dead animal abusers.—Robin Webb

So far no one on the other side has ever been seriously harmed or killed. But that may now change.—Ronnie Lee

We're a new breed of activism. We're not your parents' Humane Society. We're not Friends of Animals. We're not Earthsave. We're not Greenpeace. We come with a new philosophy. We hold the radical line. We will not compromise. We will not apologize, and we will not relent.—Kevin Jonas

Revolution is necessary in the United States, and that revolution would naturally have to involve the use of violence as well as other tactics. . . . [Violence] has to be used if people are serious about progressing social and political movements in this country.—Craig Rosebraugh, former ELF spokesperson

Without question, the major conflicts of the day in many nations, such as the UK and the US, are not over gender, race, class, or the war in Iraq, but rather globalization and the exploitation of animals and the earth. The class struggle is over; mainstream feminists, gays and lesbians, and people of color are safely marginalized in their fragmented identity politics; and Leftists and postmodernists posture as "radicals" and harmlessly conjure up esoteric theory-babble in seminars and conferences. Meanwhile, the new ecowarriors light up the night skies with their demands to free animal slaves and protect the earth. In the UK, one terrorism expert claims that since the ebbing of tensions over Northern Ireland, the animal rights movement is the main source of "violence."[2] In the US, the top two "domestic terrorist" groups are not the usual suspects of armed militiamen, violent hate groups, or rabid right-wing government foes who bomb federal buildings and murder people, but instead the balaclava-wearing men and women of the Animal Liberation Front (ALF) and the Earth Liberation Front (ELF).

In a revolutionary rethinking of humanity's relationships to other species and the natural world, entirely new ethical paradigms and cosmologies are being forged. With forces of change emanating from both underground and aboveground movements, animal rights and radical environmental activists are pushing and guiding human beings to a new evolutionary crossroads through the force of legal and illegal direct action tactics. Here, humanity can either come to terms with the omnicidal nature of capitalism and the violent pathologies of dominionist identities, or it can take a rapid ride into oblivion.

The animal and earth liberation movements are vivid examples of the escalation of conflicts over the meaning and future of the natural world: Should animals and the earth exist for their own sake or for human use? Should they thrive in wild conditions or be slaughtered, altered, colonized, genetically modified, and even destroyed by technology and invading human armies? Societies are becoming divided over the politics of nature as intensely as the US was over the politics of race decades ago.

Because the state is so strong in its monopolization of the means of violence, this is not a war of opposing tanks and troops, but rather a guerrilla war in which liberation soldiers disperse into anonymous cells, descend into the underground, maneuver in darkness, deploy hit-and-run sabotage strikes against property, and attempt to intimidate and vanquish their enemies. As shown time and time again, from Vietnam to the quagmire of Bush's invasion of Afghanistan and Iraq, guerrilla warfare favors David over Goliath; it can bedevil and even defeat the mighty machines of the US government.[3] Consequently, the state should not be overly confident about its ability to crush animal and earth liberation movements, as ecowarriors in turn should never doubt their power to shake the foundations of the nihilistic, murderous, life-devouring system of advanced capitalism.

The new battlefield is a crucial testing ground for modern nation-states (can they adhere to peaceful enforcement of the law and protect basic democratic rights like free speech?) and the animal and earth liberation movements (can they creatively exercise nonviolent approaches and refrain from harming people?). Hardly a day goes by, it seems, that the ALF and the ELF do not free animals from their cages in fur farms and laboratories or destroy the property of industries that kill animals and damage the environment. From burning biotech research labs and ski lodges to firebombing meat companies and pouring acid on SUVs, the ALF and ELF inflict substantial property damage on industries. According to FBI testimony to Congress in February 2002, since 1996 the ALF and ELF together have committed over 600 "criminal acts" that caused $43 million in damage to animal industries.[4] The toll clearly continues to mount as, for instance, the September 2003 ELF strike on six San Diego homes under construction alone wrought $50 million in damages, the costliest sabotage action to date.

With the destruction of animals and the environment on the rise, the forms of resistance themselves have become more intense, as animal rights and environmental activists do "whatever it takes" to stop the devastation of life and land. One finds clear signs of an escalating war in their rhetoric, tactics, and targets. Where once, for instance, radical environmental groups limited themselves to rural areas such as the Pacific Northwest and focused on logging issues, now the battle has moved into urban and suburban centers such as San Diego, Los Angeles, Bloomington, and Long Island. Isolated acts of monkey-wrenching against logging equipment and trees to be cut has escalated to major arson and bombing. In order to target sprawl and destruction of wilderness and wildlife, the ELF has begun to torch and attack new housing developments, SUVs, and Hummers. Some (non-ALF) animal liberation groups like the Animal Rights Militia and Justice Department advocate violence (see the Introduction), and new factions like the Revolutionary Cells use explosives, declare themselves "for animal liberation through armed struggle," and threaten, "this is the endgame for animal killers . . . there will be no more quarter given, no more half-measures taken."[5] The Revolutionary Cell bombings of Chiron Corporation in August 2003 and Shaklee Corporation in September 2003 because of their ties to Huntingdon Life Sciences signal a clear intensification of animal liberation struggles. Emergent groups that see even the ALF as too conservative are beginning to steer a part of the animal rights movement in more militant directions; they wish exploiters to sample a taste of the fear and pain they dole out to animals, and they intend to fight violence with violence.

As Rod Coronado observes, "There's a whole bunch of disenfranchised Americans resisting the lifestyles they were raised in and they want an upswing in activity."[6] The ELF emerged in 1992 as a radicalization of Earth First! tactics that activists felt were too timid, and the dynamics of struggle can easily advance beyond property destruction. Thus, Ron Arnold, executive vice president of the Center for the Defense of Free Enterprise, rightly asks, "What happens when the next generation comes along and gets tired that these arsonists, the ecoterrorists, aren't doing enough?"[7] Earth First! activist Tim Ream predicts, "There is every indication that we will see more political violence. There is a war against the earth happening today and we know the government isn't going to solve the problem."[8] Rik Scarce, author of *Eco-Warriors: Understanding the Radical Environmental Movement*, saw a turning point in environmental defense action with the ELF torching of a Vail ski lodge in 1998, such that "a whole different scale of sabotage had become acceptable." Scarce believes that "the environmental movement has been radicalized permanently. I don't rule out the next step . . . that people will be killed."[9]

When presented with ALF and ELF claims that no one has ever been injured or killed in their actions, critics respond, "Not yet." But even some insiders believe that the day will come when malcontents from the newest crop of ecowarriors will follow in the footsteps of radical anti-abortionists and begin to kill animal abusers at their homes or offices. "People who abuse animals deserve all they get," says ex-ALF activist Keith Mann. "If you live by the sword, you will die by the sword."[10] In a September 2002 communiqué, the ELF stated: "While innocent life will never be harmed in any action we undertake, where it is necessary, we will no longer hesitate to pick up the gun to implement justice, and provide the needed protection for our planet that decades of legal battles, pleading, protest, and economic damage have failed . . . to achieve." Former ELF spokespersons Craig Rosebraugh and James Leslie Pickering openly defend violence as a legitimate tactic against exploiters and urge activists to go beyond the limitations of direct action against property by small cells of individuals in order to create a radical anti-capitalist social movement: "We believe that a revolution is necessary in the United States of America to rid the world of one of the greatest terrorist organizations in planetary history, the US government."[11]

In turn, industries and the government have stepped up their own responses to the new militant direct action movements. Under Bush, Dick Cheney, Donald Rumsfeld, and John Ashcroft, the state has so far avoided the kind of murderous assaults the FBI earlier unleashed on the Black Panther Party, the American Indian Movement, and MOVE while intensifying the attack on other fronts.[12] For now at least, they have put away their guns (but not always their fists and batons) in order to play legal (and illegal) hardball with the new crop of radicals. Especially in the aftermath of 9/11, the Bush administration took firm measures to criminalize animal rights and environmental protests and, indeed, nearly every form of dissent. The corporate-state complex is applying old laws in new ways (e.g., using the Racketeer Influenced and Corrupt Organizations [RICO] act, which was originally designed to stop organized crime), enforcing oxymoronic "free speech zones," breaking up demonstrations with gratuitous force and violence, and creating new legislation, such as the "Animal and Ecological Terrorism Act" and the USA Patriot Act, that grants the state frightening powers of surveillance, search and seizure, and political repression.

Thus, in order to disrupt and destroy opposition to the prevailing economic and political order, industries and government deploy systems of intense surveillance, grand juries, witch hunts, police dragnets, and political repression. The war between activists and the corporate-state complex unfolds simultaneously on many levels: *material* (physical violence used on occasion by both sides), *paralegal* (civil disobedience by activists and unconstitutional repression by the state), *legal* (courtroom battles and statutes used against activists as they seek to enforce or create laws that protect animals and the earth), and *semantic* (the politics of the discourse of "terrorism").

With the earth in grave crisis, animals dying by the billions, democracy under attack, and the corporate-state complex besieged by liberation, anti-globalization, and antiwar movements, the US and other capitalist nations are torn asunder by intense social conflicts in which the politics of nature takes on an increasingly significant role. In conditions where compromise or negotiation seem ever more remote possibilities, the gloves are coming off as opposing sides assume positions of war.

Patriot Games

The state . . . is the most flagrant negation, the most cynical and complete negation of humanity.—Michael Bakunin

If you harbor a terrorist, if you feed a terrorist, you're just as guilty as the terrorists.—George W. Bush

After the 1993 bombing of the World Trade Center and the 1995 bombing of the Murrah Federal Building in Oklahoma City, the state created the 1996 Antiterrorism and Effective Death Penalty Act, which enhanced state powers of surveillance, repression, and deportation of foreigners as it undermined civil liberties. When terrorists hijacked and crashed planes on September 11, 2001, a new political order was born. In October 2001, one month after the attack, the Bush administration bulldozed through Congress a frontal assault on civil liberties perversely titled the "USA Patriot Act" (a surreal acronym for "Uniting & Strengthening America Providing Appropriate Tools Required to Intercept and Obstruct Terrorism Act").[13] Exploiting the new climate of fear, the Bush team claimed that a free nation must give way to a secure nation. From the offices of a questionable presidency, we now have neither.

Framed as legislation to combat terrorists, the Patriot Act proposes bold new measures to undermine the Constitution. A Trojan horse for tyranny, this 342-page tome aims to dismantle the very freedoms for which true patriots have died. It pulls together a mishmash of provisions to augment state power. Some changes eliminate existing legal loopholes that mitigate government authority, some update laws for the age of the Internet, and some grant the Justice Department powers previously proscribed by Congress but passed because of the urgency of a response to 9/11.

Perhaps most importantly, the Patriot Act builds on laws created by the Foreign Intelligence Surveillance Act (FISA), a secret court created in 1978. The purpose of FISA was to review requests for surveillance of suspected spies, terrorists, and other foreign enemies of the US in order to collect intelligence information. Unlike other courts, the FISA court did not require probable cause that a crime was being committed to obtain a warrant. Attorney General John Ashcroft has tried to argue that the Patriot Act grants the authority to use FISA to conduct a criminal investigation and expand the powers of the executive branch accordingly. This would in effect override the Fourth Amendment that "no warrant shall issue, but upon probable cause." The seven members of the FISA court—which refused only one out of 12,000 surveillance requests over the course of two decades—unanimously rejected Ashcroft's interpretation of the Patriot Act, viewing it as an abuse of government authority. In a decision that chastised the FBI for misleading them on more than 75 of the applications they had approved, they denied Ashcroft their approval in August 2002. But Ashcroft argued that the FISA court exceeded its authority, and an appeals court overturned the decision.[14]

The Patriot Act shifts the focus of FISA from foreign to domestic intelligence, thereby targeting not only foreign spies and terrorists but also American citizens. By weakening the already permissive nature of FISA and by applying these diminished standards to domestic criminal investigations, the Patriot Act reendows the government with COINTELPRO-like powers to spy, invade, disrupt, and violate constitutional rights. To use FISA secret courts and procedures for domestic investigations, the FBI need only claim that foreign intelligence gathering is a "significant"—but not necessarily the "primary"—purpose of investigation.

The Patriot Act dissolves the system of checks and balances that supports the Constitution, as the executive branch of government seizes control of legislation and the courts. Under the banner of fighting terrorism, power is becoming increasingly centralized in the

Leviathan of the state as other branches of government become rubber-stamp mechanisms and alibis for totalitarianism. The Patriot Act violates numerous constitutional rights, such as the First Amendment rights to free speech and freedom of assembly, the Fourth Amendment right to security from unreasonable search and seizures, and the Fifth and Sixth Amendment rights to basic protections during criminal proceedings. Among other things, the Patriot Act arrogates to the executive office the authority—without need to show evidence of grounds for suspicion—to demand from librarians and bookstores lists of materials checked out or purchased, to undertake clandestine sneak-and-peek operations in the homes and workplaces of terrorism suspects, to monitor any citizen communications by phone or the Internet, and to allow indefinite detention of non-citizens while denying them legal counsel. In the new Panopticon Surveillance State, government agencies can collect and share information on anyone with minimal or no judicial review, as the executive office minimizes the information citizens can gather on corporations and on government itself through Freedom of Information requests. Building on infamous Carnivore data mining techniques to buttress the "Total Information Awareness" program or state variations on it (see below) that could come straight out of George Orwell or Philip K. Dick, the state can amass an encyclopedic wealth of information on any individual they target and nullify rights to privacy and freedom of speech.[15]

Perhaps most alarmingly, the Patriot Act created a new legal category of "domestic terrorism" that is defined broadly enough to have a chilling effect on political activity. Casting its dragnet far and wide, the Patriot Act declares that the crime of "domestic terrorism" occurs when a person's action "appears to be intended to intimidate or coerce a civilian population [or] to influence the policy of government by intimidation or coercion." Interestingly, through this new form of citizen coercion the Patriot Act falls under its own definition and by logic should annul itself. Practically, however, this definition of terrorism will stretch to fit civil disobedience and virtually any protest activity. In Bushspeak, protest and coercion, citizen and terrorist, are cunningly conflated.

The new definition of terrorism is a direct challenge to liberation groups, like the ALF and ELF, that are deemed security threats. The penalties for liberation activities are far greater than previously defined. The crime of arson against a vivisection laboratory, for example, formerly carried a penalty of not more than 20 years, but the Patriot Act amends the law to read "for any term of years or for life." It also has removed the statute of limitations for specific "terrorist" offenses, including those that create a "foreseeable risk" of death or injury to another person. The maximum penalty for providing material support to, harboring, or concealing a "terrorist" increases from 10 to 15 years in prison (see Black and Black in this volume).

But, given the strategic vagueness of Patriot Act language, nearly any protest group can fit the terrorist definition. How much latitude is granted under the phrase "appears to be"? Just what is it to "intimidate or coerce a civilian population" or "to influence the policy of the government by intimidation or coercion"? Protests often are intimidating, and their entire point is to "influence" social policy. People for the Ethical Treatment of Animals (PETA), for instance, might be classed as a "terrorist organization" for their financial support of well-known animal rights "terrorists" such as Rod Coronado, Gary Yourofsky, and Josh Harper. Following bureaucratic logic, PETA is guilty of "harboring," "aiding," or "lending material support to" "terrorists," all punishable crimes under the Patriot Act. Indeed, right-wing industry front groups like the Center for Consumer Freedom have a field day smearing PETA and even more conservative organizations such as the Humane Society of the United States as "terrorist" organizations. Presumably, activists who organize a vegan bake sale to support tree-sitters or political prisoners could be indicted for "aiding terrorists." The Patriot Act is a menacing weapon in the hands of the government whereby once they vilify someone as a terrorist, they can then apply repressive Patriot Act laws and spread guilt by association.

This government repression and hysteria has weighty implications for grassroots activists, too. If an animal lover shelters dogs rescued from a laboratory by the ALF or houses a "terrorist," he or she could be arraigned under the Patriot Act. A foreign student involved with PETA, Greenpeace, or certainly the ALF, can be deported for assisting a "domestic terrorist" organization. Speaking out in support of the ALF or ELF can earn one a criminal charge, as can taking pictures of animal abuse in laboratories or factory farms and slaughterhouses. In the Orwellian dystopia of "Homeland Security," where truth is falsehood and falsehood is truth, documenting animals tortured in a slaughterhouse is terrorism, but beating and killing them in unspeakably vicious ways is free enterprise. According to an official FBI definition, "Eco-terrorism is a crime committed to save nature." It speaks volumes about capitalist society and its dominionist mindset that actions to "save nature" are classified as criminal actions while those that destroy nature are sanctified by God and Flag.

"Shock and Awe" Attacks on Democracy

The jaws of power are always open to devour, and her arm is always stretched out, if possible, to destroy the freedom of thinking, speaking, and writing.—John Adams

Under current federal law, there are unreasonable obstacles to investigating and prosecuting terrorism.—George W. Bush, September 11, 2002

Two years after the attacks, it is no longer possible to view these changes [brought on by the Patriot Act] as aberrant parts of an emergency response.—Michael Posner, the Executive Director of the Lawyers Committee for Human Rights

In the era of the Patriot Act, one can expect more state repression and less government accountability to Congress, the courts, and citizens. As stated by the Center for Constitutional Rights in their "Erosion of Civil Liberties in the Post 9/11 Era" report, "These Executive Orders and agency regulations violate the laws of the US Constitution, the laws of the United States, and international and humanitarian law. As a result, the war on terror is largely being conducted by executive fiat and the constitutional liberties of both citizens and non-citizens alike have been seriously compromised."[16] The problem is not a legitimate war on real terrorists, but the hyperbole of the threat and the exploitation of 9/11 to justify unleashing draconian rule and to advance corporate interests. According to Laura Murphy, Director of the ACLU's Washington National Office, "The [Patriot Act] goes far beyond any powers conceivably necessary to fight terrorism in the United States."[17] To borrow a phrase from Frankfurt School theorist Herbert Marcuse, the Patriot Act creates "surplus repression," that is, repression far beyond what is necessary for minimal social organization or, in this case, to fight foreign terrorists.[18]

The Patriot Act sets back the struggle for civil liberties by decades and has already created a new "normalcy" of political repression, but it was only the opening volley of the Bush administration as it launched another front in its real war—the assault on democracy.[19] Every bad horror movie has its sequels, and it is no different in this case. Whereas the Patriot Act was enacted to hurt foreigners and non-citizens the most, its successors are designed to come after American citizens themselves.[20] The Son of Patriot Act authorizes increases in domestic intelligence gathering, surveillance, and law enforcement prerogatives that are unprecedented in US history.

In February 2003 a watchdog group called the Center for Public Integrity reported that they had obtained a leaked copy of draft legislation—dated January 9, 2003 and stamped "confidential"—that the Bush administration had told the Senate Judiciary Committee did not exist.[21] The legislation is titled the "Domestic Security Enhancement Act of 2003," or, as it is unaffectionately known, Patriot Act II.[22] Like the opportunistic debut of Patriot Act I, which exploited the 9/11 tragedy and widespread fears of additional terrorist attacks, Patriot Act II reveals that the Bush administration was waiting for the next terrorist attack or its war with Iraq to spring more booby-trapped legislation on Congress requiring emergency passage. If approved, Patriot Act II will plant dangerous landmines in the path of every activist and nonconformist in this country. Many members of Congress, however, are more circumspect and skeptical this time around and are challenging further efforts to erode the Constitution (see below).

In addition to increasing secret surveillance and requiring even less juridical or political oversight of executive power, Patriot Act II creates new crimes and punishments for nonviolent activities. It calls for 15 new death penalty categories for "terrorism." It authorizes secret arrests for anyone involved with an organization deemed "terrorist," and it makes giving donations to such a group a criminal action. As the government and sundry industries involved in animal exploitation try to make the "terrorist" tag stick to groups like PETA and Greenpeace, contributors to those organizations risk being identified as "terrorists." If Patriot Act II is passed, the government will keep a DNA base on all "terrorists" and put their pictures and personal information on a public Internet site. Most alarmingly, the government could strip Americans of their citizenship and deport them if they belong or give "material support" to a "terrorist" group.

These measures go far beyond Patriot Act I. They assail legal forms of protest and dissent, while threatening to exile those who belong to or support "terrorist" organizations—PETA and Greenpeace today, the Humane Society of the United States and the Sierra Club tomorrow. With a broad brush, the state intends to paint a scarlet letter on the forehead of every activist. This proposal subverts the very principles and logic of democracy; it does so, grotesquely, in the name of patriotism.

The public exposure of Patriot Act II was a momentary setback for the Bush and champions of the new Security State, but not a fatal blow, as they have been able to sneak key elements of the Act into other forms of legislation. Fragmenting and dispersing it among other bills, couching its insidious policies in cryptic language and fine print, and attaching it to legislation sent to Congress at the last minute to preclude careful reading and possible public debate, leaders of the new administration continue to chip away at the Constitution and balance of powers. In this manner, and while the nation was focused on the capture of Saddam Hussein, Bush surreptitiously signed into law the Intelligence Authorization Act for Fiscal Year 2004 on December 13, 2003.

This act surpasses the Patriot Act to grant the FBI unprecedented power to obtain financial records from institutions without permission from a judge through a court order or need to prove just cause. Whereas the Patriot Act required the FBI to submit subpoena requests to a federal judge, now an FBI agent simply drafts a "national security letter" that claims the targeted information is relevant to a national security investigation. In addition, the law broadens the definition of "financial institution" so that it can acquire significantly more data on individuals through an expanded number of businesses that include travel agencies, real estate agents, stockbrokers, the US Postal Service, jewelry stores, casinos, and car dealerships. The law also forbids subpoenaed businesses from revealing to customers, the press, or anyone else that the government demanded financial records. Only after the law was passed did many stunned members of Congress realize what they had signed. Meanwhile, the administration and its allies continue to smuggle other aspects of Patriot Act II into proposed bills, as Senator Orrin Hatch (R-Utah) and Republican allies have drafted the Victory Act (Vital Interdiction of Criminal Terrorist Organizations) that would make drug possession a terrorist offense (creating the new crime of "narco-terrorism"), facilitate the use of illegal wiretaps, and expand federal power to intercept communications and administer subpoenas for terrorist investigations.

Lobbying for Tyranny: The Texas Eco-Terrorism McBill

This legislation takes more than "a bite out of crime," it jails

and penalizes animal and eco-terrorists and their sympathetic financial agents for what they are—domestic terrorists.
—Sandy Liddy Bourne, daughter of G. Gordon Liddy and advisor to the American Legislative Exchange Council's Homeland Security Working Group

While the ALF ransacks research laboratories and the ELF scorches SUVs and condos, the corporate-state complex is busy working to rig the rules of warfare to its advantage. The assault on animal rights and environmental organizations is happening from the top down and the bottom up, on the federal and state levels. The bills currently being debated in various states are the result of alliances between corporations and professional lobbying groups, and their goal is to thwart any challenge to industry rights to killing and predation.

Deepening a dynamic as old as our nation, corporations are finding new methods and resources to gain access to politicians and policy makers. Powerful lobbying organizations such as the American Legislative Exchange Council (ALEC) operate as think tanks and policy makers that charge corporate clients thousands of dollars a year to join.[23] Membership earns corporations privileged access to policy meetings that invite their input in drafting new laws and bring them into direct contact with politicians. According to a *Washington Post* report, "Of the country's 6,500 state legislators, 3,000 belong to ALEC, including dozens of leaders of state legislatures and senates. Twelve sitting governors are ALEC graduates, as are 77 members of Congress."[24] Corporations and trade organizations can dictate laws and public policy while hiding their tracks behind such lobbying organizations. ALEC has been in the business of corporate policy prostitution for 30 years and currently operates with an annual budget of nearly $6 million.

One key function of groups like ALEC is to draft model bills that advance corporate interests and then float them in state legislatures across the country. ALEC has written over 3,100 bills and passed 450 into law in various states. Not coincidentally, as they push legislation criminalizing dissent, ALEC has over a dozen clients involved in the prison industry and has played a crucial role in passing dozens of tough anti-crime bills such as the "three strikes" laws. The group has thereby helped to significantly increase incarceration rates in the US, and it intends to add animal rights and environmental activists to their client list.

This is obvious if one considers Texas House Bill 433, a recent draft legislation that seeks to capitalize on federal efforts to criminalize animal rights and environmental activism, and is pending in Pennsylvania, Maine, New York, and other states.[25] Texas HB 433 involved a partnership with ALEC and the US Sportsmen's Alliance (USSA), a militantly anti–animal rights organization comprised of hunters, fishermen, trappers, and "scientific wildlife management professionals." They defend their right to kill animals through grassroots coalition support, ballot issue campaigning, and lobbying efforts. In August 2002 Rob Sexton of the USSA spoke to ALEC's Task Force on Criminal Justice about the growing "terrorist threat" of animal rights groups. In December 2002 the committee, headed by Representative Ray Allen (R-Dallas), voted to accept HB 433, and in February 2003 the "Animal and Ecological Terrorism Act" was sent to the Texas legislature.

The USSA claims that they only seek to protect wildlife interests and prevent illegal actions, and do not intend to inhibit the constitutional rights of their critics. This lie is contradicted first by the fact that Texas and other states already have laws in place to prohibit criminal actions against property, and second in that the bill unambiguously attacks basic rights. The real agenda of the USSA clearly is not to stop actions that already are illegal, but to criminalize any currently legal activities, such as protests or demonstrations, that pose threats to their bloodletting.

As evidence of the interests sponsoring HB 433, the bill singles out animal and environmental industries for special legal protection. HB 433 defines an "animal rights or ecological terrorist organization" as "two or more persons organized for the purpose of supporting any politically motivated activity intended to obstruct or deter any person from participating in any activity involving animals or an activity involving natural resources." The bill criminalizes actions obstructing "any lawful activity involving the use of a natural resource with an economic value," such as mining or foresting, or obstructing a lab, circus, zoo, or other institution that uses animals for research or economic assets.

Like the Patriot Act and its more recent counterpart, the language here is willfully vague, but the purpose is quite specific: to cripple the animal rights and environmental movements by kneecapping their right to dissent. Under HB 433 and its numerous clones, two or more people can be labeled terrorists if they leaflet a circus, protest an experimental lab, block a road to protect a forest, do a tree-sit, block the doors of Neiman Marcus, or potentially impede industry profits in any fashion, presumably even through education. HB 433 clearly violates the First Amendment rights of free speech and assembly as it threatens the privacy rights of individuals and freedom of the press. Andrew Becker of the Sierra Club observes that "The legislation is so sweeping and nebulous it could also cover nonviolent civil disobedience or even ordinary environmental activism."[26] Following measures that have been attempted in states such as Illinois, Missouri, and New York, the bill classifies as a felony "terrorist" action the photographing or video-taping of animal abuse in a facility such as a puppy mill, factory farm, or slaughterhouse.[27] HB 433 and its clones intend to make it a class D felony to unlawfully enter any animal facility for the purpose of taking photographs or using a video recorder "with the intent to defame the facility or facility's owner." Missouri SB 657 declares it a felony offense "if a person photographs, videotapes or otherwise obtains images without the express written consent of the animal facility, from a location not legally accessible to the public."[28]

This means that animal abuse is no one's business but that of the "property owner," and exposés of cruelty, rather than the cruelty itself, would become outlawed, the offenses punishable by up to six months in jail.[29] Thus, it appears that the terrorists are not the monsters who club pigs to death with metal pipes, but rather the activists, whistle-blowers, or investigative reporters trying to document such sadistic abuse. Like Patriot Act II, the Texas eco-terrorist bill aims to criminalize donating money to any group smeared as "terrorist," and requires that all guilty individuals supply their names, addresses, and a recent photograph to post on a public Internet database.

After being slammed with criticism from outraged citizens and groups including the Humane Society of the United States, the American Society for the Prevention of Cruelty to Animals, the Texas Humane Legislative Network, the Sierra Club, and the American Civil Liberties Union, Allen backed off HB 433, and it died in the House Committee on Defense Affairs and State-Federal Relations in May 2003. But in March 2003 Allen resubmitted a similar bill, HB 1516, which aims to escalate criminal penalties for actions against animal and natural resource industries.

Any bills modeled after HB 433, such as those introduced or considered in Illinois, Missouri, Ohio, Oregon, Pennsylvania, Oklahoma, and New York, could take effect in any state at any time. The Missouri bill attempting to outlaw photographing animal facilities died in committee in May 2003, but a similar bill passed the Ohio senate in May 2003 and won approval in the Oregon senate in June 2003. On January 1, 2004, a new California state law went into effect, based on ALEC's "Animal and Ecological Terrorism Act" model, that banned activists from trespassing on animal farms. The law significantly raised the trespassing penalties from a citation and a $10 fine to a misdemeanor punishable by six months in jail and/or a $1,000 fine.

Clearly, animal rights and environmental activists are becoming a threat, and corporate exploiters will go to any lengths—from shredding the Constitution to creating a fascist police state—to protect their profits and plunder. Michael Ratner, a human rights lawyer and vice president of the Center for Constitutional Rights, claims that the Texas bill is unprecedented in its assault on freedom. "This is unique. Even under the definition of domestic terrorism in the Patriot Act, you have to at least do something that arguably threatens people's lives. The definitional sections of this legislation are so broad that they sweep within them basically every environmental and animal rights organization in the country."[30]

Pump Up the Volume: The War of Words

> Actions by special interests groups, including animal rights groups, are the most dangerous threat to this country.—FBI agent testifying before Congress, February 2002

> Let's call the ELF and the ALF for what they truly are—terrorist organizations. It is imperative to treat all acts of terrorism equally.—Rep. Greg Walden (R-OR)

> Make no mistake, the violent methods used by these [eco-] criminals are nothing short of acts of terror.—Rep. Scott McInnis (R-CO)

Today's animal rights and environmental movements bear the stigma of "violent extremism" and "domestic terrorism." They contain factions and figures that defend the legitimacy of violence against human beings, though they have yet to commit any. The new liberation movements must now confront spying, infiltration, harassment, and persecution by a government that exploits public anxiety about the "international terrorist threat" and paranoia over domestic security to advance its own agendas. The state's goal is not merely to felonize property destruction "crimes," but also to re-categorize them as forms of domestic terrorism, to prosecute them under racketeering laws, and, with the Patriot Act and its offspring, to considerably increase the penalties for property destruction and "support" of "eco-terrorism."

Enemies of the ALF and ELF want to change the classification of their actions from vandalism, arson, and property damage to offenses punishable under the jurisdiction of Homeland Security. After the summer 2003 ELF attacks on SUVs and Hummers in California, for instance, Chris Chocola (R-IN) introduced legislation in his home state (his district houses the main assembly plant for Hummer H2s) to make arson a federal crime that falls under the rubric of terrorism. If Chocola gets his way, a convicted offender will be punished with a jail sentence of five years to life. Instead of passing legislation to force automakers to improve emission standards, Chocola bows to his corporate bosses with a measure that would severely penalize strikes on gas-guzzling, super-polluting tanks that have no place on any road.

Just as during the anti-communist hysteria of 1950s, all the government has to do to legitimate its crackdown on dissent is to define an individual or group as "terrorist," and the repression follows as if a fait accompli. The government and exploitation industries are inciting a war of rhetoric—a Machiavellian battle that has nothing to do with truth and everything to do with monopolizing the means of communication and the power to shape public consciousness. Appropriating the lens and pages of like-minded corporate media giants, the corporate-state complex tries to delegitimate liberationists through a verbal war based on lies, slander, misrepresentation, distortion, fabrication, and outrageous hyperbole.

On September 12, 2001, as the smoke was still rising from the rubble of the World Trade Center, US representative Greg Walden (R-OR) declared that the ELF poses a threat "no less heinous that what we saw occur yesterday here in Washington and New York." When SHACtivists set off harmless smoke bombs in two Marsh insurance buildings in Seattle in July 2002, Police Chief Gil Kerlikowske called the stunt "domestic terrorism." The Center for Consumer Freedom found the prank to evoke "horrifying parallels with last September's attack on New York City" and proclaimed, "It's time to start using the 'T'-word."[31]

Never mind the difference between two smoke bombs and two passenger plane missiles, between people who were mildly irritated at most and thousands who died horrible deaths, and between an action in defense of innocent animals and a paradigmatic terrorist strike that murdered thousands of civilians. Trying to inject some sanity into the debate, an ALF representative wrote:

One simply cannot compare the events of September 11 to the

illegal direct actions taken by underground groups and individuals for animal and earth liberation. Flying fully loaded planes into office towers [resulting] in massive loss of life and injuries is something that is on a completely different level than the actions [of the ALF and ELF]. Aside from the obvious differences of philosophy between real terrorists and animal and earth activists *vis a vis* the injuring or [taking] of life, the horrific actions we witnessed on September 11 represent what real terrorism is all about, and what violent people are capable of doing. To compare this to the actions of people who work to save animal lives and our planet while explicitly not using violent means is, frankly, ridiculous. Furthermore, to label nonviolent activists as "terrorists" is a slap in the face to everyone who has been killed or who is suffering as a result of September 11.[32]

In an October 23, 2001 story, the ultra-conservative CNSNews.com hypothesized that the ALF could be behind a wave of anthrax attacks on US citizens, since they were known to invade laboratories and could be working with foreign terrorist groups such as Al Qaeda.[33] In August 2002 SHACtivists in Boston and San Antonio were brought up on the RICO act and charged with attempted extortion, threats to burn a dwelling, stalking in violation of a restraining order, criminal harassment, and conspiracy. Since the Boston activists hailed from Britain, the press suggested that, like Al Qaeda, "terrorism" was being exported through an international ring. An August 21, 2002 *Boston Herald* opinion column provides this evidence of growing readiness to malign any act of resistance today as terrorism: "If it looks like a duck, waddles like a duck and quacks like a duck, call it a duck. Members of Stop Huntingdon Animal Cruelty are engaged in nothing more than terrorism that so far hasn't killed anybody. It has no place in American life. . . . This moral monstrosity has to be nipped in the bud." Nothing, of course, is said about the sadistic cruelty toward animals at HLS and the ethical motivations of activists tried and hanged in the media.

The legal and rhetorical fronts of the war heated up in February 2002 when George Nethercutt (R-WA) introduced the Agroterrorism Prevention Act HR2795. This bill seeks to establish a five-year mandatory sentence for firebombing and would allow prosecutors to seek capital punishment against anyone who causes the death of another person during an attack on an animal or plant enterprise. Moreover,

Nethercutt's bill aims to create and maintain a national clearinghouse to collect data on ALF- and ELF-type crimes, while extending the RICO act to "ecoterrorism." Rep. Darlene Hooley (D-OR) submitted a similar bill, the Environmental Terrorism Reduction Act, thereby seeking to outlaw protests "committed in the name of the environment." House Forest and Forest Health Subcommittee Chairman Scott McInnis avers that the "ecoterrorists" are not "nature-loving hippies," but rather "hardened criminals" to be likened to Timothy McVeigh. Not to be outdone, Nethercutt called the ALF and ELF our "homegrown brand of Al Qaeda." In a move reminiscent of the McCarthy hearings in the US during the 1950s, McInnis, Nethercutt, and other members of Congress demanded that mainstream environmental groups publicly disavow the tactics of the ALF and ELF—and gave them a deadline. "National environmental organizations need to know, you are either with us or you are against us. You need to choose which side you are on, and know we will be watching," said Nethercutt.[34]

The Alice in Wonderland hyperbole that seems a genre rule of state and corporate criticism completely misrepresents animal liberation struggles as it undercuts the ability to identity real evil and violence in our social world.[35] In headlines and text, reporters affix the term "ecoterrorist" to animal rights and environmental activists as if it were a neutral or natural designator that demanded no argument or explanation. Quite commonly, media reports refer to the "violent campaign" that the ALF, the ELF, or SHAC is waging against animal exploiters without ever defining violence or suggesting that what these groups are attacking is wrong or violent. Rather, they print uncritical and false claims, as in the case of a *US News and World Report* article on SHAC, entitled "Terrorize people, save animals." The article states: "Commercial test labs like Huntingdon are a critical link in the health-care system"—ignoring a half-dozen exposés that proved HLS to be a barbaric and fraudulent operation.[36] When the corporate-state complex cautions, "It is only a matter of time before somebody gets hurt" in the direct action movements on behalf of animals, they ignore the fact that *someone already has been hurt*—the billions of animals killed every year in factory farms, slaughterhouses, vivisection laboratories, and the "entertainment" industries.

Will the Real Terrorists Please Shut Up?

I called [animal rights activists] terrorists. I grouped all [terror-

ists] together because it's really pretty hard to distinguish one
from the other.—Utah state representative Paul Ray

You could call us "terra-ists." We value animal life and more.
We strive to reduce the sum total of suffering, not only to people but to all other species and to the earth.—Ingrid Newkirk

The state and corporate deployment of the T-word in response to
nearly every challenge to their corrupt and violent authority renders
the highly charged term "terrorist" banal and meaningless. As many
activists are unwilling to endure this rhetorical fusillade without a
struggle, they have entered into the semantic battlefield with the intent
of providing more accurate and objective definitions of terrorism and
establishing the identity of the real "terrorists" (see Watson and
"Defining Terrorism" in this volume).[37]

The Center for Consumer Freedom (CCF) provides a prime example of how exploitation industries abuse terrorist discourse for their
own political agendas, as they demonize animal rights and even vegetarian groups as "fanatics," "terrorists," or "front groups for terrorism." A front group if ever there were one, CCF is a coalition of 30,000
restaurant, alcohol, and tobacco companies adamantly opposed to vegetarianism; animal rights; anti-biotechnology activists; anti-smoking
lobbying; organic foods advocates; critics of fast food, saturated fat,
and cholesterol; and any "food cop" who dares to question or regulate
consumption of the goods related to their industry.[38] A vivid illustration of economically conditioned blindness, CCF denies the dangers of
secondhand smoke and alcohol-impaired driving, the problem with
schools hawking soda pop to students for big contract money, and even
the obesity epidemic in American society, a serious problem to which
the media has given considerable attention in the last few years. No
vegetarian or animal rights groups fall outside the huge net they cast
over today's "nanny culture" of "politically correct whiners." Their
goal, completely decontextualized from weighty ethical and political
issues, is to protect "the public's right to a full menu of dining and
entertainment choices."[39] The organization aims to wage a propaganda war against activists in a position to influence consumer behavior;
hence, according to leader Rick Berman, their main strategy is "to
shoot the messenger. . . . We've got to attack their credibility as
spokespersons."[40]

Besides SHAC and PETA, CCF's favorite target is the Physicians
Committee for Responsible Medicine (PCRM), an organization led by

Dr. Neal Barnard and composed of scientists, medical doctors, researchers, and others who advocate veganism and the abolition of animal experimentation. Since 2000 PCRM has been featured regularly in the mass media, debating Dr. Robert C. Atkins over the validity of his high-protein diets and attacking the food pyramid as a form of institutionalized racism that neglects the health concerns of minority peoples in order to sell meat and dairy products.[41] PCRM also has publicly urged the government to sue meat retailers for the devastating effects of their products on public health, much in the same manner that tobacco industries have been targeted. In a September 1999 press release, Dr. Barnard warned of the health risks of meat consumption and stated, "It's time we looked into holding the meat producers and fast-food outlets legally accountable."[42]

The CCF rejects PCRM's claims to scientific legitimacy and denounces them as a "terrorist front group" for PETA and SHAC. While gunning to repeal PETA's tax-exempt status, they "expose" the financial and organizational ties between PCRM and PETA (PETA gives PCRM money, and the two groups share similar funding sources) and between PCRM and SHAC (Barnard worked with Kevin Jonas, former spokesperson of the ALF and current member of SHAC, on a major letter-writing campaign).[43] In a January 2002 press release, CCF called on PCRM to "stop portraying itself as a medical organization and come clean about its connections to extremist animal rights organizations responsible for acts of violence and millions of dollars in the destruction of property." PCRM, they say, is "no more than a puppet for PETA to use in spreading its virulent anti-choice rhetoric." PCRM's superb health education campaigns are rejected as nothing but "junk science" and efforts "to dispense dangerous animal rights orthodoxy masquerading as nutritional advice." CCF conveniently ignores certain facts, such as the 16 major research studies that link milk consumption to maladies like prostate cancer and heart disease, and they somehow neglect to disclose their own status as an organizational facade for sundry industries profiting from killing animals and poisoning the public.[44]

CCF decries the destruction of inanimate property but shows zero regard for the billions of animal lives destroyed every year in slaughterhouses and laboratories. They excoriate PCRM for their "junk science" but praise HLS—notorious for its drugged-out and drunk employees who falsify data—as scientifically respectable. They say that PETA and other groups use "scare tactics [that] are designed to intimidate people into accepting a ridiculously small set of food choices," ignoring the rich diversity of a vegetarian diet.

It's clear that public discourse and thought have shifted toward more conservative directions and a deeper bias against direct action when "progressive" groups like the anti-racist Southern Poverty and Law Center join in the fray of stigmatizing the ALF and ELF as "domestic terrorists." Their article "From Push to Shove" is a misinformed diatribe against the new direct action movements. It uncritically accepts the glib propaganda of the corporate-state complex and bemoans legitimate strikes such as the action against the notorious Coulston chimpanzee compound in Alamogordo, New Mexico (so egregious that even the US government shut it down).[45] Brian Levin, a criminal justice professor and director of the Center for the Study of Hate and Extremism at California State University-San Bernardino, lumps ALF and ELF actions against property with violent racist and homophobic assaults on people. From his blinkered perspective, both types of actions are equally "hate crimes." Levin ignores the true hate crimes—the contempt and hatred that exploiters have for animals and the earth—as he fails to grasp the love of life and nature that motivates ALF and ELF actions.

Post-Constitutional America

> The next thing you known they'll be calling in artists, actors, and anyone else they can think of to ask of them, "Are you now or have you ever been a vegetarian?"—Bruce Friedrich

A madness is sweeping the nation no less absurd, outrageous, frightening, and irrational than the Red Scare of the 1950s. The Patriot Act expands government's law enforcement powers as it minimizes meaningful review and oversight by an independent judicial body. When not altogether overridden by executive power, the disempowered courts are compelled to grant orders authorizing surveillance so long as the FBI, CIA, or Justice Department says the magic words, "This is a terrorist investigation," or simply, "Do it." The Bush administration's steps to criminalize dissent are straight out of the film *Minority Report*, where you are guilty until proven innocent, and the government condemns you even for thinking an illegal thought, arresting you before you can choose whether or not to put that thought into action.

As the US government moves ever closer to tyranny, it collapses differences between violent and nonviolent protest, between terrorist and citizen, between Al Qaeda and PETA. Patriot Act I was just the first incursion in the new war against democracy, and the enemy is quickly advancing on activist positions. *We are all under attack*—not just the ALF and ELF, but also mainstream groups and indeed any citizen who dares to rise from his or her stupor before the TV screen to assume a political stand in the streets. Every dissenting citizen is now treated like an "enemy combatant." Rather than bickering among themselves and condemning each other's tactics, animal advocates ought to be lining up against the common enemy of the corporate-state complex.

The new concept of patriotism is marketed with as much truth and logic as the packaging of Happy Meals. Government doublespeak defines peace as war and war as peace, (corporate) criminality as principled moral action and principled moral action as criminal behavior. But we need to stop expecting truth from the state and begin to see it for what it really is—a bureaucracy that monopolizes the means of violence and exists largely as a political tool for the economic interests of ruling elites. The FBI has always worked to impede domestic civil liberties and halt radical movements dead in their tracks. The stories of agent-heroes fighting to protect American democracy against gangs, the mafia, and sundry evil types are the fables (always encouraged and pre-approved by the FBI) of comic books and television shows. Since its inception the FBI has monitored domestic radicalism and dissent, and it has jailed, beaten, and murdered radicals in this country. As evidenced by their infamous counter-intelligence program (COINTELPRO) during the 1960s and 1970s, the FBI has infiltrated, disrupted, and destroyed radical social organizations, using techniques ranging from surveillance and agents provocateurs to framing and assassination. To the extent the animal rights, environment, anti-globalization, and antiwar movements grow strong, they will try to do it to them, too.

Liberty and democracy have precious little breathing space in the straitjacket of neo-McCarthyism and Homeland Security. Following a peaceful protest in 1998 against Neiman Marcus for selling fur, a Dallas court barred Megan Lewis from further animal rights protests.[46] In October 2001 the Secret Service and Durham police questioned a college freshman about an anti-Bush poster hanging in her dorm room. After the launching of the 2003 war against Iraq, national media conservatives routinely branded antiwar protestors as traitors who should be jailed. When Baghdad fell, anchor Neil Cavuto of the conservative Fox News channel, which boasts "fair and balanced" coverage, announced to critics of the war, "You were sickening then; you are sickening now." The yellow-ribbon-tying masses equate patriotism with blinkered jingoism, as Paleolithic "America, love it or leave it" cries ring throughout the wasteland of talk radio. Across the nation, antiwar activists were surveilled, harassed, and arrested for the crime of exercising their constitutional rights. The shrill attack on the Dixie Chicks (much of it organized by conservative media giant Clear Channel Communications) for voicing their right to a critical viewpoint about President Bush is a clear indicator of the barbaric impulses stirring in the nation, irrationally oblivious to the fact that if the troops in Iraq were fighting for anything, it was precisely for the Dixie Chicks' right to dissent. Hollywood blacklisting is back as outspoken critics of Bush's war against Iraq (Susan Sarandon, Tim Robbins, Martin Sheen, and others) are banned from events and suffer retaliation for their views. In February 2003 a man was arrested in a New York shopping mall for refusing to remove an antiwar T-shirt he was wearing. Many outrageous incidents involving state harassment result from one person reporting another to authorities. In 2002 John Ashcroft tried to implement Operation TIPS (Terrorist Information Prevention System), in which individuals were asked to monitor their fellow citizens and to report suspicious behavior. The program was not approved, but its Website, now defunct, claimed at one time that over 200,000 tips had been filed since September 11, 2001.[47] In the case of the man detained by FBI agents in an Atlanta coffee shop in June 2003, a fellow "citizen" turned him in for reading an article entitled "Weapons of Mass Stupidity."

For many years, conservative organizations in academia have been monitoring what "liberal" professors say about topics such as the war and the Israel-Palestine conflict. Lynne Cheney, wife of Vice President Dick Cheney, recently founded a new conservative group, the American Council of Trustees and Alumni, which blasted dozens of professors for not showing sufficient patriotism after 9/11. Cheney considers college and university faculty to be "the weak link in America's response to the attack," perhaps because in those institutions there are still some embers of free thinking glowing.[48] How long can it be before industries sponsor Websites monitoring what professors say about vegetarianism, animal rights, environmental issues, and direct action?

Increasingly, animal rights activists are being brought before grand juries and charged with violations of the RICO Act. Grand juries are nothing but repressive mechanisms designed to coerce activists to supply them with information under the threat of 18 months in prison for non-compliance, all without a right to have counsel present. On February 12, 2002, for instance, Congress summoned former ELF spokesperson Craig Rosebraugh to Washington, DC for its special oversight hearing on Eco-terrorism and Lawlessness on the National Forests. Rosebraugh pleaded the Fifth Amendment to most questions, exasperating his inquisitors. In written testimony, he defiantly championed the cause of animal and earth liberation as he took the government to task for its own state-sponsored terrorism against people all over the globe. "In fact," he notes, "the US government by far has been the most extreme terrorist organization in planetary history."[49] Surveilled and harassed continuously for exercising his right to free speech on behalf of the ELF, Rosebraugh presents a case study in state repression and the political consequences of the Patriot Act.[50]

SHACtivists in the UK and the US are getting the same treatment as they face an increasing number of grand jury subpoenas, RICO charges (that they violated federal racketeering laws by banding together in an interstate network to force companies to change their business practices), and new "exclusion zone" laws that severely inhibit their controversial protest tactics. Since the precedent set by the National Organization for Women in its use of the RICO act against abortion protesters, it has become common for corporations to use RICO to fight activists. HLS and Stephens Inc., HLS's main financial backer before it pulled out in 2002 due to relentless pressure from SHAC, filed a lawsuit against In Defense of Animals, the Animal Defense League, and SHAC, charging them with organized harassment. The state of Oregon, subject to numerous arson attacks on behalf of environmental causes, expanded RICO laws to include actions against logging. As in the 1998 case where Stephens Inc. filed a suit against PETA, many such suits are settled out of court. But they cost organizations time, money, and resources, and often result in muffling public criticism of corporate evil.[51]

Both in the US and internationally, the state is increasingly targeting activists for undercover infiltration and raids. On July 30, 2002, nine members of the Royal Canadian Mounted Police (RCMP), Canada's national police agency, smashed down the door at the home of ALF spokesperson David Barbarash. They ransacked his place, seizing computers, floppy disks, videos, photographs, mail, and personal belongings. On the flimsiest justification, an arbitrarily chosen newspaper article in which Barbarash espouses the basic animal liberation line he has championed hundreds of times, the RCMP was granted permission for a search warrant. In his August 19, 2002 statement through Frontline Information Service, Barbarash observed: "This raid was not about animal rights issues or actions; this raid was about how we all have lost a large chunk of basic civil liberties and human rights. It's about how we really do live under the rule of a police state where it's no longer allowable to speak your mind or express beliefs which oppose oppression, and which challenge the corporate/military governments. To do so risks raids, possible arrest and lengthy jail terms."[52]

Such a risk was taken in February 2003, when Fresno State University hosted a national conference on "Revolutionary Environmentalism." Could there be free speech without state surveillance and harassment, in an academic setting, featuring radicals doing no more than expressing their views? The event brought together activists from Earth First!, former members and representatives of the ALF and ELF, and prominent academic writers in order to speak to students, faculty, and a community audience of over 600 people. Local agricultural producers and SUV dealers were outraged that the university would sponsor "criminals" and "terrorists," and hired extra security to foil the midnight raids of the invading terrorists who had come only to talk about urgent social issues and explain the reasons for their radicalism. To advance the war against terrorism, the FBI planted six agents in the hotel housing the conference participants. Critics tried to stop the conference, but the university courageously defended it on the grounds of free speech and the need to understand contemporary liberation struggles. Months afterward, however, Fresno State capitulated to the FBI when the bureau subpoenaed a tape of the conference's evening community panel. The university and the state failed the free speech test.

After the controversial Fresno conference, Virginia Tech's Board of Visitors unanimously approved a resolution to ban from the campus any group or individual that has advocated or participated in "illegal acts of domestic violence or terrorism." In January, the USSA challenged Michigan State University for hosting a site for the Animal Legal and Historical Center, which serves as a resource for animal activists and legal researchers. Mining, timber, and construction lobbyists urged lawmakers to halt funding for the University of Montana's environmental studies program, claiming that it was damaging the state's economy. In late February, reports surfaced that Virginia Beach undercover officers had infiltrated three meetings of Dolphin Liberty, a group opposed to a proposed exhibit of dolphins at the Virginia Marine Science Museum. In early 2003 anti–animal rights forces launched an assault on numerous universities that sponsored forums for animal rights and environmental ethics.

During a March 2003 presentation to Minnesota law enforcement officers and emergency management officials, Captain Bill Chandler noted that although his state harbored violent neo-Nazi and right-wing militia groups like the Aryan Nation and Posse Comitatus, ALF and ELF cells were the most dangerous threats, even "more dangerous in Minnesota than Al Qaeda." In late April 2003 the FBI interrupted a University of Minnesota meeting of the Student Organization for Animal Rights, asking for the names of all members of the group during the past few years. That same day, the FBI raided both SHAC's New Jersey office and the Seattle home of ALF supporter Josh Harper. In August 2003 FBI agents descended on a California home searching for a videotaped talk by Rod Coronado as possible evidence relating to SUV attacks during his visit to the area. Two months before, Coronado had found a Global Positioning Device under his car, obviously placed there to monitor his movements. In January 2004 the FBI shut down three venues for the Total Liberation Fest in Erie, Pennsylvania before the event finally transpired thanks to the flexibility and persistence of its organizers. Federal agents placed surveillance cameras throughout the area, monitored them continuously with agents in SUVs, infiltrated and recorded the events, and asked local homeowners for permission to occupy their attics to stand guard against the high-level threats to Homeland Security from bands playing music and activists speaking.

These are not just isolated events, but rather strategic interventions by the state in a systematic and coherent policy of repression, particularly against the new militancy in the animal rights and environmental movements. Never strong, civil liberties and constitutional rights in this country are becoming ever more fragile, tenuous, and precarious. The US political system is morphing into a post-constitutional dystopia.

Creeping Fascism

We have no desire whatsoever to in any way erode or undermine constitutional liberties.—John Ashcroft

Let's go fuck 'em up.—Miami cop overheard at the November 2003 FTAA protest

When a long train of abuses and usurpations . . . evinces a design to reduce the people under absolute despotism, it is their right, it is their duty, to throw off such government, and to provide new guards for their future security. The oppressed should rebel, and they will continue to rebel and raise distur-

bance until their rights are fully restored to them and all partial distinctions, exclusions, and incapacitations are removed.
—Thomas Jefferson

In September 2003 the government announced the creation of a master "Watch List" of more than 100,000 terrorist suspects. The list tracks suspected foreign terrorists as well as citizens the government deems tied to "domestic terrorism." Ashcroft promoted it as "one-stop shopping" for police on the lookout for all possible "terrorists," including those in animal rights, environmental, or antiwar protest groups. Privacy advocates objected that the list grants the state ever-greater powers to track and compile information on citizens whose only relation to "terrorist" activities is that they are affiliated with or support legal protest and lobbying organizations.[53]

Ashcroft's list signifies a dangerous new trend involving the compilation, centralization, and sharing of information on citizens—between corporations and the state, and within government at the federal, state, and local levels. The airline industry is one area in which this dynamic is at work. To replace the current system of terrorist watch lists, the Transportation Security Administration (TSA) developed a new airline passenger–screening system called Computerized Airline Passenger Pre-Screening System II. CAPPS II uses a vast data-mining program to check names against commercial databases and a watch list of suspected terrorists and people wanted for violent crimes. While the TSA claims CAPPS II will make flying safer without impinging on individual privacy rights, critics argue that it would create yet another plank in an oppressive surveillance system. In March 2003 Delta was the first airline to volunteer to implement the CAPPS II system, which conducts background checks on all passengers and assigns them a threat level—red, yellow, or green—to determine if they should be subjected to increased levels of security or even refused boarding.[54] The TSA has put over 1,000 citizens on a "no-fly" list, targeting "security risks" such as Greenpeace activists.

In September 2003 Congress moved to delay the planned debut of CAPPS II until the General Accounting Office can certify that it will not falsely target innocent passengers. At the same time, JetBlue Airways confirmed that they had violated their own privacy policy. At the TSA's request and with their help, Jet Blue provided five million passenger itineraries to a defense contractor in order to test a Pentagon pattern recognition technology designed to screen out terrorists who might intend to infiltrate or attack US Army bases worldwide. The contractor, Torch Concepts, augmented the list of names and itineraries with additional sensitive personal information such as Social Security numbers and income level by purchasing the information from a data-aggregation company. It used the data to test the feasibility of a passenger-profiling system like CAPPS II. Thus, the TSA, the army, an airline carrier, and a data warehouse company conspired to violate the Privacy Act. Today, many companies profit off the commodification of the personal information they collect and compile—information that would allow them to create a detailed profile of a person's life to be sold or shared with law enforcement agencies. CAPPS II and its analogues, as Americans for Tax Reform president Grover Norquist has said, are clearly part of "a series of police power and informational privacy power grabs that flowed from September 11."[55] In this spirit, in January 2004, Northwest Airlines admitted that in 2002 they gave information on more than 10 million passengers to NASA to be used for anti-terrorist research. After the JetBlue scandal, Northwest publicly stated that it would not release passenger data, but, unlike JetBlue, the airline also denied that it had done anything wrong.

Across the country, the FBI, state anti-terrorist squads, and local police monitor, gather, and share intelligence on protest activities and groups. State authorities at all levels routinely surveil direct action sites like Indymedia and infiltrate announced demonstrations. The California Anti-Terrorism Information Center keeps tabs on political activity and uploads information into criminal and anti-terrorism databases used by law enforcement officials to surveil and disrupt protests. The involvement of terrorist watch organizations in legal protests blurs the boundaries between political involvement and terrorism. As former California state Attorney General's office spokesman Mike van Winkle sagaciously revealed to *Oakland Tribune* reporters, "You can make an easy kind of link that, if you have a protest group protesting a war where the cause that's being fought against is international terrorism, you might have terrorism at that [protest]. You can almost argue that a protest against that [war] is a terrorist act."[56] In May 2003 the *Denver Post* revealed that Denver police had gathered information on peaceful protestors and civil rights groups and delivered it to the FBI's Joint Terrorist Task Force and other law agencies in an eight-state region.[57] Working with the FBI, the Denver police have created files on 208 organizations and 3,200 individuals.[58] In addition, a Boulder law enforcement agency monitored Rocky Mountain Animal Defense, a peaceful local animal rights group, and sent the information to Denver for inclusion in spy files.[59] Across the nation, police in numerous states

330 / TERRORISTS OR FREEDOM FIGHTERS?

are cooperating to create a centralized database of information on citizens in forms such as the Multistate Anti-Terrorism Information Exchange (MATRIX) (see below).

Protestors of all kinds are monitored, harassed, assaulted, and prevented from congregating and demonstrating by cops in full riotgear—as they were during the November 2003 protests of the Free Trade Areas of the Americas (FTAA) meeting in Miami. Police repression was particularly intense at the May 2003 Biodevastation 7 Forum in St. Louis, organized as a critical response to the World Agricultural Forum hosted by Monsanto. Over 30 people planning on attending the conference and subsequent protest were arrested *beforehand* on petty charges such as riding a bicycle without a license. In their pre-emptive strike, the "Pre-Crime" police repeatedly interrogated activists, searched their vehicles, and raided their homes and offices. Such actions by federal agencies and local police are clear violations of constitutional rights, but in the shadow of the Patriot Act they become standard operating procedures. In October 2003 Greenpeace boarded a vessel eight miles outside of Miami and waved a banner criticizing Bush for illegal logging policies. In retaliation, Ashcroft dredged up an 1872 "sailor monger" law and charged Greenpeace with an illegal action, thereby threatening their tax-exempt status.

In November 2003 a classified FBI document surfaced that confirmed what every government critic already knew. In a directive sent out to more than 17,000 state and local police agencies on October 15, 2003, the FBI warned about planned antiwar demonstrations in Washington and San Francisco and urged authorities to report suspicious behavior to the FBI. The document proved that, similar to the COINTELPRO era of the 1960s, the FBI is advocating spying on peaceful protestors engaged in nothing more than lawful forms of dissent. In its zeal to squelch dissent against the Iraq war and discontent with the federal government, the FBI's policy is to treat citizens exercising their constitutional rights like terrorists.[60]

Free speech cannot survive in an atmosphere of surveillance, intimidation, harassment, and arrest. The thought that one's name might end up in a police file for speaking out or attending a protest, or that one might be severely beaten by police during a peaceful demonstration, is a strong deterrent for many citizens contemplating involvement in civic affairs. If one analyzes the key defining criteria of fascist regimes in Italy, Germany, and elsewhere—such as militarism, jingoism, national security obsessions, disdain for human rights, state-controlled mass media, and bogus elections—one finds uncanny similarities in the US under Bush and the Patriot Act.

A crucial element in fascist systems of domination is the loss of privacy. Clearly we live in an advanced surveillance society—what some call the "transparent society"—where our speech and movements are recorded and monitored by computers, cameras, microphones, retinal and facial recognition systems, data mining systems, and fingerprints. Some of these measures protect us from assault or identity theft, but they also erode our privacy rights and supply personal information to businesses and the government. After 9/11, retired Admiral John Poindexter resurfaced to propose a "Total Information Awareness" project designed to collect all informational footprints an individual leaves behind, ranging from doctor's visits and travel plans to ATM withdrawals, book purchases, and email correspondence. In response to public outrage, Congress cancelled funding for the totalitarian information awareness program in September 2003, but a group of 13 states were independently working on the same effort in the Multistate Anti-Terrorism Information Exchange (MATRIX). Appropriately titled, the MATRIX is a data mining system that under the pretense of ferreting out dangerous "terrorists" would allow states to collect and share a wealth of information on any citizen almost instantaneously. "I won't lie to you," said Lt. Col. Ralph Periandi of the Pennsylvania State Police, "This system is not just being used to investigate terrorism."[61]

The Patriot Act has not been around for long, but it has already dramatically altered the political landscape. On March 24, 2003, the *Washington Post* reported that since 9/11, Ashcroft personally has signed more than 170 "emergency foreign intelligence warrants," three times the number authorized in the preceding 23 years. On May 18, 2003, the *Philadelphia Inquirer* wrote that in the first two months of 2003, the FBI filed terrorist charges against 56 people, but an investigation found that 41 had nothing to do with terrorism. In the aftermath of the terrorist attacks, the FBI and the Justice Department issued dozens of "national security letters" that require businesses to turn over all electronic records on their employees' finances, phone calls, emails, and other personal information. The story makes no mention of surveillance of political activists, although from the government's perspective they may well fall into the vague category of "other national security threats" whom Ashcroft and crew can target at will.

Congress will re-examine the Patriot Act in 2005, but by then inertia may have set in and the new security culture and "war on terrorism" may still be considered the nation's top priority. On May 8, 2003, Senator Orrin Hatch, Chairman of the Senate Judiciary Committee, tried to pass a bill that would make the "anti-terrorism" powers of the Patriot Act permanent, and thereby abolish the "sunshine" review of 2005. Fortunately, Hatch was firmly checked by both Democrats and Republicans who are increasingly alarmed about the Bush agenda to erode civil liberties in the name of national security. Still, a compromise bill that expands government power to use secret surveillance against "terrorist suspects" passed in the Senate by a vote of 90 to 4. The struggle to preserve constitutional rights is eternal and ongoing. As mentioned, new laws such as the Intelligence Authorization Act for Fiscal 2004 have already been passed that widely disseminate repressive elements of Patriot I and II, making Patriot Act-style legislation more entrenched and harder to rescind. There is no shortage of legislators creating new laws to perpetually erode constitutional rights in the name of fighting terrorism.

Beginning with the Reagan administration in the 1980s, conservatives have labored to roll back the clock on the environmental and social gains of the 1960s and 1970s, and the social welfare policies stemming from the 1930s. Indeed, Bush's time machine reaches back centuries, not decades, as he and his cronies methodically work to annul the US Constitution and the historical gains of the eighteenth-century period of Enlightenment and emerging democratic sensibility. The Bush administration, corporate lobbying groups like ALEC, and pro-violence organizations such as the USSA are exploiting fear and paranoia of terrorism for their own advantage in order to justify their assault on freedom. The Bush administration in particular is shamelessly trying to gain from the tragedy that took the lives of thousands of innocent civilians on 9/11 in order to advance its own agendas and protect corporate profits, while shielding itself from public scrutiny.

The current wave of tyranny is part of a larger class warfare plan that includes subverting liberties, destroying social programs, and invading nations in order to benefit corporations and the super-wealthy. Bush quickly distinguished himself as one of the most dangerous individuals to emerge in recent history, and he is determined to fulfill what he sees as America's manifest destiny: the extension of American power throughout the world.

One Struggle, One Fight

They that can give up essential liberty to obtain a little temporary safety deserve neither liberty nor safety.—Ben Franklin

I think that it is not too soon for honest men to rebel and to revolutionize. What makes this duty the more urgent is the fact that the country so overrun is not our own, but ours is the invading army.—Henry David Thoreau

We have seen only a few of many portals through which one can view the intensifying drama surrounding the struggle between vegetarian, animal rights, and environmental activists and the corporate-state complex. From the CCF to the FBI, from the USSA to Congress, industries and their government allies are fighting back at "extreme" animal rights and environment groups, as direct activists and liberationists redouble their efforts amid ferocious repression. While opponents rev up the propaganda machines in their effort to strip away the Robin Hood mystique of liberationists, ecowarriors try to unmask the government and corporations as the repressive forces they are. As evidence of increasing tensions, and especially after the events of September 11, there has been a growing tendency here and abroad to criminalize animal rights activities and to brand them not simply as "radical" or "extreme," but rather as "terrorist"—a term that should be applied not to acts of ethical sabotage, but rather to the willful inflicting of pain and violence on innocent living beings for nefarious political or economic goals. As the CCF, George Nethercutt, Ray Allen, Brian Levin, and others impugn the ALF and ELF as extremists and fanatics, a cursory examination of their worldview, policies, and rhetoric should suffice to establish the identity of the real zealots and dangers to society.

The ironies are all too painful. When beagle puppies are crippled and punched in the face, when monkeys are strapped into restraint devices that smash their skulls, when kittens have their brains invaded with electrodes, and when rabbits and guinea pigs are pumped with toxic chemicals until they die, we are asked to believe that this is science, not terrorism. When over 10 billion animals each year in the US alone are confined and killed in unspeakably vicious ways by food industries, we are told this is business, not terrorism. In this sick and violent society, property is more sacred than life, and thus only those who destroy property are branded as criminals while the real terrorists perpetuate the "banality of evil" (Hannah Arendt) through the daily affairs of torture and killing. For every scratch an activist might inflict on an animal exploiter, a sea of blood flows from the bodies of animals; consequently, it is the height of perversity to brand activists rather than animal exploitation industries as the ethical misfits.

Clearly, in the era of the Patriot Act, the stakes of fighting for animal rights are now much higher, and this should prompt new reflection on tactics for both aboveground and underground activists. Activists must not be afraid or intimidated, but they also need to know their rights, or what is left of them, to exercise high levels of security, and to know the costs of sabotage actions.[62] Words define reality, and the animal and earth liberation movements must resist being defined as violent fanatics and extremists. They must defend themselves rhetorically and philosophically, establishing a sharp distinction between animal and earth liberation, property destruction, protests, and demonstrations on one side, and bona fide violence and terrorism on the other side. They must expose for all to see the charlatans and real terrorists in state and corporate garb who fulminate against honorable dissidents and freedom fighters from behind their Oz-like curtain.

It is imperative to spread awareness about the history and nature of state repression, from the first Red Scare of the 1920s and the COINTELPRO operations in the 1960s and 1970s to today's Patriot Act and neo-McCarthyism. It is important to know what murderous crimes the US government has committed against radical individuals and groups in the past in order to understand what it is capable of doing today.[63] Although the government has the right and the duty to stop genuine terrorists who pose threats to the nation and its citizens, it can and must do this without violating the Constitution, basic human rights, national sovereignty, and international law. The state cannot hide its own crimes under the mantle of Homeland Security. The government wants citizens to believe that security, not liberty, must be the overriding national goal for the indefinite future. If the public allows it, the state will deploy this false dualism from now on to keep chipping away at personal liberties until none are left. If the mission of terrorist organizations such as Al Qaeda is to destroy what is left of Western democracy, then, with the help of Bush and Ashcroft, they are succeeding brilliantly.

In addition to growing Congressional opposition to the tyranny of the Patriot Act,[64] there is hope in the news that 159 towns and cities—as well as the states of Alaska, Hawaii, and Vermont—have created Bill of Rights Defense Committees and passed resolutions against the Patriot Act. From Ithaca, New York to Oakland, California, city councils have condemned the Patriot Act as unconstitutional and devoid of moral legitimacy. Taking more than just symbolic action, Ithaca and other communities require city employees (e.g., librarians) to adopt a policy of non-cooperation with the Patriot Act if government action against terrorism violates the civil rights and liberties of people within their communities. In effect, entire cities and states are adopting policies of civil disobedience as they pit individual rights and state duties against the federal government. Where Congress often has proved cowardly and inept in its duties, city governments are taking on protection of the Constitution as their own responsibility. As one member of the Oakland Civil Rights Defense Committee said, "Congress hasn't been able to check this unconstitutional executive grab, so it is up to us to reclaim our fundamental rights of free speech, free association, due process and equal protection."[65]

If it is not already obvious, the struggle for animal rights is intimately connected to the struggle for human rights—for free speech, freedom of association, freedom from search and seizure, a fair trial, and so on. The animal rights community can no longer afford to be a single-issue movement, for *now in order to fight for animal rights we have to fight for democracy*. As different expressions of peace and justice struggles, progressive human and animal rights organizations need to identify important commonalities and form alliances against capitalism, militarization, patriarchy, state repression, and many other social pathologies that affect everyone, whatever their gender, sexual preference, class, race, or species.

It is time once again to recall the profound saying by Pastor Martin Niemöller about the fate of German citizens during the Nazi genocide: "First they came for the Jews and I did not speak out—because I was not a Jew. Then they came for the communists and I did not speak out—because I was not a communist. Then they came for the trade unionists and I did not speak out—because I was not a trade unionist. Then they came for me—and by then there was no one left to speak out for me."

Attacks on foreigners are preludes to attacks on US citizens, which are overtures to assaults on the animal rights and environmental activist communities, which augur the fate of all groups and citizens in the nation. In the world of Bush, Cheney, Rumsfeld, Ashcroft, the FBI, the CIA, and the corporate conglomerates, *we are all becoming aliens*, foreigners to their pre-modern barbarity by virtue of our very wish to uphold modern liberal values and constitutional rights. Like "the war on drugs," the "war on terrorism" is phony, a front for the war on privacy, liberty, and democracy. Only counter-terrorists can defeat terrorists. May the armies of the animal, earth, and human liberationists rise and multiply in a perfect war against the oppressors of the earth.

Notes

1. See Rania Masri, "The Women and Children of Iraq Are Under Siege," *The Prism*, www.ibiblio.org/prism/Mar97/iraq.html.
2. "Animal rights, terror tactics," BBC News, August 30, 2000. See news.bbc.co.uk/2/hi/uk_news/902751.stm.
3. On guerrilla warfare, see Mao Tse tung, *On guerrilla Warfare* (Urbana: University of Illinois Press, 1961) and Che Guevara, *guerrilla Warfare* (Lincoln: University of Nebraska Press, 1985). For an excellent analysis of how low-tech guerrilla warfare in Vietnam defeated the US military machines, see William Gibson, *The Perfect War: Technowar in Vietnam* (New York: Atlantic Monthly Press, 1986).
4. "The Terrorist Threat Confronting the United States," Congressional Statement, Federal Bureau of Investigation. See www.fbi.gov/congress/congress02/watson020602.htm.
5. For the text of their communiqué, see directaction.info/news_sept30_03.htm.
6. Stacy Finz, "Activists see more violence from extreme protesters," *San Francisco Chronicle*, September 6, 2003.
7. "Eco-terrorists top FBI's list," *Denver Post*, December 15, 2003.
8. Finz, op cit.
9. Greg Avery, "Eco-terror act at Vail unsolved 5 years later," *Daily Camera*, October 19, 2003.
10. Paul Harris, "Death risk as animal rights war hots up," *The Observer*, March 11, 2001.
11. See www.arissa.org. For Rosebraugh's defense of violence as a political tactic, see his book *The Logic of Political Violence: Lessons in Reform and Revolution* (Portland, OR: Arissa Media Group, 2003).
12. See Ward Churchill and Jim Vander Wall, *Agents of Repression: The FBI's Secret Wars Against the Black Panther and the American Indian Movement* (Boston: South End Press, 1990).
13. The text of the Patriot Act is available on the ACLU Website (www.aclu.org).
14. "Appeals panel rejects secret court's limits on terrorist wiretaps," CNN, November 19, 2002.
15. Wired magazine explains, "The FBI's controversial Carnivore spy system, which has been renamed DCS1000, is a specially configured Windows computer designed to sit on an Internet provider's network and monitor electronic communications. To retrieve the stored data, an agent stops by to pick up a removable hard drive with the information that the Carnivore system was configured to record." See Declan McCullagh, "Anti-attack Feds Push Carnivore," Wired, September 12, 2001.
16. See www.ccr-ny.org/v2/reports/docs/Civil_Liberties.pdf.
17. ACLU Website, October 14, 2001.
18. Herbert Marcuse, *Eros and Civilization: A Philosophical Inquiry into Freud* (Boston: Beacon Press, 1974).
19. See "Assessing the New Normal: Liberty and Security for the Post-September United States," www.lchr.org/us_law/loss/assessing/assessingnewnormal.htm. The site features lengthy criticisms of the Patriot Act.

20. After 9/11, thousands of Arab and Muslim immigrants, and various foreigners, were rounded up and jailed for months without formal charges or the right to legal counsel. None of them were charged with terrorism. See Karen Rignall, "Beyond Patriotic," www.tompaine.com/feature2.cfm/ID/9256.

21. Charles Lewis, "The Assault on Liberty," The Center for Public Integrity, September 17, 2003; for further information on Patriot Act II, see www.aclu.org.

22. The draft of the bill is available online at www.eff.org/Censorship/Terrorism_militias/patriot2draft.html. For a recent update on the political struggle in Congress over the Patriot Act and related legislation, see "The Impact of the USA PATRIOT Act: An Update," at www.fepproject.org/commentaries/patriotactupdate.html. Since the state is constantly trying to pass new anti-terrorist legislation, one must be continually vigilant and regularly monitor sites such as the Bill of Rights Defense Committee (www.bordc.org).

23. For a critical debunking of the powerful corporate interests behind ALEC, see www.alecwatch.org; see also "Private Sector Shaping Public Policy," www.opensecrets.org/newsletter/ce45/ce45.01.htm.

24. Ira Chinoy and Robert G. Kaiser, "Decades of Contributions to Conservativism," The Washington Post, May 2, 1999.

25. For the text of the bill, see www.capitol.state.tx.us/tlo/78r/billtext/HB00433I.HTM.

26. Brad Knickerbocker, "New laws target increase in acts of ecoterrorism," The Christian Science Monitor, November 26, 2003.

27. See Bill Berkowitz, "Factory Farms Fancy Secrecy," www.workingforchange.com/article.cfm?ItemID=13266. Illinois House Bill 5793—which "makes it a crime to be on a farm (or any other 'animal facility') and photograph or videotape pigs or any other animals without the consent of the owner if [there is] one" and if the "intent is to 'damage the enterprise' "—passed 128 votes to 0 in the House in April 2002, and at the time of this writing is still is up for vote in the Senate. Berkowitz cites the Peoria Journal Star, which reported, "The stated need for the law, according to legislative analysis, is to protect the food supply from terrorists." If the law were approved, unauthorized recording of waste spillage or animal abuse would become a crime punishable by up to six months in jail, while the real criminals, the mass murderers of animals, go about business as usual. Efforts to link ALF or ELF actions to threats to the American food supply are just one step away from Nethercutt-type accusations of "agroterrorism," a highly charged term that invites severe repression by the state.

28. The texts of these bills, along with updates about recent legislative action, can be found on the Website of the Humane Society of the United States, www.hsus.org. For an overview of recent state efforts to pass anti-"terrorist" legislation, see the "State Legislation Addressing Terrorism," National Conference of State Legislatures, December 2001, www.ncsl.org/programs/press/2001/freedom/terrorism01.htm.

29. As evidence of this mentality, a January 19, 2003 letter to the Salt Lake Tribune blasted the "environmental terrorists" who broke into a hog farm, but offered no criticism of the institution of factory farming and mass slaughter of pigs.

30. Karen Charman, "Environmentalists = Terrorists: The New Math," tompaine.com/feature.cfm/ID/7748.

31. The Center for Consumer Freedom, "Special Report: It's time to start using the 'T' word," www.consumerfreedom.com/headline_detail.cfm?HEADLINE_ID=1544. Other anti-animal rights lists such as AnimalRights.Net regularly feature "animal rights terrorism" in their headlines. The New York Post jumped on the bandwagon

during Craig Rosebraugh's appearance before the Subcommittee on Forests and Forest Health, with the headline "Terror Takes the Fifth," (February 18, 2002). *The Wall Street Journal* joined in the fray with "Terrorist Buds: Bombing in the name of 'Mother Earth' isn't cool" (February 14, 2002). The article berated the ELF as a "band of stoned arsonists" and "our domestic, tree-hugging Al Qaeda." The opposition is not above lying and distortion campaigns. After the national animal rights conference in summer 2002, for instance, infiltrators from the Sportsmen's Alliance quoted Paul Watson out of context to make it appear that he saw the taking of human life in order to save endangered species as nothing more than "collateral damage," and reported that "Animal Rights Conference Encourages Terrorism," a story that was picked up by newspapers around the country. For Watson's rebuttal, see "Pirate or Policeman: High Seas Activist Says He Fights to Uphold Law," abcnews.go.com/sections/us/DailyNews/seashepherd020801.html.

32. "North ALF Press Office 2001 Year-End Direct Action Report," www.tao.ca/~naalfpo/2001_Direct_Action_Report.pdf.

33. Tom DeWeese, "The Eco-Terrorist Anthrax Connection," CNSNews.com Commentary, October 23, 2001.

34. Testimony of Congressman George R. Nethercutt, Jr., Resources Subcommittee on Forests and Forest Health, Subcommittee Hearing on Ecoterrorism and Lawlessness on the National Forests, www.cdfe.org/nethercutt.htm.

35. On the negative consequences of the deployment of terrorist discourse, see "Living in Fear: How the US Government's War on Terror Impacts American Lives" and other essays in Cynthia Brown, ed., *Lost Liberties: Ashcroft and the Assault on Personal Freedom* (New York: The New Press, 2003). Also see Benjamin R. Barber, *Fear's Empire: War, Terrorism, and Democracy* (New York: W.W. Norton, 2003).

36. April 8, 2002. Critics think SHAC may lose the public relations war for itself and the ALF. As the *Boston Globe* wrote in an editorial entitled "Animal Extremism," "If SHAC activists seek to illuminate the condition of laboratory animals, they have failed. Their own tactics reveal a disturbing willingness to inflict suffering" (August 22, 2002). Other newspapers such as the *Philadelphia Inquirer* and Seattle's *Everett Herald* have also denounced SHAC as "violent criminals" and "domestic terrorists."

37. In November 2002 demonstrating an unusual example of academics involving themselves in public debate, two Portland State University professors decried the linkage of the terrorist label to environmental activism. They authored a faculty resolution that passed 46–9 condemning the use of "inflammatory terms such as 'terrorism' and 'ecoterrorism' " and sent the resolution to the mayor and city commissioners.

38. For an exposé of the Center for Consumer Freedom and the interests they represent, see "Impropaganda Review: A Rogue's Gallery of Industry Front Groups and Anti-Environmental Think Tanks," www.prwatch.org/improp/ddam.html.

39. CCF often uses this phrase at the end of their press releases; see for instance "DISMISSED: US District Court Judge Tosses Out Frivolous Fast Food Lawsuit," www.consumerfreedom.com/release_detail.cfm?PR_ID=14.

40. Berman cited at www.prwatch.org/improp/ddam.html.

41. See, for example, "Racism in the US Dietary Guidelines?", www.pcrm.org/health/Commentary/commentary9906.html.

42. PCRM News Release, www.pcrm.org/news/health990924.html.

43. See CCF, "PCRM: PETA Comrades' Ridiculous Marketing" (January 18, 2002), and activistcash.com.

44. In September 2001 PCRM received some much-deserved legitimation when the

USDA panel of experts agreed that the claims made by the "milk mustache" and "got milk?" advertisements were untruthful.

45. Intelligence Report, Fall 2002. See www.cdfe.org/splc_report.htm. See also Friends of Animals' critique of SPLC's use of terrorist discourse against animal rights groups by Lee Hall: "Of Babies, Bathwater, and the Animal Rights Movement," *Actionline*, Summer 2003, friendsofanimals.org/action/summer2003/splc.htm.

46. Will Potter, "The New Backlash: From the Streets to the Courthouse, the New Activists Find Themselves Under Attack," *The Texas Observer*, September 14, 2001.

47. See www.politechbot.com/docs/tips.deleted.112002.html.

48. See her "Defending Civilization" report at www.artsci.wustl.edu/~stone/cheneyreport_original.pdf.

49. Craig Rosebraugh, "Written Testimony Supplied to the US House Subcommittee on Forest and Forest Health for the February 12, 2002, Hearing on 'Ecoterrorism,' " www.protectcivilliberties.com/written%20testimony.pdf.

50. For details, see Craig Rosebraugh, *Burning Rage of a Dying Planet: Speaking for the Earth Liberation Front* (New York: Lantern Books, 2004).

51. For further details on these incidents and the use of law and the IRS to suppress activism, see Potter, op. cit.

52. "Canadian Secret Police Raid Anarchist Activist's Home for US Authorities," www.ainfos.ca/sup/ainfos00247.html.

53. See "Administration Creates Center for Master Terror 'Watch List,' " *The New York Times*, September 17 2003.

54. See www.boycottdelta.com/index.html, which points out that information collected on passengers can be stored for up to 50 years and can be easily hacked, and that background checks damage one's credit ratings. See also Michelle Delio, "Privacy Activist Takes on Delta," *Wired*, March 5, 2003.

55. See Ryan Singel, "CAPPS Navigates Unfriendly Skies," *Wired*, August 26, 2003. On the JetBlue scandal, see www.dontspyonus.com.

56. Ian Hoffman, Sean Holstege and Josh Richman, "Analysts saw protesters as terrorists," *Oakland Tribune*, May 18, 2003.

57. Mike McPhee, "Denver police shares its 'spy files,' " *Denver Post*, December 15, 2003.

58. Kristie Reilly, "Warning! You Are Being Watched," *In These Times*, September 19, 2003.

59. "The real extremists: Police surveillance of peaceful groups crossed the line," *Daily Camera*, May 21, 2003.

60. Curt Anderson, "FBI Publicly Denies Spying on Protesters," Associated Press, November 26, 2003.

61. Dave Lindorff, "Still Watching: Private industry moves in to compile personal data," *In These Times*, November 11, 2003. Also see Nancy Kranich, "MATRIX and the New Surveillance States," www.fepproject.org/commentaries/matrix.html.

62. For activist legal resources, see www.cala-online.org/civil_liberties.htm.

63. On the sordid history of US political repression, see Robert Justin Goldstein, *Political Repression in Modern America: 1870 to the Present* (Cambridge: Schenkman Publishing Company, 1978) and Howard Zinn, *A People's History of the United States: 1942–Present.* (New York: Harper Perennial, 2003).

64. In July 2003, for instance, the House voted 309 to 118 to advance a Republican-sponsored amendment to block Patriot Act secret "sneak and peak" searches of homes and offices.

65. See Bill of Rights Defense Committee Resolution, www.bordc.org/Oakland-res.htm.

Afterword

The ALF: Who, Why, and What?

Ingrid Newkirk

I would hazard to say that no movement for social change has ever succeeded without "the militarism component." Not until black demonstrators resorted to violence did the national government work seriously for civil rights legislation. In the 1930s labor struggles had to turn violent before any significant gains were made. In 1850 white abolitionists, having given up on peaceful means, began to encourage and engage in actions that disrupted plantation operations and liberated slaves. Was that all wrong?

Henry David Thoreau, addressing the execution of John Brown, wrote, "It was John Brown's peculiar doctrine that a man has a perfect right to interfere with the slaveholder in order to rescue the slave. I agree with him." And it was John Kennedy who said, "Those who make peaceful revolution impossible will make violent revolution inevitable." Who wants to fight? Not those who end up fighting. All they want is change, but society is complacent and society is slow, and society is too convenience-oriented to listen and voluntarily change its habits. Society has to be pushed into the future.

There is a difference between violence to property and violence to people, of course. The ALF would not hurt a mouse, but it will burn a building. To equate the two is to establish a fixed devotion to property as something holy. When carried to its extreme this is the kind of thinking that leads police officers to shoot to death people who are taking things from stores.

Thinkers may prepare revolutions, but bandits must carry them out. In the course of any public struggle there comes a time when a law obeyed reluctantly or without thought is discredited. Today, the question of violating the laws that offer a layer of extra, and I think unconstitutional, protection to those who abuse animals, that exempts them from being civilized and respectful toward animals, is discredited.

Disobedience frightens us. But Christian Bay, the author of *Civil Disobedience*, remarked, "The widespread tendency to recoil from the very concept of disobedience in a society priding itself on its liberties, is a measure of the degree of immunity to real social change that has been achieved by our present socioeconomic and political system in the US."

Today, this question of violating the laws that indemnify animal abusers looms before us just as it did in the past for those who wished to free other slaves, human slaves, from the shackles we now see on elephants in the circus, and the exploitation we now see of monkeys and rats in laboratories. We may wish for change to spring out of pleasantries, but it won't. As Frederick Douglass said, "Power concedes nothing without a demand. It never did and it never will."

If a concentration camp or laboratory is burned, that is violence, but if it is left standing is that not more and worse violence? In a broiler house, 30,000 chickens are crammed into crates every six to eight weeks, breaking their wings; then they are thrown like sacks onto trucks, whisked down the highway in the cold or heat, hung upside down by their feet, and, protesting as best they can, panic in their hearts and eyes, their throats are slit. Isn't the chicken house today's concentration camp?—or do we not believe that it is wrong to make victims and to deride and persecute those we do not relate to? Will we condemn its destruction or condemn its existence? Which is the more violent wish?

If a property stands as a mechanism, a platform, or a vehicle for violence, shouldn't it be destroyed?

We have to ask why there is a need for an ALF. No doubt it is because there are people whose sense of urgency at the pain and slaughter of others does not allow them to wait for a couple of decades for change. Perhaps their pain is more intense than the pain of those of us who weep and know things are wrong and work within the framework of an exploitative society, geared to continue that very exploitation, in the hope that "one day" things will be different.

Perhaps the ALF exists because of complacency. After all, if peaceful dialogue worked, there would be nothing for the ALF to do; it would not have a job. So, when a hundred years or more of writing polite letters fails to effect vital change, should we condemn those who are compelled to try something stronger or condemn those who refused to change?

How many of us would be content writing letters to the editor and politely talking about the situation if our very own loved ones had been snatched away from us and were being imprisoned and tortured? Would we sit back if our sisters were being force-fed bleach? Well, someone's sister is being force-fed bleach as I write this. We know about it, but we continue sitting here. Should we blame the ALF for getting up and trying to stop it?

In Europe, the ALF is large and its agents are fearless. People will go to jail if they must. They understand that from the outset. It is no surprise to them. They do not whine and ask for much if they draw the short straw. They go, learn, wait, and inspire from inside. They know their lot is far superior to that of those they fight for. Rod Coronado, a Native American animal liberationist who spent several quiet, dignified years in a federal penitentiary in the US, calls them "warriors."

It is these warriors who provide the prod in the ribs to both conservative animal protectors and animal exploiters alike. Their very existence is an indictment of how society changes. It is also, perhaps, the animals' greatest hope.

Appendices

1: My Experience with Government Harassment

Rod Coronado

As animal liberationists, it is important to recognize that, in society's eyes, we support terrorism. Of course, ALF actions have never resulted in even one injury, let alone death, yet the Department of Justice labels the ALF as a domestic terrorist organization. The laws of the land have decided that private property shall take precedence over life and, as such, any actions to preserve life are likely to be deemed criminal.

Feds Cry "Terrorism"

This is not something unique to the animal liberation movement. Ploughshares activists, many of whom are Catholic priests, for many years have attacked the equipment of the US military death machine whose sole intent is killing people and, as a result, have served long prison sentences. Earth First! activists, whose only targets were ski lifts and power lines serving mines and pump stations, were infiltrated for two years by an FBI agent who then busted them in the act of cutting down a power line in Arizona in 1989.

All of this means that the nonviolent actions we participate in and support are likely to be viewed by the federal government as the work of extremists who may employ terrorism to achieve their goals. Of course, this same charge has historically applied to anti-slavery advocates, African-American community organizers, American Indian Movement members, anti-Vietnam war activists, and now us. And, as proven in 1973 in Wounded Knee, South Dakota, the US federal law enforcement community and military forces are prepared and willing to use deadly force to stop their own citizens whom they have deemed enemies of the state. Now, we can argue until we're blue in the face that we're not real terrorists and those in the labs, slaughterhouses, fur farms, hunting blinds, factory farms, military and police forces are; but our voices matter little to the big money interests who place politicians, the police, and judges in power—those who just so happen to be the very same people we oppose. The pharmaceutical, medical, "food" and agriculture, military, timber, mining and petrochemical industries control the courts, Congress and the media, so it's best if we just recognize the likelihood that our beliefs will be criminalized and prepare for the government repression that has already began.

First Encounter

My first encounter with the FBI was in 1988 after the ALF and Animal Rights Militia (ARM) had firebombed a veal processor, a slaughterhouse, a poultry plant and a butcher shop in Santa Clara County, California. FBI agents wanted to speak with me because of the obvious escalation in illegal animal liberation activities, my history with Sea Shepherd, and my arrest in Canada for ALF smash attacks.

My first mistake was just talking to the FBI. I felt I had nothing to hide. The agent was cordial and simply asked if I had been approached by the ALF or ARM, asking to be recruited or to be their spokesperson. I said no. But, as I was willing to talk, his calls persisted. Finally, he asked me to come down to his office and tell him about Sea Shepherd's 1986 raid on the Icelandic whaling industry—an action for which I had accepted personal responsibility.

The FBI agent said that Iceland was soon to file an extradition application and that it would be in my best interest to cooperate. He asserted that if I didn't cooperate, the FBI would be forced to arrest me if the extradition order was granted. The agent also said that if I made a signed statement, it would help to show the courts that I was cooperative, which would help me should I be officially charged.

I called his bluff and refused, and never heard from him again. I now realize that, had I made the official statement he was requesting, it would have been used against me in the grand jury proceedings when federal prosecutors were trying to convince jurors that I was a criminal. What might appear as a harmless confirmation of a publicly known fact can easily haunt you in the future as a sworn statement made to a federal agent. That is why we should never speak to the FBI.

In 1989 I was contacted again by the FBI, who asked me point-blank what I knew about the ALF. I told the agent to either present a subpoena or a warrant. He asked where I could be served a subpoena; I gave him my address and never heard from him again.

When you know your right to remain silent, you make the FBI's job 10 times harder. In 1990 the FBI approached my parents. They were accompanied by a man who my mom said "looked just like one of your friends, with long hair and a beard." The agents showed my mother photos of activists and asked if she had seen any of them hanging around with me. The FBI said the activists were suspects in the fire-bombing of an army recruitment center. They asked that I contact them, which I did in the hopes that by seeing the photos I could then warn the activists that they were under surveillance.

When I realized it was a stupid idea to try to beat the FBI at their own game, I canceled my meeting with them. No activists should feel they can gain information by talking with the FBI. The moment you begin talking to the FBI, the more they will approach you, knowing you will talk. There will always be two agents, as one is trained in asking questions while the other will evaluate your body language for subliminal messages as to which subjects you are comfortable discussing and which ones trouble you. So, even though you may say nothing, the FBI are still able to gather intelligence.

Feds Target Visible Warriors

In 1990 the Earth Night Action Group toppled power lines from a coal-fired power plant, and soon the FBI was swarming northern California. They were successful in pressuring the former girlfriend of an animal rights activist into being wired with a recording device to try to gather information from other activists about the sabotage. That is why activists should never openly speculate as to who might have done what action, either in person or on the phone, as we are only doing the FBI's job for them.

Once the FBI has associated a particular illegal act with political idealism or a cause, then the way is paved for surveillance, wiretaps, grand jury subpoenas, and other forms of governmental repression of the individuals or groups associated with that cause. Once again, we can be outraged at this and scream bloody murder that our civil rights are being violated, but that's not going to change a damn thing. We can either accept that the ALF, animal liberation and earth defense in general are major targets for police repression and act accordingly, or we can go back to supporting only the ineffective tactics controlled and allowed by our opposition. But there is no room in any legitimate, illegal, direct action struggle for those who want to be seen as militants— who talk the talk but don't walk the walk. Those are the people who bring down the heat yet can't stand the fire. Prove to the animals and the earth where your heart lies and to no other.

Later in 1990 two Earth First! organizers were the targets of a car bomb. Following the assassination attempt, the two victims themselves were accused of transporting explosives, and, while the real bombers went free, myself and many other northern California activists began to be questioned and put under police surveillance. During this time, Santa Cruz County was seen in the government's eyes as "a breeding ground for eco-terrorists."

A sympathetic reporter even told us of seeing "an eco-terrorist's flow chart" in the Sheriff's Department, listing as "eco-terrorists" any activists who had been arrested for civil disobedience. No evidence of actual criminal involvement was necessary; just the willingness to get arrested for earth defense and animal liberation was enough for you to be seen as a potential terrorist. There is every reason to believe that when investigating ALF activities, the FBI first surveys activists with civil disobedience arrest records.

The FBI sees it as a logical progression that one will first protest, do CD and then commit illegal direct action. I have seen ALF activists who never had any encounters with law enforcement officials, nor even had their names mentioned by the FBI, all because they never went to demos and never did CD.

Witch Hunts: The ALF Betrayed

In 1991 ALF actions moved to the Northwest and with them the FBI's focus on animal liberation investigations. Grand juries were convened in Oregon and Washington to investigate arson attacks on fur industry targets. At this time, the Coalition Against Fur Farms (CAFF) and PETA were the only organizations speaking out in defense of the ALF and, as a result, made easy targets for the FBI. The FBI repression of the animal rights movement from 1987 to 1991 had the chilling effect of silencing previously vocal supporters of the ALF.

In this way, the ALF was abandoned by all but a few. Where in the past it had become popular to support the ALF, now, with the price of that support being FBI harassment, the ALF was left with few to defend their actions to the movement and media.

What frustrated me the most during this time (while I both partici-pated in ALF actions and publicly defended them) was the fact that other activists would whisper their support yet were afraid to pen an article about the ALF and their anti-fur farm raids, let alone participate or offer physical or financial support.

It must be said that, for all the criticisms I've heard about PETA, they at least were not afraid to voice public support for the ALF and report ALF raids in their newsletters and to the media. And, when activists were subpoenaed to the grand juries, PETA offered financial and legal support where others had failed.

As the coordinator for CAFF, I wrote numerous articles for *The Animals' Voice* and the *Earth First! Journal* about the ALF's recent raids. I also gave media interviews much in the same fashion as SOAR and CAFT do now.

FBI Terrorize Family and Friends

Following these actions, the FBI's focus shifted to me. Had a wider body of vocal and visible support been evident for the ALF during 1991, I might have been able to last longer as an ALF activist. Had more activists been aware of their rights and not been afraid of the FBI, especially when they themselves were not even guilty of any crimes, the government would have seen widespread support for the ALF and not known where to begin its investigations.

I'll be the first to admit that, as an ALF activist, I should have been the last person to publicly defend them and their actions. But with the evidence we had gathered over the last year of fur farm animal abuse and with ALF attacks on that same industry, I felt it was necessary for someone to explain the ALF's actions and not miss an opportunity to strike an additional blow to the fur industry through the media.

By fall of 1991 the FBI had returned to my parents' home and work, accusing me of being an ALF member and telling them that I was working with explosives. The FBI tried to intimidate my family into cooperating by telling them that I needed to be stopped before some-one was injured or killed. By this time, the FBI had realized that I myself would not talk with them. They began to focus pressure on my family, friends, and former girlfriend.

In the beginning of 1992 the FBI upgraded its ALF investigations when a package containing stolen records from a torched mink research lab was intercepted. The package was addressed to the house of a former PETA employee. When a search warrant was executed, night-vision goggles, radios, balaclavas and maps of labs in Louisiana were found.

It had always been known that if the FBI could make a connection between the ALF and PETA, the latter organization could be destroyed by Racketeer Influenced Corrupt Organizations (RICO) laws. The government was already planning on charging the ALF under the RICO law as it also covers arson, interstate transportation, and organizing the committing of a crime. This was and probably still is one of the goals of the FBI.

Closing In

While I watched as friends and other activists were served subpoenas, and PETA was targeted for their alleged association with the ALF, the rest of the animal rights movement began to waver. Individuals and groups saw what was happening to vocal supporters of the ALF and chose to remain silent.

One individual who was subpoenaed to the grand jury told me that the questions asked were solely about me. One by one, activists were harassed and subpoenaed, as well as former roommates, journalists who had interviewed me, and Earth First! activists. Certain activists were threatened with having their children taken from them by the FBI and, in southern Oregon, a former home of mine was raided with a helicopter by the FBI and ATF (Bureau of Alcohol, Tobacco and Firearms), despite the fact that the feds had been saying that I was only a "person of interest" and not the subject of an arrest warrant. An activist who had purchased my car was subpoenaed and harassed, and the marine mammal protection ship Sea Shepherd was raided by the FBI and ATF and twice by US Customs when it was suspected I was aboard.

What was most despicable was the treatment of activists' parents and families who were targets of grand juries:

- One family I had visited in Michigan was specifically targeted. A family friend was approached by the FBI and told that if he was able to get an activist to speak a suspect's full name (only the suspect's first name was known) on the telephone, the Feds would pay his police academy tuition. He refused.
- The sister-in-law of a suspect was approached at her work and told that if she helped the FBI she would be eligible for a $35,000 reward. She refused.

- The FBI staked out the church where an activist's father ministered and, at one point, threatened the church's secretary with imprisonment, accusing the church of hiding fugitives.

Non-Cooperation: Our Best Defense

What angered the FBI most was the stubbornness of people they tried to question. Individual activists' families and friends complicated the FBI's job by refusing to answer any questions without a subpoena. My parents were targeted by a particularly vile agent who stopped by their house to show them my wanted poster and to tell them that, if they really loved me, they would tell him where I was before some fur farmer or local cop shot me.

Another time, the FBI arrested a Guatemalan refugee who worked for my family, handcuffing him and dragging him downtown. When my father protested, the FBI released him, apologizing that they had mistakenly thought he was me. Later it was discovered that when my parents were away on vacation, their house had been broken into and a floor plan drawn up for future surveillance.

Finally, when my mother was served with a subpoena to the grand jury, she told the agent at the door that she wouldn't talk to him because she was already taking medication for the stress the FBI was causing her. The agent replied, "This ought to help your stress," and handed her a subpoena.

By tracing phone records from calls I had made with a credit card, one by one, the FBI questioned everyone with whom I had come in contact. Of course, the attention directed at me was in a large part due to the fact that I was the subject of a grand jury investigation, rather than someone subpoenaed to testify.

To this day, I have never been questioned by the FBI or a grand jury. Those who were called to testify either answered a few simple questions and were granted immunity from prosecution or refused to testify. By the time of my arrest in 1994, four people had spent between five and six months in jail for refusing to testify. Meanwhile I avoided more close calls with the FBI.

In the Crosshairs

In one particularly chilling incident, activists visited me in one of my hideouts. I had instructed them not to drive their own vehicle for fear that a satellite tracking device might be placed on the vehicle, as one activist was a known acquaintance of mine. The activists met me at a previously agreed location, driving their own vehicle. We left the vehicle 30 miles from where I was staying, my anger overtaken by my joy at seeing a friend. When we picked up the vehicle a few days later, I instructed the driver to follow me at a distance and maintain an open channel on our radios.

We gassed up at different gas stations. But, as we were leaving a small town, I noticed a late-model American car in perfect condition but with mud splattered all over it. The car was backed into a road bank; I recognized it as one of the few cars to have passed us in the small town where we had gassed up. I radioed my friend about it and instructed them to meet us at a pre-arranged destination. When they did, they were frantic because they had surprised that same car, which had pulled off the road at another location, with its lights off.

The area where we met was very remote, and as we talked we could see the approaching headlights of the car behind us; the lights went off before the car reached us. It is my conclusion that, with the aid of a satellite tracking device, the FBI were using my friend as bait to lead them to me while I was on the run.

Help the Underground Resistance

Two things are required by any movement sincere about its attempts to sustain an underground resistance. The first is a structure to support those warriors who choose to live life in the underground away from all aboveground politics and who can be supported financially and morally by their legal counterparts. Every legitimate revolutionary struggle has this structure.

The other requirement is the uniform recognition by aboveground supporters that one must refuse to speak about other activists to any law enforcement agency. Of equal importance is an understanding and acceptance to never speculate over the phone or computer as to who might be an ALF member or how you heard so-and-so talking to so-and-so about how he or she wanted to strike a particular animal abuse target.

The consequences of such actions could easily result in your being subpoenaed to a grand jury or, even worse, being targeted yourself, as well as endangering other activists. Speaking with law enforcement officials can provide investigators with enough information to obtain search warrants and authorization for phone and wire taps. All these things are made much easier to obtain in light of recent "anti-terrorism" legislation, ranging from the Effective Death Penalty and Antiterrorism Act of 1995 to the Patriot Act.

A grand jury will be convened to gather information with the hopes of presenting enough evidence to issue an indictment. In the case of ALF actions, a grand jury will attempt to prove a suspect's association with animal rights and then, hopefully, use testimony from various sources to prove that there is reasonable cause to believe an individual committed a crime. Articles, letters, press releases, and statements all can be used against you. It is your job to prove your innocence rather than their responsibility to prove your guilt. Standard statements of support of ALF actions can be seen by the usual conservative grand jurors as incriminating. All this should not intimidate you into deciding not to support or join the ALF—just be careful of what you say and even more careful about what you do.

My own situation may seem grim, but the fact that after five Federal grand juries that lasted over four years, subpoenaed over 70 individuals and investigated six major ALF raids, I was the only activist indicted and only received four and a half years—I believe it shows that we did pretty well. And my indictment would not have been possible had it not been for preventable mistakes I made that resulted in providing the feds with physical evidence.

Stand Up For Your Rights

If you are to be a vocal ALF supporter, turn the tables on interviewers or editors. When doing interviews or writing letters to the editor, refuse to acknowledge ALF actions as violent or terrorist. I often respond with the question that if the media and police are so concerned with violence and terrorism, why not ask the same questions of those who operate in the light of day with human blood on their hands, like the ATF, FBI, US military, police and arms manufacturers. That usually shuts them up.

We cannot let the FBI or anyone else intimidate us into withdrawing our support from actions that cause no harm, yet save countless lives. All that is necessary is that we educate ourselves regarding the intimidation tactics of our opposition and familiarize ourselves with what few rights we have left. Remember that there is nothing illegal about opposing government and police repression of our movement or any other free-speech or protest tactic that fights for peace and justice.

The Bill of Rights guarantees our obligation to overthrow any government of our own that no longer respects the rights of its citizens. It is important that we learn the lessons that our counterparts in Britain have learned. Despite major police repression, the ALF continues to be a force to be reckoned with in the UK. All that prevents us from creating the same in the US is our degree of willingness to take greater personal responsibility, overcome our fears and sacrifice a little bit of our own comfort and freedom.

Just remember: Whatever we go through, and I say this even as someone who has sat in prison for four years, that whatever we as First World human beings go through in courts, jails or prisons, it is little compared to what political activists in other countries endure to fight for their beliefs. It is also nothing compared to the animals whose freedom lies in our own hands.

The FBI, ATF, police and corporations are the ones with blood on their hands, and they try to intimidate us with harassment, injury, imprisonment or death. What is most fearful is doing nothing as our one earth and her animal children are ruthlessly exploited and destroyed. Remember that, and good luck!

2: Letters from the Underground, Parts I and II

ANONYMOUS

The following article, the first and second in a three-part series printed in No Compromise, *is one person's story of her involvement with the ALF. In Part I, she explains how she overcame her fear and excuses and started conducting solo ALF actions. In Part II, she describes how she found partners to help her with her actions and how they worked together as a team. These are useful statements of how and why individuals decide to go underground in order to fight for animal rights.*

Part I: How I Came to Join the ALF

To begin, let me say that while associating with animal rights activists (something I try to avoid), I often hear people rhapsodizing about articles they've read in the press or seen on the news about animals being liberated, laboratories being trashed, lorries being torched, fast food restaurants being burned to the ground, etc. In the course of these conversations it is practically guaranteed that one or more persons will praise the action and wonder, "Gee, how do I hook up with these people?" or "Why don't these lads contact me?" or "How do I get involved with that group?" This is how I found the answer to that question.

After reading stories about lab break-ins and fur stores being torched, I, too, desperately wanted to join this group. But how? There was really no place to start. All of my friends in the animal rights movement had less interest in illegal direct action than I did, and even those who showed some interest were completely clueless as to how to meet these people.

At one point, I wrote an animal rights group to let them know that I would be willing to help them raid a lab. Needless to say, that letter went unanswered. Finally I realized what I was doing—I was waiting for someone with a plan to drop in out of the blue and ask me to join in a lab raid. Now, stop and think about this. Would anyone who had put hundreds of hours into planning a covert, illegal direct action that could land them in prison for years risk asking a basic stranger for help simply because he or she was a vegetarian or belonged to the local animal rights chapter? NO! (At least not if they want to stay active and out of jail.)

So how did I, or a better question is, how do you, end up "joining" the Animal Liberation Front? That's easy. Come up with your own plan! Really. It's not as hard as you think. Let me repeat this important point: *Come up with your own plan.*

One of the reasons there is not a lot more illegal direct action happening is that there are only a few people willing to invest the time and energy necessary to choose a viable target, research the facts, re-con the place, and conduct any other work necessary to execute a successful direct action. There are always plenty of people who want to help in the actual execution of the plan—people are always willing to share in the "excitement," but not in the actual work. Simply put, no one wants to help bake the bread, but everyone wants to eat it.

Overcome the Excuses

People dismiss the idea of planning a direct action for many reasons. Nearly all are mere excuses that could easily be overcome. Most commonly, people tell themselves they don't know anyone who could help in the final execution of the plan. For example, they don't know who could find homes for X number of animals; they don't know whom they could trust as a lookout; they don't know who could loan or rent them a vehicle to use, etc. I want to emphasize here that if you are faced with a problem like this, continue on!

There are many bridges that one can foresee that look uncrossable during the planning of an action. These problems seem irresolvable and often discourage people from continuing on with their plan. Again I must emphasize, *continue*. These problems either solve themselves or are more easily solved when you actually reach that point of the plan. And in some cases, the plan is aborted for some other reason long before the problem ever has to be confronted. It is important to add that you should expect about four out of five plans into which you've invested time and money to fall through. Again, this shouldn't deter you. If you approach direct action with the knowledge that most of your plans may not work, then you should not be discouraged from battling on if some of your plans do fall through.

While it is not necessary, it is advisable before taking any direct action to read as much literature as possible on the topic. This is much easier to do now thanks to a "revival" in the grassroots animal rights/liberation movement. If possible, any literature pertaining to illegal activities should be mailed to a fake name at a post office box or private mailbox center. If this is not possible, perhaps a well-trusted friend (who could handle police/federal harassment and is not personally involved in illegal activities) would be willing to have it sent to his or her place. Another possibility would be to get this information off a Website (from a library, campus, or cyber-coffee shop computer).

Though some of these security precautions may seem ridiculous, paranoid, and unnecessary, you will be thankful you followed them if you continue to increase the frequency, severity, and effectiveness of your actions, thus producing more intense local and federal investigations.

An Army of One

But, wait a minute! You still don't know if there is anyone you can trust. This does not mean that you shouldn't consider doing an action. When I realized that no one was going to drop in and ask me to help them with their plan—when I finally realized that I was the ALF—I decided to target a fast food restaurant that I had noticed as appearing vulnerable. Though I still didn't know who could help me with this plan, I proceeded to scope it out the next few nights, still thinking I would find someone to help me.

Though I had no experience at "casing a joint," it came very easily and naturally. Between 2:00 and 3:00 A.M. (the time I decided would be safest to strike the place) I carefully scoped it out. Some nights, dressed head to toe in my jogging gear (now is not the time to be caught there in your balaclava), I jogged up and down the street past the restaurant. I was careful to look for possible activity inside the building, check on any employees' cars in the parking lot, judge the amount of traffic and police presence, determine how well the parking lot and building were lit, scan for any drive-through or security cameras (to look out for and to sabotage!), etc.

Other nights I walked my boyfriend's dog up and down the street looking for the same things. In no time at all I was very familiar with the activity of the area (and had walked two emergency escape routes I would take should I be interrupted). I was soon confident with this target. Unfortunately, I still didn't know anyone I would trust enough to divulge my plans to. I knew what I wanted to do.

The day before I was going to execute my plan, I drove to a neighboring town and bought super glue, spray paint, and some garden gloves from three different stores, making sure to pay in cash at each store. That evening I went for a walk wearing my gloves and ended up picking up two large rocks and half of a brick that I determined was small enough to carry around and handle, yet big enough to smash through the thick plate glass windows of a fast food restaurant.

The First Action

Though I would have felt a bit more comfortable with a partner to look out for me, I was tired of waiting around for apathetic and unmotivated people. That night, dressed in black from head to toe, I went jogging. As I got near the restaurant I slowed to a walk. Seeing that there was no traffic around and facing a dark and empty-looking building, I approached the restaurant.

Walking briskly across the lot, I pulled my mask down over my face. At the rear of the building I quickly took off my black backpack and got out my supplies. I quickly filled the two back door locks with super glue and small pieces of paper clips that I had snipped especially for this occasion. I then proceeded to spray paint slogans over the entire back of the building and on the side with the drive-through window.

This done, I peeked around the building. Headlights were approaching from up the street, so I just remained calm and motionless. My stomach dropped when I saw it was a police car, but the cop drove by without slowing down or looking my way.

Delighted, I walked around to the front of the building and quickly tossed all three projectiles through three separate windows! I saved this part of the action for last because of the loud sound it would make. And, with the three explosions of glass, I quickly sprinted through one of my pre-arranged exits and into a residential area where I quickly vanished. I then removed my black turtleneck and balaclava, ditched them in an apartment complex dumpster, and went home.

My point here is that with enough planning, determination, and self-confidence, one person can pull off a successful action! Of course, the "bigger" or "more severe" the action, the better it may be to have a lookout with clear communications to you. Nevertheless, one person shouldn't feel helpless and inactive because he or she doesn't know others who are willing to take illegal direct action. Besides, taking action is your first step in feeling out potential comrades who share the same philosophy as you and are ready and willing to take action.

Part II: Looking for Partners

It is really very difficult to explain how to find close, trustworthy partners who are willing to take the same risks and are knowledgeable and strong enough to withstand heavy bouts of police interrogation, intimidation, and harassment. Though you never plan to be faced with this situation, it is a realistic risk, and you and anyone you work with should understand with a firm knowledge that if this situation arises, you and anyone you work with will not cooperate at all with any law enforcement agencies!

There is no cut and dried pattern or formula for choosing or finding partners. THIS IS GOOD. If there were a pattern or formula, it would open the door for infiltration of law enforcement and corporate agents.

However, executing the fast food action by myself led me to a second person whom I later hooked up with.

Friends and Comrades

Another member of our current cell really was not "chosen." We had merely known and trusted each other since high school, when we used to forge passes out of study hall so we could skip school and go swimming in the river.

We had both been vegetarians (and outcasts) in high school, and I taught him about animal rights as he shared with me his views of deep ecology. It wasn't long before we started working together. My point here is that there was no formula with which to evaluate my friend. I had spent years with him as a best friend and we pretty much knew each other inside and out.

These are the best kind of partners to have, since you already have an established relationship and friendship that no law enforcement agent would be able to break up. So I'd like to emphasize that this is the best way of "finding" a partner: working with someone you have a history with. And always trust your intuition. If someone doesn't feel right or you get "weird vibes" from him or her, *don't work* with that person! The opposite is true here also, but I don't need to explain that, since when you find that true connection, the feeling is pretty much unmistakable.

The other partner I connected with after the fast food restaurant action had a long history in the environmental movement. I only shared my interest in illegal direct action with her after she had complained to me consistently about a billboard advertising animal products and how someone should correct the billboard so consumers would know exactly what suffering that product really hid.

After hearing repeated complaints from my friend (was she checking me out, too?), we went for a walk. Here I told her that the billboard she hated so much appeared to be easily accessible (I had already re-conned it) and that if she wanted to help redecorate it, that would be jolly.

Needless to say, she thought this was a grand idea, and, within a matter of days, the billboard had been corrected. Red paint bombs made from Christmas ornaments also gave the appearance of blood running down the advertisement.

Critiquing the Action

The day after the billboard action, my friend and I went on another walk (we *never* talked in a house or car!) to discuss and critique our action. This may seem silly to some, but it is the best way to learn from your mistakes and make improvements for further actions.

Meetings like this—restricted to only those involved with the action—are great to learn from. Other than that they should never be discussed again. In this case, we realized that the system we had set up to warn of cops (a loud whistle) didn't work. I had been warned twice of police in the area by her whistle, but I was never sure when to resume work on the billboard. Also, the whistling merely attracted attention to my partner rather than to me.

Because of this, we ended up putting together our savings and buying a police scanner, frequency book, and a cheap pair of two-way radio headsets. Because of the headset's low price ($49.95 for the pair), I knew they would not be reliable for an action where the lookout is a long distance away. Nevertheless, they would suit our needs for more billboard, fast food restaurant, and fur shop actions.

Building Trust and Solidarity

These are the actions that should be done most often to build up confidence, unity, and comradeship. The more of these types of actions done, the more competent, confident, and experienced you and your cell will become, and you can soon "move up" to bigger and better actions (bigger and better being defined here as larger actions with more severe amounts of damage being done to the target. This, of course, includes arson attacks).

These actions will come in time if you and your partners stay active and build up a unity and confidence that becomes almost intuitive. Myself and the two individuals I currently work with have almost a psychic connection in which we usually know what the other two people are thinking. This will not happen overnight, and if you expect it to, you will be let down. That is why I must emphasize motivation and persistence.

It took me about two years of actions like this, and now I currently work regularly with two separate cells and a handful of other people who occasionally seek my assistance. Through persistence and perseverance you will build up a network of resources including tools, money, people, and experience.

If you tell yourself that there are no suitable targets to strike, you should stop and ask yourself if this is what you really want to be doing. If it is, just go to the nearest phone book and let your fingers do the walking. The *Yellow Pages* will give you the names, phone numbers, and addresses (and a map of the local area) of countless animal exploiters. This is an invaluable and easily accessible resource, available 24 hours a day in any city or town you may find yourself in.

In one instance, our cell drove two states away to "remodel" an establishment profiting off of animals' deaths. Once there, however, we realized this would not be possible. Instead of going home disappointed, we simply went to the nearest pay phone and let our fingers do the walking. Before we left that state, one animal abuse establishment had been completely destroyed!

3: Defining Terrorism

STEVEN BEST AND ANTHONY J. NOCELLA, II

> It is important to bear in mind that the term "terrorism" is commonly used as a term of abuse, not accurate description. It is close to a historical universal that our terrorism against them is right and just (whoever we happen to be), while their terrorism against us is an outrage. As long as that practice is adopted, discussion of terrorism is not serious. It is no more than a form of propaganda and apologetics.—Noam Chomsky

> There has never been any consensus definition of terrorism. —Richard Betts, director of the Institute of War and Peace Studies, Columbia University

> It is only worth entering into definitions if something hangs on them. In this case, something does.—Adam Roberts, Professor of International Relations, Oxford University

Barely a few years into it, the twenty-first century already is clearly marked as the "Age of Terrorism." The attacks of September 11, 2001 marked a salient turning point in the history of the US and indeed of global geopolitics. The US declared its number one priority to be the "War on Terrorism," and its domestic, national, and international policies have changed accordingly. In his address to the nation shortly after the 9/11 attacks, Bush used the terms "terror," "terrorism," and "terrorist" 32 times without ever defining what he meant.

In the amorphous name of "terrorism," wars are being fought, geopolitical dynamics are shifting, the US is aggressively reasserting its traditional imperialist role as it defies international law and world bodies, and the state is sacrificing liberties to "security." One of the most commonly used words in the current vocabulary, "terrorism" also is one of the most abused terms, applied to actions ranging from flying fully loaded passenger planes into buildings to rescuing pigs and chickens from factory farms.

Semantic Chaos

Everyone uses the term, but who really understands it? What precisely is terrorism? What causes it? Who engages in it? Should terrorists be identified according to their intentions, ideologies, tactics, or targets?

Who wreaks the most violence? When is violence justified so that it is not "terrorism"? How is terrorism different from assault, murder, and other violent "criminal" acts?

Does terrorism involve violence toward one person or many? How can one distinguish morally culpable terrorists from legitimate guerrillas, insurgents, counter-terrorists, or freedom fighters? Does terrorism require a political motivation or can it also be a random hateful attack? If so, how does one define "political motivation"?

Does terrorism include threats of violence as well as actual acts of violence? How important to the concept is the intent to create a psychological state of fear and intimidation, and thereby to inhibit freedom of action and peace of mind? How broadly should one define psychological terms like "fear" and "intimidation"?

What is it to be an "innocent" victim of terrorism? Who is "innocent" and who is "guilty"? Can there be terrorism against military targets or only against "civilians" and "non-combatants"?

Does terrorism involve a sudden, singular, direct dramatic action such as a bomb strike, or can it also include an economic or political policy that unfolds slowly, indirectly, yet devastatingly (such as decisions by a government that lead to poverty, hunger, homelessness, and sickness for millions of its own citizens, or the actions the World Bank takes to suppress justice struggles and enforce economic austerity policies on the underdeveloped world)?

How does the new world of information and computers require changing the definition of terrorism (e.g., "cyber-terrorism")? And in a world of high-tech chemistry and genetics, what about the new threats of "bio-terrorism" (involving the use of a biological agent to infect a large population) and "agroterrorism" (which deploys a pathogen against crops, livestock, and poultry)? In addition to injury to people, can there be terrorism against an economic system? Is it reasonable to speak of the "human terrorism" against the animal world?

It seems that the meaning of the term terrorism becomes clear in inverse relation to the frequency with which it is used.[1] This is true in part because "terrorism" is inherently a complex concept, but more so because it is a subjective, highly loaded, emotionally and politically charged term whose meaning is relative to one's political ideology and agenda, and even one's culture. Since no individual, group, or government wants to accept the negative consequences of the term, "terrorism" is always what someone else does.

There is no universal consensus definition of terrorism. One recent survey of definitions by leading researchers found 109 different definitions.[2] Beset by political differences, the United Nations General Assembly was unable to pass a resolution denouncing terrorism until 1985. A recent book discussing attempts by the United Nations and other international bodies to define terrorism is three volumes and 1,866 pages long yet still reaches no firm conclusion. As the UN puts it, "the question of a definition of terrorism has haunted the debate among States for decades." The European Union also has been unable to formulate an adequate definition of terrorism acceptable to all member states. Yet another illustration of the diffuse nature of the term lies in the fact that the US State Department, the Department of Defense, and the Federal Bureau of Investigation all employ different definitions.

The Exploitation of Language

US industries and the state capitalize on the vagueness of the term "terrorism" to apply it in any way they see fit to suit their purposes. In post-9/11 America, the term is used so broadly and promiscuously by state and industry interests that a "terrorist"—or "eco-terrorist," if an action challenges the interests of those exploiting animals or natural resources—is simply anyone who disagrees with, challenges, or inhibits their profit-driven agendas. We could not put it better than Dan Berry, who wrote on the Clearinghouse for Environmental Advocacy and Research: "If environmental groups cost business money, then they're eco-terrorists." Under the current administration, protesters, demonstrators, and government critics are denied their constitutional rights, surveilled, harassed, beaten, jailed, and defamed as treacherous conspirators and terrorists.

The political relativity of the concept is manifest in the trite but true phrase "one man's terrorist is another man's freedom fighter." Depending on the interpreter, violence against a perceived enemy can be seen as terrorism or counter-terrorism, as aggressive offense or legitimate defense. To Israel and the US government, Palestinian organizations are terrorists, but to Palestinians they are freedom fighters opposing the occupation of their homeland. The Indian government consid-

364 / TERRORISTS OR FREEDOM FIGHTERS?

ers groups working to liberate Kashmir from Indian oppression to be terrorists, while many Pakistanis embrace them as liberators. The US calls its violent allies friends and impugns its foes as terrorists. If we use violence against our enemies, it is a just war or strike; if they use it against us, it is terrorism. The Reagan administration championed the *contras* as freedom fighters, whereas the Nicaraguan people who endured their bombs and bullets viewed them—more accurately—as terrorists. In November 2001 Bush publicly referred to the Afghan Northern Alliance as "our friends," ignoring the fact that "Since 1992, the various Alliance factions have killed tens of thousands of civilians every bit as innocent as America's 9/11 victims; their rap sheets includes rape, torture, summary executions and 'disappearances.' "3 The US hailed Osama bin Laden and his comrades as freedom fighters in the 1980s, while many government officials denounced Nelson Mandela as a terrorist. The Western world reviled the 9/11 attacks as a paradigm of evil, but Al Qaeda and other enemies of the US upheld it as a legitimate strike in their jihad, while decrying US bombings of Afghanistan as terrorism. The US corporate-state complex censures the ALF as terrorists, while many activists champion them as freedom fighters.

The problem raised by pluralistic perspectives on terrorism is that of establishing some kind of non-arbitrary foundation by which to condemn heinous terrorist acts. Yonah Alexander proposes the norms of international law as the way to distinguish terrorism from a "lawful war." Others find the critical issue to be whether or not the immediate target is civilian. Still others insist that the term is inherently loose and imprecise.

One important point of clarification is that, while the terms "violence" and "terrorism" are used interchangeably, they are two different concepts. All terrorism involves violence, but not all violence is terrorism. For example, violence may be used in cases of self-defense or against legitimate targets—"combatants" rather than "non-combatants"—in conditions of war. Quite conveniently, however, the US military says, "We also consider as acts of terrorism attacks on military installations or on armed military personnel when a state of military hostilities does not exist at the site, such as bombings against US bases."4 Even the US military can be the target or object of a terrorist attack—but will never admit to conducting terrorist attacks itself.

The USA Patriot Act shrewdly exploits semantic vagueness. It defines terrorism so broadly (see below) that virtually all political struggle falls under its rubric. The inclusion of attacks on property (see the FBI definition below) means that groups like the ALF and ELF can be considered terrorists by those who accept this definition. Talk of "harboring" terrorists throws out into the political arena a vast net of guilt by association.

Clearly, "terrorism" is not just a word; it is a weapon. The definition is politically motivated by the user in order to target certain individuals or groups.[5] Speakers routinely brand their adversaries as terrorists to malign their cause and demonize them while, conversely, legitimating their own cause and any means necessary to secure it. Regarding the politically motivated use of terrorist accusation, Tomis Kapitan acutely observes:

> There is a definite political purpose. . . . Because of its negative connotation, the "terrorist" label discredits any individuals or groups to which it is affixed. It dehumanizes them, places them outside the norms of acceptable social and political behavior, and portrays them as people who cannot be reasoned with. By delegitimating any individuals or groups described as "terrorist," the rhetoric:
>
> Erases any incentive an audience might have to understand their point of view so that questions about the nature and origins of their grievances and the possibility [of] legitimacy of their demand will not even be raised.
>
> Deflects attention away from the policies that might have contributed to their grievances.
>
> Repudiates any calls to negotiate with them.
>
> Paves the way for the use of force and violence in dealing with them and, in particular, gives a government "freedom of action" by exploiting the fears of its own citizens and stifling any objections to the manner in which it deals with them.
>
> Fails to distinguish between national liberation movements and fringe lunatics.[6]

Those who monopolize power and the means of communication monopolize meaning; they can advance fraudulent definitions of terrorism that become widely accepted and internalized as common sense.

Definitional Exclusion #1: The US and State-Sponsored Terrorism

For self-serving purposes, the prevailing definitions of terrorism leave out two key facets of violence: state and state-sponsored terrorism, and species terrorism.

First, they define terrorists as lone individuals like Ted Kaczynski or sub-state groups like the Red Brigade. They thereby exclude state or state-sponsored violence, such as the longstanding US policies that financed and directed coups and political violence against civilian populations in Guatemala (1954), Lebanon (1958), the Dominican Republic (1965), Vietnam (1954–75), Laos (1964–1975), Cambodia (1969–1975), Nicaragua (1980–1990), Grenada (1983), Panama (1989), and Iraq (1990–1991, 2003–) to name just some rogue interventions.[7]

Terrorism is something that can be directed against a government, but not directed by a government.[8] US definitions of terrorism include the actions of insurgency movements—social justice movements always demeaned as "communist" in the past—but never the horrors perpetuated by US clients like Somoza in Nicaragua, Pinochet in Chile, and sundry dictators and right-wing death squads.[9] The chemical warfare the US unleashed against the people of Vietnam was far greater in scope and casualties than anything perpetuated by Saddam Hussein (using chemicals and weapons given to him by the US). In its imperialist war against Vietnam alone, the US killed over four million people.[10]

Official US government definitions of terrorism always deploy Manichean Good vs. Evil dramas. This strategy allows a double standard whereby the forces of Good ignore or downplay their own violence and legal violations, while hysterically denouncing comparable or lesser infractions by the Evil side. But, as Noam Chomsky observes, the US itself presents a textbook case of any reasonable definition of terrorism. In the United States Code and army manuals, terrorism is defined as "the calculated use of violence against civilians to intimidate, induce fear, often to kill, for some political, religious, or other end." The problem with the official definition, however, is that it "turns out to be almost the same as the definition of official US policy," though the latter is masked as "counter-insurgency" or "low-intensity conflict." The official definition, Chomsky claims, makes the US "a leading terrorist state because it engages in these practices all the time. . . . It's the only state, in fact, which has been condemned by the World Court and the Security Council for terrorism, in this sense."[11]

Similarly, if one adheres to the official FBI definition of violence, it is clear that in country after country, as systematic and deliberate policy, the US government has used deliberate "force or violence" "unlawfully," "to intimidate or coerce a government, civilian population, or segment thereof," in order to achieve "political or social objectives." In Philip Cryan's deconstruction, the US has been "directly responsible for acts of terrorism, and for the 'harboring' of terrorists, on an almost unimaginable scale in terms of human death and the creation of fear. When Green Berets trained the Guatemalan army in the 1960s—leading to a campaign of bombings, death squads, and 'scorched earth' assaults that killed or 'disappeared' 200,000—US Army Colonel John Webber called it 'a technique of counter-terror.' "[12]

The US coup against the democratically elected Socialist leader Salvador Allende led to tens of thousands of civilian deaths and torture on a mass scale. Terrorist Henry Kissinger, a key architect of the coup, was awarded the Nobel Peace Prize in 1973 and continues to be upheld in the media as a sage, credible policy expert, and ambassador to peace. The US backing of the infamous *contras* fomented massacres and bloodshed in Nicaragua in the early 1980s, and its backing of the fascist government of El Salvador resulted in 70,000 civilian deaths. The US "harbors" terrorists and rogue states on a global scale. Bin Laden's main line of support stems from Pakistan and Saudi Arabia, two major US allies, and the CIA trained and funded the Afghan resistance movement that became the epicenter of terrorist training camps. Speaking of terrorist training camps, let us not forget that at the infamous School of the Americas in Fort Benning, Georgia, the US instructed thousands of Latin American military personnel, humanitarian soldiers like Manuel Noriega who went on to become some of the best dictators, torturers, and mass murderers money can buy.[13]

Definitional Exclusion #2: Species Terrorism

Virtually all definitions of terrorism, even by "progressive" human rights champions, banish outright from consideration the most excessive violence of all—that which the human species unleashes against all nonhuman species. Speciesism is so ingrained and entrenched in the human mind that the human pogrom against animals does not even appear on the conceptual radar screen. Any attempt to perceive nonhuman animals as innocent victims of violence and human animals as planetary terrorists is met with befuddlement and derision.

But if terrorism is linked to intentional violence inflicted on innocent persons for ideological, political, or economic motivations, and nonhuman animals also are "persons"—subjects of a life—then the human war against animals is terrorism. Every individual who terrifies, injures, tortures, and/or kills an animal is a terrorist; fur farms, factory farms, foie gras, vivisection, and other exploitative operations are terrorist industries; and governments that support these industries are terrorist states. The true weapons of mass destruction are the gases, rifles, stun guns, cutting blades, and forks and knives used to experiment on, kill, dismember, and consume animal bodies.

The numbers of animals slaughtered by human beings is staggering. Each year, in the US alone:

- Over 10 billion farmed animals are killed for food consumption;
- 17–70 million animals are killed for testing and experimentation;
- Over 100 million animals are killed in hunting; and
- 7–8 million animals are trapped or raised in confinement for their fur.[14]

These figures do not include the millions of animals killed by the Wildlife Services division of the US Department of Agriculture (formerly known as Animal Damage Control) to protect livestock industry cattle; the 55,000 horses killed in the United States and processed for human consumption; the countless numbers of animals exploited and killed by various facets of the animal "entertainment" industry; and other forms of killing by human predators.

For the animals, every second is a 9/11 attack.

The FBI concept of terrorism *defines terrorism as attacks on property, but not on life.* Thus, by a definitional fait accompli, the ALF is a terrorist group, but not the animal exploitation industries that murder billions of animals every year. The corporate-state complex coined the neologism "eco-terrorism," and currently is expanding and exploiting the meaning of "agroterrorism," to bring acts of sabotage against property by groups like the ALF and ELF within the conventional parameters of heinous and despicable forms of violence and evil.[15] Whether directed against people or property, those flexing the term "eco-terrorism" proclaim that violence is violence and terrorism is terrorism. Despite the fact that laws against property destruction already exist throughout the land, the destroyers of animals and the earth are intent on reframing sabotage as "terrorism," thereby maximizing their ability to vilify and punish material strikes against exploitation industries.

What is Terrorism?

As suggested by the Austrian philosopher Ludwig Wittgenstein, one cannot always precisely specify the necessary and sufficient elements of a definition, but one can provide of cluster of related concepts. There is no single, universally accepted definition of terrorism, nor is there ever likely to be. Key aspects of terrorism—such as political or ideological motives, violence, targeting noncombatants, the aim of terrorizing, the goal to modify behavior—are relatively clear, but formulating them in a clear, compact, quasi-objective definition has proven to be an enormous challenge. As terrorism expert Walter Laqueur writes, "Even if there were an objective, value-free definition of terrorism, covering all its important aspects and features, it would still be rejected by some for ideological reasons."[16]

Any broad, abstract definition of "terrorism" is always open to attack by counter-example, will leave out some important element, will be vague to the point of meaninglessness, and may lend itself to political repression. The State Department definition focuses on subnational groups and leaves out nation states. Government definitions exclude from their definitions of terrorism political and economic policies that slowly but surely kill thousands of millions of innocent people. No definitions of terrorism, even those advanced by "progressives" like Chomsky, ever take into consideration the human war against animals.

Our own definition below does not incorporate a psychological aspect involving attempts to create "fear" or "intimidation," as we find these terms lend themselves to overly broad interpretations that legitimate political repression of activist groups. Understanding that terrorists aim to frighten and intimidate their targets, we prefer to focus on physical violence against all forms of life. We also exclude from our definition of terrorism acts of property destruction against industries as: (1) these acts are defensible in principle; (2) such illegal actions already have names and penalties that do not merit being upgraded from sabotage, vandalism, or arson to terrorism; and (3) the real terrorism involves the crimes that corporations and governments commit against human beings, animals, and the earth.

Capturing a diversity of definitions of terrorism is a way to begin building a fair and just working definition. Although co-opted by and for the interests of US industries and elites, the meaning of the term "terrorism" is worth struggling over, because in this obscenely violent world there are real terrorists whose actions need to be defined, condemned, and deterred. The task of shaping an accurate definition of terrorism is of enormous consequence today; nothing less than democracy and the right to dissent is at stake. Vague definitions of terrorism give government greater latitude in persecuting dissent. Rather than be standing targets for the terrorism of "terrorism," activists and the voices of opposition need to provide sound definitions and expose the real terrorists for who and what they are.

The following definitions are examples of attempts to define terrorism, and include general statements and US government definitions. The repetition of terms and meanings is unavoidable, but it points to key elements that may be necessary or part of a future consensual definition. Save for our own, no definition below directly includes the violence a human being, industry, state, or human species directs against animals.

That is a key philosophical and political task of the present era.

I. General Definitions

The unlawful use or threatened use of force or violence by a person or an organized group against people or property with the intention of intimidating or coercing societies or governments, often for ideological or political reasons.
—The American Heritage Dictionary of the English Language, Fourth Edition

Terrorism is the intentional use of physical violence directed against innocent persons—human and/or nonhuman animals—to advance the religious, ideological, political, or economic purposes of an individual, organization, corporation, or state government.
—Steven Best and Anthony J. Nocella

Terrorism is the deliberate use of violence against civilians in order to attain political, ideological, or religious aims.
—Boaz Ganor, Executive Director of the Institute for Counter-Terrorism

Terrorism is the threat and use of both psychological and physical force in violation of international law by state and sub-state agencies for strategic and political goals.
—Yonah Alexander, Director of the Institute for Studies in International Terrorism, State University of New York

Terrorism is the use or threatened use of force designed to bring about political change.
—Brian Jenkins, founder of the RAND Corporation's terrorism research program

Terrorism constitutes the illegitimate use of force to achieve a political objective when innocent people are targeted.
—Walter Laqueur, Chairman of the International Research Council at the Center for Strategic and International Studies, author of *The Age of Terrorism*

Terrorism is the premeditated, deliberate, systematic murder, mayhem, and threatening of the innocent to create fear and intimidation in order to gain a political or tactical advantage, usually to influence an audience.
—James M. Poland, Emeritus Professor, Criminal Justice, California State University, Sacramento

Terrorism is the use of force or the threat of force by an individual, group, or nation-state against a civilian population to achieve a political end.
—Robert Jensen, Professor in the School of Journalism, University of Texas at Austin

Terrorism is the systematic use of coercive intimidation against civilians for political goals. . . . The goals of terrorism are always political. . . . Terrorism as a political act is a primary means of expression and not a last resort. . . . The targets of terrorist coercion are the civilian population.
—Pippa Norris, Montague Kern, and Marion Just, authors of *Framing Terrorism: The News Media, the Government and the Public* (2003)

Terrorism is the deliberate use of violence, or the threat of such, directed upon civilians in order to achieve political objectives.
—Tomis Kapitan, Professor of Philosophy, Northern Illinois University

Intrinsically, terrorism is a state of mind. Political terrorism, presumably, is the state of mind of political actors who are

paralyzed by the threat of unpredictable attack. By default the concept has come to be employed to characterize the kinds of actions that are assumed to induce "terrorism." The circularity of this definition is obvious.
—Ted Robert Gurr, founder and director of Maryland's Center for International Development and Conflict Management

Terrorism is the calculated use of violence or threat of violence to attain goals that are political, religious, or ideological in nature through intimidation, coercion, or instilling fear.
—Noam Chomsky, Professor of Linguistics, Massachusetts Institute of Technology

Terrorism is an act carried out to achieve an inhuman and corrupt objective and involving threat to security of any kind, and in violation of the rights acknowledged by religion and mankind.
—Ayatulla Taskhiri, Iranian religious scholar

Terrorism is the half-thinking man's conditioned reflex to sustained oppression and lack of personal empowerment.
—Shaukat Qadir, retired Pakistani soldier and political analyst

Terrorism has become an invective that opposing sides hurl at each other for propaganda. The word means those who deliberately harm innocent life for the purpose of forcing behavioral change.
—Mark Somma, Chair of the Political Science Department, Fresno State University

"Terrorism" is a word people use to refer to armed struggles they don't like.
—John Burdick, Associate Professor, Syracuse University

II. State and Political Definitions

All criminal acts directed against a State and intended or calculated to create a state of terror in the minds of particular persons or a group of persons or the general public.
—League of Nations (1937)

Any act intended to cause death or serious bodily injury to a civilian, or to any other person not taking an active part in the hostilities in a situation of armed conflict, when the purpose of such act, by its nature or context, is to intimidate a population, or to compel a government or an international organization to do or to abstain from doing any act.
—United Nations

Terrorism is an anxiety-inspiring method of repeated violent action, employed by (semi-) clandestine individual, group or state actors, for idiosyncratic, criminal or political reasons, whereby—in contrast to assassination—the direct targets of violence are not the main targets. The immediate human victims of violence are generally chosen randomly (targets of opportunity) or selectively (representative or symbolic targets) from a target population, and serve as message generators. Threat- and violence-based communication processes between terrorist (organization), (imperiled) victims, and main targets are used to manipulate the main target (audience(s)), turning it into a target of terror, a target of demands, or a target of attention, depending on whether intimidation, coercion, or propaganda is primarily sought.
—UN Office of Drugs and Crime, Academic Consensus Definition (Schmid, 1988)

Regardless of the differences between governments on the definition of terrorism, what is clear and what we can all agree on is any deliberate attack on innocent civilians, regardless of one's cause, is unacceptable and fits into the definition of terrorism.
—United Nations Secretary-General Kofi Annan

Terrorism is the unlawful use or threat of violence against persons or property to further political or social objectives. It is usually intended to intimidate or coerce a government, individuals or groups, or to modify their behavior or politics.
—US Vice-President's Task Force, 1986

It is premeditated—planned in advance, rather than an impulsive act of rage.
It is political—not criminal, like the violence that groups

such as the mafia use to get money, but designed to change the existing political order.

It is aimed at civilians—not at military targets or combat-ready troops.

It is carried out by subnational groups—not by the army of a country.

—Paul Pillar, former deputy chief of the CIA's Counterterrorist Center

Terrorism is the calculated use of unlawful violence or threat of unlawful violence to inculcate fear; intended to coerce or to intimidate governments or societies in the pursuit of goals that are generally political, religious, or ideological.

—US Department of Defense

The term "terrorism" means premeditated, politically motivated violence perpetrated against noncombatant targets by subnational groups or clandestine agents, usually intended to influence an audience. The term "international terrorism" means terrorism involving citizens or the territory of more than one country. The term "terrorist group" means any group practicing, or that has significant subgroups that practice, international terrorism.

—State Department

Terrorism is the unlawful use of force or violence against persons or property to intimidate or coerce a government, the civilian population, or any segment thereof, in furtherance of political or social objectives.

—FBI Definition (revised July 2001)

III. Definitions of "Domestic Terrorism" and "Animal Rights and Ecological Terrorism"

Domestic terrorism involve[s] acts dangerous to human life that (A) are a violation of the criminal laws of the United States or of any State; and (B) appear to be intended (or to have the effect): (i) to intimidate or coerce a civilian population; (ii) to influence the policy of a government by intimidation or coercion; or (iii) to affect the conduct of a government (or any function thereof) by mass destruction, assassination,

or kidnapping (or threat thereof); or (C) occur primarily within the territorial jurisdiction of the United States.
—USA Patriot Act (Section 802)

Animal rights or ecological terrorist organization means two or more persons organized for the purpose of supporting any politically motivated activity intended to obstruct or deter any person from participating in an activity involving animals or an activity involving natural resources.
—Texas House Bill 433, "Animal Rights and Ecological Terrorism"[17]

IV. Definitions of "Bioterrorism" and "Agroterrorism"

Bioterrorism is the use of biological agents to intentionally produce disease or intoxication in susceptible populations.
—USDA's Animal and Plant Health Inspection Service

Bioterrorism is the use of biological agents in terrorism. This includes the malevolent use of bacteria, viruses, or toxins against people, animals, or plants.
—Onnalee Henneebery, Centers for Disease Control and Prevention

Bioterrorism can be described as the use, or threatened use, of biological agents to promote or spread fear or intimidation upon an individual, a specific group, or the population as a whole for religious, political, ideological, financial, or personal purposes. These biological agents, with the exception of smallpox virus, are typically found in nature in various parts of the world. They can be, however, weaponized to enhance their virulence in humans and make them resistant to vaccines and antibiotics. This usually involves using selective reproduction pressure or recombinant engineering to mutate or modify the genetic composition of the agent. Bioterrorism agents may be disseminated by various methods, including aerosolization, through specific blood-feeding insects, or food and water contamination.
—Arizona Department of Health Services

Agroterrorism is the act of any person knowingly or mali-

ciously using biological agents as weapons against the agricultural industry and the food supply.
—Steve Cain, Agricultural Communications Specialist

Agroterrorism is the use of biological or chemical agents directed against crops and livestock in an effort to disrupt the food supply to a population.
—Vermont Health Alert Network

Notes

1. For an excellent historical and political analysis of the complexity of terrorism, see "The Criminology of Terrorism: History, Law, Definitions, and Typologies," faculty.ncwc.edu/toconnor/429/429lect01.htm.
2. Ray Takeyh, "Two Cheers from the Islamic World," *Foreign Policy*, 2002, 128, January–February, pp. 70–71.
3. Cited in Dennis Hans, "Bush's Definition of Terrorism Fits Northern Alliance Like a Glove; TV Interviewers Don't Notice," Common Dreams News Center, November 23, 2001, www.commondreams.org/views01/1123-05.htm.
4. "Terrorist Group Profiles," library.nps.navy.mil/home/tgp/tgpmain.htm.
5. For an analysis of the self-interested nature of the definition of terrorism, see Brian Whitaker, "The Definition of Terrorism," *The Guardian*, May 7, 2001.
6. Thomas Kapitan, "The Terrorism of 'Terrorism,' " in James Sterba, ed., *Terrorism and International Justice* (Oxford: Oxford University Press, 2003), pp. 47–66. Kapitan's essay is enormously important for the task of creating a credible definition of terrorism that does not render invisible the bulk of violence today and does not demonize peace and justice movements. Kapitan also describes various ways in which sloppy and politically motivated "terrorist" rhetoric increases terrorism, such as by encouraging a cycle of violence and revenge (p. 53).
7. For a dated but still valuable account of US state-sponsored terrorism, see Edward S. Herman, *The Real Terror Network: Terrorism in Fact and Propaganda* (Boston: South End Press, 1982).
8. A 1937 League of Nations Convention, for instance, defines terrorism as "all criminal acts directed against a State and intended or calculated to create a state of terror in the minds of particular persons or a group of persons or the general public." Title 22 of the US Code defines terrorism as "premeditated, politically motivated violence" against "noncombatant targets by subnational groups" usually with the goal to influence an audience.
9. These fascist dictatorships created and financed by the US were euphemistically called (right-wing) "authoritarian" governments to distinguish them from the allegedly far more evil (left-wing) "totalitarian" governments. See Herman's *The Real Terror Network* on this distinction.
10. Edward S. Herman, "Global Rogue State," www.zmag.org/zmag/articles/feb98herman.htm.
11. Stephan Marshall interview with Noam Chomsky, www.guerrillanews.com/counter_intelligence/207.html.
12. Philip Cryan, "Defining Terrorism," *CounterPunch*, November 29, 2001, www.counterpunch.org/cryan1.html.

13. See School of the Americas Watch at www.soaw.org/new. Their site notes that "SOA graduates have included many of the most notorious human rights abusers from Latin America. SOA graduates have led military coups and are responsible for massacres of hundreds of people. Among the SOA's nearly 60,000 graduates are notorious dictators Manuel Noriega and Omar Torrijos of Panama, Leopoldo Galtieri and Roberto Viola of Argentina, Juan Velasco Alvarado of Peru, Guillermo Rodriguez of Ecuador, and Hugo Banzer Suarez of Bolivia. SOA graduates were responsible for the Uraba massacre in Colombia, the El Mozote massacre of 900 civilians in El Salvador, the assassination of Archbishop Oscar Romero, and the Jesuit massacre in El Salvador, the La Cantuta massacre in Peru, the torture and murder of a UN worker in Chile, and hundreds of other human rights abuses. In September 1996, under intense pressure from religious and grassroots groups, the Pentagon released seven Spanish-language training manuals used at the SOA until 1991. *The New York Times* reported, 'Americans can now read for themselves some of the noxious lessons the United States Army taught thousands of Latin Americans. . . . [The SOA manuals] recommended interrogation techniques like torture, execution, blackmail and arresting the relatives of those being questioned.' "

14. These numbers are from the years 1999–2000; fur figures vary greatly according to consumer demand. Hunting numbers have been steadily dropping as factory-farmed animal deaths continue to rise.

15. In June 2001, at the Frontiers of Freedom ecoterrorism conference, Rep. George Nethercutt (R-WA) unveiled his "Agroterrorism Prevention Act of 2001." The bill proposed expanding the 1992 Animal Enterprise Protection Act to protect the property interests of biotech, timber, and various agricultural and biological industries from "terrorists" and saboteurs. As noted by PR Watch, "The bill contains increased sentencing for all levels of violation and an expanded definition of types of businesses defined as 'plant enterprises,' including stores that sell 'plant products' (i.e., paper or wood). Under this extremely broad definition, blocking access to an office supply store, or 'conspiring' to limit profitability of paper products, could be considered 'agroterrorism' if the loss of revenue met the law's threshold. Likewise, putting 'frankenfood' stickers on GMO products in grocery stores, if the profit loss could be proven, would be considered a terrorist act. Tree-sitting or road blocking to prevent a timber sale would almost certainly qualify as a disruption that would meet the revenue loss threshold." See "Post 9/11 Anti-Environmentalism Threatens Green Activism," www.prwatch.org/documents/clear_v9n1.html. In June 2002 President Bush signed into law the "Public Health Security and Bioterrorism Response Act of 2002" (also known as the "Bioterrorism Preparedness Act of 2001"). The act is available online at www.theorator.comm./bills107/hr2795.html.

16. Walter Laqueur, *The Age of Terrorism* (Boston: Little, Brown and Company, 1987), pp. 149–150.

17. For the text of the bill, see www.capitol.state.tx.us/tlo/78r/billtext/HB00433I.HTM.

Contact Resources

ACADEMIC

Center on Animal Liberation Affairs (CALA)
Department of Philosophy,
University of Texas, El Paso, TX 79968
Website: www.cala-online.org
E-mail: info@cala-online.org

ALF INFORMATION WEB LINKS

Animal Liberation Front
www.animalliberationfront.com
Animal Liberation Frontline Information Service
www.animalliberation.net
Earth Liberation Front
www.earthliberationfront.com

MEDIA

Arkangel magazine
BCM 9240, London WC1N 3XX
E-mail: info@arkangelweb.org
Website: www.arkangelweb.org

Bite Back magazine
222 Lakeview Ave, Ste. 160-231, West Palm Beach, FL 33401
E-mail: biteback@directaction.info
Website: www.directaction.info

No Compromise magazine
740A 14th Street #125
San Francisco, CA 94114
Phone: 831-425-3007
E-mail: nc-info@nocompromise.org

PRESS OFFICE

ALF Press Office
BM4400, London WC1N 3XX, UK
Phone/Fax: + 44 (0) 1623 746470
Mobile phone: + 44 (0) 7752 107515
E-mail: alfpressoffice@yahoo.com

PRISONER SUPPORT GROUPS

Auckland Animal Action
PO Box 7523, Wellesley St, Auckland, New Zealand
E-mail: aucklandanimalaction@yahoo.com

Earth Liberation Prisoners—Poland
PO Box 43, 15-662 Bialystok 26, Poland
E-mail: ELP4321@hotmail.com
Website: www.spiritoffreedom.org.uk

UK Earth Liberation Prisoners Support Network
BM Box 2407, London, WC1N 3XX, UK
E-mail: ELP4321@hotmail.com
Website: www.spiritoffreedom.org.uk

EVTR [ALF SG Finland]
PO Box 223, 33201 Tampere, Finland
E-mail: yllapito@elaintenvapautus.net
Website: www.elaintenvapautus.net

ALF Supporters Group [The Netherlands]
Postbus 3607, 1001 AK Amsterdam, The Netherlands
E-mail: alf-sg@zonnet.nl

Italian Earth Liberation Prisoners Support Network
E-mail: italianelp@yahoo.com

North American ALFSG
PO Box 428, Brighton, Ontario, K0K 1H0
E-mail: naalfsg@resist.ca

North American Earth Liberation Prisoners Support Network
E-mail: naelpsn@graffiti.net

DFF SG [Norwegian ALF SG]
PO Box 386, 5001 Bergen, Norway
E-mail: torchvial@yahoo.com

Spanish ALF SG
APDO 50390, 28080 Madrid, Spain

Spirit of Freedom (Earth Liberation Prisoners)
c/o Cornerstone Resource Centre
16 Sholebroke Avenue, Chapelton, Leeds, LS7 3HB, UK
E-mail: earthlibprisoner@mail.com
Website: www.spiritoffreedom.org.uk/

DBF-SG [ALF SG Sweden]
Box 919, 114 79 Stockholm, Sweden
E-mail: dbfsg@hotmail.com

Turkey Earth Liberation Prisoners Support Network
E-Mail: elp_tr@hotmail.com

United Kingdom ALF SG
BCM 1160, London, WC1N 3XX, England
E-mail: 100302.1616@compuserve.com
Website: www.animalliberation.net/support/ukalfsg.html

Vegan Prisoners Support Group
Box 194, Enfield, Middlesex, EN1 3HD, UK
E-mail: vpsg@cares.demon.co.uk
Website: www.animalliberation.net/support/naalfsg.html

About the Authors

Nicolas Atwood
A Minnesota native, Nicolas Atwood is now an activist in Florida. He received an MPA from New York University, and an undergraduate degree from Macalester College.

Judith Barad
Dr. Barad is Chairperson and Professor of Philosophy and Women's Studies at Indiana State University. She is the author of three books: *Consent: The Means to an Active Faith According to St. Thomas Aquinas, Aquinas on the Nature and Treatment of Animals,* and *The Ethics of Star Trek.* She has published numerous articles and has spoken at dozens of conferences.

Mark H. Bernstein
Dr. Bernstein is Professor of Philosophy at the University of Texas, San Antonio. He previously taught at Wesleyan University. Bernstein has published many articles in both metaphysics and applied ethics. He is the author of *Fatalism* and *On Moral Considerability: An Essay on Who Morally Matters.* He has hosted both a television show and a radio series in Austin on animal rights and has lectured throughout Texas and other states on the nature and extent of our moral obligations to animals.

Steven Best
Dr. Best is Associate Professor and Chair of the Philosophy Department at University of Texas, El Paso. He is Vice President of the Vegetarian Society of El Paso and President of the El Paso animal rights group Stop Animal Neglect and Exploitation (SANE). He is a journalist for Animal Rights Online and, with Anthony Nocella, a founding member of the Center on Animal Liberation Affairs (CALA). He is co-host of

the animal rights/vegan radio show, Animal Concerns of Texas (ACT), and regularly gives talks to the community and local schools on issues relating to health, animal rights, and environmentalism. Many of his writings on animal rights, vegetarianism, philosophy, and related issues can be found at utminers.utep.edu/best.

Jason Edward Black
Jason Edward Black (MA, Wake Forest University) is a doctoral student in rhetorical studies at the University of Maryland examining social movement discourse and American nationalism. He has written extensively on American Indian identity, the ideologies of animal welfare and rights, and greyhound protection. Black's current research program traces the construction of "Indianness," beginning with Jacksonian nationalism and moving to contemporary milieus, to uncover animal metonyms used to justify American colonization. Black is an activist for greyhound protection and the eradication of the dog racing industry.

Jennifer Laurie Black
Jennifer Laurie Black (MA, Wake Forest University) is a public relations and marketing professional interested in championing social change and animal activism. She concentrates her work on new communication technologies, and writes about the impact of persuasion on the Internet to further socio-political progression. When not working and consulting in Washington, DC, Jennifer volunteers as a greyhound adoption counselor and anti-track educator.

Ward Churchill
Ward Churchill (Keetoowah Band Cherokee) is a Professor of Ethnic Studies and Coordinator of American Indian Studies at the University of Colorado in Boulder, where he is also associate director of the Center for Studies of Ethnicity and Race in America. He is co-director of the Colorado chapter of the American Indian Movement and vice chair of the American Indian Anti-Defamation Council. His many books include *Marxism and Native Americans*, *Fantasies of the Master Race*, *Struggle for the Land*, *From A Native Son*, *The COINTELPRO Papers*, *Indians R Us?*, and *A Little Matter of Genocide: Holocaust and Denial in the Americas*.

Rod Coronado
Coronado served with the Sea Shepherd Conservation Society on five

campaigns defending whales and dolphins in the North Pacific and Atlantic. As a Sea Shepherd agent in 1986, Coronado was one of two operatives responsible for the sinking of two illegal Icelandic whaling ships and the crippling of that nation's only commercial whaling station. In 1987 Coronado co-ordinated hunt sabotage campaigns against trophy bighorn sheep hunts in California and was arrested in Canada for a series of ALF attacks on fur shops. In 1990 Coronado infiltrated the US fur farm industry and obtained graphic evidence of cruelty on American fur farms that was later nationally televised. That same year Coronado organized the rescue, rehabilitation and reintroduction of Canada lynx, bobcats and mink from a Montana fur farm. In 1993 Coronado was federally indicted for six ALF raids on research laboratories and fur farms at Utah State University, Oregon State University, Washington State University, and Michigan State University. In 1994 Coronado was captured and sentenced to 57 months in federal prison. Coronado was released in 1999 and currently lives in Tucson, Arizona, where he works at a high school for indigenous youth.

Karen Davis
Dr. Davis is the founder and President of United Poultry Concerns, a nonprofit organization that promotes the compassionate and respectful treatment of domestic fowl. She is the editor of UPC's quarterly Newsletter *PoultryPress*, and the author of numerous articles and books including *Prisoned Chickens, Poisoned Eggs: An Inside Look at the Modern Poultry Industry, Instead of Chicken, Instead of Turkey: A Poultryless "Poultry" Potpourri* (a vegan cookbook), *A Home for Henny* (a children's book), and *More Than a Meal: The Turkey in History, Myth, Ritual, and Reality*. Karen Davis is also the director of UPC's chicken sanctuary, located at UPC's headquarters in Machipongo, Virginia.

Karen Dawn
Karen Dawn created and runs DawnWatch.com., a service that updates subscribers on media stories relevant to animal rights issues and encourages audience and reader response. Dawn saw the impact of audience feedback while working as a researcher and writer on the Australian nightly news show *The 7:30 Report* and writing for various Australian publications in the mid-1980s. She launched DawnWatch in 1999 and started lecturing in 2001 at FARM and Farm Sanctuary (2003) conferences on activists' use of the media. She is on the voting committee for the HSUS Hollywood Genesis Awards—awards given to

members of the media who spotlight animal rights issues. She has been a spokesperson for the animal rights movement on TV and radio, hosting various interviews with movement leaders on KPFT radio in Houston, and recently the "Why Animal Rights?" series on KPFK in Los Angeles in 2003.

Bruce Friedrich

Friedrich has been an animal rights activist since 1987 and is dedicated to anti-imperialist nonviolent activism. Friedrich spent more than six years working full-time in a Catholic Worker shelter for homeless families and a soup kitchen in Washington, DC without pay (part of Gandhi's nonviolent program). He is presently Director of Vegan Outreach for People for the Ethical Treatment of Animals (PETA).

Kevin Jonas

Kevin Jonas is a campaign coordinator for Stop Huntingdon Animal Cruelty (SHAC) USA. Since 1999 he has been a full-time volunteer in the international effort to close down the notorious animal-testing lab Huntingdon Life Sciences. Kevin has led demonstrations and spoken out against vivisection in over 15 states and in several countries. He has been featured in scores of media interviews for US and international publications, including *US News and World Report*, the *New York Times*, the *Washington Post*, the *Financial Times*, and others. Prior to his involvement with SHAC, Kevin engaged in several acts of civil disobedience with his student animal rights group at the University of Minnesota, filmed undercover footage of factory farm cruelty, and spoke out nationally for direct action with the North American Animal Liberation Front Press Office.

pattrice jones

As cofounder of the Eastern Shore Sanctuary and Education Center, pattrice jones cares for chickens while promoting agriculture reform in a rural region dominated by the poultry industry. Jones also coordinates the Global Hunger Alliance, which unites animal, environmental, and social justice organizations to promote plant-based solutions to the worldwide hunger and water crises. She has spoken up for animals in venues as diverse as the World Food Summit in Rome, the World Social Forum in Porto Alegre, and the Sustainable Development Conference in Islamabad. An activist since age 15, when she gave up meat and joined the gay liberation movement, jones has organized rent strikes, kiss-ins, street theatre, and extremely unlikely coalitions. At the Baker-

Mandela Center for Anti-Racist Education, she designed programs concerning racism, sexism, and economic exploitation. She taught a University of Michigan course on social change activism until the course was canceled in retaliation for her own activism. A founding member of Global Boycott for Peace, jones agitates for economic direct action against war in the same spirit in which she advocates veganism. Her articles linking animal and social justice issues have appeared in Bangladesh, Italy, Pakistan, and South Africa as well as in the US and Canada.

Noel Molland

Noel Molland has been involved with many animal liberation and eco-defense campaigns over the years. He was sentenced to three years' imprisonment for allegedly conspiring to incite animal liberation and earth liberation direct action through the dissemination of Animal Liberation Front and Earth Liberation Front information. Noel is currently volunteering with Earth Liberation Prisoners Support Network (ELP), which he helped to found in 1993.

Ingrid E. Newkirk

Ingrid Newkirk is cofounder and president of People for the Ethical Treatment of Animals, the largest animal rights organization in the world. Newkirk's campaigns to save animals have made the front pages of *The Washington Post* and other national newspapers. She has appeared on *The Today Show*, *Phil Donahue*, *The Oprah Winfrey Show*, *West 57th*, *Nightline*, and *20/20*, among others. She is the author of *Free the Animals*; *Save the Animals! 101 Easy Things You Can Do*; *Kids Can Save the Animals! 101 Easy Things to Do*; *The Compassionate Cook, 250 Ways to Make Your Cat Adore You*; and *You Can Save the Animals: 251 Simple Ways to Stop Thoughtless Cruelty* as well as numerous articles on the social implications of our treatment of animals in our homes, slaughterhouses, circuses, and laboratories. Newkirk served as a Maryland state law enforcement officer for 25 years with the highest success rate in convicting animal abusers. She has been the director of cruelty investigations for the second-oldest humane society in the US and Chief of Animal Disease Control for the Commission on Public Health in the District of Columbia. Newkirk achieved the passage of legislation to create a spay/neuter clinic in Washington, DC and coordinated the first arrest in US history of a laboratory animal scientist on animal cruelty charges and helped achieve the first anti-cruelty law in Taiwan. She spearheaded the closure of Department of Defense underground "wound laboratory" and has initiated many other campaigns against animal abuse, including ending General Motors' crash tests on animals.

Anthony J. Nocella, II

Nocella is a Social Science doctoral student in the Maxwell School at Syracuse University, where he is focusing his attention on peacemaking with international and domestic revolutionaries and extremist groups, political violence, strategic and tactical analysis of social movements, multiculturalism, and conflict studies. He holds an MA in Peacemaking and Conflict Studies and a graduate certificate in mediation from Fresno Pacific University. His long devotion to peace activism has led him to work with such groups as the Catholic Worker, Peace Action, Texas; American Friends Service Committee; Mennonite Central Committee; and Earth First!. He has also worked as a peacemaker in Colombia with the Mennonite Central Committee, and as a lobbyist for Sierra Club's End Commercial Logging campaign. He has taught workshops in mediation and tactical analysis, and has assisted in a number of defense committees. He is a co-founder of the Institute for Revolutionary Peacemaking and Education with Richard Kahn, an institute dedicated to expanding the theory of revolutionary pedagogy. He has written in more than a dozen publications and is the author of *Introducing Restorative Justice to Activists* and *A Peacemaker's Guide for Building Peace with a Revolutionary Group*.

Tom Regan

Tom Regan (Emeritus Professor of Philosophy, North Carolina State University) is universally recognized as the intellectual leader of the animal rights movement. During his more than 30 years on the faculty, he received numerous awards for excellence in undergraduate and graduate teaching, was named University Alumni Distinguished Professor, published hundreds of professional papers and more than 20 books, won major international awards for film writing and direction, and presented hundreds of lectures throughout the United States and abroad. Upon his retirement in 2001, he received the William Quarles Holliday Medal, the highest honor NC State University can bestow on one of its faculty. In that same year, using his donated papers and his extensive personal library as the foundation, the North Carolina State University Library established the Tom Regan Animal Rights Archive. Enriched by the addition of newly donated materials, the collection is the world's leading archival resource for animal rights scholarship.

Information about Tom Regan's career and the archive named in his honor is available at www.lib.ncsu.edu/arights. He is married to the former Nancy Tirk, with whom he co-founded The Culture & Animals Foundation.

Lawrence Sampson

Sampson is a Delaware (Lenape) on his mother's side, and Eastern Band Cherokee through his father. He was born on the Qualla Boundary Cherokee reservation in North Carolina. At the age of five, he was sold for $10,000 through the illegal Indian baby adoption/selling programs the US government secretly engaged in. Raised until the age of 14 by a non-Indian family, he eventually ran away and was reunited with his father. He graduated from Stephen F. Austin State University, in Nacogdoches, Texas, with a Bachelor of Social Studies degree. He enlisted in the US Army, where he was a paratrooper, and engaged in combat operations in Panama and Iraq. He was also accepted to Warrant Officer Candidate School to be a helicopter pilot. Since his separation from the Army, he has been very active in the Indian community, establishing or helping to establish several organizations to address the myriad of needs in their communities. Most of his attention has been directed into the Warrior Society known as the American Indian Movement, where he has engaged in direct action against United States authorities in order to assist Indian people in asserting sovereignty and self determination. He is currently the Southern Regional Spokesperson of AIM, where he works to reduce the gulf of misunderstanding between the Indian and the non-Indian.

Maxwell Schnurer

Schnurer is currently an assistant professor and debate coach at Marist College in Poughkeepsie NY. A long time animal rights activist, Schnurer's work focuses on social movements, cultural change and activist strategies. He is the co-author of *Many Sides: Debate Across the Curriculum* (Idea Press, 2000).

Kim Stallwood

While a student in 1973, Kim Stallwood became a vegetarian after working in a chicken processing plant in England, and went on to become a vegan in 1976. He helped direct Compassion In World Farming (1976–1978), British Union for the Abolition of Vivisection (1978–1986), and People for the Ethical Treatment of Animals (1987–1992). In 1993 Stallwood became editor of *The Animals'*

Agenda and executive director of its nonprofit publisher, the Animal Rights Network. He also founded the ARN Collection, which became the world's largest library in animal rights. Currently, he is reestablishing ARN as the Institute for Animals and Society (IAS), the first think tank in the world devoted exclusively to advancing the moral and legal status of animals in public policy. The IAS collaborates with North Carolina State University on the Tom Regan Animal Rights Archive, which recently acquired the ARN Collection. The IAS also works with the Community College of Baltimore County (MD) on a premier training program in animal advocacy. Stallwood has edited two anthologies of *Animals' Agenda* articles (*Speaking Out for Animals* and *A Primer on Animal Rights*) and *The Animals' Agenda Directory of Organizations*

Paul Watson
Paul Watson, a conservationist and environmental activist, is internationally renowned for his daring, innovative, and aggressive approach to the field of wildlife conservation. As one of the founding members of the Greenpeace Foundation, Paul Watson sailed into a nuclear test site in Alaska in 1971, and in 1975 became the first man to place his body between a harpoon and a whale, capturing the attention of the media worldwide. Watson founded the Sea Shepherd Conservation Society in 1977, an organization registered in Canada, the US, Great Britain, Ireland, Australia, and Sweden. Under his leadership, the society has been in the forefront of marine wildlife conservation, and is known for its direct confrontation and use of the media to bring attention to conservation and environmental issues. Paul Watson's nautical knowledge results from his work in the Norwegian and Swedish merchant marines and Canadian Coast Guard. He has been written about in scores of books and magazines, and has been the subject of hundreds of radio and television programs worldwide. A major motion picture is being produced about his life and work. Paul Watson has authored five books and lectures worldwide on marine wildlife conservation, the politics of conservation, and his personal experiences in environmental movements and campaigns.

Robin Webb
Robin Webb has been the British ALF press officer since 1991, following a radical activist line that has seen him targeted by many police forces, including SO-13, the anti-terrorist unit. Mr. Webb is unique in the UK's legal history, having been the victim of *quadruple* jeopardy

(being charged an unprecedented four times on the charge and evidence), but continues to speak out on behalf of the Animal Liberation movement.

Western Wildlife Unit

Western Wildlife Unit was a cell of the Animal Liberation Front.

Freeman Wicklund

Freeman Wicklund currently serves as the President of Eco-Animal Allies, a Minneapolis-based animal rights nonprofit whose mission is to promote respectful and responsible treatment of people, animals, and the environment. During his 16 years as an animal activist he has started six animal rights organizations, including the Student Organization for Animal Rights—or SOAR—at the University of Minnesota; the Animal Liberation League, which later became Compassionate Action for Animals; the humane education program Bridges of Respect; and Eco-Animal Allies. Freeman's direct action advocacy had led to him being arrested for animals 13 times to date. For several years Freeman served as a media spokesperson for the Animal Liberation Front. He also founded and edited the periodical *No Compromise*, the magazine of the grassroots direct action animal liberationists and their supporters. In conformity with the principles of Gandhian nonviolence, Freeman organized the first open rescue of hens in the United States while serving as Executive Director for Compassionate Action for Animals. For the past four years, he has worked as a Humane Educator for Bridges of Respect providing several hundred presentations a year on animal rights and environmental issues to students in local schools.

Gary Yourofsky

Between 1997 and 1999 Gary Yourofsky was arrested 13 times for random acts of kindness and compassion, once serving 77 days in maximum security for freeing 1,542 mink in an ALF raid on a Canadian fur farm. Currently, Yourofsky travels the country arguing the case for animal rights and promoting a vegan diet. Each year he gives more than 200 lectures in 75 college classrooms in courses ranging from cultural anthropology and English composition to psychology and philosophy.

INDEX

Note: Throughout this index, locators followed by "n" indicate endnotes.
The abbreviation "ALF" is used to refer to the Animal Liberation Front.

Abbey, Edward, 49, 59n17
abolition, 12–13, 75–76
abortion activism, 281
ACLU, 288–89. *see also* USA Patriot Act
activism
  abortion, 281
  Al Qaeda analogy, 327
  criminalization of, 311–12, 314
  environmental, 18–19, 67, 113–14
  future of, 57–58, 285–87
  theoretical, 142–43
  USA Patriot Act and, 288–90, 306–9, 364
activists, violence against, 19, 25, 61n31, 76,
  82
Adams, Carol, 108–9, 117, 155n8–9
Adams, John, 16, 310
agroterrorism, 376
Agroterrorism Prevention Act (HR2795),
  318
ahimsa, 88
airline industry, 328–29
ALEC (American Legislative Exchange
  Council), 313
Alexander, Yonah, 364, 370
ALF. *see also* animal liberation movement
  cell development, 354–61
  critique of tactics, 37–42
  decentralization of, 24
  future of, 285–87
  mission of, 7–8, 79
  origins of, 18–23, 74, 77, 239
  as terrorists, 294–96
  understanding, 197–201
  and USA Patriot Act, 296–98
  violence and, 36, 84–85, 283 (*see also* non-
    violence)
ALF Supporters Group (ALF SG), 84–85
Alinsky, Saul D., 195

Allen, Ray, 314
All Heaven in a Rage, 76–77
Al Qaeda, 327
American Civil Liberties Union. *see* ACLU
American Legislative Exchange Council
  (ALEC), 313
Amory, Cleveland, 19
anarcha~feminism, 143–44
anarchy, 126n24
Anderson, Curt, 339n60
anger
  causes of, 168–70
  defined, 160, 164–68
  as motivator, 171–75
  physiology of, 162–63
  revenge and, 160–61
Animal and Ecological Terrorism Act (Texas
  HB 433), 314
Animal Enterprise Protection Act of 1992,
  289
Animal Liberation Front. *see* ALF
animal liberation movement. *see also* ALF
  history and origins of, 1–2, 67–74
  justification for, 95–96, 101–4
  meaningfulness of, 93–96
  objections to, 96–97
  open rescues, 40–41, 202–12, 219, 248
  society and, 13–14
  as terrorist activity, 308–9
  uniqueness of, 255–56
  vs. animal rights, 26–27
animal rights, 26–27, 61n35, 335. *see also* animal liberation movement
Animal Rights Militia (ARM), 35–36, 77–78,
  301, 304
Animal Rights National Index (ARNI), 78
Animal Rights Network Inc., 81
animals. *see also* specific animals

attitudes toward, 13–14, 140
desires of, 153
exploitation of, 14–15, 58n2, 105n5, 146–47
Gandhi on, 129, 231
numbers killed, 58n4, 368
objectification of, 202–4
similarities to humans, 94–95
violence toward, 31, 33
Animals' Agenda, The, 81, 87
animal welfare, 12, 26–27, 38, 61n35
Animal Welfare Act, 38
Annan, Kofi, 372
Antiterrorism and Effective Death Penalty Act (1996), 306
Aquinas, Thomas (Saint), 62n43, 160–71
Arendt, Hannah, 333
Aristotle, 205
Arkangel, 195
ARM. *see* Animal Rights Militia
ARNI. *see* Animal Rights National Index (ARNI)
Arnold, Melanie, 292, 299n11
Arnold, Ron, 304
arson
actions, 20, 23, 42, 69–70, 78, 119
justification of, 62n47, 148
problems of, 36–37, 258
and USA Patriot Act, 290–93
Ashcroft, John, 10, 293, 307, 324, 327
Atwood, Nicolas, 53
Revolutionary Process and the ALF, 272–75
Auschwitz, 121–23, 126n24
Avery, Greg, 336n9

Bakunin, Michael, 306
Band of Mercy (20th-century group), 20, 68–74, 76–77, 82, 239
Bands of Mercy (19th-century RSPCA group), 19, 68, 82
Barad, Judith
Aquinas's Account of Anger Applied to the ALF, 51, 159–77
Barbarash, David, 23, 25–26, 44–45, 62n55, 205, 300, 325
Barber, Benjamin R., 338n35
Bari, Judy, 61n31
Barnard, Neal, 321
Barnes, Don, 29, 131
Barr, Judi, 60n18
battery hens, actions for, 206–9
Bay, Christian, 342
beagles, rescue of, 73, 77, 83, 264–65
Beauvoir, Simone de, 140
Becker, Andrew, 315

Begin, Menachem, 281–82
Bekoff, Marc, 61n66
bellum justum (just war doctrine), 101–2
Berger, John, 203
Berkowitz, Bill, 337n27
Berman, Rick, 320, 338n40
Bernstein, Mark, 33, 50, 104n2, 105n4
Legitimizing Liberation, 93–105
Berry, Dan, 363
Best, Steven, 10, 36, 59n6, 59n8, 61n35, 62n52, 370
Behind the Mask: Uncovering the Animal Liberation Front, 9–63
Defining Terrorism, 55, 361–77
It's War! The Escalating Battle Between Activists and the Corporate-State Complex, 54, 300–339
Betts, Richard, 361
Bible, The, 103, 249
Bicester Two, 20, 72–73
Biehl, Janet, 59n14
Bill of Rights Defense Committees, 334–35
Bin Laden, Osama, 294–95
Bin Wahad, Dhoruba, 125n11
Biodevastation 7 Forum, 330
Birkenau, 121–22, 126n24
Bismarck, Otto von, 43
bison, 188
Bite Back, 195
Black, Jason and Jennifer, 10
The Rhetorical "Terrorist": Implications of the USA Patriot Act for Animal Liberation, 54, 288–99
black cat symbolism, 137–39
blacklisting, 324, 328
Black Panthers, 125n11
bombs, use of, 62n45, 86, 222–23, 306
Bookchin, Murray, 59n14
Boots (pharmaceutical company), 79
Boston Tea Party, 15–16
Bourne, Sandra Liddy, 313
Britain. *see* United Kingdom
British Union for the Abolition of Vivisection (BUAV), 84
Brower, David, 61n63
Brown, Christopher, 265
Brown, Cynthia, 58n1, 338n35
Brown, John, 125n14
BUAV (British Union for the Abolition of Vivisection), 84–85
Buckeye egg farm, 207
buffalo, 188
Burdick, John, 372
bureaucracy, functions of, 122–23
Burke, Edmund, 157

burnout, 173
Bush, George W., 292, 306, 310, 332

cages, battery, 206–9
Cain, Steve, 376
CALA. *see* Center on Animal Liberation Affairs (CALA)
California Anti-Terrorism Information Center, 329
capitalism and oppression, 117–18
CAPPS II (Computerized Airline Passenger Pre-Screening System II), 328
Carnivore, 308
Carruthers, Peter, 104n1
Cartesian view of animals, 93–94
Cates, Diana Fritz, 169
cats, 265–66
Cavel West horse slaughterhouse, 178
Cavuto, Neil, 323
Center for Constitutional Rights, 310
Center for Consumer Freedom, 317, 320–21
Center on Animal Liberation Affairs (CALA), 195
Chain, David Gypsy, 61n31
Chamfort, Alain, 46
Chang, Nancy, 58n1
Chantraine, Pierre, 176n14
Charman, Karen, 337n30
Cheney, Dick, 305
Cheney, D.L., 104n3
Cheney, Lynne, 324
Cherney, Darryl, 60n18, 61n31
chickens, actions for, 71, 206–9
Chinoy, Ira, 337n24
Chiron Corp., 62n45, 222–23, 304
Chocola, Chris, 317
Chomsky, Noam, 361, 366, 372
Churchill, Ward, 60n29, 336n12
  Illuminating the Philosophy and Methods of Animal Liberation, 1–6
civil disobedience, 15–17, 334–35
civil rights. *see* USA Patriot Act
Civil Rights Movement, 101, 241–43
Clausewitz, Karl von, 301
Cleaver, Eldridge, 1
Clemitson, Ivor, 72
Cleyre, Voltairine de, 15, 17
Clifton, Merritt, 211n8
Coalition Against Fur Farms (CAFF), 348–49
cockfighting, as feminist issue, 141
coercion *vs.* persuasion, 238
COINTELPRO, 41, 323
Cole, David, 58n1
collateral damage, 103, 282
Collins, Michael, 281

Compassionate Action for Animals (CAA), 207
Compassion Over Killing (COK), 207–9, 215
Confucius, 157
Consort Kennels, 265
cooperation, 151–53
Coronado, Rod
  on apathy, 57
  Direct Actions Speak Louder than Words, 51, 178–84
  media coverage and, 213–15
  motivation of, 51, 295
  My Experience with Government Harassment, 54, 345–54
  on violence, 62n47, 223, 304
  on "warriors," 343
  mentioned, 42, 87, 127, 293, 299n11, 16
corporations, and government, 313–16
Coulston Foundation, 178–79, 322
critical pedagogy, 197–201
Cryan, Philip, 367

Darwin, Charles, 94
data, aggregation of, 308, 329
Da Vinci, Leonardo, 57
Davis, Karen, 40, 81, 87, 140
  Open Rescues: Putting a Face on Liberation, 52, 202–12
Dawn, Karen, 39
  From the Front Lines to the Front Page: An Analysis of ALF Media Coverage, 52, 213–28
DayLay egg farm, 207
death penalty, 311
deaths, human, 35, 224–26, 305
definitions of terrorism, 30–37, 279–80, 288–90, 362–64, 367–68, 370–76
Delio, Michelle, 339n54
DeMeo, James, 155n14
democracy, 16–17, 310–12, 335
Demosthenes, 277
Denton, Robert E., Jr., 297, 298n3
Des Jardins, Traci, 218–19
Detweiler, Rachelle, 202, 212n21
DeWeese, Tom, 338n33
Dillard, Courtney, 240
direct action. *see also* lab animals
  costs of, 240–41
  definition of, 137–38
  effectiveness of, 138, 178–79, 246–47
  as empowering women, 19–20
  future of, 248–50
  Gandhi on, 245–46
  history of, 16–18, 238–39
  planning, 354–61

of SHAC, 266–67
  strategy and, 273–74
dissent
  criminalization of, 305–6, 311–12, 314, 323
  repression of, 41
  as terrorism, 10–11, 288–89
diversity of tactics, as strength, 44–46
Dixie Chicks, 324
doctrine of double effect, 103
dolphins, 21, 60n23, 215–16
Domestic Security Enhancement Act of 2003
  (Patriot Act II), 311–12
domestic terrorism, 302, 374–75
domestic violence, as animal issue, 141
Donovan, Josephine, 155n8
Douglass, Frederick, 15, 143, 193, 342
Dowie, Mark, 59n15
ducks. see foie gras
Dunayer, Eric, 208–9
Dylan, Bob, 42

Earth. see environmental activism
Earth First!, 19, 60n17–18, 113
Earth Liberation Front (ELF), 18, 126n30,
  283–87
Earth Night Action Group, 347
ecofeminism, 142–43
economic incentives for abuse, 130–31, 179
ecotage. see environmental activism
eco-terrorism, 283–84, 309–10, 314, 318–19,
  375
education, 28–29, 61n39, 248–49, 334
Einstein, Albert, 157
ELF. see Earth Liberation Front (ELF)
Ellerman, Joshua, 241
Emerson, Ralph Waldo, 240
emotions, physiology of, 162–63
empowerment, 111–12
England. see United Kingdom
environmental activism, 18–19, 67, 113–14
Environmental Terrorism Reduction Act, 319
ethics, 46–49, 110–18, 146–51. see also nonviolence
experimentation. see lab animals
exploitation of animals, 14–15, 58n2, 105n5,
  146–47
explosives. see bombs, use of
extremism, benefits of, 285
extremists, 130, 144–45, 285
Exxon, 283
Eyerman, Ron, 114
Ezekiel, Rafe, 156n18

factory farm animals, 203–4
fascism, 327–32

FBI (Federal Bureau of Investigation), 323,
  329–30, 346–47, 349–54
fear, 100, 223–26
Fedor, Katie, 206, 240
feminism
  animal liberation and, 139–42, 151–53
  ethics of, 146–51
  symbolism of, 137–39
  types of, 142–45
  vegetarianism and, 145
Finkelstein, William, 227
Finsen, Lawrence, 60n26, 81, 127
Finsen, Susan, 60n26, 81, 127
Finz, Stacy, 336n6, 8
fire. see arson
FISA (Foreign Intelligence Surveillance Act),
  307
Flaubert, Gustave, 65
Flynn, Elizabeth Gurley, 137
foie gras, 217–20
Foreign Intelligence Surveillance Act (FISA),
  307
Foreman, Dave, 19, 60n17–18, 61n31,
  113–14, 127
Fosdick, Harry Emerson, 238
Fossey, Dian, 61n31
Foucault, Michel, 117, 127
Fouts, Roger, 261
Fox, Mitchell, 222
Francione, Gary, 45, 58n5, 61n35, 62n50
Francis of Assisi, Saint, 18
Franklin, Benjamin, 333
freedom fighters, ALF as, 23–24
freedom of animals. see animal liberation
  movement
Freire, Paulo, 196, 198–99, 200n8
Friedrich, Bruce G., 322
  Defending Agitation and the ALF, 53, 252–62
Fullmer, Dari, 273
Fund for Animals, 19
fur industry, attacks on, 23, 42, 119, 131–36,
  178, 220–22, 239–40
future of activism, 57–58, 285–87

Gandhi, Mohandas K.
  on animals, 129, 231
  strategies of, 245–46, 255–56
  on truth, 135, 199
  on violence, 80, 182, 262
  mentioned, 17, 130, 252–54
Ganor, Boaz, 370
Garfield, James A., assassination of, 225
geese. see foie gras
gender stereotypes, 19–20
Genesis Awards, 226

Geoghegan, Erin, 211n17–18
Gibson, William, 336n3
Gilligan, Carol, 146
Gioseffi, Daniela, 156n17
Goethe, Johann Wolfgang von, 9, 57
Gold, Mark, 81
Goldstein, Robert Justin, 339n63
Goodall, Jane, 197, 261
Goodman, Cliff, 20, 68, 72, 82–83
Goodman, James, 16, 59n11
Goodwin, J.P., 239–40
government, U.S., terrorism by, 305, 325,
  366–67
Gramsci, Antonio, 155n12
grand juries, 239, 324–25, 353
Greenpeace, 18–19, 59n16, 330
Grieder, William, 59n12
Griffin, D.R., 61n66, 104n3
guidelines, ALF, 8
Guither, Harold D., 127, 290, 299n14
Gurr, Ted Robert, 371–72

Halifax, George Savile, Marquess of, 29
Hall, Lee, 339n45
Hans, Dennis, 376n3
Harper, Josh, 293
Harris, Paul, 336n10
Harshav, Barbara, 124n2
Hatch, Orrin, 312, 332
Haywood, Bill, 127
Hegins (Pa.) pigeon shoot, 243–45
Henneebery, Onnalee, 375
hens, actions for, 71, 206–9
Hentoff, Nat, 58n1
Herman, Edward S., 376n7, 9–10
Hill, Julia Butterfly, 155n11
Hill, Mike, 82
Hillgrove Cat Farm, 265–66
Hindi, Steve, 29, 61n39
Hitler, Adolf. *see* Holocaust
Hoechst Pharmaceuticals, 20, 69–70
Hoffman, Ian, 339n56
Holocaust
  analogy to ALF, 23, 101, 105n4, 113–16,
    124n3
  Auschwitz, 121–23
  empowerment and, 110–13
  infrastructure attacks, 118–20
  psychology of, 108–9
Holstege, Sean, 339n56
hooks, bell, 198
Hooley, Darlene, 319
Hope for the Hopeless (video), 207–9
Horne, Barry, 78, 91
Howard, Robin, 82

HSA. *see* Hunt Saboteurs Association (HSA)
HSUS. *see* Humane Society of the United
  States (HSUS)
Hughes, Tom, 211n8
Humane Society of the United States
  (HSUS), 43–44, 214, 224–26, 285
human rights movement, 255–56, 335
humans
  affected by animal exploitation, 14–15,
    105n5
  attitudes toward animals, 13–14, 140
  similarities to animals, 94–95
  violence toward, 62n46, 223–26
hunger strikes, 72–73
hunting, 19–20, 68–74, 76–77, 82, 239
Huntingdon Life Sciences, 28, 62n46,
  125n18, 126n18, 263, 304. *see also* SHAC
Hunt Retribution Squad, 77, 301
Hunt Saboteurs Association (HSA), 19–20,
  60n19, 67–68, 76, 82, 238–39
Huskisson, Mike, 83

identification with others, 170–71
image of activists, 195
inaction, responsibility for, 181
incarceration, 259–60
Indians, 186–88
indirect action, 137–38
informants, 73
infrastructure, attacking, 118–20
Inge, William, 129
Intelligence Authorization Act for Fiscal Year
  2004, 312
intent, importance of, 30–31, 294–96
Ireland, 281
ISE-America, 207–9
Israel, 281–82

jail, 72, 82, 259–60
Jamieson, Andrew, 114
Jasper, James M., 127
Jefferson, Thomas, 328
Jenkins, Brian, 371
Jensen, Robert, 371
Jesus, 130
JetBlue Airways, 328
Jonas, Kevin, 46, 214, 302
  Bricks and Bullhorns, 53, 263–71
jones, pattrice, 15, 25
  *Mothers with Monkeywrenches: Feminist
    Imperatives and the ALF,* 51, 137–56
justice, 160
Justice Department (activist group), 35–36,
  78–79, 300–301, 304
"just war doctrine," 101–2

Kaiser, Robert G., 337n24
Kapitan, Thomas, 365, 371
Kelley, Robin D.G., 120
Kellner, Douglas, 59n8
Kennedy, John F., 218, 257, 341
Kheel, Marti, 151
King, Martin Luther, Jr.
  quoted, 46, 56, 134, 193, 198–99, 229
  strategies of, 17, 233, 241–42, 245–46,
    252–56
  mentioned, 130
Knickerbocker, Brad, 337n26
Kornegger, Peggy, 143
kotos (rancor), 164
Krakowski, Shmuel, 118, 127n32
Kranich, Nancy, 339n61
Krishnamurti, 9

lab animals, actions for, 21–23, 71, 73, 239,
  260–61
Lamartine, Alphonse de, 65
Langer, Ellen, 108
language, lack of, 94
language, politics of, 34–37
Laqueur, Walter, 369, 371
LaVeck, James, 61n39
Law and Order (TV show), 226–27
laws, animal, 38, 289, 313–16
Ledwith, Margaret, 198
Lee, Ronnie
  arrests of, 72, 82
  Band of Mercy and, 20, 68
  hunger strike of, 72–73
  on mission of ALF, 18
  on SHAC, 263
  as TV character, 227
  on violence, 83–84, 302
legal system, as barrier, 18, 38, 272
legislation, animal, 38, 289, 313–16
Leneman, Leah, 155n15
Levin, Brian, 322
Lewis, Charles, 337n21
Lewis, Megan, 323
liberation, animal. see animal liberation move-
  ment
Liberation Leagues, 77, 85–86, 88–89
Liberator, The, 84
Lindorff, Dave, 339n61
Linzey, Andrew, 44, 62n52
lobbying, 312–16
love, as motivation, 198–200
Lyman, Howard, 29, 131
Lynn, Gina, 115

Machiavelli, Niccolo, 277

Makah nation, 187
Mandela, Nelson, 49, 130, 182, 229, 286
Manes, Christopher, 61n64
Mann, Keith, 305
Mao Tse-tung, 336n3
Marcuse, Herbert, 310, 336n18
Mark, Patty, 52, 204–6, 210
Marx, Karl, 18
Mason, Jim, 59n9
Masri, Rania, 336n1
MATRIX (Multistate Anti-Terrorism
  Information Exchange), 330–31
McAllisterm, Pam, 156n17
McCarthy, Joseph, 10
McCarthyism, neo-, 323
McClain, Carla, 126n20
McCullagh, Declan, 336n15
McInnis, Scott, 316, 319
McLaren, Peter, 195–96, 200n3
McPhee, Mike, 339n57
McVeigh, Timothy, 282
Mead, Margaret, 196
meat industry, 78
media coverage
  of actions, 207–8, 217–26, 244–45, 249,
    283–84, 319
  biases of, 89–90, 131–34, 182–83, 319, 323
  good vs. bad, 39–41, 83, 214–17, 227–28,
    240–41
mekhabbel (terrorist), 282
Mendes, Chico, 61n31
menis (ill will), 164
Mercy for Animals (MFA), 207, 215
Merton, Thomas, 236n4
methods. see tactics
Milgram, Stanley, 107–9
Milhaven, John Giles, 174, 177n36
military actions. see under terrorism
milk, as feminist issue, 140
Miller, Chris, 211n8
Milton Keynes. see Hoechst Pharmaceuticals
mindlessness, 108
mink, actions for, 23, 42, 131–36, 220–22
Molland, Noel, 19
  Thirty Years of Direct Action, 50, 67–74
moral law, 26, 130–31, 280–81
Morrison, Adrian, 125n17
motivation, 171–75, 189–92, 198–200, 284
Multistate Anti-Terrorism Information
  Exchange (MATRIX), 330–31
Murphy, Laura, 310
Murrah Federal Building attack, 306

NALL (Northern Animal Liberation League),
  85

narco-terrorism, 312
Nash, Roderick, 59n6
Native Americans, 186–88
nature and society, 186–88, 302–6
Nazis. *see* Holocaust
Neimöller, Martin, 335
Nelkin, Dorothy, 127
neo-Cartesian view, 93–94
neo-McCarthyism, 323
Nethercutt, George, 318–19, 338n34, 377n15
Newkirk, Ingrid
    Afterword: The ALF: Who, Why, and What?,
      54, 341–43
    quoted, 21, 23, 171, 203, 240, 320
    mentioned, 210, 218, 293
New Zealand action, 36
Nigeria, ecofeminism in, 155n11
Nocella, Anthony J., II
    Behind the Mask: Uncovering the Animal
      Liberation Front, 9–63
    Defining Terrorism, 55, 361–77
    Understanding the ALF: From Critical Analysis
      to Critical Pedagogy, 52, 195–201
No Compromise, 195
nonviolence. *see also* violence
    commitment to, 25–26, 36, 83, 88, 182–84
    effectiveness of, 244–45
    failure of, 102, 301
    strategic, 252–54
    women and, 147–49
Norquist, Grover, 329
Norris, Pippa, 371
Northern Animal Liberation League (NALL),
    85

Oates, Stephen B., 233
O'Barry, Ric, 60n23
objectification, 108–9, 112–17, 202–4,
    209–10
Oklahoma City bombing, 306
Oliver, Daniel T., 299n22
open rescues, 40–41, 202–12, 219, 248
Operation Bite Back, 42, 178
Operation TIPS (Terrorist Information
    Prevention System), 324
oppression, 41, 108–9, 112–19, 202–4,
    209–10, 284
Orwell, George, 34
Oxford Laboratory Animal Colonies, 20

Pacelle, Wayne, 43–44, 61n39, 214
Pacheco, Alex, 172–73, 297
pacifism. *see* nonviolence
Palestine, 281–82
Parenti, Michael, 59n12

Paris, Susan, 43
Park, Miyun, 208
Parks, Rosa, 130
pastoralism, 139–40, 144–45
patriarchy, 144–45
Patriot Act. *see* USA Patriot Act
Patriot Act II (Son of Patriot Act), 311–12
Patterson, Charles, 109, 117, 124n3, 125n12,
    127n33, 212n24
PCRM (Physicians Committee for
    Responsible Medicine), 320–21
Peace News, 85
Peel, John, 77
People for the Ethical Treatment of Animals.
    see PETA
Periandi, Ralph, 331
"person," defining, 33, 62n41
persuasion *vs.* coercion, 238
PETA (People for the Ethical Treatment of
    Animals)
    PCRM and, 321
    support of ALF, 22, 86, 213, 349
    USA Patriot Act and, 293–94, 309
Physicians Committee for Responsible
    Medicine (PCRM), 320–21
Pickering, James Leslie, 305
pigeons, 243–45
Pillar, Paul, 373–74
Platt, Theresa, 222
pleasure, and revenge, 160–61
Poindexter, John, 331
Pojman, Louis, 161
Poland, James M., 371
political change, methods of, 16–18
politics of nature, 302–6
Posner, Michael, 310
Potter, Will, 339n46
Premarin, 141, 155n10
Prescott, Heidi, 244, 250n3
press. *see* media coverage
Prestige, John, 67, 82
Principle of Utility, 104
prison, 259–60
privacy, loss of, 288, 308, 331–32
Procter and Gamble, 99
profit, as incentive for abuse, 130–31, 179
property destruction, 99–100, 130, 179. *see*
    also tactics
    justice and, 16
    justification of, 24–25, 46–49, 205
    minimizing, 89
    as nonviolence, 61n40
    as violence, 30, 32–33
    vs. vandalism, 32–33
Provisional RSPCA, 77

Qadir, Shaukat, 372

rabbits, actions for, 266
radicals, 130, 144–45, 285
Rainbow Warrior, 61n31, 283
rape, as animal issue, 140–41
Ratner, Michael, 316
Ray, Paul, 320
Ream, Tim, 304
Regal Rabbits, 266
Regan, Tom, 38, 58n4, 61n35, 206
    How to Justify Violence, 52–53, 231–36
Reilly, Kristie, 339n58
repression. see oppression
rescue. see animal liberation movement
research animals. see lab animals
retribution, 161
revenge, 160–61, 165
Revolutionary Cells Animal Liberation
    Brigade, 35–36, 223, 300–301, 304
Rice, Catherine, 240
Richman, Josh, 339n56
RICO Act, 305, 325
Ridge, Tom, 293
Rignall, Karen, 337n20
Roberts, Adam, 361
Robota, Roza, 122–23
Rollin, B., 104n3
Rosebraugh, Craig, 61n68, 302, 305, 324–25,
    336n11, 338n31, 339n49–50
Roselle, Mike, 60n18
Rosenberg, Kirsten, 87
Rotem, Simha, 111, 124n2, 8
Rowe, Martin, 58n4
RSPCA, Provisional, 77
RSPCA (Royal Society for the Prevention of
    Cruelty to Animals), 19, 68
Ruby, Hilma, 134
Ryder, Richard, 59n7, 81

sabotage. see property destruction
Sampson, Lawrence
    Touch the Earth, 51, 185–88
satyagraha (truth-action), 182, 255
Scarce, Rik, 59n16, 60n18, 304–5
Schimmel, Solomon, 176n25
Schnurer, Maxwell
    At the Gates of Hell: The ALF and the Legacy
        of Holocaust Resistance, 50, 106–27
Scholtz-Klink, Gertrude, 15
School of the Americas Watch, 377n13
Scott, Ron, 42
Seabrook, Charles, 62n50
seals, actions for, 38–39, 70

Sea Shepherd Conservation Society, 19, 39,
    283
secrecy, 347–48, 352
self-purification, 242
September 11, 2001 (terrorist attack), 9–10,
    128–30, 257–58, 288–89, 294–95, 317–18
Severson, Kim, 218
Sexton, Rob, 314
Seyfarth, R.M., 104n3
SHAC (Stop Huntingdon Animal Cruelty),
    28, 214, 222–23, 266–71, 318–19, 325. see
    also Huntingdon Life Sciences
Shaklee Corporation, 62n45, 304
Shamir, Yitzhak, 281–82
Shapiro, Paul, 62n53, 206, 211n19–20
Sharp, Gene, 243
Sharpe, Richard, 176n27
Sicard, Jim, 212n23
Sierra Club, 285
Silent Suffering (film), 207
Singel, Ryan, 339n55
Singer, Isaac Bashevis, 112, 124n3, 209
Singer, Peter, 28–29, 31, 59n7, 61n34, 62n41
sins vs. vices, 176n25
slaughterhouses, 122, 178
slavery, 12–13, 75–76
Smith, Craig Allen, 297, 298n3
Smith, Paul, 127
Smithies, Catherine, 68
Solomon, Robert, 162
Somma, Mark, 372
Son of Patriot Act (Patriot Act II), 311–12
speciesism, 13, 24, 31–32, 113, 139–42, 270.
    see also worldview
species terrorism, 33, 367–68
Spiegel, Marjorie, 59n9, 227
spokespeople, 148
Stallwood, Kim, 25, 40, 50
    A Personal Overview of Direct Action in The
        United Kingdom and the United States,
        81–90
state-sponsored terrorism, 305, 325, 365–67
statute of limitations, 291, 309
Steelman, Sara, 245
Stein, Jenny, 61n39
Steinem, Gloria, 224
Stern Gang, 281
Stewart, Charles J., 297, 298n3
Stop Huntingdon Animal Cruelty. see SHAC
Stowe, Harriet Beecher, 193
Strand, Rod and Patti, 299n13
strategic nonviolence, 87, 252–54
strategies. see tactics
strategy, importance of, 273–74

suffering, of activists, 242–43
Suffragettes, 75, 101
tactics. *see also* property destruction
  arson (*see* arson)
  for avoiding capture, 85–86
  bombings, 222–23
  civil disobedience, 15–17, 334–35
  combined, 264–66, 268
  comparison of, 213–14, 245–46
  criticisms of, 27–29, 70–71, 98–101, 180, 249
  intensification of, 300–301, 304–5
  as justified by goals, 79–80
  nonviolence (*see* nonviolence)
Takeyh, Ray, 376n2
targets, 11–12, 273–74, 279, 304
Taskhiri, Ayatulla, 372
Taub, Edward, 125n17
terrorism. *see also* violence
  against animals, 33
  contrasted with ALF actions, 23–24
  defined (*see* definitions of terrorism)
  military actions, 279–80
  overuse of term, 320–22, 361
  punishments for, 290–92, 308–9
  purposes of, 100, 294–95
  SHAC and, 268–70
  by U.S. government, 305, 325, 365–67
  USA Patriot Act, 288–90, 306–9, 364
  vs. violence, 30–37, 364
  war on, 9–10
Terrorist Information Prevention System (TIPS), 324
Texas HB 433 (Animal and Ecological Terrorism Act), 313–16
theoretical activism, 142–43
Thomas Aquinas, Saint, 62n43, 160–71
Thoreau, Henry David, 15, 26, 130, 333, 341
TIPS (Terrorist Information Prevention System), 324
Title 18 (United States Code), 288–93
Total Information Awareness program, 308, 331
Tracy, James, 59n10
training, activist, 242
Treadwell, Gary, 83
Troen, Roger, 293
True Friends, 261
Trull, Frankie, 224
Truth, Sojourner, 139
Tubman, Harriet, 130, 139

Underground Railroad, 23–24, 75–76, 130
Undersea Railroad, 86

understanding the ALF, 195–201
Union Carbide, 283
United Kingdom, 19–20, 67–74, 76, 238–39
United Poultry Concerns, 81, 87, 205–7
United States, 21–23, 86. *see also* U.S. government
unity among activists, 261–62
universities, actions at, 22–23, 86, 178–79, 326
Unnecessary Fuss (film), 22, 86
U.S. government, as terrorist, 305, 325, 366–67
USA Patriot Act, 9–10, 58n1, 288–93, 296–98, 306–9, 331–32
USSA (US Sportsmen's Alliance), 314
US Sportsmen's Alliance (USSA), 314
Utility, Principle of, 104

"Valerie," 21
value, of individuals, 96
values, core, 88–89
vandalism. *see* property destruction
Vander Wall, Jim, 60n29, 336n12
Van Winkle, Mike, 329
Vaughan, Claudette, 211n10
veganism, 145
vegetarianism and feminism, 145
vengeance. *see* revenge
vices *vs.* sins, 176n25
Victory Act, 312
videos of rescues, 206–8
violence. *see also* nonviolence; terrorism
  advocacy of, 84, 231–36, 305, 341–43
  argument against, 44, 88–90
  as attracting the disaffected, 149
  as complementary, 254–56, 283, 285
  domestic, 141
  feminism and, 149–50
  Gandhi on, 80, 182, 231, 262
  in media, 282–83
  non-physical, 31
  proportional use of, 103
  terrorism *vs.*, 30–37, 364
  toward activists, 19, 25, 61n31, 76, 82
  toward animals, 31, 33
  toward humans, 62n46, 109, 223–26
virtue, 169
vivisection, 23, 78, 179, 265
Von Clausewitz, Karl, 301

Walden, Greg, 316–17
Walker, Alice, 128
Wand, Kelly, 60n26
war analogy, 101–2, 305–6

war on terrorism, 9–10
Watch List, 328
Watson, Paul
    ALF and ELF: Terrorism Is as Terrorism Does,
        53–54, 279–87
    on illegal actions, 21
    marine activities of, 18–19, 38–39
    on violence, 33, 300
    violence against, 61n31
    mentioned, 31, 320
Webb, Robin, 11, 19, 37, 42, 301–2
    Animal Liberation—By "Whatever Means
        Necessary," 50, 75–80
Webb, Ronnie, 30
Werner, Harold, 110, 118
Western Wildlife Unit, 189–92
whales, 38–39, 42, 187
Whitaker, Brian, 376n5
Wicklund, Freeman, 61n67, 81, 87, 127, 206,
    252
    Direct Action: Progress, Peril, or Both?, 53,
        237–51
Wiesel, Elie, 91
Wild Earth, 60n18

Wittgenstein, Ludwig, 369
Wolkie, Howie, 38
women, 19–20, 108. see also feminism
Worby, Thomas, 82
World Trade Center attack (1993), 306
World Trade Center attack (2001). see
    September 11, 2001
worldview, 113–16

Yourofsky, Gary, 29, 293
    Abolition, Liberation, Freedom: Coming to a
        Fur Farm Near You, 50–51, 128–36

Zinn, Howard, 339n63
zoos, 203–4
Zygmunt, Bauman, 127